بسم الله الرحمن الرحيم

"The house of al-Arqam is the house of Islām"

Al-Ḥākim (d.403h.) in *al-Mustadrak 'ala al-Ṣaḥiḥayn* (6185)

Defining Legends

An Analysis of Afrocentric Writings Against Islam

DAR AL-ARQAM

ISBN: 19164756 1 8

British Library Cataloguing in Publishing Data
A catalogue record for this book is available from the British Library

Prepared and published by Dar al-Arqam Publishing
Birmingham, United Kingdom

www.daralarqam.bigcartel.com
Email: daralarqam@hotmail.co.uk

Authored by AbdulHaq al-Ashanti
(abdulhaq77@hotmail.com)

Printed in Turkey by Mega | export@mega.com.tr

DEFINING LEGENDS

AN ANALYSIS OF AFROCENTRIC WRITINGS AGAINST ISLAM

AbdulHaq al-Ashanti

DAR AL-ARQAM

Contents

يَا أَيُّهَا النَّاسُ إِنَّا
خَلَقْنَاكُم مِّن ذَكَرٍ وَأُنثَىٰ وَجَعَلْنَاكُمْ شُعُوبًا وَقَبَائِلَ لِتَعَارَفُوا
إِنَّ أَكْرَمَكُمْ عِندَ اللَّهِ أَتْقَاكُمْ إِنَّ اللَّهَ عَلِيمٌ خَبِيرٌ ۝

O people, indeed We have created you from male and female and made you peoples and tribes that you may know one another. Indeed, the most noble of you in the sight of Allāh is the most righteous of you. Indeed, Allāh is Knowing and Acquainted.

[al-Hujurāt (49): 13]

'Ubayy ibn Ka'b (may Allāh be pleased with him) narrated that the Messenger of Allāh (may the peace and blessings of Allāh be upon him) said "If anyone proudly asserts his descent in the manner of the people of Jāhiliyyah (pre-Islamic days of ignorance) tell him to bite his father's penis, and do not use a euphemism."[1]

Abū Hurayrah (may Allāh be pleased with him) reported that the Messenger of Allāh (may the peace and blessings of Allāh be upon him) said "Let the people cease to boast about their ancestors who have died, who are merely fuel for the Hell-fire, or they will certainly be of less account with Allāh than the beetle which rolls dung with its nose. Allāh has removed from you the pride of the pre-Islamic period and its boasting of ancestors. One is only a pious believer or a miserable sinner. All men are sons of Ādam, and Ādam, peace be upon him, came from dust."[2]

---

1 *Sharh us-Sunna*h of al-Baghawī noted in Waleeyuddeen al-Khātib at-Tabrizī, translated by James Robson (Emeritus Professor of Arabic, University of Manchester) *Mishkat ul-Masabih* (Lahore, Pakistan: Sh. Muhammad Aṣhraf Publishers, 1994 Reprint), p.1021.

2 Ibid. *hadeeth hasan*, transmitted by Abū Dāwood, Musnad Ahmad and similar wordings in at-Tirmidhī.

Acknowledgements

Indeed, all praise is due to Allāh, we praise Him, we seek His aid, and we ask for His forgiveness. We seek refuge in Allāh from the evil of our actions and from the evil consequences of our actions. Whomever Allāh guides, there is none to misguide and whoever Allāh misguides there is none to guide. I bear witness that there is no god worthy of worship except Allāh and I bear witness that Muhammad is the servant and messenger of Allāh.

يَا أَيُّهَا الَّذِينَ آمَنُواْ
اتَّقُواْ اللّهَ حَقَّ تُقَاتِهِ وَلاَ تَمُوتُنَّ إِلاَّ وَأَنتُم مُّسْلِمُونَ

O you who have believed, fear Allāh as He should be feared and do not die except as Muslims (in submission to Him).

[*Āli-Imrān* (3): 102]

يَا أَيُّهَا النَّاسُ اتَّقُواْ رَبَّكُمُ الَّذِي خَلَقَكُم
مِّن نَّفْسٍ وَاحِدَةٍ وَخَلَقَ مِنْهَا زَوْجَهَا وَبَثَّ مِنْهُمَا رِجَالاً كَثِيرًا وَنِسَاء
وَاتَّقُواْ اللّهَ الَّذِي تَسَاءلُونَ بِهِ وَالأَرْحَامَ إِنَّ اللّهَ كَانَ عَلَيْكُمْ رَقِيبًا

O mankind, fear your Lord, who created you from one soul and created from it its mate and dispersed from both of them many men and women. And fear Allāh through whom you ask things from each other, and (respect) the wombs. Indeed Allāh is ever, over you, an Observer.

[*an-Nisā* (4): 1]

يَا أَيُّهَا الَّذِينَ آمَنُوا

ٱتَّقُوا ٱللَّهَ وَقُولُوا قَوْلًا سَدِيدًا يُصْلِحْ لَكُمْ أَعْمَالَكُمْ وَيَغْفِرْ لَكُمْ ذُنُوبَكُمْ وَمَن يُطِعِ ٱللَّهَ وَرَسُولَهُۥ فَقَدْ فَازَ فَوْزًا عَظِيمًا ﴿٧١﴾

O you who have believed, fear Allāh and speak words of appropriate justice. He will amend for you your deeds and forgive your sins. And whoever obeys Allāh and His Messenger has certainly attained a great attainment.

[*Al-Ahzāb* (33): 70-71]

To begin:

Thanks to: 'AbdulMālik Edwards, Jibreel 'Abdus-Shakoor, Hamzah Lewis, 'Alī Sierra Leonī, 'Eesā Caliste, Yūsuf Adam and 'Abdur-Raheem Green, for their support during composing this original project back in 1420 A.H./1999 C.E.[3] I would also like to extend my thanks to 'Adnan Karim from Dar al-Arqam Publishing who has also been helpful in assisting and facilitating the publication of this work.

3 A.H. stands for 'After Hijrah,' the Islamic dating system beginning after the Hijrah of Muhammad and his companions to Madeenah correlating to 622 C.E. C.E. stands for 'Common Era,' Muslims do not use 'A.D.' as it stands for 'Anno Domini' a Latin word meaning 'in the year of our lord,' 'lord' here meaning Jesus. However Jesus, peace be upon him, is not 'lord' for Muslims rather the Lord of Jesus is also the Lord of Muslims and the Lord of all people.

Foreword

By Shaykh, Dr. Khālid al-Anbarī[4]

The foundation of Islām is against the claim that Islām is intrinsically against black people, the Prophet (*sallallāhu 'alayhi wassallam*) says "There is no virtue of the red over the black, or the black over the red, except in *taqwā* (God-consciousness)."[5] The Divinely Legislated texts from the Qur'ān and Sunnah oppose the claim (that Islām is intrinsically against black people). As from the aspect of history then from the time of the companions and the Prophet (*sallallāhu 'alayhi wassallam*) to our present time, also demonstrates that Islamic history opposes the claim and nullifies it. To the extent that the writings of the just Orientalists also indicate that this claim is false and a lie upon Islām, 'Umar ibn al-Khattāb (*radi Allāhu 'anhu*) said with regards to Bilāl (*radi Allāhu 'anhu*): "Bilāl is our master."[6] So if 'Umar ibn al-Khattāb and Abū Bakr as-Siddeeq (*radi Allāhu 'anhuma*) said "Bilāl is our master" and Bilāl was a black man, how can this claim be true? To the extent that some leaders of the Arabs and the Muslims, or many of them in fact, were black, so Islām and the history of Islām is the only path which does not distinguish between the black and the white.

As for slavery, then if you read Islamic history you will see that slaves

---

4 Former Associate Professor of *Sharee'ah* at King Abdul-Aziz University, Riyadh and formerly associate professor at Imām Muhammad Bin Saud University and 'Ajman University UAE.

5 *Musnad Ahmad.*

6 The full hadeeth is narrated by Jābir ibn 'Abdullāh (*radi Allāhu 'anhu*) that 'Umar ibn al-Khattāb (*radi Allāhu 'anhu*) used to say "Abū Bakr is our master and he freed our master Bilāl." The hadeeth is in *Saheeh Bukhārī* in the chapter on 'The Virtues of the Companions of the Prophet', Volume 5, Book 57, Number 98.

were both black and white, just as the masters were both black and white! No difference! So this claim is denied by the books of Islamic history and when you read the books of Islamic history you will see this clearly, beginning from the time of the Prophet (*sallallāhu 'alayhi wassallam*) and his *Sīrah*, then from the biographies of the companions (*radi Allāhu 'anhum*), then the biographies of the successors and then within the biographies in Islamic history. And all praise is due to Allāh because when black people were not getting their rights in America, the black people in the Islamic countries were not discriminated against by the Muslims and during these times the Muslims were in a state of weakness and not technologically developed or as progressed as the West.

All praise is due to Allāh, the Muslims do not distinguish between the white and black, and if you were to go to any Muslim country you will find that there is no difference between the white and black and you will find them as families and friends without any difference and this is from the guidance of Islām. This racial discrimination was known before Islām in the pre-Islamic period and also within the contemporary Western setting and in recent times, as demonstrated in the riots and revolts that have taken place in America. Such race riots did not take place within the Islamic countries, rather some Orientalists have noted that black people had major positions, therefore racial discrimination is neither found at all within the texts of Islām nor within the mind of a Muslim, because it is firmly established within the mind and soul of a Muslim that both the white and the black are slaves to Allāh and His worshippers and that there is no difference between the black and the white except with *taqwa* (God-consciousness). How many Muslim leaders and rulers were black? How many ministers in Islamic history were black? How many presidents, even up to this day, were black? Therefore, this racial discrimination is not to be found at all, even within modern history! The most famous example of this being Muhammad Anwar Sadat, a former President of Egypt who was a black man, I saw him myself. So we have leaders and rulers who have been black and there is no difference among us between the black and white. So it is not correct to say that Islām looks upon black people as merely being slaves! This is a false view of Islām and is also a view that has been presented within films, because in films they depict the slaves as always being black and the masters as always being white! This is a clear mistake and opposes the reality of

Islamic history, many slaves were white. Suhayb ar-Rūmī, in Islamic history, was from Rome and he was a slave who was white. Therefore, this is a major false claim and 'AbdulHaq has researched well and found the reality.

Dr Khālid al-Anbarī
Former Associate Professor
King Abdul'Azeez University, Jeddah
15 January 2007

Introduction

In the Name of Allāh, the Most Beneficent, Most Merciful

Indeed all praise is due to Allāh, we praise Him, we seek His Aid and ask for His forgiveness, whomsoever Allāh guides there is none to misguide and whomsoever Allāh misguides there is none to guide. I bear witness that there is no god worthy of worship except Allāh and I bear witness that Muhammad is His Messenger, to proceed:

Since the 1960s there has been a rapid and phenomenal increase of people in the West embracing Islām and the majority of those in the West who are turning to Islām are people of African origin in the UK and the USA. At the same time, Afrocentric ideology has also spread in the West which has, since the 1970s, argued that Islām itself was a religion of Arab conquerors that plundered Africa to the detriment of the African peoples themselves and this (Kemet Afrocentricity, various Hebrew Israelite cults or 'black Orientalism') has emerged to counter this growth of people of African origin turning to Islām. Moreover, Afrocentrics have initiated writings with reference to Islām and have claimed that Islām as a religion had, and has, no benefit and is only relevant to the 'Arab' cultural mind and milieu and as a result cannot be applied to people of African origin or their lands. This school of thought attempts to claim that the involvement of black people in Islām is contradictory and even tries to accuse Islām of being something that was used to enslave and discriminate against people of African origin, by referring to instances within history which indicate racial prejudice within Muslim lands or amongst some ignorant Muslims.

Furthermore, black Orientalism and Kemet Afrocentricity has a number of surprising unconscious associates who are in agreement, ranging from Zionists to evangelical Christian missionaries to different Hebrew

Israelite cults, so in Defining Legends the claims and assertions of these partisan elements in promoting claims that Islām itself includes, nay promotes, racism, slavery of black people, discrimination, injustice and prejudice will be critically evaluated in light of the Qur'ān, Sunnah, the understandings of the early Muslims (*salaf*) and historical evidence. Indeed, much of the sources that this school of thought refers to are usually directly taken from Orientalist sources or via cross-referencing from those who have a similar intention, i.e. from those elements who seek to discredit Islām in the eyes of people of African origin.

Defining Legends will critically evaluate mainstream black Orientalism and extremist Afrocentric claims about Islām and bring new evidence to challenge their false assumptions. The documentary evidence presented in some Afrocentric literature about Islām will be analyzed and dismissed where necessary. This study will mainly dismiss the anti-Islamic trend within some Afrocentric perceptions of Islām along with recourse to more corroborated criteria and demonstrate the incoherence of their arguments against Islām. Defining Legends also demonstrates how much of Afrocentric thought regarding Islām is in fact entrenched in a Eurocentric origin, therefore based upon anti-Islamic European Christian, Freemasonic and Zionist sources.

The importance of Muslims writing on history, and on some of the more difficult aspects of history, should not be avoided by Muslims. As how can a people go forward in the future if they do not take lessons from the past? This is what Muslim historians have highlighted throughout history, along with the importance of being impartial, honest, truthful and non-biased. Al-Akfānī stated in his book *ad-Durr an-Nadheem fī Aqsām il-'Ilm wa't-Ta'leem* as relayed by 'Izzaddeen al-Kinānī al-Hanbalī in *Shurūt ul-Mu'arrikh fī Kitābat it-Tārīkh wa't-Tarājim* [Conditions of the Historian in Writing History and Biographies], which will be discussed shortly:

> History books are benefitted from in order to investigate reports of the 'Ulama [scholars] and the 'Uqalā' [wise people] and their realities, events, biographies and what remains of their virtues and spiritual illnesses after they have passed.

When embarking on a serious historical study of any subject it is incumbent that one makes his chronicles as impartial as possible so as not to present a biased view of past events. This impartiality is based on a quality of the scholars of Ahl us-Sunnah and Ahl ul-Hadeeth, for:

> أهل العلم يكتبون مالهم وما عليهم ، وأهل الأهواء لا يكتبون إلا ما لهم .
>
> The People of Knowledge write what is for them and what is against them; while the People of Desires do not write except for what is for them.[7]

The Mujaddid of the era, Imām al-Albānī *(rahimahullāh)*, noted:

> لأن هذا هو الذي عليه أهل الحديث أن يذكروا الحقائق سواء كانت لهم أو عليهم، خلافا لأهل الأهواء، كما يذكر ذلك ابن تيمية كثيرا في رده عليهم
>
> ...as this is what the People of Hadeeth are upon, that they mention the realities whether they are for them or against them; as opposed to the People of Desires as Ibn Taymiyyah has mentioned many times in his refutations against them.[8]

Imām as-Suyūtī stated in *ash-Shamārīkh fī 'Ilm it-Tārīkh* [Fireworks in Historiography] in regards to the benefit of history:

> Its benefit is in taking lessons and advice from it and obtaining practical lessons from it by stopping at the changing of times

---

7 Ibn Taymiyyah ascribes this statement to 'AbdurRahmān bin Mahdī in *al-Jawāb as-Saheeh*, vol.6, p.343; it has also been ascribed to Wakī' ibn al-Jarrāh (the trustworthy Hāfidh and pious worshipper) by ad-Dāraqutnī, See Imām 'Ali bin 'Umar ad-Dāraqutnī, *Sunan ad-Dāraqutnī* (Beirut: Dār ul-Ma'rifah, 1422 AH/2001 CE, 1st Print, eds. Shaykhs 'Ali Ahmad 'AbdulMajūd and 'Ali Muhammad Mu'awwidh), vol.1, p.26, no.32, p.77-78.

Ad-Dāraqutnī's *sanad* is as follows: Ahmad bin Muhammad bin Sa'eed narrated to us: Ibrāheem bin 'Abdullāh bin Muhammad bin Sālim as-Sulūlī, Abū Sālim said: I heard my father say: I heard Wakī' say... – the narration.

8 Imām Muhammad Nāsiruddeen al-Albānī, *Silsilah Ahādeeth ad-Da'eefah wa Mawdū'ah wa Atharahā as-Say'i fi'l-Ummah* (Riyadh: Maktabat ul-Mā'rif, 1425 AH/2004 CE), vol.12, p.551.

so as to be protected from the harmful examples and obtain beneficial examples.

As-Sakhāwī *(rahimahullāh)* stated in his landmark work on historiography *al-I'lān bi't-Tawbīkh liman Dhamm Ahl it-Tārīkh* that Tāj as-Subkī stated in his book *Mu'īd un-Ni'am*:

> The historian has to be a scholar, who is credible and possesses knowledge of the conditions of those who he is writing about. There should neither be any friendship between them which can lead the one documenting the history to *ta'assub* [bias] for the one he is writing about, nor any enmity which can lead the one writing the history to have hatred towards the one he is writing about.[9]

Subkī also stated in *Tabaqāt al-Kubrā*, in the biography of Ahmad bin Sālih al-Misrī:

> The historians can possibly debase a people or raise a people due to *ta'assub* or *jahl* [ignorance], or due to merely relying on a transmission of someone who cannot be trustworthy, or any other reason.[10]

Dr Muhammad bin Sāmil as-Sulamī, the former head of the College of Sharee'ah and Islamic Studies at Umm ul-Qurā' University stated in his book *Manhaj Kitābat it-Tārīkh il-Islāmī* [The Methodology of Writing Islamic History] when discussing 'Sought-After Conditions for a Historian In Order for his Narrations to be Accepted', he stated under point 5:

> Leaving Personal Interests and Desire
>
> This is a matter which is difficult to find except in rare cases. However with the previous condition [about avoiding suspicion], along with the sense of responsibility and fear of Allāh and evoking this in the mind, he is able to be free of misleading

9 Muhammad bin 'AbdurRahmān bin Muhammad Shamsuddeen as-Sakhāwī (831-903 AH/1427-1497 CE), *al-I'lān bi't-Tawbīkh liman Dhamm Ahl it-Tārīkh* (Beirut: Mu'assasat ur-Risālah, 1407/1986 CE, ed. Franz Rosenthal), p.122.

10 Ibid., p.123; quoting from *Tabaqāt ush-Shāfi'iyyah* (Cairo, 1324 AH), vol.1 p.197.

desires by Allāh's Aid.[11]

While Dr Muhammad Rashaad Khaleel (Professor of Islamic Heritage at the University of Riyadh) stated in his book *al-Manhaj al-Islāmī li-Dirāsat it-Tārīkh wa Tafseerihi* [The Islamic Method for Studying and Interpreting History] some conditions which have to be maintained for the one who attempts to embark on a history. Of these conditions is *'al-Ikhlās wa't-Tajarrud'* [Sincerity and Impartiality], Dr Muhammad Rashaad Khaleel states about this condition:

> ...that is because the goal of the researcher has to be to search for the truth wherever it is and not seek proofs and evidences which merely support his own personal view or preconceived idea; or supports a particular *madhhab*, belief or genus [of people]. Much distortion has thus entered Islamic history past and present from this door. In the past, those who hated Islām corrupted reports and fabricated them so as to plot against Islām and defame its adherents. While presently the same thing has occurred from people of innovation and desires and the people of fanatical bias to *madhhabs*, politics and racism in a similar way to which we presented prior from the words of al-Qādī Abū Bakr Ibn al-'Arabī.[12]

Furthermore, when one undertakes the responsibility of documenting and presenting history, one has to be prepared to also mention, if authentically transmitted, details of a sensitive nature that may challenge the mythical and romantic aspects of history. If this sensitive aspect of historical documentation is circumvented or completely ignored, this invariably will lead the commentator to present a flawed, historical narrative. By leaving out "sensitive" and "awkward" memories of the past, some historical commentators seek to present a sanitised history

11 Dr Muhammad bin Sāmil as-Sulamī, *Manhaj Kitābat it-Tārīkh il-Islāmī Ma'a Darāsat li Tatawwur it-Tadween wa Manāhij il-Mu'arrikheen Hatta Nihāyat al-Qarn ath-Thālith al-Hijrī* [The Methodology of Writing Islamic History With a Study of the Development of the Codification of the Methodology of the Historians Up Until the End of the Third Century After The Hijrah]. Dammām, KSA: Dār Ibn ul-Jawzī, Shawwāl 1429 AH, p.249.

12 Dr Muhammad Rashād Khaleel, *al-Manhaj al-Islāmī li-Dirāsat it-Tārīkh wa Tafsīrihi* [The Islamic Method for Studying and Interpreting History]. Casablanca: Dār uth-Thaqāfah, 1406 AH/1986 CE, pp.122-123.

of events.

Towards the end of the first section of the study, it is shown that one of the main architects of pan-African thought, Edward Wilmot Blyden, had great respect of Islām and viewed it as the only religion that could provide a real change for the whole continent of Africa. In fact, many non-Muslim pan-Africanists and black historians had a similar respect for Islām such as Franz Fanon, Dr Walter Rodney, W.E.B. Dubois, Kwame Nkrumah, J.A. Rogers, Dr Ivan Van Sertima, Cheikh Anta Diop and many others. The Islamic adherence of the African Muslims that were enslaved in the Americas and the Caribbean will also be assessed and it will be seen that the African Muslims enslaved maintained their Islām and preserved their own terms of reference and values, making it clear that neither the European Christian world nor a creolised identity appealed to them.

I
The Afrocentric Assault on Islām

One of the most vehement Afrocentric writers who criticized Islām was the late Chancellor Williams, especially his book *Destruction of Black Civilisation.*[13] This book is important as it is used by the hostile Afrocentrics when attacking Islām and Muslims. The book has also been heavily relied upon by Christian evangelists in their missionary work. Williams himself was a committed Christian and he admits this in the book, this probably explains his deep hatred for Islām and this effectively made his book emotionally biased. Joseph 'Jay' Smith,[14] the Anglo-American evangelical flag-bearer of late 1990s Christian polemic against Islām in the UK had also referred to this book. One of Smith's side-kicks who goes by the peculiar name 'Brother Banda,' even wrote a feeble criticism of Islām and alleged racism within Islām and William's work was heavily relied upon.[15] This propaganda tract was distributed at Hyde Park Speaker's Corner in the mid to late 1990s. The Afrocentrist

---

13 First published in 1971, re-printed in 1987.

14 The 'arch-deacon' and senior Christian missionary polemicist against Islām in the UK. Smith is an Anglo-American born in India from an evangelical background and has a variety of degrees and diplomas. He has studied 'divinity theology' in America and also studied at the School of Oriental and African Studies, University of London. Smith however is not even regarded highly by the de-mythologiser orientalists at SOAS. When asked by myself in 1998, a former lecturer of Smith's, G. Hawting, described Smith as being: "A Christian missionary with his own agenda, obviously extreme in his theories, too radical in his claims to be accepted at a scholarly level and a trouble maker." Enough said! As stated to me by Professor Hawting in 1998 at SOAS, University of London.

15 This was called '*An African Asks Some Disturbing Questions of Islam,*' and was made into one of the Hyde Park Christian Fellowship's '99 Truth Tracts.'

Molefi Asante has also made historical mistakes and inaccurate claims:

> The Arabs with their Jihads, or holy wars, were thorough in their destruction of much of the ancient culture. It is also as if small bands (of fleeing Egyptian priests) keeping ahead of the Islamic onslaught managed to preserve certain aspects of the traditional culture of Egypt.[16]

Molefi Asante thus asserts that these "aspects of ancient Egyptian culture" were kept amongst the Wolof, Yoruba, Ashanti and other West African tribes. Other characters that have axes to grind are writers such as Wole Soyinka, claiming that Islām and Arabs are responsible for "the cultural and spiritual ravaging of the continent,"[17] and all of this is noted without a shred of historical evidence from either African, Arabic or European sources, and if any sources are mentioned then they are actually white European ones!! Soyinka has even gone so far as to suggest that north Africa should not be considered part of Africa! Soyinka's deep hatred for Islām and Arabs owes a lot to his internal Nigerian political schism, though this is never openly acknowledged or admitted by Soyinka.

This is merely polemic, and Lange notes in his book *The Philosophy of Historiography*:

> Polemical histories need not be false, of course, strictly, but they are likely to be one-sided, with a vengeance.[18]

Lange then states in the footnote to the above paragraph:

> The best propaganda, and the hardest to detect, as is well known, is that which tells only the truth, but tells it selectively, leaving out the qualifying truths, or the counter-truths, and spins its truths in such a way as to induce and support a particular ideological viewpoint.[19]

---

16 Molefi Asante, '*Afrocentricity and Culture*' in Asante and Kariamu Welsh Asante (eds.), *African Culture – The Rhythms of Unity* (Westport, CT: Africa World Press, 1985).

17 Wole Soyinka, *The Burden of Memory, The Muse of Forgiveness* (New York: Oxford University Press, 1999), p.42.

18 John Lange, *The Philosophy of Historiography* (New York: E Reads, 2010), p.59

19 Ibid., p.60.

Chancellor Williams' book is a fictitious race war between black Africans and Arabs and promotes a number of popular misconceptions about Islām namely: Islām was spread by the sword and Islām is an Arab religion. The front cover of the book itself regurgitates stereotypes by displaying an Arab on a horse with a sword fighting a semi-naked African in leopard skin with a spear in his hand!? Even this image is not exactly Afrocentric as it seems to be based on medieval and colonial European stereotypes of both peoples. Williams argues, with no solid historical evidence, an amazing story reminiscent of medieval European Christian polemical writings against Islām. Sherman (AbdulHakeem) Jackson notes regarding this:

> More directly, however, if the Arab invasions are responsible for the destruction of African civilisation, why did such black eyewitnesses as Edward Blyden, Martin Delaney and others fail to report this? And if the Arab invasions led to the destruction of African civilisation, why did it not lead to the destruction of all those other civilisations over whose lands the Arabs seized control? Why would the "Arab invaders" destroy every peeve of civilisation they could put their hands on in sub-Saharan Africa but leave the statue of Buddha standing in Afghanistan, the ruins of Persepolis standing in Persia, and the Sphinx, Abu Simbel, and countless pagan gods and temples standing in Egypt? Clearly the analogue here is, once again, the black experience in America. The Arabs *had* to destroy the culture and civilisation of the Africans in Africa because the white Americans destroyed the culture and civilisation of the Africans in America.[20]

This lack of evidence was also noted by Cheikh Anta Diop who was one of the most respected and knowledgeable scholars of African history, he was also a physicist and director of the Radiocarbon Laboratory at I.F.A.N. at the University of Dakar, Senegal, and a noted Egyptologist, his most famous work is *The African Origin of Civilization.* He mentioned in his book *Precolonial Black Africa*, in contrast to the anti-Islamic Afrocentrics,

> The Arab conquests dear to sociologists are necessary to their theories but did not exist in reality. To this day no reliable

20 Sherman Jackson, *Islam and the Blackamerican: Looking Toward the Third Resurrection* (New York: Oxford University Press, 2005), p.113.

historical documents substantiate such theories.[21]

Williams mentioned that the Arabs used tactics such as interbreeding with Africans in order to create an Islamically brainwashed mongrel hybrid race that he calls a *"Mulatto."* Destruction of black artworks, monuments and writings, enslavement of Africans and invasions also typified the "Arab Muslim" invasions. However, Dr Walter Rodney, who gained a Ph.D in history and authored the famous book *How Europe Underdeveloped Africa*, did not mention Muslims as being involved in destroying the continent, on the contrary Walter Rodney highlighted Islām's positive influence within Africa:

> As in other parts of the world, literacy in Africa was connected with religion, so that in Islamic countries it was a Koranic education...Moslem education was particularly extensive at the primary level, and it was also available at the secondary and university levels. In Egypt there was the Al-Azhar University, in Morocco the University of Fez, and in Mali the University of Timbuktu - all testimony to the standard of education achieved in Africa before the colonial intrusion.[22]

W.E.B. Dubois notes:

> Gao, Timbuktu, and Jenne were intellectual centers, and at the University of Sankore gathered thousands of students of law, literature, grammar, geography and surgery...From this Africa a new cultural impulse entered Europe and became the Renaissance.[23]

Blyden mentioned:

> The introduction of Islam into Central and West Africa has been the most important, if not the sole, preservative against the desolations of the slave trade. Islam furnished a protection to the tribes who embraced it by effectively binding them together in one strong religious fraternity and enabling them

---

21 Cheikh Anta Diop, *Precolonial Black Africa*, trans. by Harold Salemson (New York: Lawrence Hill Books, 1987), p.102.

22 Walter Rodney, *How Europe Underdeveloped Africa* (Washington: Howard University Press, 1974), p.240.

23 W.E.B. Dubois, *The World and Africa* (New York: International Publishers Inc, 1969), pp. 211 and 223.

> by their united efforts to baffle the attempts of powerful pagan slave hunters. Enjoying this comparative immunity from sudden hostile incursions, industry was stimulated among them...Large towns and cities have grown under Islam's energy and industry. Dr Barth[24] was surprised to find such towns or cities such as Kano and Sokoto in the centre of Africa – to discover the focus of a complex and widely ramified commerce, and a bust hive of manufacturing industry, in a region which most people believed to have been a desert.[25]

In terms of Muslims allegedly causing destruction and mayhem, we find that the Prophet Muhammad *(sallallāhu 'alayhi wassallam)* when he ordered the Muslim armies stated: *"Do not kill women, children or the elderly. Do not cut down fruit-bearing trees. Do not destroy an inhabited place. Do not slaughter sheep or camels except for food. Do not burn trees and do not scatter them. Do not steal from the booty and do not be cowardly."*[26] Regardless of how cruel the enemy, Islām forbids their mutilation, torture or slaughter. The Prophet Muhammad also forbade killing by deceit and treachery and the violation of treaties and cease-fires. So even during war, the believers are ordered with compassion and to continue the great Jihād of calling to truth:

وَإِنْ أَحَدٌ مِّنَ الْمُشْرِكِينَ اسْتَجَارَكَ فَأَجِرْهُ

حَتَّىٰ يَسْمَعَ كَلَامَ اللَّهِ ثُمَّ أَبْلِغْهُ مَأْمَنَهُ ذَٰلِكَ بِأَنَّهُمْ قَوْمٌ لَّا يَعْلَمُونَ ۝

> And if any of the polytheists seeks your protection, then grant him protection so that they may hear the words of Allāh [i.e. the Qur'ān]. Then deliver him to his place of safety. That is because they are people who do not know.
>
> [*at-Tawbah* (9): 6]

As for non-combatants or civilians we read,

---

24 Heinrich Barth was one of the early European Saharan and West African travelers. His published works include the five volume *Travels and Discoveries in North and Central Africa – A Journal of an Expedition Undertaken Under the Auspices of H.B.M's Government in the Years 1849-1855*.

25 *Christianity, Islam and the Negro Race*, p. 215.

26 *Muwatta'* of Imām Mālik.

لَا يَنْهَاكُمُ اللَّهُ عَنِ الَّذِينَ
لَمْ يُقَاتِلُوكُمْ فِي الدِّينِ وَلَمْ يُخْرِجُوكُم مِّن دِيَارِكُمْ أَن تَبَرُّوهُمْ وَتُقْسِطُوا
إِلَيْهِمْ إِنَّ اللَّهَ يُحِبُّ الْمُقْسِطِينَ ۝ إِنَّمَا يَنْهَاكُمُ اللَّهُ عَنِ الَّذِينَ قَاتَلُوكُمْ
فِي الدِّينِ وَأَخْرَجُوكُم مِّن دِيَارِكُمْ وَظَاهَرُوا عَلَىٰ إِخْرَاجِكُمْ أَن تَوَلَّوْهُمْ
وَمَن يَتَوَلَّهُمْ فَأُولَٰئِكَ هُمُ الظَّالِمُونَ ۝

Allāh does not forbid you from those who do not fight you because of religion and do not expel you from your homes – from being righteous toward them[27] and acting justly toward them.[28] Indeed, Allāh loves those who act justly.[29] Allāh only forbids you from those who fight you

27 Ibn Katheer (*rahimahullāh*) says about this: to be gentle with them.

28 Ibn Katheer (*rahimahullāh*) says about this: to be fair with them.

29 Ibn Katheer (*rahimahullāh*) transmits in regards to this in the *ayah*: Imām Ahmad recorded that Asmā' bint Abū Bakr said, "My mother, who was an idolatress at the time, came to me during the Treaty of Peace, the Prophet conducted with the Quraysh. I came to the Prophet and said, "*O Allāh's Messenger! My mother came visiting, desiring something from me, should I treat her with good relations*" The Prophet said,

«نَعَمْ صِلِي أُمَّكِ»

"Yes. Keep good relation with your mother." The Two *Saheehs* recorded this *hadeeth*. Imām Ahmad recorded that 'Abdullāh bin Zubayr said, "Qutaylah came visiting her daughter, Asmā' bint Abī Bakr, with some gifts, such as Dibab, cheese and clarified (cooking) butter, and she was an idolatress at that time. Asmā' refused to accept her mother's gifts and did not let her enter her house. 'Ā'ishah asked the Prophet about his verdict and Allāh sent down the ayah,

لَّا يَنْهَىٰكُمُ اللَّهُ عَنِ الَّذِينَ لَمْ يُقَٰتِلُوكُمْ فِى الدِّينِ ۝

Allāh does not forbid you with those who fought not against you on account of religion…

…Until the end of the *ayah*, Allāh's Messenger ordered Asmā' to accept her mother's gifts and to let her enter her house." Allāh's statement,

إِنَّ اللَّهَ يُحِبُّ الْمُقْسِطِينَ ۝

Indeed Allāh loves those who act justly.

> because of religion and expel you from your homes and aid in your expulsion – (forbids) that you make allies of them.[30] And whoever makes allies of them, then it is those who are the wrongdoers.
>
> [*al-Mumtahinah* (60): 8-9]

Therefore, the Prophet Muhammad expressly forbade Muslim armies from attacking women and children, the sick and elderly, Monks, Rabbis, hired labourers etc. he also outlawed the wanton killing of animals, the burning of crops and vegetation, the polluting of waters and the destruction of homes and places of sanctuary. The Qur'ān, 1400 years ago, mentioned

وَلَوْلَا دَفْعُ اللَّهِ النَّاسَ
بَعْضَهُم بِبَعْضٍ لَّهُدِّمَتْ صَوَامِعُ وَبِيَعٌ وَصَلَوَاتٌ وَمَسَاجِدُ يُذْكَرُ فِيهَا
اسْمُ اللَّهِ كَثِيرًا وَلَيَنصُرَنَّ اللَّهُ مَن يَنصُرُهُ إِنَّ اللَّهَ لَقَوِيٌّ عَزِيزٌ

> For were it not that Allāh checks one set of people by means of another, monasteries, churches, synagogues and mosques wherein the Name of Allāh is mentioned often, would surely have been destroyed.
>
> [*al-Hajj* (22): 40]

Once, when news reached the Prophet Muhammad *(sallallāhu alayhi wassallam)* that children had been killed in a battle, he exclaimed *"What is with some people that the killing today caused them to go so far as to kill children?!"* A man answered: *"O Messenger of Allāh, they are just children of polytheists!?"* The Prophet replied: *"Verily, the best of you are children of polytheists. Do not kill children! (I say again) do not kill children! For every soul is born upon a natural (Islamic) disposition (innocent, monotheistic and good) – until its tongue speaks on its behalf..."*

The Qur'ān further highlights,

---

30 Ibn Katheer (*rahimahullāh*) states about this part of the verse:

> Allāh forbids you from being kind and befriending with the disbelievers who are openly hostile to you, those who fought against you, expelled you and helped to expel you. Allāh the Exalted forbids you from being their friends and orders you to be their enemy.

يَا أَيُّهَا الَّذِينَ آمَنُواْ كُونُواْ
قَوَّامِينَ لِلّهِ شُهَدَاء بِالْقِسْطِ وَلاَ يَجْرِمَنَّكُمْ شَنَآنُ قَوْمٍ عَلَى أَلاَّ تَعْدِلُواْ
اعْدِلُواْ هُوَ أَقْرَبُ لِلتَّقْوَى وَاتَّقُواْ اللّهَ إِنَّ اللّهَ خَبِيرٌ بِمَا تَعْمَلُونَ۝

O you who believe, stand steadfast for Allāh as witnesses of justice, and let not the hatred of a people prevent you from justice towards them. Be just, that is closer to righteousness and fear Allāh. Indeed, Allāh is Well-Acquainted with what you do.

[*al-Mā'idah* (5): 8]

Yet these sources of Islām are not quoted in their 'scholarly' works about Islām, as those who have an agenda against Islām selectively misquote the sources in order to suggest that Islām encourages the wanton persecution and slaughter of non-Muslims. However, an honest holistic study of the Qur'ān and *Sunnah* reveals that those passages dealing with warfare are explicit in calling for equity and justice; always taking the side of the oppressed against the oppressor, whether believer or disbeliever, encouraging leniency and a halting of war in favour of peace.[31] Later in the book, examples will be given of how other systems and beliefs do not have such an emphasis in their source texts. Cheikh Anta Diop also notes:

> The primary reason for the success of Islam in Black Africa, with one exception, consequently stems from the fact that it was promulgated peacefully, at first by solitary Arabo-Berber Travelers to certain Black kings and notables, who then spread it about them to those under their jurisdiction...What is to be emphasized here is the peaceful nature of this conversion, regardless of the legend surrounding it.[32]

Some note that 'Arabs' invaded Egypt and killed the indigenous populace, oppressing them under Islām. The reality however is that during the initial spread of Islām Egypt was being ruled by the Byzantines who were of European descent, Egypt was not under the rule of Africans from the Nile Valley civilizations. Cheikh Anta Diop, the expert of Egyptian history from an African perspective, highlights:

---

31 *'Islamic Terrorism – Exploded'* by AR Mahdi from www.Quran.nu

32 Cheikh Anta Diop, *Precolonial Black Africa*, p.163.

> During the period of our study, from the third to the seventeenth centuries, not one conquest was ever launched by way of the Nile...Nor was there ever an Arab conquest of Mozambique or any other East African country.[33]

When one of the Muslim commanders, 'Ubādah ibn as-Sāmit (*radi Allāhu 'anhu*), who was a darker skinned Arab, went to these rulers, the Egyptian leaders said about him *"get that black man away from us!"* Therefore, the Greek-speaking Christian Byzantines (of European origin) were controlling Egypt at this time in any case, not black Egyptians of the Nile Valley! Indeed the Muslims if anything were bringing a respect of blackness to Egypt. This exchange between 'Ubādah ibn as-Sāmit and the then ruler of Egypt Muqawqis illustrates this point superbly:

> وعندما جاء المسلمون لفتح مصر وتوغلوا فيها حتى وقفوا أمام حصن بابليون رغب المقوقس في المفاوضة مع المسلمين فأرسل إليهم وفداً ليعلم ما يريدون ، ثم طلب منهم أن يرسلوا إليه وفداً ، فأرسل إليه عمرو بن العاص عشرة نفر فيهم عبادة بن الصامت ، وكان عبادة أسود شديد السواد طويلاً حتى قالوا إن طوله عشرة أشبار ، وأمره عمرو أن يكون هو الذي يتولى الكلام . فلما دخلوا على المقوقس تقدمهم عبادة بن الصامت فهابه المقوقس لسواده وقال لهم : نحوا عني هذا الأسود وقدموا غيره يكلمني ، فقال رجال الوفد جميعاً إن هذا الأسود أفضلنا رأياً وعلماً وهو سيدنا وخيرنا والمقدم علينا ، وإنما نرجع جميعاً إلى قوله ورأيه ، وقد أمره الأمير دوننا بما أمره ، وأمرنا ألا نخالف رأيه وقوله ، فقال لهم : وكيف رضيتم أن يكون هذا الأسود أفضلكم وإنما ينبغي أن يكون هو دونكم ؟ قالوا : كلا ! إنه وإن كان أسود كما ترى فإنه من أفضلنا موضعاً وأفضلنا سابقة وعقلاً ورأياً وليس

33 Ibid., p.101.

ينكر السواد فينا ، فقال المقوقس لعبادة : تقدم يا أسود وكلمني برفق فإني أهاب سوادك ، وإن اشتد كلامك عليّ ازددت لك هيبة ، فقال عبادة – وقد رأى فزع المقوقس من السواد : إن في جيشنا ألف أسود هم أشد سواداً مني .

When the Muslims arrived to conquer Egypt and penetrated the defences of the land until they reached the fortified areas, Muqawqis wanted to negotiate with the Muslims and sent a delegation out to them to enquire about their demands. He then requested that a delegation, from the Muslims, go out to see him so 'Amru bin al-'Ās sent out ten men which included 'Ubādah ibn as-Sāmit. 'Ubādah was very black in complexion and also very tall, to the extent that it was said that he was as tall as ten arm spans (about two and a half metres), and 'Amru instructed him to convey the terms. When they entered to speak to al-Muqawqis, 'Ubādah was put forward and Muqawqis became scared due to 'Ubādah's blackness, and said to the Muslims: "Get this black man away from me and put someone else forward to speak to me." The men from the delegation said: "this black man is the best of us in terms of opinion and knowledge, and he is our master and the best of us and preferred among us. All of us refer back to his word and view. The leader gave him command instead of us and to adhere to what he instructs. He also instructed us not to oppose his view and word." Muqawqis said to them: "How can you be pleased with this black man being the most virtuous of you, he should rather be the lowest of you?!" They [i.e. the Muslims] said: "No, not at all! Though he is black, as you can see he is the best of us in rank, priority, intelligence, sense and judgement. Blackness is not something rejected among us." Muqawqis then said to 'Ubādah: "Come forward then O black one and speak gently to me as your blackness frightens me and if you speak sternly with me I will become even more fearful." When 'Ubādah saw that Muqawqis was scared he said to him: "In our army are a thousand men blacker than me!"[34]

There are some important points to append to this:

---

34 This is relayed in a number of historical texts, the earliest of them being Ibn 'Abd al-Hakam, *Futuh Misr wa Akhbāruhā* [The Conquest of Egypt and its Reports] (New Haven, CT: Yale University Press, 1922), ed. C.C. Torrey, p.66.

One. Islam in its initial inception among the Muslims emphasised a meritocracy regardless of race and colour. This equality was taught and is documented, and was not theoretical. Such equality was previously unheard of among civilisations prior and even if it may have been found there was no core teaching about this facet and hence, Islam's universality.

Two. Some Arabs self-identified as *'aswad'* [i.e. 'black'] and without colourism or any notion that this was negative.

Three. Blackness was not looked down upon among the first Muslim generation.

Four. The early Muslims taught respect for blackness, while the other 'civilisations' did not.

Five. Some historians suggest that al-Muqawqis, who made this remark, is not to be identified with Cyrus, the Patriarch of Alexandria but rather with a Sassanid governor of Egypt at that time. The term 'Muqawqis' is the Arabic-derived name of the Coptic 'Pikaukasos' which means 'Caucasian', as the Sassanid Empire reached up to the Caucasus. The term 'al-Muqawqis' came to be applied to all Egyptian Patriarchs by Muslim historians. However, due to the close role in treaty arrangements between Cyrus and the Sahābah as noted in the historical record, 'Muqawqis' most likely refers to him than anyone else. Allāh knows best.

Six: Byzantine Romans were ruling over Egypt at the time of the Islamic conquest, not the followers of Imhotep! Stewart Gibson states in *Shackles of Iron: Slavery Beyond the Atlantic*:

> This source and several others suggest that many African soldiers were not slaves but free Africans living in the Arabian Peninsula at the time. The references are, however, too meagre to establish whether these Africans were freed slaves or had emigrated from Africa. That freed soldiers were somehow recruited from Africa also cannot be ruled out.[35]

Adh-Dhahabī in *Siyar A'lām un-Nubalā'* relayed that Ibn Yūnus said:

35 Stewart Gibson, *Shackles of Iron: Slavery Beyond the Atlantic* (Indianapolis and Cambridge: Hackett Publishing Company, 2016), p.39.

Muhammad ibn Maslamah (*radi Allāhu 'anhu*), one of the companions who climbed over the fortress with az-Zubayr during the conquest of Egypt" and relayed that 'Ibāyah bin Rufā'ah described him as being "black, tall and huge".[36] According to the historian al-Qudā'ī, there were Ethiopian troops involved in the conquest of Egypt and settled in Fustat.[37] It is also well known that the Christians of Egypt ('Aegyptus' in Latin) welcomed the Muslim conquest of Egypt as they would be liberated from their Christian Byzantine co-religionists.[38] Indeed, regarding one of the Sudanese kingdoms, Suba, which operated in the region of present day Kabashiyyah and extending south towards Sennar, had bishops appointed by the Patriarch of Alexandria, it was documented that "their king enslaves whom he wishes of his subjects, whether they have committed a crime or not."[39] Dr Ivan Van Sertima, a well-known non-Muslim historian, has noted that:

> I think it should also be pointed out, contrary to myths about the Muslims, that they did not force their religion down the throats of the Christians...We have been given no evidence that this

---

36 Imam Shamsuddeen Muhammad bin Ahmad bin 'Uthman adh-Dhahabi (d. 748 AH/1374 CE), *Siyar A'lam un-Nubala'* (Beirut: Mu'assasat ur-Risalah, 1402 AH/1982 CE, ed. Shu'ayb al-Arna'ut), vol.2, p.370.

37 See Timothy Power, *The Red Sea from Byzantium to the Caliphate, AD 500-1000* (American University of Cairo Press).

38 'Amr ibn al-'Ās (*radi Allāhu 'anhu*) who led the campaign into Egypt, left the Christians in peace. According to *The Chronicle of John, Bishop of Nikiu*, trans. RH Charles (London: William and Norgate, 1916), in chapters 120-121:

> On the twentieth of Maskaram Theodore and all his troops and officers [the Byzantines] set out and proceeded to the island of Cyprus, and abandoned the city of Alexandria. And thereupon 'Amr the chief of the Muslims made his entry without effort into the city of Alexandria. And the inhabitants received him with respect; for they were in great tribulation and affliction... And 'Amr became stronger every day in every field of his activity. And he exacted the taxes which had been determined upon, but he took none of the property of the churches, and he committed no act of spoliation or plunder, and he preserved them throughout all his days...And he increased the taxes to the extent of twenty-two batr of gold till all the people hid themselves owing to the greatness of the tribulation, and could not find the wherewithal to pay.

39 J.S. Trimingham, *Islam in the Sudan* (London: Frank Cass, 1983), p.62.

changed dramatically in later Muslim dynasties.[40]

Seven. There was no wholesale invasion of Nubia by the Muslims, there were some skirmishes but no significant battle or invasion.

Hence, blackness was present among the Arabs, indeed it was present among the Quraysh and the Bani Hāshim as a result of generational intermarriage. Classical Arabic geographical works and lineage works note terms such as '*Aswad*' [black], '*Udmah*' [intense blackness] and '*Adlam*' [intense blackness]. The Arabs of the pre-Islamic times categorised people as either '*Aswad*' which included those of black and brown complexions (i.e. '*Asmar*' [brown]), or '*Ahmar*' [red] which included those who were of fairer complexions described by the Arabs as '*Asfar*' [lit. 'yellow', i.e. blonde] or '*Abyad*' [white]. Moreover, in *Tanweer ul-Ghabash*, Ibn ul-Jawzī lists those from the Quraysh who were born to Ethiopian mothers. This was also due to the fact that, and this was noted by al-Jāhidh, the pre-Islamic Arabs preferred to have children with Ethiopian women in order to strengthen their progeny and promote chivalry among them, which Africans were renowned for during antiquity. Dr Jawād 'Ali stated in his book *al-Mufassal fī Tārikh il-'Arab Qabla'l-Islām* [The Detail Regarding the History of the Arabs Before Islām], vol.7, p.311:

> Some of the black Arabs were famed for bravery and valour [*iqdām*]...some of the tribes were predominantly black to the extent that they are referred to as 'Dalam' and 'ad-Dalam' is used to refer to a man who is intensely black in colour...this may indicate an origin from Africa as is apparent.

Jawad 'Ali also suggests that when the Islamic conquests encapsulated the world and the Arabs came into contact with other peoples, they then began to prefer to marry from those other peoples rather than the Africans with whom they had been having contact for centuries. Moreover, Dr 'Ali even argues that the low view of black people which these other non-Arabs had was then passed over to the Arabs and that such anti-black sentiment was not found among the Arabs initially. This is an interesting point and there does seem to be some accuracy in this, as the Arabs during the Pre-Islamic Era were not only interacting

40 Ivan Van Sertima (ed.), *Golden Age of the Moor* (New Brunswick and London: Transaction Publishers, 1992), pp.18-33.

regularly with Ethiopia but also were under the rule of the Ethiopians at one stage and dominated by them, the Year of the Elephant proving this. These connections between the pre-Islamic Arabs and Ethiopia was also noted by Dr Jawād 'Ali in *al-Mufassal*, p.449-450.

Moreover, there has been the line of thought that considers Islām as an 'Arab' religion that was designed in order to mainly "unite the Arabs" upon its initial inception. However, the words of the Prophet Muhammad (*sallallāhu 'alayhi wassallam*) himself do not indicate such an Arab nationalist concept, for he said: "*Every other Prophet was sent to his nation exclusively, while I have been sent to all of humanity.*"[41] He also said "*Indeed my friends and allies are not the tribe of so and so. Rather, my allies and friends are the pious, wherever they may be.*"[42]

The idea that Islām is an "Arab religion" is still persistent even though the fact remains that most Muslims are not Arabs and not all Arabs are Muslims!? Furthermore, it is rather absurd to consider Islām as representing a culture that includes belly-dancing, *sheeshah* smoking and other absurdities that are found amongst the Arabs. Arab countries only constitute about seventeen per cent of the Muslim world, not even twenty per cent. In fact the largest population of Muslims in the world today is found in Indonesia, wherein the people historically accepted Islām via peaceful conversions. Islām is not something that is exclusive to Arabs and the first Muslims of non-Arab origin opposed Arabs in order to spread Islām. As the former Mufti of Saudi Arabia, the noble Shaykh 'Abdul'Azeez ibn 'Abdullāh ibn Bāz (*rahimahullāh*)[43] noted:

> So the Prophet distanced Abū Tālib and Abū Lahab (his uncles) – because they were not Muslims and drew near Salmān the Persian, Suhayb the Roman and Bilāl the

41 Al-Bukhārī.

42 Al-Bukhārī and Muslim.

43 The late Shaykh 'Abdul'Azeez ibn 'Abdullāh ibn Bāz was the leading scholar of Saudi Arabia and the head of Dār ul-Iftā. He was blind from youth and excelled in Islamic studies due to his tremendous memory. He was also the first chancellor of the Islamic University of Madeenah and a lecturer on *Saheeh ul-Bukhārī* which he knew by memory. He wrote a number of treatises on a variety of topics including editing *Fath ul-Bārī* of Ibn Hajar al-'Asqalānī, the commentary of *Saheeh ul-Bukhārī*.

> Ethiopian. This is because they possessed *īmān* (faith) and piety and they followed the Prescribed Laws and traversed the Straight Path.[44]

The Qur'ān was revealed in the Arabic language as the last revelation, yet many Prophets and Messengers before spoke ancient Ethiopic,[45] ancient Nubian or Hebrew, Syriac, Aramaic and many other languages. Jesus did not speak English and neither did the ancient Egyptians. In Muslim Africa, the Arabic language is studied alongside the other indigenous languages as it is in other parts of the Muslim world. In fact one of the main formulators of Arabic language and grammar was as-Sibawayh who was not an Arab but a Persian and his book is universally celebrated.[46]

The position of Ethiopia during the time of Islām is also neither addressed nor assessed by Williams and those who blindly followed his 'destruction of black civilisation' thesis. Ethiopia at this time was a strong and powerful land, and in the period prior to the Prophet Muhammad (*sallAllāhu 'alayhi wassallam*) Ethiopia was a major world power which in fact dominated a variety of lands in the Arabian Peninsula. Indeed, they ruled with an iron-fist and an arrogance which no doubt led to their own destruction during the Year of the Elephant (in the 6th century CE) and that would then lead to an anti-Ethiopian sentiment among the Arabs. 'AbdulHakeem Jackson emphasises:

> Now, every student of Muslim history knows that the Ethiopians invaded Arabia in the sixth century C.E., a fact alluded to by the Qur'ān itself (Soorah 105: 1-5). But because the black experience in America contradicts such a role for blacks, Williams completely overlooks an example that could place black people in the

44 Shaykh Bin Bāz, *Majmū' al-Fatāwā wa Maqālāt Mutanawwi'ah* (vol. 3, pp.100-103); '*Marriage, Casts and Compatibility*' in *al-Istiqāmah* newsletter, no.7 (Rabī' ul-Awwal 1418AH/ July 1997).

45 In fact there are some words in the Qur'ān which are from the ancient Ethiopian language of Ge'ez, which was a language which became extinct in northern Ethiopia and in what is now Eritrea by the 13th century CE but is still used in Ethiopic Christian worship. The modern Ethiopian language of Amharic is based on Ge'ez and is the second largest Semitic language spoken in the world today after Arabic. For more on this see chapter six.

46 For more on this in Islām see the chapter '*Does Islām Teach Racism*?'

company of those whose achievements constitute the benchmark for his comparisons.[47]

The fact that the early Muslims sought refuge and safe-haven in Ethiopia under the rulership of the Christian Ethiopian king Najāshī at the time demonstrates that Africa and Africans supported the spread of early Islām and that early Islām was composed of non-Arab elements that were vital to its spread around the world. A Muslim scholar, Shaykh Muhammad Amān bin 'Alī al-Jāmī stated[48] that the companions of the Prophet Muhammad migrated to Ethiopia to escape the abuse and

47 Jackson, *op cit.*, p.113

48 In his explanation of *Usūl uth-Thalāthah*. Shaykh Muhammad Amān bin 'Ali Jāmī 'Ali was born in the town of Taga Tab in Harer, Ethiopia in 1349 AH/1930 CE. He memorised the Qur'ān at an early age and studied Arabic in his hometown with Shaykh Muhammad Ameen al-Harerī. He then migrated to study in another town and studied *Nadham uz-Zubd* of Ibn Raslān with Shaykh Mūsā, also the text of *al-Minhāj* with Shaykh Abādir. He also studied other Islamic sciences at this town. He also met a colleague, Shaykh 'AbdulKareem, and the two of them wanted to fulfil the Hajj and so they left Ethiopia for Somalia and took a ship from there to Aden in Yemen. They experienced many hardships in Yemen but persevered and arrived in Hudaydah where they fasted the month of Ramadān. They had travelled by foot on this arduous journey through Yemen and while in Yemen they were warned against the Salafi *da'wah* by some of the ignorant Yemeni *shaykhs* who referred to the *da'wah* as "Wahhabiyyah". They continued on their journey passing through as-Sāmitah and al-'Arīsh until they gained permission to enter Makkah.

After completing the Hajj in 1369 AH (1950 CE), Shaykh Muhammad Amān Jāmī began to seek knowledge in Masjid al-Harām and studied with Shaykh 'AbdurRazzāq Hamza, Shaykh 'AbdulHaqq al-Hāshimī, Shaykh Muhammad bin 'Ali as-Sumālī and others. While in Makkah, Shaykh Muhammad Amān became acquainted with Shaykh 'Abdul'Azeez bin Bāz and travelled with him to Riyadh in the 1970s when the Educational Institute was opened. During his secondary studies at the Educational Institute, Shaykh Muhammad Amān's colleagues included Shaykh 'AbdulMuhsin al-'Abbād al-Badr and Shaykh 'Ali bin Mahnā, former judge at the Central Court in Madeenah. In Riyadh, Shaykh Muhammad Amān studied with Shaykh Muhammad Ameen ash-Shanqītī from Mauritania and also the *muhaddith* Shaykh Hammād al-Ansārī from Mali, and he was also close to Shaykh 'AbdurRahmān al-Afreeqī from Mali. Shaykh Muhammad Amān also studied with Shaykh 'AbdurRazzāq al-'Afīfī, Shaykh Muhammad Khaleel Harrās and Shaykh 'Abdullāh al-Qar'āwī.

oppression of the polytheists in the Arabian peninsula and at this time Ethiopia was not a Muslim land, the Shaykh said:

> ... It was a journey for the sake of calling and conveying the message (of Islām), and so that they could spread the new call to the African continent.[49] This is what alarmed the people of Makkah to the point that they said: "The Call has left. The Call of the man (Muhammad) has gone to Africa, to Najāshī." He was known to them. So they were worried so much so that they chose and dispatched a delegation led by the cleverest amongst the leading men of the Arabs, 'Amr bin al-Ās.[50] They equipped him with all the information he would need and the gifts that were loved by the kings and the members of his palace.[51] And they covered the land with gifts, as it is commonly said, in order that their request could be accepted. What was their request? It was that they hand over that delegation to them.
>
> 'Amr described them as being foolish. This is how the people of falsehood always are – they describe the people of truth as being foolish, crazy and having little understanding. They said "They have abandoned the religion of their forefathers and won't accept your religion either!" It was as if he meant to say: "There doesn't exist any religion except for our religion and your religion O Najāshī. And these individuals do not adhere to your religion

---

He authored *as-Sifāt al-Ilāhiyyah fi'l-Kitāb wa's-Sunnah an-Nabawiyyah fī Daw' il-Ithbāt wa't-Tanzeeh* [The Divine Attributes in the Qur'ān and Prophetic Sunnah in Light of Affirmation and Exaltation], *Adwā 'ala't-Tareeq id-Da'wah ilā'l-Islām* [Lights on the Path of Da'wah to Allāh], *Haqeeqat ud-Daymoqrātiyyah wa Annahā Laysat min al-Islām* [The Reality of Democracy and That It Is Not from Islam], *Haqeeqat ush-Shūrā fi'l-Islām* [The Reality of Consultation in Islām], *al-'Aqeedat al-Islāmiyyah wa Tāreekhuhā* [The Islamic Creed and Its History], *Nidhām ul-Usra fi'l-Islām* [The Family Unit in Islam]. He also explained classical creedal works such as *Tajreed ut-Tawheed* by al-Maqrīzī, *'Aqeedat ut-Tadmuriyyah* by Ibn Taymiyyah, *Thalāthat ul-Usūl* and *Shurūt us-Salāh* by Muhammad bin 'AbdulWahhāb, and other works. The *shaykh* returned to Allah on 26th Sha'bān 1416 AH/Thursday January 18th 1996 CE.

49 This indicates the role and importance of Africa in the early era of Islām.

50 Before 'Amr became a Muslim (*radi Allāhu 'anhu*).

51 The fact that they bestowed him with gifts shows that they were concerned and wanted to impress him, so if the Arabs did not respect black people then would they have done this?

or the religion of your forefathers.[52] And the proof for this is that when they enter into your presence, they don't prostrate to you with the greeting due to Ethiopian kings since they are irrational."

Upon hearing this about them, he (Najāshī) summoned them and they were standing outside.....they entered into his presence, with Ja'far bin 'Abī Tālib leading them, and their heads raised up and not bending their backs (i.e. standing without prostrating). At this, an-Najāshī asked: "Why don't you prostrate to me, i.e. greet me like my people greet me?" Ja'far replied, "We only prostrate to the One who put you in charge, not to you." "We only prostrate to the One who put you in charge" refers to Allāh, "the One who made you a king. He gives the rule to whom He wills and takes it away from whom He wills. The One who made you a king is the One that deserves to be worshipped and prostrated to."

This moved an-Najāshī, so he began asking them about the new religion and about the new messenger and what he came with and what befell him. In brief, he acknowledged the truth, gave back the gifts to the delegation from Quraysh, and then expelled them. So they returned home debased and unsuccessful. When an-Najāshī honoured these companions of Allāh's Messenger, which consisted of members from the Prophet's household, not to mention some of his daughters, Allāh honoured him with Islām. So he became the first king of his time that believed in the Messenger of Allāh (may Allāh's peace and blessings be upon him)[53] and openly professed his faith. This is what is meant by the companions' "*hijrah*" (migration) to Ethiopia – it was not the well known and recognised form of *hijrah*. Rather, it was a means of calling to Allāh, conveying His message, and explaining His new religion so that the people there could be aware of it, and so that the call could spread and transcend the Arab peninsula...based on this understanding, it is correct to apply the term "*hijrah*", in the religious sense, to the journey the companions of Allāh's Messenger (may Allāh's peace and blessings be upon him) made to Ethiopia...and the objective behind it was, as we stated before, to spread the call and to convey the new religion and the message of the last of the prophets, Muhammad (may Allāh's peace and

52 A familiar and common argument indeed!

53 Hence the honoured and respected position that an-Najāshī has in Islām, the first king to accept Islām was from Africa and Islām was aided by Africa.

blessings be upon him), to the people in Africa.[54]

Therefore, the Ethiopians and other black African states were recognised, respected and honoured by the Arabs due to their strength and position. One of the famous Muslim scholars Ibn Katheer mentions in his *tafseer* of the Qur'ān:

> In their courage, and obedience to Allāh and His Messenger, the Companions reached a level never seen before by any nation or generation before them, or any nation that will ever come. Through the blessing of the Messenger (*sallallāhu 'alayhi wassallam*) and their obedience to what he commanded, the Companions were able to open the hearts, as well as, the various Eastern and Western parts of the world in a rather short time. This occurred even though they were few, compared to the armies of the various nations at that time. For example, the Romans, Persians, Turks, Slavs, Berbers, Ethiopians, Sudanese tribes, the Copts and the rest of the Children of Adam.[55]

Ibn Katheer also mentions a narration in regards to a verse of the Qur'ān (Sūrah al-Anfāl, verse 26) from Qatādah bin Di'āmah as-Sadūsī Abu'l-Khattāb al-Basrī[56] who stated:

> Arabs were the weakest of the weak, had the toughest life, the emptiest stomachs, the barest skin and the most obvious misguidance. Those who lived among them lived in misery; those

54 Abridged and adapted from Husayn bin 'Awdah al-'Awāyishāh, *al-Fasl al-Mubeen fee Mas'ala wa Mufāraqat al-Mushrikeen*, trans. Aboo Maryam Ismā'eel Alaracon, *A Conclusive Study on the Issue of Hijrah and Separating from the Polytheists* (New York: al-Ibānah, Safar 1427 AH/March 2006 CE) pp.107-112.

55 *Tafsir Ibn Kathīr* (Abridged), Vol.4: Surat Al-A'raf to the end of Surah Yūnus (Riyadh, Houston, New York and Lahore: Darussalam Publishers and Distributers, 2000), p.331

56 He lived from circa 61-1157AH/693-765 CE, he was a precise, reliable and trustworthy narrator of *hadeeth* and it was also said that he was born blind. He took knowledge from Anas ibn Mālik, Sa'eed ibn ul-Musayyib, Ibn Seereen and others. There is a book entitled *an-Nāsikh wa'l-Mansūkh*, Dr Hātim Sālih ad-Dāmin, (ed.), (Beirut: Mu'assisah ar-Risālah, 1404 AH) which is ascribed to him. Imām Ahmad ibn Hanbal said about him "the strongest memoriser from the people of 'Irāq." Refer to Ibn Hajar al-'Asqalānī, *at-Taqreeb*, vol.2, p.123; *Tahdheeb ut-Tahdheeb*, vol.8, p.351 and adh-Dhahabī, *Tadhkirat ul-Huffādh*, vol.1., p.115.

> who died went to the Fire. They were being eaten up, but unable to eat up others! By Allāh! We do not know of a people on the face of the earth at that time who had a worse life than them. When Allāh brought Islām, He made it dominant on the earth, thus brining provisions and leadership for them...It is through Islam that Allāh granted all what you see, so thank Him for His favours, for your Lord is One Who bestows favours and likes praise. Verily, those who thank Allāh enjoy even more bounties from Him.[57]

Yet at the same time, the people who propound the argument that Islām represents "Arab teachings" do not apply a similar criterion to themselves in order to render their own views as promoting 'European and Anglo-American teachings.' Considering the fact that they are based in the West, speaking English exclusively, and basing their arguments against Islām from anti-Islamic Eurocentric sources. However, due to the pervasiveness of the dominant Western culture and the *Islamophobic* tendencies that have developed in recent years, many people are not actually aware that they are regurgitating the same prejudices. What is of further concern is that people of African origin in the West are also beginning to share in the hatred of Islām that is being revealed within some communities. For example, in the early 2000s in the UK, the far right scare-mongering political party, the BNP, were calling on people of African-Caribbean origin, along with Sikhs and Hindus, to join them and used an anti-Islām agenda. While more recently in 2018, anti-Islamic hate-mongers like 'Tommy Robinson' have been defended and protected by new-age Kemet Afrocentrics like 'SaRa' and 'Kalam'. As a result, far-right movements in the UK have managed to recruit a number of people of African and Asian origin to their political aims and ambitions in some cities within the UK. Therefore, the apprehension that many Muslims have over certain stereotypes about Islām is not imagined by Muslims but is rather becoming a reality.

In the UK the anti-racism think-tank, the Runnymede Trust, conducted a report in 2004 (a flagship report on Islamophobia) that noted that Islamophobia was pervading the UK. In the report, Dr Richard Stone, a former advisor to the Stephen Lawrence Inquiry,[58] warned that key

57 *Tafsir Ibn Kathīr* (Abridged), Vol.4: Surat Al-A'raf to the end of Surah Yunus, pp.293-4

58 Stephen Lawrence was a British youth of West Indian origin who was violently

recommendations that were highlighted in an earlier report in 1997 had been ignored. The report also noted that anti-racist organizations had done little to combat anti-Muslim prejudice. Dr Richard Stone noted that a key idea in the Stephen Lawrence Inquiry, institutional racism, should be adapted in order to tackle institutional Islamophobia. The report highlighted from several examples of anti-Muslim hostility,

> ...Widespread and routine stereotypes in the media, including the broadsheets, and in the conversations and 'common sense' of non-Muslims – people talk and write about Muslims in ways that would not be acceptable if reference were to Jewish people, for example, or to black people.

The term 'Islamophobia' implies that it is a kind of mental sickness, and the following quotes that we read shortly will actually sound as if those holding such views are somewhat unstable. The stereotypes and assumptions are not only simplistic and extreme, but they are not systematically challenged in western countries. As a result, many sections of the community within western societies also blindly adopt the same images, stereotypes and ideas, without challenging them. Therefore, one website which claimed to be the "voice of black people in the UK" allows, promotes and endorses such polemics against Islām. The following are some quotes from the site:

Posts from a British Afrocentric website, May 2005:

> *Islamic b*******...it is not a BLACK religion...these religions were forced upon us...DROP 'EM NOW!!!! It's turning Black people weak and crazy!* (Evo0, Tuesday May 24th 2005)

> *Islam is a barbaric religion that does not tolerate freedom of speech, that prefers the sword to dialogue, is backward and repressive...all of this backed up by scholars who say that this is the will of allah...it is amazing that in the 21st century people hold on to this foolishness and call it wisdom. That you would which to bow down to a God that represented the backwardness of Arabia 1400 years ago is amazing...* (calculator2, Tuesday May 10th 2005)

> *We need a religion and appreciation of the divine for ourselves. Not hand me down religions...nah aint ready for no Arab man religion.*

---

killed by a gang of racist white thugs in Eltham, South East London in the 1990s; nobody was ever convicted of his murder.

> *No matter how many Africans are brainwashed into it. And looking for brotherhood with arabs is repeating the mistakes of antiquity. No doubt.* (mansamusa, Thursday January 6th 2005)
>
> *...But from my experiences with muslims...all of them I have met hide behind their religion, especially the men... (bluehoney, Monday May 30th 2005) Absolutely right about these religions turning Black people crazy. That was the whole point of taking them to Black people!* (Backatya, Monday May 30th 2005)

The above comments were disseminated on a certain Afrocentric website in which the moderators themselves join in against Islām and support the likes of such comments about Islām and Muslims. This not only indicates a lack of balance but also that there is no recourse given to Muslims to respond to such extreme statements in a concise manner. The website therefore wishes to promote a one-sided and partisan view of Islām even if stereotyping and wild generalizations are made.[59]

---

59 Incidentally, this is the same website that shut down its forum for a few months in 2006 due its invitation of ignorant comments from uncorroborated sources which contributed to racial tensions, culminating in a riot in the city of Birmingham between 'blacks' and 'Asians' (terms which are used in the UK to simplistically describe two different minority groups)! Due to its foolish promotion of ignorant comments on their forums, some of which were calling for murder (!) and other postings which were sending people on wild goose chases from London up to the city of Birmingham, the website had to close down its forums! It took a race riot which resulted in the deaths of two young people and some shootings, for the thoughtless moderators of this forum to realize that they were facilitating the promotion of ignorance, hatred and uncorroborated claims from unknown people. Only now do they have on the forums, before entering into the main forums: "You may not post any content which is racist, violent, incites violence, threatens violence, or contains harassing content or hate speech."!? The riots resulted in the murder of a young black man named Isiah Young-Sam by Waqar Ahmad, Azhil Khan and Afzal Khan from Handsworth. The three tried to escape by booking one-way tickets to Pakistan, but they were later arrested in Dubai and found guilty. Also during the riot Dwayne Maye accidentally shot dead his best friend Aaron James, as the pair ran from police ("Three guilty of riot night murder", BBC Online edition, Monday 22 May 2006). Furthermore, in Brixton some Afrocentrics were distributing a one-page so-called '*fatwa*' that had been allegedly compiled by Asian Muslims which called to a *jihād* against people of African origin and called for a "holy war against blacks"!!? The so-called '*fatwa*'

Moreover, one could be mistaken into thinking that some of the remarks are from anti-Muslim white nationalists, yet they are from those who call to Afrocentricity!? In some of these examples obscene language was used yet in others elementary conventions of spelling, punctuation and grammar were utilized. Whilst they do not propose violence against Muslims they do describe Muslims as "barbaric", "crazy", "brainwashed", "backward" and "in hiding". It is quite disturbing that small sections of the society who themselves suffer from racial profiling and stereotyping, have themselves adopted a similar stance in talking about Muslims and Islām. One of the persons quoted in the box above even utilized the name of a famous West African Muslim as a forum name, yet still displayed negative opinions about Islām?! The *Runnymeade* Trust in their report on *Islamophobia* in the UK noted that there is a collective failure in addressing it, the report stated, adapting from the Stephen Lawrence Inquiry report:

> It can be seen or detected in processes through unwitting prejudice, ignorance, thoughtlessness and stereotyping which disadvantage Muslims.[60]

had no authors and was allegedly put together by some Muslims yet there were no names, no indication of the Muslim organisation who allegedly put together the '*fatwa*', no references, no sources, nothing at all to authenticate and validate the document.

60 *Islamophobia – Issues, Challenges and Action – A Report by the Commission on British Muslims and Islamophobia* (Stoke on Trent, UK and Sterling, USA: Trentham Books, 2004), p.14.

II

Did Either the Arabs or the Almoravids Conquer West Africa?

The Role of Dubious Arabic and Orientalist Sources

Conquest theories have been popular with Afrocentrics, Orientalists, Christian missionaries, Zionists and other arm-chair 'experts'. Yet the reality is that there is no historical proof whatsoever that Arabs conquered West Africa and subsequently forced and coerced black Africans to become Muslims in the process. In fact, much of the literature on the history of Islam in West Africa will posit that the Almoravids, who were Berbers in origin, were the ones who "conquered" the empire of Ancient Ghana and Islam gained sway that way. Essentially, the suggestion buttresses notions of Islam being "spread by the sword". Perhaps the best assessment of these "conquest" theories of and "invasion" is by Pekka Masonen and Humphrey J. Fisher in their research paper *Not Quite Venus from the Waves: The Almoravid Conquest of Africa in the Modern Historiography of Western Africa.*[61] They state:

> Similarly, there is no direct evidence for any conquest, still less a violent and destructive conquest, of Ghana by the Almoravids. The conquest hypothesis is a European creation.

The Ghana referred to here is not modern-day Ghana (which was formerly known as the Gold Coast) but rather Ancient Ghana which is where present-day Mali and eastern Senegal is today. Islām was

61 Originally published in the journal *History of Africa*, vol.23, 1996, pp.197-232. The version of the paper being used here however is an updated edition from http://www.uta.fi/~hipema/Venus.htm

spreading in Ancient Ghana already before the time of the Almoravids (1054-1147 CE). This is confirmed by Arabic sources such as al-Bakrī who wrote circa 1068 CE; the historian az-Zuhrī writing circa 1137 CE (not to be confused with Ibn Shihāb az-Zuhrī who was from the early Islamic scholars); al-Idrīsī writing circa 1154 CE; ash-Sharīshī, writing circa 1222 CE and the unknown authors of *Kitāb ul-Istibsār* (1191 CE) and *al-Hulal al-Mawshiyyah* (1381 CE).[62] Therefore, how did the theories of the "invasion", "destruction" and "conquest" of ancient Ghana come about and what were the ideological factors which led to the theory to become widespread. Furthermore, there are connections between this theory about West Africa and ideas that all of Africa was introduced to Islām in this way, as a result, it is important for us to look at the background.

The idea that ancient Ghana was conquered by the Almoravids has its roots in the writings of Leo Africanus. He was a Moroccan Muslim who was sold into slavery in his early twenties and then ended up at the Papal Court in Rome where he was baptised as a Christian. In 1526 CE he wrote *Descrittione dell' Africa*, which is written in Italian. This was Leo's work on African history, anthropology and geography and was first published in Venice in 1550 then there were a few reprints along with translations into French, Latin, English and then into Dutch and German. In the West, Leo Africanus came to be regarded as the highest authority on the geography and history of Africa and this was the case for about 400 years.

Leo Africanus claimed that the "Land of the Blacks" (i.e. West Africa) was not necessarily "conquered" but rather over-powered in 380 AH/1012 CE and that it was a land "inhabited by people who lived like brutes, without kings, lords, republics, government and any customs, and without knowing husbandry." Leo Africanus also mentions that the blacks were dominated by "the five nations of Libya" and intending by this "the Zenaga, Guenziga, Terga, Lemta and Berdeua." Yet what is interesting to note is that these tribes are black anyway, just from different tribes that are found in Africa! In fact these Berber tribes that Leo Africanus mentions are probably the same tribes that Ibn Khaldūn mentioned as being the main Berber peoples, i.e. "Gudala, Lamtuna,

62 "*The Embroided Cloaks*", was completed circa 1381 CE in Granada.

Masufa, Watzila, Targa, Zaghawa and Lamta."[63]

Here the Zaghawa are included and they are none other than one of the tribes currently present in Darfur. However, within all of Leo Africanus' account there is no reference to the Almoravid leader Abū Bakr Ibn 'Umar who was the leader of the Almoravids at the time of the alleged "conquest". Africanus makes mention of a "King Joseph" referring no doubt to Yūsuf ibn Tashfeen who ruled from 1087-1106, yet nothing at all of Abū Bakr ibn 'Umar. This is important as it shows that Leo Africanus did not have full knowledge of ancient Ghana and its history, let alone of Morocco and its history, he merely regurgitated that ancient Ghana was over-powered due to it being taken as a given that it occurred. So his account sets the scene of not a clear conquest, but of "northerners" over "southerners" and "whites" over "blacks". In such a framework, notions of a "conquest" may have been easy to accept, even if there are absolutely no historical documents or accounts to corroborate this.

Less than 25 years after the first two editions of Leo Africanus' work had been published, came the Spanish scholar from Granada Luis del Mármol Carvajal who published his *Descripcion general de Affrica.* This work was published in three parts, two in 1573 CE and one in 1599 CE. Mármol relied mostly on Leo, but he did have knowledge of other Arabic sources as he had been captive in Tūnis as a galley slave after being caught on an expedition there. On several occasions he mentions El Mocaudi (al-Mas'ūdī); el Bebquer/Bubquer (al-Bakrī); Ibni Alraqiuq (Ibn ur-Raqeeq); Abdul Malic (Ibn 'AbdulMālik al-Marrakushī) and others. In dealing with the "Land of the Blacks" (intending by this West Africa), he more or less gives a word-for-word account straight from Leo Africanus! Including the alleged uncivilised state of the blacks, their domination by "King Joseph" and the "five Libyan nations"! However, there is no mention here whatsoever of any military intervention against the blacks in the context of their conversion to Islām. Indeed, even Mármol mentions one "Yahaya son of Ali Benbucar" and that while he undertook military action against Spain and Egypt, conquering and attacking them in the 11 century CE, there is no similar action said to have been taken against the blacks. Masonen and Fisher highlight that

63 N. Levtzion and J.F.P. Hopkins (eds.), *Corpus of Early Arabic Sources for West African History* (Cambridge: Cambridge University Press, 1981), pp.321, 327.

the history of the Almoravids was used to provide understandings for contemporary politics and philosophy.

Ahmad Bābā at-Timbuktī (*rahimahullāh*) in his famous book *al-Kashf wa'l-Bayān li-Asnāf Majlūb is-Sūdān* (*Explaining and Clarifying the Types of People from the Black Lands that can Legitimately be Enslaved*), which was written in the 17th Century CE, mentioned that those who became Muslims from amongst the people of the Black Lands did so voluntarily "without being conquered by anybody."[64] His statement here carries weight as he was writing from the place involved and thus would have had access to a variety of sources and he also quotes from Ibn Khaldūn to support his theory. Masonen and Fisher state:

> The fact that the "conquest hypothesis" never clearly emerged in Africa, despite the attractive justification it could have offered for indulging in the slave trade, does lend support to the contention that the conquest never occurred.

The writings of Ahmad Bābā however were unknown to Europeans for about three hundred years and as a result all Europeans knew about West Africa in the 19th century was based on the works of Leo Africanus, al-Idreesī[65] and Mármol. In 1738, Francis Moore an English trader in Gambia compared the "conquest" of the blacks by Libyan tribes, as described by Leo Africanus, to the Spanish conquest of the New World!? Moore stated:

> The Libyan tribe of Sanhagia... coming amongst these harmless and naked people[66], made as rapid conquests as the Spaniards did in America, and contemned the Natoves as much, looking upon them as brutes, because they were not Mahometans, nor instructed in avarice, nor ruled by tyrants; for which the Moors upbraided them as wanting the knowledge of religion, property

64 Bernard Barbour and Michelle Jacobs, "The Miraj: A Legal Treatise on Slavery by Ahmad Baba" in John Ralph Willis (ed.) *Slaves and Slavery* in Muslim Africa, vol.1 (London: Frank Cass, 1985), pp.125-159. See English text, p.128; Arabic text, p.142. Also cited in 'Uthmān ibn Fūdī (Dan Fodio), F.H. al-Masri (ed.), *Bayān Wujūb ul-Hijrah 'ala'l-'Ibād* (Khartoum University Press and Oxford University Press, 1978 CE), p.51.

65 His *Nuzhāt ul-Mushtāq* had appeared as an abridged Latin translation in 1619 CE.

66 This is a rather paternalistic view of "the blacks".

and government.[67]

This view is remarkably similar to that of the Afrocentrics and black Orientalists not only in its description but also in the utter lack of proof and sources. Mungo Park also copied more or less word-for-word from Leo Africanus too, blindly accepting Leo's account as fact, Park also mentioned the claims about Libyan's dominating blacks. Then came William Desborough Cooley who authored *The Negroland of the Arabs, Examined and Explained; or, An Enquiry into the Early History and Geography of Central Africa* which attempted to study West Africa based upon Arabic sources. Cooley states:

> Ghánah merged in the empire of the Moabites, an event which may be assigned, with much probability, to the year of the Hijra 469, when the Mohammedan faith was forcibly imposed on the pagan nations of Negroland contiguous to the Western Desert.[68]

Three sources are cited by Cooley and two of these, namely Mármol and *al-Hulal al-Mawshiyyah* are his main sources for the "forced conversion" myth. However, Cooley does not refer to al-Bakrī at all for this "forced conversion" conclusion even though al-Bakrī is Cooley's main reference in his entire study! Al-Bakrī mentions neither a "conquest" nor an "invasion" of ancient Ghana by the Almoravids in 469 AH/1076-77, because he was writing circa 460 AH/1067-7 CE, yet Cooley thought that a "conquest" account was present in al-Bakrī!! Cooley also mistakenly took the conquest of Awdaghust as being the capital of ancient Ghana, when the capital was Kumbi![69]

Cooley had used the Arabic manuscript of Ibn Khaldūn's *Kitāb al-'Ibar*, but a partial Arabic edition of it was prepared by Baron William MacGuckin de Slane, a French Arabist, this edition was published in two volumes in Algeria in 1263-7 AH/1847-51 CE. A complete Arabic

67 Francis Moore, *Travels in the Inland Parts of Africa* (London: Edward Cave, 1738), p.v in "Letter to the Editor".

68 William Desborough Cooley, *The Negroland of the Arabs, Examined and Explained; or, An Enquiry into the Early History and Geography of Central Africa* (London: J Arrowsmith, 1841 and London: Frank Cass and Co., 1966), p.66.

69 See Basil Davidson, *African Civilisation Revisted* (Trenton, New Jersey: African World Press, 1993), p.85. Quoting from D. Tamsir Niane and Jean Suret-Canale, *Historie de l'Afrique Occidentale* (Paris: 1961), p.23.

edition was published in 1284 AH/1867 CE at Bulaq in Cairo in seven volumes. In 1852-6, after the completion of the Arabic volumes, de Slane published a French translation of these entitled *Histoire des berbères et des dynasties musulmanes de l'Afrique septentrionale* (4 volumes, Paris).[70] De Slane states that "the veiled people" (referring to the Almoravids and the West African Saharan style of wrapping the turban or *'imāmah* across the face):

> "*Étendit sa domination sur les Noirs, dévasta leur territoire et pilla leurs propriétes*" ("extended their domination over the blacks, devastated their territory and pillaged their property")[71]

However, in the Arabic editions there is no mention of "devastation" or "pillaging"[72] so it is strange that de Slane added it for the translations. In any case, due to this addition of "devastation" and "pillaging" this text contributed to the conquest theory of West Africa by the Almoravids.

Heinrich Barth, the famous German explorer who was the first European to gain access to the literary past of the Songhay Empire, published his *Travels and Discoveries in North and Central Africa ... in the years 1849-1855* appeared in three editions in 1857-59.[73] The book mainly revolves around Barth's own travels, adventures and experiences and also contains an in-depth chronology of West African history from 300 CE. Barth notes:

---

70 Masonen and Fisher note that this was re-edited by Paul Casanova and reprinted in 3 volumes (Paris, 1925-34). De Slane published also French translations of al-Bakri (*Journal Asiatique*, 5. série, vols. 12-14, 1858-9) and Ibn Khaldun's *Muqaddima* (*Notices et Extraits des Manuscrits de la Bibliothèque Imperiale*, vols. 19-21, 1862-68).

71 Ibn Khaldoun, *Histoire des berbères* (Paris 1852-6), vol.2, 110

72 Ibn Khaldoun, *Histoire des berbères et des dynasties musulmanes de l'Afrique septentrionale* (Alger 1847-51), Arabic text prepared by M. de Slane, vol. I, 263, lines 16-17

73 Barth's *Travels and Discoveries* was published in five volumes in English (London 1857-8), and in German (*Reisen und Entdeckungen* in Nord- und Central-Africa, Gotha 1857-58). The English version was very soon afterwards published in three volumes in New York, in 1857-59. The modern reprint, "Centenary edition", published in London in 1965 by Frank Cass, is based on the American edition with additional maps from the English edition. This is available from the SOAS Library, London.

> A.D. 1076. A.H. 469. Ghanáta conquered by the Senhája, and great part of the inhabitants, as well as the neighbouring districts of Negroland, compelled by the Mórabetin to embrace the Mohammedan faith. Abú Bakr ben Omar takes up his residence in this part of Negroland.[74]

Barth's only sources for this "forced conversion" are only Mármol and the book by an anonymous author *al-Hulal!* Barth also neglects any further analysis of this and even Cooley does not claim that the Almoravids displaced the native rulers of Ghana. Masonen and Fisher argue that the conquest and forced conversion may have been taken from de Slane's work which may have been known to Barth. Then came Ernest Mercier who in his work published in *Revue Africaine*, in 1868-69[75] and also blindly accepts the capital of ancient Ghana to be Awdaghust. Mercier in his work however increased the violence and even claims there was a massacre! He states:

> ... The Almoravids, who seemed to have interrupted their conquests in the rich areas of the north, returned to the south and went to attack the land of the Negroes, which was called in those times by the name R'ana.[76] They conquered this country easily, and entered victoriously into Aoudar'ast, a flourishing city and capital of the country and a residence of the ruler who was also called R'ana by the inhabitants. The victors destroyed and pillaged the peaceful population, and these acts of violence were legalized, in their eyes, by the idolatry of the vanquished; they massacred the men, violated the women, and took a considerable booty which they carried into their country.[77]

In 1888 René Basset, a French Orientalist published a short article on the ancient West African empires and feebly attempted to look at relations between what he narrowly viewed as "white Muslim

---

74 1965, vol.3, p.660. In the original English and German editions this table is included in the fourth volume.

75 "*Notice sur les Almoravides et les Almohades d'après les Historiens arabes*", nos. 69, 71, 76, 77 (in vols. 12 and 13 of the Kraus reprint of 1968).

76 Mercier's spelling reflects the old-fashioned rendering of the Arabic consonant *ghayn* with r', which is nowadays represented with "gh".

77 1868-69, no. 69, 222.

pastoralists" and "sedentary black animists".[78] Basset blindly followed Cooley's conquest theory and propagated a forced conversion myth which became well-rooted in French writing on West African history. This would later contribute to French notions of "*Islām noir*". In 1892 CE Louis Binger, another Frenchman whose work was blindly followed in Europe, reinforced this "conquest" theory and strangely cites al-Bakrī as his main source reference that ancient Ghana was conquered. Binger states, remarkably similar to Mercier writing in 1868 CE, that:

> El-Békri added that after this conquest [of Ghana] a great part of the population was forced to embrace Islam by the Merabétin, as well as many of the neighbouring areas.[79]

The conquest theory became solidified and accepted when Maurice Delafosse published his *magnum opus* three-volume *Haut-Sénégal-Niger* for which he was awarded medals in France.[80] Soon after, Delafosse was regarded as the highest authority in early West African history not only in France but also in the Anglophone world, though *Haut-Sénégal-Niger* was never translated into English. Delafosse stated:

> The conquest seems to have been complete: not only did the Almoravids take the city, pillage the goods of the inhabitants, massacre a part of the Soninke population, forcing the rest either to flee or to embrace the Muslim religion, but they obliged the emperor to recognise the suzerainty of Abu Bakr and to pay him tribute, and they annexed to their political domain all the dependencies of Ghana, as far as and including the auriferous mountains of Bambuk.[81]

Yet Delafosse, who was awarded medals and exalted as the definitive expert of West African history, did not bring a shred of evidence for this! There is no footnote, reference or source mentioned whatsoever yet certain names within his bibliography tell us from whence he arrived at

---

78 "*Mélanges d'histoire et de littérature orientales II*", Le Muséon, vol. 7 (1888), 49-60 and 137-151. Also cited under the title "*Essai sur l'histoire et de la langue de Tombouctou et des royaumes de Songhaï et Melli*", which is the opening sentence of the article.

79 *Du Niger au Golfe du Guinée*, (Paris), vol. 2, p.383.

80 Paris; reprinted, with a preface by Robert Cornevin, in 1972 (3 volumes, Paris).

81 Delafosse 1912, vol.2, p.54

this: Cooley, Barth, Basset, Mercier, Binger et al.! Masonen and Fisher highlight "This picture of Delafosse ruled virtually unchallenged in West African historiography for half a century." As a result, Delafosse's opinion was accepted in African historiography for fifty years. Even J.S. Trimingham who is known for his largely positive work on the history of Islām in Africa regurgitated a conquest hypothesis in regards to this issue and repeats the "massacre" and "forced conversion" myths.[82]

How and Why Did These "Conquest" and "Invasion" Myths and Theories Become Popular?

Imperialism and colonialism brought with it many distorted ideas about African history which were not based on actual sources and rather reflected racist views which some Europeans held. Masonen and Fisher note that a reason for this among the French in particular was due to the increasingly negative view of Tuaregs and equating them with the Almoravids of the past, partly due to the practice of veiling the face which the Arabic sources mention was also a practice of the Almoravids of the past. Mungo Park stated that:

> The Moors were at once the most vainest and proudest, and perhaps the most bigoted, ferocious, and intolerant, of all the nations on earth; combining in their character the blind superstition of the Negro, with the savage cruelty and treachery of the Arab.[83]

At this time a number of French and European travellers had been murdered in the West African Sahara such as Daniel Haughton in 1791; Alexander Gordon Laing in 1826; Alexine Tinne in 1869; the Flatters expedition massacre in 1881 and other similar incidents. Mungo Park also stated for example:

> The enterprising boldness of the Moors, their knowledge of the country, and, above all, the superior fleetness of their horses, make them such formidable enemies, that the petty Negro states

---

82 *A History of Islam in West Africa* (London 1962; reprinted 1970), p.55; see also pp.25, 29-30, 33.

83 "An Abstract of Mr. Park's Account of his Travels and Discoveries, abridged from his own Minutes by Bryan Edwards, Esq. 1798", *Proceedings of the African Association*, 1810/1967, vol.1, p.349.

> which border upon the Desert are in continual terror while the Moorish tribes are in the vicinity and are too much awed to think of resistance.[84]

Hereby portraying the indigenous West Africans as being a rather passive and weak entity unable to mount any challenge whatsoever! This actually contradicts the Arabic sources which state that the West African states had huge armies. Indeed, al-Bakrī stated about Ancient Ghana in 1067 CE that:

> Ghana is the title of the kings of this people, while the name of their country is Aoukar. The king who governs them at present... is called Tenkaminen; he came to the throne in 455 AH... Tenkaminen is the master of a large empire and a formidable power...The king of Ghana can put two hundred thousand warriors in the field, more than forty thousand being armed with bow and arrow...[85]

Masonen and Fisher highlight:

> From this point of view, the conquest (and destruction) of Ghana by cruel Almoravids could be seen as an historical example of the negative impact of Islamic fanaticism, justifying European "protection" in sub-Saharan Africa. And the French truly believed that part of their mission in Western Africa was to save the local black population from Muslim slavery and oppression: in Upper Niger they deliberately sought the assistance of the animist Bambara in their fight against Ahmadu of Segu and Samory. We should also notice that historiography had an important role in late 19th-century France in raising the national spirit...

Probably the first modern scholar to express any doubts over the "invasion" and "conquest" theories was Paul Semonin in an article published in 1964.[86] The main impetus for Semonin was the finding of a new Arabic source for Almoravid history by Ibn al-Idharee which required some historians to reconsider some of their previous views about Almoravid

84 Ibid. 1799, p.159. Furthermore, Park claimed that the Moors ruled all the areas reaching from the Senegal to the borders of Abyssinia (pp. 112-13)!!?

85 Abdullāh Abū 'Ubayd al-Bakrī, *al-Kitāb al-Masālik wa'l-Mamālik*, quoted in Basil Davidson, *op.cit.*, p.86

86 "The Almoravid movement in the western Sudan. A review of the evidence", *Transactions of the Historical Society of Ghana*, vol. 7 (1964).

history, like for example the founding of Marrākush (Marrakech).[87] In the same year, Vincent Monteil noted that the conquest theory of Delafosse had to be done away with because it was unsubstantiated.[88] Semonin did not however deny that a conquest may have taken place but he did at least throw doubt on its occurrence by stating "there has been a lack of critical attention to the problems presented by the source material". He concluded with:

> The Sack of Ghana is so poorly documented that it is questionable what precedents it may have set, or what real impact it may have had, beyond that of a calamitous but momentary disturbance in the Sahil with limited resources for a continuing influence upon the Islamization of the area.[89]

After Semonin came Paulo Fernando de Moraes Farias in 1967, he mentioned the "supposed destruction" of the power and capital of Ghana by Abū Bakr ibn 'Umar, saying "it is well known that the date of the Almoravid 'victory' over Ghâna is poorly documented."[90] In 1974, Mahamadou Coulibaly endeavoured to seriously and critically assess

87 Masonen and Fisher note that the document was: "A previously unknown part of a manuscript concerning the Almoravids, written by Ibn Idhari in early 14th century, became familiar to western scholars in the mid-1950s, although the Arabic text was not published until 1961 by Ambrosio Huici Miranda ("*Un fragmento inédito de Ibn Idhari sobre los Almorávides*", *Hespéris-Tamuda*, 2). The author's full name is Abu'l-Abbās Ahmad bin Muhammad Ibn Idharī, and the full title of his work *Al-Bayān al-Mughrib fi Akhbar al-Andalus wa'l-Maghrib* [The Amazing Exposition on the History of al-Andalus and the Maghrib]. A French translation of Bayan by E. Fagnan (*Histoire de l'Afrique et de l'Espagne intitulée al-Bayano'l-Mogrib*, 2 vols, Algiers) had been published in 1901-4, but it lacks the important account of the Almoravids."

88 *L'Islam Noir*, Paris 1964, pp.58-62, it was re-edited in 1980.

89 Semonin 1964, pp.42, 59. Masonen and Fisher highlight that "Semonin (42n.2) derived this idea from Huici Miranda who had expressed his doubts on Ibn Abi Zarc's reliability in this matter already in 1961 (see "*El Rawd al-Qirtas y los Almorávides*", *Hespéris-Tamuda*, I, 523-24). See also Monteil 1964, 62: "Some years later the Almoravids islamized the land of Ghana, in 1076 (469 AH), a date given by one author only, az-Zuhri.""

90 "The Almoravids: some questions concerning the character of the movement during its periods of closest contact with the western Sudan", *Bulletin de l'I.F.A.N*, s,r. B, vol. 29, pp.848-49.

the invasion and conquest theories.[91] Coulibaly correctly emphasised that the historian az-Zuhrī, the source for the conversion of Ghana in 1076 CE and not to be confused with Ibn Shihāb az-Zuhrī from the epoch of the *Salaf*, makes no reference to any military victory. There is no evidence for the destruction of Ghana, not even of its dismemberment, nor any substantive political or military domination of Ghana by non-black Muslims forcing the people to convert.[92]

Furthermore, Coulibaly highlighted the results of the archaeological excavations in Tegdaoust (the putative site for Awdaghust) and Kumbi Saleh (the putative site for Ghana) as arguments against the conquest, because no indisputable remains of Almoravid presence have been found at either site![93] In 1980 John Hunwick argued that the Almoravids did not actually conquer Ghana, but had great influence on its affairs, helping a Muslim faction of the ruling house rise to power.[94] This idea had been introduced in 1970 by Jean Devisse, who speculated that the relationship between the new ruler of Ghana and the Muslim population might have changed for worse after the death of King Basi in 455 AH/1063 CE, who had been famous for his friendship with Muslims, eventually causing an Almoravid intervention.[95] However, al-Bakrī reports that Basi's successor, Tunka Manin, had many Muslim counsellors within his court.[96] Other Western scholars who rejected the simplistic "conquest" theory of Delafosse were Daniel F. McCall in 1971, Harry Norris in 1982 and Dierk Lange in 1991, due to the lack of evidence and the weak premise.[97] Indeed, as Conrad and Fisher bluntly

---

91 "*L'Attaque de Ghana* (*XIe siècle*)", *Afrika Zamani*, no. 2 (1974), pp.55-77.

92 *Ibid.*, 57-8. Masonen and Fisher note that Coulibaly used fragments of al-Zuhri (Arabic text with French translation) published in Youssouf Kamal's *Monumenta Cartographica Africae et Aegypti* (vol. III, fasc. 3, Cairo 1933, pp.801-3), although a more complete version had been published by Mahammad Hadj-Sadok in 1968, in *Bulletin d'études orientales,* vol. 21. Yet in Hadj-Sadok's edition the date for the conversion is 496, instead of 469.

93 *Ibid.*, 60-61 and 73

94 "*Gao and the Almoravids: a Hypothesis*", in B. Swartz Jr and R. Dumett (eds.), *West African Cultural Dynamics* (The Hague, 1980), p.420.

95 "*La question d'Audagust*", p. 153.

96 N. Levtzion and J.F.P. Hopkins (eds.), *op. cit.*, pp.79-80

97 McCall, 1971, 14; Norris, *The Berbers in Arabic Literature* (London and Beirut

put it "there was no Almoravid conquest of ancient Ghana."[98] David C. Conrad and Humphrey Fisher made the most detailed critique of the "conquest of ancient Ghana" theory, first in Humphrey J. Fisher's review article Early Arabic Sources and the Almoravid Conquest of Ghana, and then in a two-part joint article by David C. Conrad and Fisher, *The conquest that never was: Ghana and the Almoravids*, 1076.[99] Masonen and Fisher conclude in their excellent research paper *Not Quite Venus from the Waves*:

> We have described in this paper important periods of historiographical transformation, which were more or less, we have suggested, ideologically led. First there was the Moroccan interpretation of Almoravid history, embedded within Arab and Berber attitudes towards the blacks; both this interpretation and the attitudes were carried over to the Renaissance European literature of Africa. Later there were Europeans' own experiences in early 19th-century Africa, which also affected their conceptions of African past. And finally there was the rise of a new science, and a new philosophy to go with it, in Europe itself, towards the end of the same century, contributing to the new politics of colonialism in Africa, and stimulating changes to the historical record of Almoravid days in particular, calling up the conquest of Ghana.[100]

To conclude then, ironically the only actual conquest of a Northern African state over a West African one occurred in the 16th century when the Sa'dī Dynasty of Morocco, in cooperation with some of the Portuguese, invaded the Songhay Empire for its resources. This actual conquest is never at all discussed by any of these writers who regurgitate the mythical conquest of West Africa by the Almoravids.

1982), 133-34; Lange, "*Les rois de Gao-San, et les Almoravides*", *Journal of African History*, 32 (1991), 275.

98 Conrad and Fisher, "The local oral sources", in *History in Africa*, 9 (1982), p.45.

99 *Journal of African History*, 23 (1982), 549-60; Part I: "The external Arabic sources", and then: "The local oral sources", *History in Africa*, 9 (1982), 19-59, and 10 (1983), 53-78.

100 See http://www.uta.fi/~hipema/Venus.htm for the full article

III
Sudan

The political and ethnic situation in Sudan[101] greatly influenced Chancellor Williams' ideas about Islām even though the Sudan situation has nothing to do with Islām, but rather power and politics. The stereotype that has been given in the West through the media is that the civil wars in Sudan have been between 'Arabs' and 'black Africans' and much of this is in order to discredit Islām in the eyes of people of African origin.

In the 1990s, the Southern Sudanese Marxist Socialist, John Garang and his SPLA had used Christianity in order to gain wider support from Western agencies such as Tearfund, World Vision, Christian Solidarity International, Caroline Baroness Cox of the UK and others. Even the Archbishop of Canterbury at the time illegally visited Southern Sudan during the civil war and gave his support and backing to the SPLA.[102] The civil war in Southern Sudan, which is now over due to the peace deals and the subsequent break up of the country, furthered the Islamophobia agenda and the amount of articles written by the media in the West reflect this. Many people have obviously blindly accepted these reports as the anti-Islām Afrocentrics maintain exactly the same as the Western media, for example:

- Peter Graff in Time Magazine[103] stated: "On one evening in 1987,

101 Recently the civil war in Sudan between the SPLA and the government is currently over as a peace deal has been made between the government and the southern Sudanese rebel groups.

102 "*Christians have no right to dictate to Muslims*," in The Muslim News (28th August 1998), p.2.

103 November 3 1997, pp.50-51

Arabs in Khartoum were calling for a holy war against the blacks."

- Andrew G. Bostom writing for the neo-con mouthpiece *FrontPage Magazine* on April 18 2005 stated in a poorly researched article entitled *Black Slaves, Arab Masters*: "All these elements of jihad slavery- its juridical rationale, employment as a method of forcible Islamization (for non-Muslims in general, and directed at Sub-Saharan African Animists, specifically), and its association with devshirme-like levies of adolescent males for slave soldiering- are apparent in the contemporary jihad being waged against the Animists and Christians of southern Sudan, by the Arab Muslim-dominated Khartoum regime."
- Bruce W. Nelan, with additional reports from William Dowell of the United Nations, Clive Mutiso in Khartoum and Douglas Waller in Washington DC in *Time Magazine*[104] again, stated: "Africa's largest country is really two: an Islamic and Arabised north and a Christian and Animist African south."
- Patrick Sookhdeo[105], director of the obscure think-tank known as

104 July 27 1998, pp.24-28

105 Patrick Sookhdeo, an alleged former Muslim originally from Guyana, who is now a British Anglican Canon and director of the obscure '*Institute for the Study of Islam and Christianity*' in London. Also known for his context-dropping, cut and paste quotations and wild claims about Islām and Muslims, he is the author of *Islam: The Challenge to the Church* (Pewsey: Issac Publishing, 2006); *Islam in Britain: The British Muslim Community in February 2005* (Pewsey: Issac Publishing, 2005); *Understanding Islamic Terrorism: The Islamic Doctrine of War* (Pewsey: Issac Publishing, 2004); *A People Betrayed: The Impact of Islamisation on the Christian Community in Pakistan* (Fearn, Ross-shire: Christian Focus Publications, 2002 and Pewsey, Wiltshire: Issac Publishing, 2002) and other works. In the London Spectator magazine in July 2005 Sookhdeo wrote an article entitled "*The Myth of a Moderate Islam*" wherein he claimed that as the likes of the terrorists and extremists merely say that they are doing their actions in the name of Islām they are therefore to be seen as representing Islām!? Sookhdeo also states within the article that "Muslims must with honesty, recognise the violence that has existed in their history" as if Muslims do not recognise or comment on it!!? Even Bernard Lewis noted that "the Christian attitude towards Islam was far more bigoted and intolerant than that of the Muslims towards Christianity." See Bernard Lewis, *The Muslim Discovery of Europe* (London: Phoenix, 1982), p.297.

The fact of the matter for Sookhdeo to admit himself is that Christian civilisation has given rise to more atrocities than the Muslim world has. Saint Augustine stated "lead them in"—i.e. "force them to convert" and the Qur'ān says the exact opposite: **"There is no compulsion in religion"** [*Baqarah* (2): 256]. Most of the wars in the 20th century have had little to do with Muslims and the vast majority of the estimated 250 million deaths out of warfare during the 20th century have mostly come from the Western 'Christian' world, with the Muslims accounting for about 10 million of these deaths. The greatest death totals come from World War 1, about 20 million, at least 90 % of which were inflicted by "Christians", and World War 2, 90 million, at least 50% of which were inflicted by "Christians," the majority of the rest occurring in the Far East. There was also the slaughter of 900,000 Rwandans in 1994 in a population that was over 90% Christian, this in fact led to Rwandans embracing Islām! See: http://news.bbc.co.uk/1/hi/world/africa/3561365.stm Also the genocide of over 300,000 Muslims and systematic rape of over 100,000 Muslim women by Christian Serbs in Bosnia between 1992 and 1995. So statistically, Christian Civilization is the bloodiest and most violent of all civilizations in all of history, and is responsible for hundreds of millions of deaths. Here is a quotation from Pope Nicholas the fifth, who gave Alfonso the fifth of Portugal in Romanus Pontifex 1454 CE the right to:

> … Invade, search out, capture, vanquish, and subdue all Saracens and pagans whatsoever, and other enemies of Christ wherever they live, along with their kingdoms, dukedoms, principalities, lordships and goods, both chattels and real estate, that they hold and possess … to reduce their persons to perpetual slavery and to take for himself and his heirs their kingdoms...

Quoted in James Muldoon, *Popes, Lawyers and Infidels: The Church and the Non-Christian World* 1250-1550 (Liverpool: Liverpool University Press, 1979), p.134.

At its outset, the Anglican Church had no better a record of toleration in regard to non-Anglican communions. Of course, time-bound references cannot be taken as our criterion. Here is another time-bound reference; the Charter which the Muslim ruler, Umar, agreed with the Christians of Jerusalem:

> In the name of God, the Compassionate, the Merciful. This charter is granted by 'Umar, Servant of Allah and Prince of the Believers, to the people of Aelia. He grants them security for their persons and their properties, for their churches and their crosses, the little and the great, and for the adherents of the Christian religion. Neither shall their churches be destroyed, nor their substances or areas, nor their crosses or any of their properties, be reduced in any manner. They shall not be coerced in any matter pertaining to their religion, and they shall not be harmed. Nor will any Jews be permitted to live with them in Aelia. Upon the people of Aelia falls the obligation to pay the jizyah; just as

'The Institute for the Study of Islam and Christianity' stated: "The tragic suffering of Sudan arises from a war which is a response to a ruthless campaign by the northern government to Arabise and Islamise the non-Muslim black African south of the country."[106]

- Sam Keily writing for the *Times* (of London) quoted a Christian minister who claimed: "The slavery is racially biased. Black people are considered as slaves by the regime…"[107]

An interesting lecture was also conducted at The School of Oriental and African Studies (SOAS, University of London) by *'The Centre for African-Arab Studies, Kush Institute'*[108] in association with the SOAS

> the people of Mada'in (Persia) do, as well as to evict from their midst the Byzantine army and the thieves. Whoever of these leaves Aelia will be granted security of person and property until he reaches his destination. Whoever decides to stay in Aelia will also be granted the same and share with the people of Aelia, in their rights and the jizyah. The same applies to the people of Aelia as well as to any other person. Anyone can march with the Byzantines, stay in Aelia or return to his home country, and has until the harvesting of crops to decided. Allah attests to the contents of this treaty, and so do His Prophet, his successors and the believers. Signed: 'Umar ibn al-Khattab Witnessed by: Khalid ibn al-Walid, 'Amr ibn al-'As, 'Abd al-Rahman ibn 'Awf and Mu'awiyah ibn Abi Sufyan. Executed in the year 15 AH.

Quoted in Alistair Duncan, *The Noble Sanctuary* (London: Longman Group Ltd, 1972), p.22.

Sookhdeo has since been convicted for sexual assault, for which a court found him guilty by a majority of 10-2 at Swindon Crown Court for sexual assault against two women and intimidation. He served a three-month community sentence and was ordered to pay £3500 in prosecution costs. On 21 November 2015, Sookhdeo was arrested by London's Metropolitan Police at Heathrow Airport for indecent assault. In March 2016 it was reported that Sookhdeo was facing historic sexual assault charges going as far back as 1977.

106 "*The Blood of the Martyrs*", in *The Daily Telegraph* (Wednesday June 3rd 1998) p. 26.

107 "*Sudanese Children Sold as Slaves,*" in *The Times* of London (16th March 1996).

108 Another obscure 'institute' that is an anti-Islamic think tank that shares much of the ideology of Afrocentricity. The inclusion of the 'Kush', which was an ancient Ethiopian civilisation also indicates their Afrocentric ideals, they are also pro-Christian and vehemently anti-Islamic in many ways reflective of Chancellor

East African Society on Friday 29th January 1999 CE in the Brunei lecture theatre. The public lecture was on the theme of 'The Politics of Islamism, Islamic Fundamentalism and Multi-Party Democracy in the Sudan.' The main speakers of this event were Dr. Den Dongrin Akuany (BA, MA, PhD, Leeds University) and Dr. Kunijwok Kwawang (BA, MA, Ph.D, Oxford University). The main lecture was given by Dr. Deng and was highly anti-Islamic and replete with Christian missionary-cum-evangelical propaganda and buttressing of the SPLA! This is not to suggest that there were/are not major short-comings in how situations have been dealt with in the Sudan yet Dr. Deng blindly equated the practices of ignorant Muslims as being from Islam itself with no adequate research or reflection. His lecture therefore was a very biased endeavour, with the internal Sudanese dynamic an evident factor in his bias. After giving the simplistic and erroneous 'Chancellor Williams' account of how Islām entered into Africa, he simply mentioned about such incidents that "these are the facts" yet these are not "the facts" as any serious student of African history knows. He argued that slavery was persistent in the Sudan and this has also been argued by various other agencies, who all note that "Arab militias" perform regular slave raids on "black tribes".

Sudan and Christian Missionary Activity

This topic requires an investigation into some of the background history of Sudan and a study of the origins of this over-emphasised issue in the West that has caused a great deal of confusion. Sudan was very significant for the colonial and Christian missionary powers who viewed Sudan as being the gateway for the evangelisation of the rest of the African continent. As a result, these elements had to concoct a systematic plan in order to scare Africans from Islām and create division in the country, this tradition is still sadly being blindly followed to this day, especially by the contemporary Christian evangelical organisations and their propaganda efforts, which has been effective in asserting that slavery was still present in the country. Therefore, we will give some of the historical background to their propaganda work and why they had to disseminate false ideas such as what has been developed in the form of the 'black slavery in Sudan' industry.

Williams.

Catholic Missionaries in Sudan

Roman Catholic policies were shaped around the desire to reach the great lakes region of Eastern Africa before the Protestants and to stop the spread of Islām at the same time. As a result, they sought to exploit the political and economic influence of the other Europeans residing in Khartoum. Monsignor L.G. Messai, in a letter to a French diplomat, said that:

> The Roman Catholic missionaries...are inevitably fated to play a great part on the White Nile to the advantage of the protecting power, and it will be in the interests of the whole of Europe because...our mission is called upon to acquire the commerce of Africa permanently for Europe.[109]

In 1857 CE the *Mazza Institute* in Verona, in an endeavour to continue missionary efforts, sponsored and organised a mission to Sudan via the Nile. The mission consisted of five priests, one of whom was Daniel Comboni[110], the infamous 'father of Catholicism' in modern Sudan. They penetrated Sudan along the Nile, about 1000 miles to the south of Khartoum, where they established a Christian missionary base and even though two of Comboni's companions died there he vowed "I will never give up, Africa or death." Comboni created a Christian village known as Malbes which was in Kordofan, the intent of this was to create a Christian community in the heart of a Muslim area in order to create friction and tension. Comboni established the training of African

---

109 Hassan Makki Mohamed Ahmed, Sudan – The Christian Design (Leicester: The Islamic Foundation, 1989 CE/ 1410 AH) p.23, quoting from Daud al-Jamal Abdulillah, *A Social History of the Christian Church in Northern Sudan 1820-1956*, (University of Khartoum: Department of History, Faculty of Arts, 1985), p.17.

110 Daniel Comboni was born in Italy in 1831 CE and studied at *Mazza Institute* in Verona, he died in Khartoum on October 1881 CE. He first went to Sudan in 1857 CE and returned to Italy in 1859 CE. In 1864 CE he vowed to dedicate his life to establishing Christianity in central Africa and Sudan and he achieved some success in mobilising Europe for this task. He thus met Francis Joseph, Emperor of Austria, the Empress Eugene, the Czar of Russia, Leopold of Belgium and many others including princes and rulers. In 1867 CE he established a college for African mission in Cairo and compiled a dictionary of the Nubian language and published studies on the Dinka and Bari language and some works on African history.

children and built "homes which are a day and a half's journey away from Kordofan, so that they might not come into contact with Muslims and lose their faith."[111] Comboni's plan was that:

> This group will eventually become a village, a town, a city, inhabited only by Catholics under the direction of the missionaries and sisters – wherever there is a Muslim predominance this system will be used…As for Islām, all the obstacles that Islam puts in the way of the conversion of its followers will fall. The power of evil will no longer maintain its hold over Africa…especially in those areas which have not been corrupted by Islam…I solemnly baptised fourteen non-believers, some pagan, some Muslims. The most joyful of them all was a young Muslim girl of fourteen… After five years of begging the permission of her Moslem mother for her to receive baptism, this was granted by the illiterate mother, and was done publicly through the Austro-Hungarian Consul. The only thing that matters to me, I say, is that Africa should be converted.[112]

Comboni thus laid the foundations for the modern catholic movement within Sudan and introduced the first Dinka Catholic priest, Deng Surur (d.1899), who worked in Suakin from 1881 to 1891 and died in Cairo. There are currently many institutions and missionary centres within the Central African Republic and Sudan which have been named after Comboni. Far from being 'promoters of peace' the Catholic missionaries in Sudan acted as tools for European powers, particularly the British, by providing arms to southern Sudanese during the colonial period, one of these missionaries said: "We gave the Nuba seventy rifles from the mission, and they then prepared an ambush for the unsuspecting Arabs…"[113]

---

111 Ahmed, *op.cit.*, p.25 quoting from Aldo Gill, *Daniel Comboni, The Man and His Message – A Selection from the Writings of Bishop Daniel Comboni (1831-1881)* (Bologna: Editrice Missionaria Italiana, 1980), p.158.

112 Gill, *op.cit.*, p.60

113 Ahmed, *op.cit.*, p.31 quoting from F.R. Wingate, *Ten Years' Captivity in the Mahdi's Camp 1882-1892*, from the original manuscript of Father Joseph Ohrwalder, 2nd Edition (London, 1892), p.31. Father Ohrwalder died in Sudan on August 7 1913.

Other Missionaries in Sudan

As for Protestant Christianity, then American missionaries began to travel to Sudan in the 1880s and Anglican Christianity was carried into Sudan by explorers and Christian representatives of the then Egyptian government, such as General Charles Gordon.[114] As for Gordon, then he wished to establish Christian missions in Sudan and encourage traditional African tribal leaders to adopt Christianity. Gordon thus co-operated with Comboni in order to establish Christianity in the equatorial regions and invited the Church Missionary Society (CMS) to evangelize the Sudan in 1878 CE. It was Gordon who tried to appoint Zubayr Pasha, a well known slave-dealer, to succeed him and it was Gordon who restored the institution of slavery after his appointment in 1884, when he declared that no immediate emancipation of slaves would be attempted.[115] British policy at this time was mainly concerned with the Sudan and when Gordon was killed in 1885 the British were shocked, considering his death to have been the result of Muslim barbarians. As a result, most of the European Christian literature after the death of Gordon focused on European interests in Sudan and strategies in how to introduce secularism, nationalism and Christianity in Sudan. All of this was in order for Sudan to become a place wherein Christian missions could be established for missionaries to take Christianity to the rest of Africa and also to block the spread of Islām to Africa by creating a buffer zone in Southern Sudan to hinder the natural daily interactions between Muslims and non-Muslims.

---

114 General Charles Gordon was born in January 1833 in Woolwich and he graduated as a 2nd Lieutenant in 1852, in 1860 he went to China, where he put down the Taipings Revolution which was headed by an Islamic ruler. In 1874 he went to Sudan and stayed there for nearly six years. In 1885 he became the Governor-General of Sudan, he also spent some time in Palestine and wrote 'Reflections in Palestine.' Lord Salisbury described Gordon as a "Christian hero" yet Gordon stated once about his fellow Christians: "I am sick of your burnt offerings and your prayer meetings. My soul hateth them, they are a trouble to me. I am weary of them. I like the Musulman, he is not ashamed of his God, his life is a fairly pure one." Refer to *Pictorial Records of the English in Egypt* (London) which contains a full description of the life of General Gordon.

115 *Pictorial Records of the English in Egypt: with a Full and Descriptive Life of General Gordon*, (London and New York: F. Warne, 1885), pp.250-6

Modern missionary activity in Sudan is connected to Rev. Llewellyn H. Gwynne[116] who came to Sudan full of enthusiasm and zeal to Christianise Sudan. Before the coming of Gwynne, Egypt and Sudan was considered as part of the '*See of the Church of England in Jerusalem and the East*', but after his coming they were considered a separate independent diocese. In 1900, Cromer asked Bishop Gwynne to open a fund in order to build an Anglican church in Khartoum. Cromer also supported the Catholic missionaries in certain areas which were thus assigned as being 'closed districts' wherein no one, not even natives from Northern Sudan, could visit without a special permit from the British authorities in Khartoum. At the same time, British administrators and Christian missionaries had roamed various areas of the Sudan encouraging distrust of Northern Sudan and there were warnings that "only the British could keep the Arabs in check."[117]

Gwynne began a programme to unite all of the different Christian groups in Sudan and this co-operation led to the development of the Council of Churches in the Sudan and included, the Church of England, the Greek Orthodox Church, the Coptic Church, the Armenian Orthodox Church, the Syrian Orthodox Church, the Evangelical Church of Egypt, the American Presbyterian Church and the Royal Army Chaplains Department.[118] More churches were admitted to this council later. A counterpart of the Sudan Council of Churches was the Inter-Mission Council, which put in efforts into a joint missionary venture in southern

116 Llewellyn Henry Gwynne was born in South Wales on 11 June 1863 in a strong Christian household, with three of his brothers being priests. His brother Howel had accompanied 'lord' Kitchener's army to the Sudan and he himself left for Sudan on 2 November 1899. He was successful in establishing relations with Shaykh Bābikar Badrī of Sudan (*rahimahullāh*), King Fārūq of Egypt, the rector of al-Azhar University, al-Marāghī and other Egyptian politicians. Gwynne was considered the first to open a girl's school in Sudan in 1902 for Coptic girls in competition with Shaykh Bābikar Badrī. He participated in the First World War as Deputy Chaplain under General Kitchener. He retired in May 1948, after working for nearly half a century in Sudan. Gwynne was anti-Zionist and died on 7 December 1957.

117 Hussein Zulfakar Sabry, *Sovereignty for Sudan* (London: Ithaca Press, 1982), p.10.

118 Ahmed, *op.cit.*, p.44 quoting A. Morris Gesthorpe, *Introducing the Diocese of Sudan* (London: Mcorquodale & Co., 1946), p.50

Sudan in order to weaken Islamic interaction there and to implement Christianity in the south of Sudan. The mission's members were the Gordon Memorial Sudan Mission, the CMS, the American Presbyterian Mission and the Sudan United Mission.[119] The last mission was brought in being by Gwynne in 1912 CE, its missionaries were mainly from New Zealand and Australia,[120] later the Sudan Interior Mission (SIM)[121] and the African Inland Mission (AIM) were developed.

The Beginnings of Missionary and Evangelical Propaganda in Sudan

In terms of Christian missionary and evangelical propaganda related to Sudan then this did not just emerge in the contemporary era but actually began as soon as missionaries entered Sudan. A Vatican missionary tract[122] claimed that:

> It is interesting to note that the population of Southern Sudan had already reduced from 2,400,000 to 550,000 during the period when the Northerners occupied the South from 1885-1903 (!!)

Dr. Hassan Makki Mohamed Ahmed, a senior research fellow at the Islamic African Centre in Khartoum states:

> Such a statement is baseless, since there was no reliable estimate of Southern Sudan's population before the Mahdiyyah or after it in 1903. No major war took place there during the period.[123]

---

119 An Australian based international mission founded by Dr. K. Kunan and was established in 1904 CE in response to an appeal from leaders in several British denominations for a joint effort to prevent the advance of Islām in Central Africa.

120 Ahmed, *op.cit.*, p.45

121 A Canadian Protestant Mission which moved its headquarters from Toronto to Sudan in 1937 after its missionaries were expelled from Ethiopia during the Italian invasion. It established its main centre in the Upper Nile north-eastern area and opened four stations with schools in the south of Sudan. They translated some portions of the Gospel into the Auduk and Anwak languages and prepared textbooks in local languages. In 1964 they had thirty-six missionaries at nine stations in Southern Sudan but by 1970 there were only five missionaries.

122 Church of Rome, *The Black Book of the Sudan, On the Expansion of the Missionaries from Southern Sudan: An Answer* (Milano, Italy: Instituto Artigianelli, 1964), p.95.

123 Ibid., p.54

In fact, the Catholic Church was the most vehement in its propaganda and the Vatican were responsible for mobilising the world press and informing them of inaccuracies. The April 1963 issue of Verona Fathers' *Nigrizia* magazine was devoted entirely to the Southern Sudan and at the same time *Frontier Call*, the mouthpiece of the Verona Fathers Mission, published in Cincinnati, USA, devoted a whole issue to the Sudan:

> Southern Sudan is an immense jail from which all citizens who could, have escaped...Christianity must go, because a united Sudan is not conceivable unless it is Moslem down to its last citizen. This flagrant disregard for the rights and liberties of millions of people goes on today in the Sudan.[124]

The Policy of Dealing With Islām in Sudan

Despite all of this effort, for about ten years the missionaries failed to convert, using this period (1905-1915) for planning and co-ordinating missionary ideas.[125] So the missionaries could only look on while people were accepting Islām in areas which were of interest to the missionaries. Archdeacon Shaw, writing in 1909 CE, said:

> Unless all these black tribes are evangelized within the next few years they must inevitably become Mohammedan, its area is a strategic position for the purpose of evangelism. It is just about the centre of East Africa, half-way from the Cape to Cairo. In it is the junction between the highlands where European settlement is possible and the lowland where all crops are native grown... Here if anywhere, the church of Christ needs a stronghold to check the spread of Islam...[126]

Wingate wrote to Gywnne on 17 May 1911 CE saying:

> If you are going to put up a strong barrier to the advance of Islam you will have to stir up the various missionary societies for greater

124 Ahmed, *op.cit.*, pp.120-1

125 W. Wilson Cash, *The Changing Sudan* (London: Church Missionary Society, 1930), p.74.

126 A.L. Kitching, *From Darkness to Light: Pioneer Missionary Work on the Upper Nile* (London: SPCK, 1935), p.16.

activity.[127]

In the summer of 1911, Gwynne demanded the removal of Muslim troops, officials and merchants from the south of Sudan.[128] W. Wilson Cash, writing for the *CMS* stated:

> The river Nile flows through *CMS* history, and now this mighty waterway is a strategic line of development for commerce and Islam as well as for Christianity. Muslim influence is spreading south and Christian missions are expanding north. The meeting place and the battleground today is the Sudan. Christianity must either win the pagans of the Sudan for Christ and through them establish a strong witnessing church or confess to failure in the face of Moslem aggression.[129]

The strategic importance of Sudan attracted top officials such as the earl of Cromer and President Roosevelt, to the extent that these two individuals actually visited the Sudan to observe the work of their fellow missionaries in southern Sudan.[130] After the *World Missionary Conference* in Edinburgh in 1910, one of the main findings from it was,

> ...The threatening advance of Islam in Equatorial Africa, presents to the Church of Christ, the decisive question whether the Dark Continent shall become Mohammedan or Christian.

In discussing this report, Rev. George Robson stated:

> Pagan Africa is becoming Mohammedan more rapidly than it is becoming Christian. Among all the inland routes of trade, Mohammedan traders are steadily advancing southward and every Mohammedan trader is a Mohammedan missionary. The very first thing which requires to be done, if Africa is to be won for Christ, is to throw a strong missionary force right across the centre of Africa to bar the advance of Islam.[131]

---

127 Lillian Passmore Sanderson and Neville Sanderson, *Education, Religion and Politics in Southern Sudan* (London: Ithaca Press and Khartoum University Press, 1981), p.84.

128 Ibid.

129 Cash, *op.cit.*, p.82

130 Ahmed, *op.cit.*, p.64

131 Charles R. Watson, *The Sorrow and Hope for the Sudan: A Survey of Missionary Conditions and Methods of Work in the Egyptian Sudan* (Philadelphia: The Board of

In 1926, a comprehensive statement prepared by a commission appointed by the *Missionary Council of the Church Assembly* declared that:

> This double scheme of building up a church and at the same time training it to face Islam is the real answer to what has been called the Moslem menace in Sudan and from the east and west into the interior...The history of missions in Moslem lands was at one time, to a large extent a history of educational work...The changing conditions of the Moslem world make it imperative that the church should reconsider its educational policy of Islam...We emphasise the fact that from the north Islam is spreading through the Sudan and the CMS mission in the Southern Sudan is hopelessly weak at present and unable with its present staff to stem the tide. Unless this mission can be greatly strengthened, we see no hope of preventing ultimately a solid mass of Mohammedanism right up to the borders of Uganda, and who can say what this may mean to the growing native church there?[132]

Indeed, this mission was strengthened by inflating the claim that Muslims perform slave raiding attacks on non-Muslim black tribes in the south of Sudan on the regular![133] British colonial policy then paved the way to what is known as the 'Southern Policy', which was a policy which emphasised segregation and disintegration. It was an aggressive cultural strategy aiming to make Southern Sudan a missionary field monopolised by missions, and a bulwark against Islām in Sudan. The main engineer of this was the Civil Secretary of the time, Harold MacMichael, who even though opposed to the missionaries in some

---

Foreign Mission of the Presbyterians, 1913), p.186.

132 The Missionary Council of the Church Assembly, *The World Call to the Church, The Call from the Muslim World* (Westminster, London: 1926), pp.58-9, 60, 138.

133 The main instance of the slave trade in the Sudan was during the 19th century during the time of the Albanian ruler of Egypt Muhammad Ali Pasha, the one who fought against the First Saudi State, later fought against the Ottomans and then negotiated with the British for his own control of Egypt. Due to the Turko-Egyptian conquest of Sudan, the regional balance was upset and there was greater demand for Sudan's resources. It has been asserted by some historians that the Northern Sudanese tribes which were conquered by the Turko-Egyptian alliance may have resorted to the slave trade in order to pay the demands on them from the Turko-Egyptian ruling powers.

issues, he was a stubborn believer in the necessity of eradicating Islām from Southern Sudan. The missionaries, Protestant and Catholic welcomed the 'Southern Policy' as it furthered their efforts of urging the colonial government to culturally and linguistically segregate Southern Sudan. The Southern Policy was defined in MacMichael's letter:

> It is the aim of the government to encourage as far as possible (Christian) Greek and Syrian traders rather than the Gallaba (Northern traders) type...The limitation of Gallaba trade to towns or established routes is essential...Every effort should be made to make English the means of communication...In short, whereas at present Arabic is considered by many natives of the South as the official, as it were, the fashionable, language, the object of all should be to counter this idea by every practical means.[134]

The civil secretary directed that Northern officials should be gradually eliminated from the Southern Sudanese provinces. The governor of Bahr al-Ghazal wrote to his subordinate:

> To further this policy of encouraging local language, tribal consciousness and English and suppressing Arabic, everything which in the smallest degree may contribute to this should be done.[135]

The MacMichael '*Memorandum on Southern Policy*' put into effect the missionary enterprise and aided the missionaries and evangelicals in Christianising Southern Sudan, and as a result the Muslims of Sudan cannot be accused of segregating Sudan. On 10 August 1928 MacMichael stated that the '*Southern Policy*' was in order to "Create a solid barrier, protecting the South against the insidious political intrigue, which must in the ordinary course of events increasingly beset our path in the North." The colonial governors of the Southern Sudan and their district controllers began to implement:

- Arabic language should not be spoken in Southern Sudan and Christian names should be used, the inhabitants of Bahr ul-Ghazal

134 Muddathur Abd-Rahim, *Imperialism and Nationalism in the Sudan: A Study of Constitutional and Political Development, 1899-1956* (Oxford: Clarendon Press, 1969), p.77.

135 Ibid.

should be forced to become Christians;

- Arab traders to be screened; the Fellata/Fulānī tribe of emigrant Muslims from West Africa should be ordered to go north;
- The forming of a buffer zone and a no-man's land between the Muslim tribes and the pagan tribes, halting the long process of interaction between the Northern and Southern tribes with the Ngok Dinka tribes not allowed to mix with the Hamr Arab tribes with whom they were freely mixing with and inter-marrying;
- The elimination of Islām in the Western district of Dar Fertit and a purge of Arabic and Muslim influence. Muslims were expelled from Raja and Kafia Kingi and pilgrims were diverted northward through Darfur.[136]

Southern Sudan thus became a closed off area in the 1930s and the missionaries began to control issues affecting the region. Dr Hassan Makki Muhammad Ahmed notes:

> In mission schools, the Southern students were taught that their brothers in the North were the source of all their hardship. In the teaching of religion and history every opportunity was taken to keep the memory of slavery alive.[137]

Now let's refer to a non-Muslim Southern Sudanese intellectual, Bona Malwal, he stated:

> Some blame can be traced to the system of education in the South at that time. There were teachings in some of the Christian missionary schools in the South which used to portray Arabic for instance, as a bad language compared to English or Italian. There were times when talking Arabic in any school in the South could be punished by dismissal from the school. Southerners were brought up as Christians in missionary schools. In these schools, the only ones that were available at that time, Christianity was presented as a superior religion in competition with other inferior religions. Islam was not allowed free access to Southern villages in the way Christianity was...it was not too difficult to build a Southern prejudice against the North in Southern schools where the Arab role in selling and buying Africans into slavery was part

136 R.O. Collins, *Shadows in the Grass* (London, 1984), p.189.

137 Ahmed, *op.cit.*, p.76

> of the history that was taught.[138]

Ahmed notes:

> By emphasising the English language and Christianisation, mission education increased existing barriers between the North and the South. Although by the fifties the CMS had accepted the unity of Sudan and there was no question of their missionaries dragging up the 'biased slavery' story it seems that came too late, as reflected in the 1955 mutiny. For several decades the educated elite had been agitating in an underhand way against the North. The missionaries had sown in the hearts of many the seeds of hatred that were to be with them always and embitter their lives.[139]

In the 1980s the efforts of foreign missionaries and evangelist organisations were co-ordinated by the Sudan Council of Churches Commission on Relief and Rehabilitation (SCCCRR) with a monthly expatriates payroll of $56,000. The World Council of Churches had some success in attracting Church organisations to participate in Southern Sudan's relief and rehabilitation programme. Such participating agencies included the Basel Mission of Switzerland, Christian Aid of the UK, Church World Service of the USA, Dan Church Aid of Denmark, Dienste over Chenzen of Holland, Dienste in Uebersee of Germany, Mennonite Central Committee of the USA and Canada, the *Lutheran World Federation* of Geneva, the National Christian Council of Kenya, Norwegian Church Relief, the United Presbyterian Church (The Program Agency) of the USA, the National Christian Church of Kenya, the Church Missionary Society and the Roman Catholic Church!!

Each of these organisations sent one or more expats with *Church World Service* sending up to twelve and the Mennonite Central Committee sending eleven. All of these organisations worked under the supervision of the *SCCCRR*, some provided money, material help, expats, propaganda and 'advice.' Therefore, a modern-day missionary and evangelical base was establishing itself in Southern Sudan along with planes, communications, boats, landing strips, cars and thousands

---

138 Bona Malwal, *People and Power in Sudan: The Struggle for National Stability* (London: Ithaca Press, 1981), pp.35-6.

139 Ahmed, *op.cit.*, pp.85-6

of employees.[140] Millions of pounds were provided to Southern Sudan by a wide variety of missionary and evangelical organisations. A contemporary example of the missionary and evangelical effort in Sudan was also observed at the evangelical website www.sudan101.com which even featured 'prayers' against 'the spirit of Islām.' The site is now defunct.

More recently, the US Christian evangelist of North Carolina, Franklin Graham son of evangelist Billy, has attacked Islām in the context of fundraising for his international relief organisation *Samaritan's Purse.* Graham stated during the aftermath of the 9/11 attacks that Islām "is a very evil and wicked religion." Graham's Samaritan's Purse rebuild churches in a project that is estimated to cost $5 million/4 million Euros, and it also includes bringing in evangelical Christian fundamentalists from other Arabic speaking countries for one-month stays in Sudan.[141]

Slavery in Sudan Hoaxes

Due to the mass hysteria caused by certain elements (evangelical and political), the "black slavery in Sudan" narrative had become popularised. The reality, as we have outlined, was not a simple issue and much confusion had been caused due to people not understanding the dynamics of that particular situation. Furthermore, the Southern Sudanese SPLA themselves were guilty of slavery and oppression, if not more so than they and their Christian evangelical cohorts were claiming were happening to them. Yet as usual, biased accounts only detail the abuses enacted by ignorant Muslims and nothing else is mentioned. Sean Gabb, director of the *Sudan Foundation* in London, noted in 1997 CE that:

- Since John Garang[142] has led the SPLA from 1983 he has yet to account for kidnappings, abductions, forced labour, forced

140 Ibid., pp.114-5

141 See "*Christian evangelist Franklin Graham blasts Islam, says will rebuild churches in Sudan*", Associated Press, October 9 2006

142 John Garang headed the Southern Sudanese rebels and would later jointly participate in a united Sudan. He was from the Dinka tribal grouping and educated in Tanzania and the US, he also conducted military training in Israel. He died in a helicopter crash in 2004 CE, which some consider to be mysterious.

conscriptions and other slavery-related practices that his 'Christian' organization has been involved in.[143]

- The 1990 *US State Department's Country Reports on Human Rights Practices* records that the SPLA forced southern Sudanese men to work as labourers or porters and forcibly conscripted them into SPLA ranks.[144]
- Inter SPLA fighting also resulted in the taking of slaves.[145]
- The *1991 Country Reports on Human Rights Practices* placed on record that the SPLA had "forcibly conscripted at least ten thousand minors."[146]
- *Human Rights Watch – Africa* in its 1994 report entitled '*Civilian Destruction – Abuses By All Parties in the War in Southern Sudan*', a 279 page study, reported that: "The SPLA has conducted forcible recruitment…since at least the mid-1980s…forcing civilians to porter supplies is a chronic abuse."[147]
- *Human Rights Watch – Africa* further noted that the SPLA was guilty of, amongst other things, indiscriminate attacks on civilians, abducting civilians, mainly women and children, torture, summary executions, the deliberate starvation of civilians, forced recruitment, forced labour, theft of civilian animals, food and grain and the holding of long term political prisoners in prolonged arbitrary detention.[148]

Are these the actions of "oppressed black African Christians under the rule of Islamic extremists," or exploitation by those who are following their own interests and desires for power? The answer is clear. Importantly, it has to be known that the actions of ignorant Muslims in any country cannot be taken to be representative of Islām. For example in Sudan, Hasan at-Turābī had been refuted by Muslim scholars for his Mu'tazilah (rationalist) understanding of Islām which have led him to reject sound

143 See: *MSA News, Sudan Foundation - Allegations of Slavery and Slavery-Related Practices, Part 2; Open Letter to Caroline Baroness Cox* (Saturday 22nd March 1997).

144 *Country Reports on Human Rights Practices for 1990*, p. 387.

145 *Country Reports on Human Rights Practices for 1991*, p. 391.

146 Ibid., p.382

147 *Civilian Devastation*, pp.174, 189, 192

148 Ibid., p.3

and authentic hadeeth from the Prophet Muhammad (*sallallāhu alayhi wassallam*). Thus, the late Ethiopian scholar of Madeenah University, Shaykh Muhammad Amān al-Jāmī (*rahimahullāh*) exposed the philosophical leanings and modernist interpretations advocated by Turābī.[149]

The Sudanese people will admit that historically there has always been a problem of intra-tribal violence which has resulted in abductions and kidnappings between traditional ethnic rivals such as between the Baqqarah nomads and the pastoral Dinka over access to grazing and water in parts of Bahr al-Ghazal and Kordofan, which has also been a part of life between the Nuer and Dinka tribes, and among other tribes in the Southern Sudan aswell.[150] Indeed, there was a *Dinka-Nuer West Bank Peace and Reconciliation Conference* that was held at Wunlit in Bahr al-Ghazal between 27 February and 8 March 1999. Dinka and Nuer chiefs, elders and community leaders met under the auspices of the *New Sudan Council of Churches* in an attempt to end years of bitter conflict between the Dinka and Nuer ethnic groups, both of them Southern Sudanese tribes![151] Since this, there have been hundreds of peace deals, accords and initiatives for peace and reconciliation in Sudan.

---

149 Muhammad Amān al-Jāmī, *Rud 'alā't-Turābī* (lecture in Arabic)

150 In connection to this, Nasseem and Marjan (1992: 213) state that a characteristic feature of slavery in the region (of Sudan and northern Uganda) was that the slave could own property, claim freedom if treated cruelly, and on becoming Muslims,

> ... Provided he was learned in Islam, he could act as "*Imam as Salat*" (Prayer Leader). The slave had the full right to arrange for his own marriage and therefore could marry as many as four. The slave wife enjoyed equal attention with the free wives (in its legal context). Unlike the practice in the European slave trade in the Muslim areas, the slave could buy his freedom, and above all, manumission was permitted by Shari'a. These are the positive features of slavery in our part of the Muslim world which many an Orientalist couldn't ignore.

See Zubairi B. Nasseem and Doka Wahib Marjan, "*The 'Nubians' of East Africa: A Discussion" in Journal of the Institute of Muslim Minority Affairs*, vol.13: 1, Jun.1992, p.213 (ff.20).

151 See '*Sudan tribes agree ceasefire' BBC World, BBC Online Network*, Wednesday 10 March 1999.

At least one Christian magazine, *Christianity Today*, admitted this scenario in an article entitled '*Slave Redemption: Americans are becoming instant Abolitionists, but is the Movement Backfiring*?' on 9 August 1999. Therefore, for the likes of Christian Solidarity International (CSI) and Christian Solidarity Worldwide, Boston-based American Anti-Slavery Group and other evangelical groups to describe this situation as 'slavery' and 'slave-raiding' would be like describing modern rival gang violence and criminality in the West as being 'slavery'! Subsequently, these evangelical organisations claim to 'redeem' those who were once 'enslaved' in Sudan!?[152] Christian Solidarity International (CSI) and Christian Solidarity Worldwide have claimed to have 'redeemed' 65,000 "slaves", yet these claims have been called into serious question. Alex de Waal was a co-director of *Human Rights Watch – Africa* and has worked for Inter-Africa Group. He is currently a director of the human rights group Justice Africa and a fellow of the Global Equity Initiative at Harvard University, he stated regarding the claims of CSI:

---

152 Slave redemption and ransoming as acts of charity and piety were based on the example of two redemptive Christian orders, the Trinitarians founded in France by Jean of Matha and Felix of Valois in 1193 CE; and the Mercedarians begun by Pedro Nolasco in Barcelona in 1203 CE. Both had been primarily initiated for freeing Christian slaves or captives during the crusaders at the hands of Muslims and both of these orders flourished throughout the Middle Ages. The Mercedarians were converted to a military order by King Jaime the first in 1218 CE and as a result they remained heavily involved with the Spanish Crown and its ensuing crusading activities in the *Reconquista*. The Trinitarians focused on their network of monastic houses, which by the mid-1200s numbered at 50 and by the mid-1500s numbered over 800. They committed themselves to donating a third of its income to ransoming slaves and slave redemption. See Robert C. Davis, *Christian Slaves, Muslim Masters: White Slavery in the Mediterranean, the Barbary Coast and Italy, 1500-1800* (Basingstoke and New York: Palgrave Macmillan, 2004) p.149.

During the epoch of Barbary Coast slavery by Muslims (of white European Christians) in the sixteenth and seventeenth centuries CE, the Trinitarians and the Mercedarians freed some Christians enslaved in North Africa. However, even during their time they were accused of "spreading a thousand fables, in order to enhance the merit of those services they do to the public..." The current issue in regards to Sudan is a continuation of this 'redemption' tradition along with further contemporary fables!

> Overeager or misinformed human rights advocates in Europe and the US have played upon lazy assumptions to raise public outrage. Christian Solidarity International, for instance, claims that "Government troops and Government-backed Arab militias regularly raid black African communities for slaves and other forms of booty." The organisation repeatedly uses the term "slave raids", implying that taking captives is the aim of government policy. This despite the fact that there is no evidence for centrally-organised, government-directed slave raiding or slave trade... The issue is a slippery one: slavery slides off into issues such as hostage-taking. The difference between a hostage and a slave is important. It shows how Sudanese history must be seen in its local context, and how it is a mistake to impose stereotypes from elsewhere.[153]

Peter Verney, the author of an official 1997 *Anti-Slavery International* report on allegations of Sudanese slavery, commented: "The charge that government troops engage in raids for the purpose of seizing slaves is not backed by the evidence."[154] In May 1999 the *Christian Science Monitor* noted that:

> There are increasingly numerous reports that significant numbers of those 'redeemed' were never slaves in the first place. Rather, they were simply elements of the local populations, often children, available to be herded together when cash-bearing redeemers appeared.[155]

In February 2002, four newspapers, The *Irish Times*, London's *Independent on Sunday*, The Washington Post and the *International Herald Tribune*, published articles exposing the fraud and corruption of the claims of 'slave redemption' industry in Sudan. The *Washington Post* reported that in numerous documented instances "the slaves weren't slaves at all, but people gathered locally and instructed to pretend they were returning from bondage."[156] The *Independent on Sunday* reported that it was able to

153 Alex de Waal, '*Sudan: Social Engineering, Slavery and War,' in Covert Action Quarterly*, Spring 1997.

154 Peter Verney, '*Slavery in Sudan*', in *Sudan Update and Anti-Slavery International*, London, May 1997.

155 "*Slave 'Redemption' won't save Sudan*" in *Christian Science Monitor*, 26 May 1999.

156 "*Ripping Off Slave 'Redeemers': Rebels Exploit Westerners Efforts to Buy*

"reveal that 'redemption' has often been a carefully orchestrated fraud."[157] The *Irish Times* set the stage for how "slave redemptions" had hitherto been presented:

> The slave redemption makes for powerful human drama. A line of women and children emerges from the African bush. A slave trader in front, wrapped in the white robes of an Arab. And before them, waiting with a bag of money at this feet, is a white, Christian, man. The procession halts under the shade of a tree. There is discussion, then money changes hands. Suddenly the trader gives a nod, the slaves walk free and there are cries of joy as families are re-united. Freedom at last. Who could fail to be stirred by this emotional sight?...The highly publicised redemptions have touched millions of hearts – and wallets – across the world but particularly in the US.
>
> Celebrities and politicians have chained themselves to railings in protest. Pop stars have given free concerts. Little girls have given their lunch money....There is another side to the redemption story. According to aid workers, missionaries, and even the rebel movement that facilitates it, slave redemption in Sudan is often an elaborate scam...the process is nothing more than a careful deceit, stage-managed by corrupt officials. In reality, many of the 'slaves' are fakes, rebel officials round up local villagers to pose for the cameras. They recruit fake slavers – a light skinned soldier, or a passing trader, to 'sell' them.
>
> The children are coached in stories of abduction and abuse for when the redeemer, or a journalist, asks questions...CSI can spend more than $300,000 during a week of redemptions at various bush locations. After their plane takes off, the profits are divided up – a small cut to the "slaves" and the "trader" but the lion's share to local administrators and SPLA figures... The warning signs have been there for years. Within the SPLA, whispers of suspicion have swelled into a chorus of criticism in recent years. Acrimonious rows have broken out and accusations profiteering levelled at individuals...It seems almost incredible that tens of thousands of abducted civilians could cross a dangerous frontline

Emancipation for Sudanese," in *The Washington Post*, 26 February 2002.

157 "*Scam in Sudan: An Elaborate Hoax Involving Fake African Slaves and Less-than Honest Interpreters is Duping Concerned Westerners*" in *The Independent on Sunday* (London), 24 February 2002.

> undetected by government forces…Put simply, the numbers didn't add up. And yet no questions were asked. The dollars rolled in and the redemptions continued.

A Roman Catholic Italian missionary, Mario Riva, who was operating in the region wherein 'slavery' and 'slave-raiding' was supposed to be occurring in Southern Sudan and who spoke local tribal languages said that he had personally seen Southern Sudanese rebel interpreters misleading foreign evangelical Christians, such as John Eibner (of *Christian Solidarity International*),[158] with regards to 'slaves' and 'slave redemption'!! Mario Riva said that the incident happened near the village of Mariel Bei in the late 1990s and he saw Eibner standing under a tree with a group of 'slaves' who were none other than Riva's own parishioners!? Marion Riva stated: "The people told me they had been collected to get money. It was a kind of business." He reported that Eibner would ask if a slave had been held in captivity.

The official interpreter would translate the question as "have you suffered in the war?" The villager would reply in the positive. The translator would then tell Eibner that the man had been abducted by Arabs, treated inhumanely and was grateful to CSI for saving his life!![159] A catholic priest quoted in the *Independent on Sunday* stated: "Interpretation was the key to deception."[160] In an open letter in 2000, senior SPLA commander Aleu Ayieny Aleu stated that "slave redemption" had become a "racket of mafia dimensions." He also revealed that one of his lighter-skinned relatives for example, SPLA captain Akec Tong Aleu, had been forced several times to pretend to be an Arab and simulate the

---

158 Eibner's account of "redeeming slaves in Sudan" entitled *My Career Redeeming Slaves* was published by the Zionist neo-con propaganda mouthpiece (founded by Daniel Pipes) *Middle East Quarterly*, December 1999, vol.4, no.4. This account was used as a source by Andrew G. Bostom in his article *Black Slaves, Arab Masters* which was published by *FrontPage Magazine* on April 18 2005. The article is no longer available but a similar article, which echoes much of the same misconceptions, and is more or less the same article but with a different title, entitled '*The Living Legacy of Jihad Slavery*' can be viewed here: https://myislam.dk/articles/en/bostom%20the-living-legacy-of-jihad-slavery.php

159 "*The Great Slave Scam*" in *The Irish Times*, 23 February 2002.

160 "*Scam in Sudan: An Elaborate Hoax Involving Fake African Slaves and Less-than Honest Interpreters is Duping Concerned Westerners*"

sale of free children to CSI on camera.[161]

Dr Annette Weber, a human rights activist, while researching her thesis in 1999, reported that she came across evidence that rebel officials were instructing parents to lend their children to pose as slaves in order to increase the numbers of "slaves" for visitors to "redeem."[162] This version of events, the *Washington Post* noted, "…coincides with descriptions of the scam offered by Sudanese officials and Western aid workers, who said the sheer volume of money flowing into the South made corruption inevitable."[163] The newspaper also reported that "prevalent fraud is acknowledged by senior rebel officials." SPLA members are said to have built houses, married an exorbitant number of wives and financed other businesses due to the money earned from the 'slavery' scam![164] The former deputy commander of the *Sudan Relief and Rehabilitation Association* (the SPLA's aid wing), Mario Muor Muor, stated in an interview in October 2001 that "redemption is just a scandalous act."[165] Bona Malwal the southern Sudanese intellectual, in an open letter to Baroness Cox, criticised her for her deceptive techniques of so-called 'slave-redemptions.'[166]

Conclusions

Due to all of these missionary and evangelical machinations in Sudan, their propaganda drive became effective and they were able to hoodwink the masses by disseminating a vast array of inaccuracies and hysteria concerning the situation in Sudan, including attacks on the Divine Legislation of Islām (Sharee'ah) and over exaggerated and unverified reports concerning slavery. Ahmed notes:

> Some Church leaders tried to cover up their impotence to do something for the Church by becoming involved in a crusade against the Arabs of Kordofan province and Sudan by introducing

---

161 "*The Great Slave Scam*".

162 "*Ripping Off Slave 'Redeemers*".

163 Ibid.

164 "*The Great Slave Scam*" and "*Scam in Sudan…*"

165 "Ripping Off Slave 'Redeemers'".

166 Letter from Bona Malwal to Baroness Cox, 23 January 2000, posted on the '*South Sudan*' website.

> a fabricated shock-report about the prevalence of slavery in the Sudan.[167]

Mohamed Omer Beshir, a former professor at the *University of Khartoum* and also served as the Head of the African Department in Sudan's Ministry of Foreign Affairs stated "The myth of rapacious Arab slave traders has been used to embitter relations between North and South."[168] In his book on the background to the conflict in Southern Sudan, Beshir refuted the claim that only Northern Sudanese 'Arabs' were responsible for the repugnant slave trade arguing how Europeans who gained easy access to Sudan after the Turko-Egyptian conquest were even more culpable. One of the most notorious examples concerning the issue of slavery relates to the activities of a person by the name of Khojali al-Hassan.

Beshir highlights that Khojali al-Hassan developed a thriving slave trading enterprise with the help of his wife Amna, who was based in the Sudan's Blue Nile province on the eastern frontier with Ethiopia. Beshir notes that the trade came to an end in 1929, yet Ethiopian sources contradict this as they shed some light on a more intriguing aspect of this trade which involved none other than Negus Tefari, the future emperor Haile Selassie the first, who the Rastas worship as a god!! Selassie's personal prestige and influence had grown considerably in the Western provinces after his coronation in November 1930. Here through his close relationship with Kholaji al-Hassan, Selassie benefited from the gold tribute that was mined with slave labour provided by the sons of Kholaji and Amna.

In ending this section, we do not deny that some Muslims commit injustice, but rather we merely emphasise that in regards to the Sudan situation much propaganda and falsehood has been exacerbated by a wide variety of partisan evangelical and political parties who have only contributed to disseminating blatant lies and manufacturing distortions to the international community. Moreover, in terms of the slavery accusation then Sudan is not a suitable example of this in the modern era, as a country like Mauritania for example would be and as the sex

---

167 Ahmed, *op.cit.*, p.138

168 Mohamed Omer Beshir, *The Southern Sudan: Background to Conflict* (London: C. Hurst & Co., 1968), p.13.

slave trade in Europe and America would also.[169]

The Darfur Crisis

Similarly, highly inaccurate claims were made regarding the Darfur[170]

---

169 The *Department of Health and Human Services Rescue and Restore Campaign* defines sex trafficking as "a modern day form of slavery in which a commercial sex act is induced by force, fraud or coercion." Europe currently has a problem with a huge "sex-slave" smuggling and trafficking trade and estimates are that as many as 120,000 women every year are smuggled into Western Europe! (See "*EU 'to protect' sex slaves*", *BBC Online*, Thursday 8 March 2001). A US government report published in 2002 estimated that 50,000 people a year are trafficked into the US and in 2003 said that the figures were about 18,000 to 20,000. A *US Department of Justice* report in June 2004 said that 14,500-17,000 women were smuggled into the US annually, the majority of these sex slaves from Eastern Europe and East Asia. More on this will be mentioned in the subsequent chapter regarding slavery.

According to a 2013 Eurostat European Commission Working paper entitled *Trafficking in Human Beings* (p.10), the percentage of victims of trafficking for sexual exploitation is increasing each year whereas the percentage reported as victims of trafficking for labour exploitation dropped from 28% in 2008 to 23% in 2010. Victims of sexual exploitation are predominantly female (96% in 2010) whereas the majority of victims of labour exploitation are males (77% in 2010). The report also noted that in 2010 EU Member States reported a total of 9528 identified and presumed victims. See: http://ec.europa.eu/anti-trafficking/sites/antitrafficking/files/trafficking in human beings - dghome-eurostat en 1.pdf

170 The name 'Darfur' is from the Arabic "*Dār Fur*" (the land of the Fur), historically it was an Islamic sultanate located in the western Sudan. The Fur were the ruling ethnic group in the Darfur region before 1916 CE. The Fur embraced Islām in the 1300s and in 1596 CE the Darfur sultanate was established and Islām declared the state religion. The Darfur sultanate remained independent throughout various conflicts in the Sudan, including the Anglo-Egyptian conquest of Sudan in 1898 CE, before finally being subjected to the British in 1916 CE and made part of Western Sudan. As a result, Darfur has a long history of independence and resistance to various other entities that sought control of it. Darfur is home to nearly 80 different tribes and ethnic groups which are divided between nomads and sedentary communities. Darfur is one of the most remote regions of Sudan and even under normal circumstances the region is hard to reach because it is so far from the capital Khartoum. Tribal and ethnic conflicts are not new in Darfur and incidents of both small and large scale conflicts are recorded as far back as

region in Western Sudan.[171] Again journalists have made the inaccurate claim that 'Arabs' are committing genocide on 'black Africans.'[172] Suffice to say that both in this case are 'Africans' and 'Arabs'! Yet the media are just not mentioning the colour of these Arabs. A few journalists have made honest and accurate accounts of the situation. Even the *New York Times*, a fierce critic of the Sudanese government, featured an article "*Sudan – No Clear Difference Between Arab and African*," highlighting facile stereotyping.[173] To the extent that in 2006 CE a so-called current affairs programme on the BBC in the UK claimed that "Arab Militias with guns and tanks were fighting against black Africans armed with spears and bows"!!?[174] In Darfur the so called 'black Africans' speak

---

1939 CE arising from disputes over access to natural resources like range lands and water points as well as livestock trespassing (grazing on farmlands), closure of herd routes and cattle raiding. Larger conflicts emerged from tribal disputes, banditry and disputes with transnational migrating communities. The influx of small arms since the war in Chad contributed to the increased loss of life.

171 The Darfur crisis erupted in 2003 when two armed movements, the *Sudan Liberation Army* and the *Justice and Equality Movement* began a rebellion against the Sudanese government and co-originated a number of terrorist attacks on government buildings and establishments. In response, militias known as '*Janjaweed*' which means 'outlaws' or 'rabble' in local Darfurian dialect mobilised against them, but there is no clear evidence that the Sudanese government are co-ordinating the so-called "*Janjaweed*", and some Sudanese from Khartoum have even said that the "*Janjaweed*" themselves are not Arabs but rather from Chad. Since 1987 there have been clashes between militias and villagers and peace recommendations have resulted in nothing. The conflicts were over sparse resources of land and water, made worse by the fact that Darfur is the most impoverished region of Sudan, moreso than the south of Sudan, having the fewest schools and hospitals. In the 1990s de Wāl notes that in imitation of the southern Sudanese SPLA Darfurian groups began to use the term 'African' but an attempted alliance with the SPLA failed. Yet as the SPLA gained high international recognition by applying over-simplified terms, in Darfur the rebel separatist groups thus began to do the same, becoming 'African' victims of an 'Arab' regime.

172 An excellent example of these inaccuracies can be seen here: http://news.bbc.co.uk/1/hi/world/africa/3791713.stm

173 "*In Sudan – No Clear Difference Between Arab and African*," in *The New York Times*, 3 October 2004.

174 This was stated by Andrew Marr on his programme on Sunday June 18 2006 CE on BBC1 in the UK!? Merely demonstrating that many within the media

mainly Arabic, John Ryle of the *Rift Valley Institute* has noted that:

> It is only recently that the division between 'Arab' and 'African' has achieved its present level of political significance in Darfur. The distinction is not straightforward... Non-Arabs who are physically indistinguishable retain their indigenous languages, although Arabic is spoken as the lingua franca of the country.[175]

Dr Abdur-Rahman Abu Doum, the former Deputy Minister of Humanitarian Affairs in Sudan recalled in 2004 a recent reconciliation conference between different ethnic groups from Darfur. He noted that one of the Fur representatives was light-skinned and the so-called Arab representative was dark-skinned! So the ethnic ideas have clearly been invented and exaggerated as there are no clear ethnic demarcations. He stated:

> Let me tell you about a meeting that took place between the residents of Darfur, the so-called the Arabs and the Non-Arabs. It so happened that the representative of the Fur tribe was a fair-skinned person, while the representative of the so-called Arabs was black. So who is who? It is all invented. You cannot say where the demarcation line is. The Fur were known to be the native tribe in that part of the country, but since ages ago the so-called Arabs came and they lived together in peace. They had intermarriages. It is very difficult to say these are Arabs and these are non-Arabs. Now the Arabic culture, the Arabic language is the common medium of communication between the peoples in that part of the world. The religion between them is that they are all Muslims. But as I told you, when it came to the issue of resources...everybody claims his/her right. I can't deny inter-tribal problems break out here and there, but some people who are interested in different aspects - some want to rule and others feel that nobody should share these resources with them – have built up the conflict. I mean, as you start hitting and the others [hit you back], it builds up and flares, and if wisdom does not prevail, if nobody intervenes to bring people together, then this will

---

merely regurgitate whatever is spoon-fed to them with little or no reflection about what is actually being given to them.

175 John Ryle, "*Disaster in Darfur*" in *The New York Review, vol. 51, no.13* (August 12 2004).

> continue...[176]

Dr Abu Doum also importantly highlighted:

> One of the leaders of the Darfur rebellion was one of the government militia leaders fighting the rebels in the south of Sudan. Therefore, was he as an 'African,' trying to kill other Africans in the south!? And by the way, he is a friend of mine...[177]

Dr Abu Doum was then asked:

> **Q:** When people talk about ethnic cleansing, is it appropriate to use that description in Darfur?
>
> **A:** I hate it and it's really hurting to me. I describe myself as a real Sudanese with Arab blood, with African blood, with Egyptian blood and I find this word very hurting ... very hurting.
>
> **Q:** Why?
>
> **A:** Because Sudan is unique, and Sudanese people have something very special: the way they live together, the way they coexist with each other. The other day, I was attending a conference at Addis Ababa. It was a summit. Lam Akol, who was a leader of the Sudan rebels, came late and I was sitting just at the beginning of the room. When he saw me, he embraced me in the Sudanese way [...]. And there was a Westerner sitting next to me. He asked me: "Are you a member of the SPLA?" I said "that's something you don't know, and you cannot perceive. It is very difficult for you to digest." Anyway, the man is a friend of mine and we used to fish when we were teenagers together. And at the end of the meeting he asked me to take care of his mother, who is in Khartoum, at a time when he was with the rebels. These are the Sudanese people.

Alex de Waal was a co-director of *Human Rights Watch – Africa* and has worked for *Inter-Africa Group*. He is currently a director of the human rights group *Justice Africa* and a fellow of the *Global Equity Initiative* at *Harvard University*, has made the following accurate observations based on his experience:

---

176 See the *IRIN* interview and the documentary *Peace Under Fire – Sudan's Darfur Crisis*, produced by the United Nations' Integrated Regional Information Unit (IRIN), April 8 2004.

177 Ibid.

> Characterising the Darfur war as 'Arabs' versus 'Africans' obscures the reality. Darfur's Arabs are black, indigenous, African and Muslim – just like Darfur's non-Arabs who hail from the Fur, Masalit, Zaghawa and a dozen smaller tribes. Until recently, Darfurians used the term 'Arab' in its ancient sense of 'Bedouin.' These Arabic-speaking nomads are distinct from the inheritors of the Arab culture of the Nile and the Fertile Crescent. 'Arabism' in Darfur is a political ideology, recently imported, after Colonel Gadaffi[178] nurtured dreams of an 'Arab belt' across Africa, and recruited Chadian Arabs, Darfurians and West African Tuaregs to spearhead his invasion of Chad in the 1980s. He failed, but the legacy of arms, militia organisation and Arab supremacist ideology lives on. Most of Darfur's Arabs remain uninvolved in the conflict, but racist ideology appeals to many poor and frustrated young men...In response, non-Arab groups (some of them Bedouins too – there's a clan related to the Zaghawa that even has the name Bedeyāt) have mobilized, adopting the label 'African', which helps to gain solidarity with the southern-based Sudan People's Liberation Party, and is a ticket to sympathy in the West.[179]

Therefore, we can clearly see that an idea of Arab nationalism has influenced some Muslims, which is an ideology that Islamic scholars have refuted. The former Mufti of Saudi Arabia, the noble Shaykh 'Abdul'Azeez ibn 'Abdullāh ibn Bāz (*rahimahullāh*) said in his refutation of Arab nationalism:

> And there is no doubt that the call to nationalism is from these calls of *jāhiliyyah* (pre-Islamic days of ignorance), since nationalism is a call to other than Islām and an aiding of other than the truth. And how many ills, evils and wars have such calls of *jāhiliyyah* caused to their people, causing great harm to their souls, their wealth and their possessions. The consequences of such calls (for the Muslims) are a splitting-up of their unity and hatred

---

178 The Libyan leader al-Gaddaffi has a number of heretical and deviated statements some of which amount to nullification of Islam, such as his considering his 'Green Book' as being above the Qur'ān and Sunnah. Gaddaffi even attempted to revise how to recite the Qur'ān! The 'Green Book' says that the black man will rule the earth and at other times calls for Arab nationalism!?

179 Alex de Waal, *'Darfur's deep grievances defy all odds for an easy solution'* in *The Guardian* (UK), Sunday July 25 2004

of each other in their hearts and a fragmentation and splitting between tribes and nations. Ibn Taymiyyah (*rahimahullāh*)[180] said: "Everything which is outside the call of Islām and the Qur'ān, with regards to lineage, land, nationality, schools of thought and ways, then it is from the calls of *jāhiliyyah.*"[181]

And there is no doubt also, that the call to nationalism is a call to transgression, pride and arrogance, since nationalism is not a divinely-revealed way of life which prevents its people from oppression and proud-boasting. Rather it is an ideology from the time of *jāhiliyyah* which leads its people to boasting about it and having *'asabiyyah* (partisanship and party-spirit) for it – even if

180 Ahmad ibn 'AbdulHaleem Ibn Taymiyyah (1263 CE – 1328 CE/728 AH) was born in Harrān near Edessa which was in northern 'Irāq but is now called Orfa and is a part of Turkey. His father and grandfather were themselves leading scholars of the Hanbalī school of Islamic jurisprudence. He grew up in Damascus where he mastered at an early age the various sciences and disciplines of Islām. Much of his time and effort was spent in defending the early Islamic understandings against the deviations that were current during his era. Apart from being incredibly well versed in the Islamic sciences he also refuted with scholarly endeavour the tenets of Christianity, Shi'ism, Sufism, *Kalām* [speculative theology, philosophy and rhetoric] etc. He was also prominent in fighting the Mongol invaders whilst other Muslims were fleeing Syria with their wealth. Due to his strong stand for the truth against those who were distorting Islām for their own desires, a great deal of his later life was spent in prison in Cairo and Damascus. His outspoken lectures against the excessive theological and philosophical scholars of his time cost him his post as professor. Whilst in prison in Cairo, Ibn Taymiyyah was responsible for changing the prison into more of a library for the other prisoners, teaching and helping them to study instead of waste their time. This further angered his pitiful enemies from amongst the Sūfīs who had already taken to praying to dead 'saints' in graves, it would be those Sūfīs who would instigate futile arguments against him. Shaykh ul-Islām Ibn Taymiyyah refuted these fault finders with clear evidences, leaving them dumb-founded to this day. However, even in jail Ibn Taymiyyah was still a prolific writer. Some of his famous published works are: *Majmū' al-Fatāwā, Minhaj us-Sunnah, as-Siyāsah ash-Shar'iyyah, al-Īmān, al-Furqān, ar-Rasāil, at-Tawassul wa'l-Waseelah, al-Jawab as-Saheeh, Iqtidā Ahl us-Sunnah* and many others. It was this massive intellect and extraordinary ability to keep Islām in its pure form inherited from the early Muslims, whilst still master other sciences without incorporating them into Islām itself, which earned Ibn Taymiyyah the title *'Shaykh ul-Islām.'*

181 Ibn Taymiyyah, *Majmū' al-Fatāwā* (vol. 3, p.456)

they are the oppressors and the others are the oppressed! So – O noble reader – consider this and the truth will be clear to you… this is what the calls of *jāhiliyyah* lead to, whereas Islām is in opposition to this. Rather Islām calls to modesty, humility, *taqwā* and to having love for the sake of Allāh, and that the true and sincere Muslims are merely one of the categories of the children of Ādam (*'alayhis-salām*)… So I call you in the name of Allāh! Does your nationalism call you to these noble manners of mercy and kindness to the Muslims – the Arabs and non-Arabs – and of having mutual sympathy and concern for them, and feeling pain at their pain? No by Allāh! Rather it calls you to having allegiance with those who have evil character and it calls you to cultivating enmity and hatred for those who deny this fake creed of nationalism…[182]

182 Abridged translation from Shaykh 'Abdul'Azeez Bin 'Abdullāh Bin Bāz, *Naqd Qawmiyyatul-'Arabiyyah*, (Cairo: Dār Imām Ahmad, 1425 AH/2004 CE), pp.23-27. Also translated as *'The Evils of Nationalism,'* by *Al-Istiqāmah* Newsletter, no.2 (Safar 1417 AH/July 1996 CE).

IV
Slavery and Early Islām

فَلَا اقْتَحَمَ الْعَقَبَةَ ۝

وَمَا أَدْرَاكَ مَا الْعَقَبَةُ ۝ فَكُّ رَقَبَةٍ ۝ أَوْ إِطْعَامٌ فِي يَوْمٍ ذِي مَسْغَبَةٍ ۝ يَتِيمًا

ذَا مَقْرَبَةٍ ۝ أَوْ مِسْكِينًا ذَا مَتْرَبَةٍ ۝ ثُمَّ كَانَ مِنَ الَّذِينَ آمَنُوا وَتَوَاصَوْا

بِالصَّبْرِ وَتَوَاصَوْا بِالْمَرْحَمَةِ ۝

> But he has not broken through the difficult pass. And what you will make you know what is (breaking through) the difficult pass? It is the freeing of a slave. Or feeding on a day of severe hunger an orphan of near relationship or a needy person in misery and then being among those who believed and advised one another to patience and advised one another to compassion.
>
> [*al-Balad* (90): 11-17]

This chapter aims to be an extensive assessment of slavery in Islam and also how it manifested in the Muslim world. The chapter will be frank and will reveal some concerning instances in Muslim history wherein there were gross contraventions of the teachings of the Qur'an and the Sunnah in regards to slavery. At this juncture it will be worth us assessing the slavery in several countries to not only assess their reality, and how far in some cases there was a complete incongruity with the teachings of the Prophet Muhammad (*sallallāhu 'alayhi wassallam*), but also to deal directly with the issue about which many Muslims unfortunately are totally unaware.

Moreover, despite many practising Muslims today having romantic notions about the role of Muslims in regards to slavery during the initial epoch of Islam, relaying the story of Bilāl ibn Rabāh (*radi Allāhu 'anhu*), while also at the same time condemning trans-Atlantic slavery, the reality is that the vast majority of modern Muslims are totally ignorant about the reality of slavery in the Muslim world over the last 1000 years and that over the last 200 years. It is important therefore that Muslims do not, out of ignorance, become apologists for slavery and downplay the reality of how it actually manifested in the Muslim world. Murray Gordon in his book *Slavery in the Arab World* (1989: xi) argues that there is a "conspiracy of silence" which has "blocked out all light in this sensitive subject". Though there is an aspect of truth in this as it relates to the Arab world, due to ignorance, lack of education and historical denial in some instances, within the Islamic tradition and Muslim scholarship the matter of slavery has been addressed frankly and in detail, as will be evident in this section. A non-Muslim academic Bernard Freamon for instance stated in a lecture held at Yale University in 2008 entitled *Slavery and the Slave Trades in the Indian Ocean and Arab Worlds: Global Connections and Disconnections*:

> I begin by noting that, in spite of the rich and rapidly developing historiography in the Western academies on slavery and abolition in the Muslim world, discussion and understanding among Muslims of that history remains deeply impoverished and shockingly uninformed. There is effectively no real knowledge of the modern history of slavery or its abolition, especially in the realms of popular knowledge and in the content of educational curricula in secondary schools and universities, particularly in the Arab world. The modern Muslim mind is essentially in denial when it is asked to reflect on the Muslim world's long and deep connections with slavery and slave-trading systems. Many Muslims do possess a kind of superficial, idealized and normatively instrumental knowledge supplied by certain aspects of their religious history but this knowledge simply will not support the kind of critical analysis required if Muslims are to truly understand and benefit from their history. [183]

183 Bernard K. Freamon, *Slavery and the Slave Trades in the Indian Ocean and Arab Worlds: Global Connections and Disconnections*, pp.3-4, see: https://glc.yale.edu/sites/default/files/files/indian-ocean/freamon.pdf Accessed March 2018.

Freamon himself is perhaps also unaware of the critiques of slavery which abound and which will be brought to light in this section especially from classical Islamic scholars and the *Shari'ah* tradition. Although Freamon's remarks are somewhat of a generalisation, he is however correct to note that in the Muslim world in particular there is an acute silence on the topic. Yet this is largely due to a limited understanding of history as if history of their countries started post-colonialism. As a result, it may be the case that this limited historiography can be due to not only ignorance, but also denial, in cases, but also largely due to poor education and the fact that many countries which were pivotal in slavery in the Muslim world experienced upheaval during colonialism and many of the existing counties retrace their main history to only the last one hundred years or so of the modern era in keeping with the current regimes and their relationships with colonial powers. Any history prior to these times is either not known, not studied, ignored, denied, brushed under the carpet, not seen as important, distant, non-existent and irrelevant. Freamon continues:

> In point of fact, the horrific thirteen hundred year history of the Indian Ocean, Mediterranean and trans-Saharan slave trades, and of chattel slavery in Muslim communities belies the strident Islamic egalitarianism that characterizes the normatively top-heavy uses of history noted above. Even though this strident egalitarianism is, in many ways, one of the hallmarks of the Islamic religion, the historical evidence, it is argued, suggests that Islamic egalitarianism, in spite of its success as a powerfully galvanizing force in spreading the religion, made virtually no contribution to the closing of the slave trades and the eventual widespread elimination of chattel slavery in Muslim communities. Slavery in the Muslim world was never really abolished, the argument runs, it just disappeared, largely as a result of pressure from Western governments, including British naval anti-slaving patrols, treaties with and financial reward schemes for local indigenous *Shaykhs*, and the shaming exhortations of European and American abolitionist movements. It was the hegemony of colonialism that ended slavery in the Muslim world, substituting one pervasive

---

From The Gilder Lehrman Center's 10th Annual International Fall Conference *Slavery and the Slave Trades in the Indian Ocean and Arab Worlds: Global Connections and Disconnections* November 7-8, 2008 Luce Hall Auditorium, Yale University, New Haven, Connecticut.

> regime of inequality and hierarchy for another. Now that the colonialist legacy has receded, it is argued, slavery may indeed reappear in Muslim communities. Recent events suggest that chattel slavery and apartheid-like inequalities are still a problem in some Muslim communities in the Sahel, Sub-Saharan Africa, and in the Persian Gulf.[184]

This is the unfortunate viewpoint which many non-Muslims have of Muslims, that Muslims have done little to challenge such inequalities in the world and have been passive observers of such abuses of not only people but of Islam itself. However, Freamon tries to utilise to buttress his argument, that slavery and inequality is apparent in the contemporary Muslim world, by making reference to the situation in Sudan – however, as has been noted earlier in this book, there are some huge issues in the 'slavery in Sudan' narrative which was widespread throughout the 1990s. Nevertheless, what Freamon posits is absolutely true, that it was only due to pressure of British colonialism that Muslim countries (such as Oman, Egypt, Algeria and Morocco) abolished the mass slavery of, predominantly black people, from the interior of Africa. Then Freamon notes:

> These facts should be deeply disturbing to Muslims and others sympathetic to the Islamic project. They suggest that the Islamic conceptions of equality are not truly universal and may not be very useful to Muslims seeking to establish egalitarian political and social orders in the modern world. This leads to the further intimation that Islamic egalitarianism is nothing more than a rhetorical device in the hands of the proponents of the religion, useful for political propaganda and religious proselytizing but without real moral force in influencing the everyday behaviour of observant Muslims.

As I noted above, mere regurgitation of simplistic notions of the equality of Islam are not enough and Muslims have to also take action in the face of oppression, transgression and injustice on all levels in society. However, Freamon must also take into consideration that the *'Ulama* made huge efforts in condemning slavery and the trade in people and the barbarity involved which totally contravened Islam, which will be documented within this chapter.

---

184 Ibid. p.9.

In the traditions of the Prophet Muhammad *(sallallāhu 'alayhi wassallam)* we find that he encouraged those who kept slaves to make contracts which facilitated the release and manumission of slaves. For example, when Sīrīn, the father of Muhammad Ibn Sīrīn asked his master Anas to make a manumission agreement with him, Anas refused. On hearing about this 'Umar Ibn al-Khattāb whipped Anas saying, "*It is Allāh's command to enter into a manumission agreement.*"[185] The Prophet Muhammad (*sallallāhu 'alayhi wassallam*) said, "*Feed slaves from the food you eat, and clothe them from the clothes you wear.*"[186] A *hadeeth* mentions that a person will have two rewards in the after-life if they had slaves and then educated them and then freed them.[187] The Prophet Muhammad also said "*slaves are your brothers...never give them more to do than they are capable of doing. If you ever do so, then help them do it.*"[188] He also said (*sallallāhu 'alayhi wassallam)* "*No one should say "my slave," as all of you are slaves of Allāh.*"[189] He also said (*sallallāhu ' alayhi wassallam*), "*Whoever frees a slave, Allāh will free his body from the hellfire, just as he freed the body of the slave.*"[190] There are many other *hadeeth* to this effect from the Prophet Muhammad (s*allallāhu 'alayhi wassallam*). Islām also made no distinction in terms of the religion of the slaves to be emancipated except for a slight difference in the reward for a Muslim who frees them. Imām ash-Shawkānī stated in *Nayl ul-Awtār Sharh ul-Muntaqā ul-Akhbār*:

> ولا خلاف أن معتق الرقبة الكافر مثاب على العتق
>
> And there is no denying that one who emancipates a disbelieving slave will also be rewarded.[191]

Ibn Qudāmah al-Maqdisī stated, emphasising the encouragement to liberate non-Muslim slaves:

185 Bukhārī

186 Bukhārī, Muslim and Abū Dāwood

187 Bukhārī, Muslim, Nasā'ī and Ibn Mājah

188 Bukhārī, Muslim, Abū Dāwood, Tirmidhi and Ibn Mājah

189 Bukhārī, Muslim, an-Nasā'ī and Ibn Hibbān

190 Bukhārī

191 Muhammad bin 'Ali bin Muhammad ash-Shawkānī, *Nayl ul-Awtār*, vol.6, *Kitāb ul-'Itq*, [Chapter of Freeing Slaves].

وإنما يكون له استرقاقهم إذا كانوا من أهل الكتاب أو مجوسا

Only those from the people of the book, magians or the like can be freed from slavery.[192]

One of the contemporary Muslim scholars of the Sunnah, Shaykh Mashhūr Hasan Āl Salmān frm Jordan answered when asked about slavery, captives and prisoners of war in Islamic jurisprudence:

> The question says "'Ubūdiyyah" [servitude] he intends by this 'ar-Riqq' [i.e. slavery], our brother is asking about ar-Riqq. Has ar-Riqq been abrogated? During the time of the Prophet *(sallallāhu 'alayhi wassallam)* was there ar-Riqq? Yes, there was during his time. Is ar-Riqq in existence now or not? Is Islām pleased with it? No, Islām interacted within a society in which there was slavery and the Prophet (*sallallāhu 'alayhi wassallam*) said: "The curse of Allāh is on a person who sells a free person and then consumes the price for that."[193] A free person cannot be taken into slavery.

192 Muwaffaq ud-Deen Abū Muhammad 'Abdullāh Ibn Qudāmah al-Maqdisī al-Hanbalī, *al-Mughni, Kitāb ul-Jihād* [Chapter on Jihād].

193 Translator's Note ['AbdulHaq al-Ashanti]: Reported by al-Bukhārī on the authority of Abū Hurayrah (*radi Allāhu 'anhu*) and also reported by Ibn Mājah and Imām Ahmad in his *Musnad*. There is another *hadeeth* wherein the Prophet Muhammad (*sallallāhu 'alayhi wassallam*) stated: "Three types of people will not have rewards for their prayer: a man who forces himself as an *Imām* on a group of people; a man who postpones prayer until its time has gone and a man who enslaves a free person." This *hadeeth* is reported by Abū Dāwūd and Ibn Mājah, however both on the authority of 'AbdurRahmān bin Zayd bin Aslam al-Ifrīqī who is very weak due to his fabrication of narrations attributed to his father, as mentioned by al-Hākim in his book of weak narrators entitled *ad-Du'afā*. Imām al-Bukhārī stated about 'AbdurRahmān ibn Zayd that "his *hadeeth* are not authentic" as relayed in *at-Tārīkh al-Kabeer*, vol.1, p.618; Ibn Hibbān stated about 'AbdurRahmān ibn Zayd that "he deserves to be abandoned" as stated in al-*Majrūheen min al-Muhaditheen wa Du'afā wa'l-Matrūkeen*, edited by Mahmūd Ibrāheem Zāyid (Halab: Dār ul-Wa'ī, 1396 AH, 1st Edition and 1402 AH for the 2nd Edition), vol.2, p.57; Ibn Sa'd stated that 'AbdurRahmān ibn Zayd "reported many *hadeeth* and was very weak" as found in *at-Tabaqāt al-Kubrā*, vol.5, p.413; al-Fasawī noted in *al-Ma'rifah wa't-Tārīkh*, vol.3, p.43 placed 'AbdurRahmān ibn Zayd amongst those who should not be narrated from; Abū Hātim stated that "he is not strong in *hadeeth* but was righteous". The only scholar who graded 'AbdurRahmān bin Zayd as above the level of *da'eef* (weak) was Ibn 'Adī who

If we as Muslims take prisoners of war from the disbelievers [during a legislated period of war] we are to protect them and not harm and not enslave them so as to protect our captives [which they have]. Would that they would implement how our *deen* teaches slaves to be treated. Our Lord Says,

وَيُطْعِمُونَ الطَّعَامَ عَلَىٰ حُبِّهِ مِسْكِينًا وَيَتِيمًا وَأَسِيرًا ۝

> And they give food in spite of love for it to the needy, the orphan, and the captive…
>
> [al-Insān (76): 8]

This is in regards to one who has tried to fight us, kill us and shed our blood when he becomes a captive we are to give him food in spite of our love of it, and in regards to "in spite of love it" the Mufassireen have two views:

One: That it means he gives food from what he loves

Two: That it means that he gives food due to his love of Allāh

Thus, it is not possible to abrogate slavery however they preserve our captives and do not rape our women and our captives can attain their rights, then we are to treat the enemies the same and better. The first to lay down principles for the rights of captives was Imām Muhammad ibn Hasan ash-Shaybānī in his book *as-Siyar* and Abū Yūsuf in his book al-*Kharāj*.[194] They both

---

stated that "there are *hasan* (good) *hadeeth* from him and some of them (i.e. scholars) attested to his truthfulness, and he was from those who they recorded *hadeeth* from." For more see Ibn Hajar al-'Asqalānī, *Tahtheeb at-Tahtheeb*, vol.6, p.178. Ibn Taymiyyah has also highlighted his weakness in narration.

194 [TN]: Many non-Muslim Western academics and researchers have also credited Imām Muhammad bin Hasan ash-Shaybānī for his efforts in this regard. Rudolph Peters (ed.) in *Jihad in Classical and Modern Islam: A Reader* (Princeton, New Jersey: Markus Weiner Publishers, 1996), pp.3-5 stated:

> During the second half of the eighth century the first comprehensive treatises on the law of jihad were written by al-Awzai and Muhammad al-Shaybani.

Peters also admits that: "the protection of non-combatants, lawful methods of warfare, treatments of prisoners of war [and] safe-conduct to enemy persons" were all issues defined in the books on law covering Jihad. Peters also stated (p.137) that

> mentioned that captives have the right to learn a trade while imprisoned, and that he has the right to learn his religion, to establish *Jumu'ah*, pray in congregation and gain understanding of his religion, contact his wife, children and relatives.[195]

T.W. Arnold notes in light of this:

> Some historians suppose that a slave gained freedom after he accepted Islam but that is not so, for it is dependent on the will of the master. However, often their masters confirmed that if they became Muslims, slaves would be set free without having to buy their freedom. If the Christians slaves proved to be good servants, their Muslim masters set them free, although they persisted to practice Christianity. Also, in the old age of slaves, masters provided them with something to subsist.[196]

Another of the contemporary Muslim scholars, Shaykh Sālih bin 'Abdullāh bin Humayd (Imām of *Masjid al-Haram*, Makkah and a former Professor of Islamic Law at *Umm ul-Qurā' University* in

---

as-Siyar was "devoted exclusively to Islamic law dealing with relations with non-Muslims." This was also noted by Charles Clinch in his 2005 article *Jihad: How it can save Just War Doctrine: An analysis of Just War Doctrine* in the UCLA International Institute: http://www.international.ucla.edu/article.asp?parentid=35780

John Strawson, a Reader of Law at the *School of Law of The University of East London*, stated in his renowned 1993 research paper *Encountering Islamic Law* that ash-Shaybānī's *Siyar*:

> …Contains detailed codes on the Law of War…its propositions on the Law of War would not seem unfamiliar to the modern student of international law.

See paper here: http://www.witness-pioneer.org/vil/Articles/shariah/jsrps.html

The role of Imām Muhammad ash-Shaybānī has also been highlighted by Recep Senturk (2005) in "Sociology of Rights: "I Am Therefore I Have Rights": Human Rights in Islam between Universalistic and Communalistic Perspectives," in the *Muslim World Journal of Human Rights*, vol. 2: issue 1, article 11.

195 From the Shaykh's Q&A session dated 22 March 2013 CE, it can be viewed here after 28 minutes: http://www.youtube.com/watch?v=SCHnlW2RQ1U

196 T.W. Arnold, *The Preaching of Islam: A History of the Propagation of the Muslim Faith*, (London: Westminster A. Constable & Co. 1896) and (Lahore: Sh. Muhammad Ashraf, 1975), p.197.

Makkah), stated

> It is interesting to note that there is no statement in the Qur'an or Sunnah ordering a Muslim to enslave, while statements abound in the hundreds which urge the setting free of slaves. At the advent of Islam the ways and means of enslavement were numerous while the outlets to freeing were almost nil; so Islam reversed this formula, by multiplying the outlets to freedom and drying up the sources of enslavement.[197]

The above quotes from the Islamic sources are of the utmost importance especially in light of the fact that new-age pseudo scholars and atheist street-preachers such as intellectually bankrupt 'Polight' from America, argue that Africans were "enslaved in the name of Islam". Such a claim is not only a complete an utter lie, as one cannot be forced to submit to God, but also is not substantiated by any historical evidence whatsoever.[198] This will also be dealt with later in this chapter.

Slavery was widespread throughout antiquity and was found in Europe, Africa, China, India, and the Middle East and was so widespread that it was like a worker and boss relationship in a contemporary context. But what is important to note is that in antiquity slavery did not have any racial connotations; the racial connotations only emerged around the sixteenth century CE after trans-Atlantic slavery. In fact, the English word 'slave' comes from 'Slav' which applies to many Eastern Europeans, in the name 'Slovakia' for example, this was due to the Eastern Europeans being a main source of slaves in antiquity for both the Romans and the Turks. To the extent that in some lands if a blond haired person was seen in the southern Mediterranean lands of the Roman Empire the person would be considered to be a slave. While in some of the Islamic sources slaves are referred to as being "red-skinned". For example, in *Saheeh Muslim*, the Book of Oaths: Ayyūb said: "We were sitting in the company of Abū Mūsā when he called for food and it consisted of fowl meat. Then a person from Banu Tameem visited him, his complexion was red as if he was a slave." Ibn Hajar al-'Asqalānī stated in *Fath ul-*

---

197 Saleh Abdullah Bin Humaid, Abdul Lateef S. Al-Khayat (trans.), *A Refutation of Doubts About Current Issues* (Jeddah and Makkah: Al-Manara, 1415 AH/1994 CE), p.39.

198 For example, see one of Polight's simplistic rants here: https://www.youtube.com/watch?v=QdpUGnlU4Wk

Bārī, vol.11, p.611:

> قوله: "أحمر كأنه مولى" تقدم في فرض الخمس "كأنه من الموالي" قال الداودي: يعني أنه من سبي الروم، كذا قال فإن كان اطلع على نقل في ذلك وإلا فلا اختصاص لذلك بالروم دون الفرس أو النبط أو الديلم.
>
> His statement 'red as if he was a slave' preceded in regards to the fifth share of the spoils of war, "as if he was a slave", ad-Dāwūdī said: "meaning: that he was of the Roman prisoners of war" this is what he said. He had either come across a transmission in this regard otherwise there is no specification of this to the Romans with the exemption of the Persians, Nabateans or the Daylamites.[199]

Imām adh-Dhahabī stated in *Siyar A'lām un-Nubalā'*, vol.2, p.168:

> والحمراء في خطاب أهل الحجاز هي البيضاء بشقرة، وهذا نادر فيهم
>
> 'Red' in the dialect of the [Arab] peoples of the Hijāz refers to white with blonde, this is rare among them.

Many, but by no means all, of the companions were from what in contemporary terms we could call the 'lower classes.' As a result, the slaves that were in Arabia at that time were not from one particular racial group, they were from any racial group because it was based upon one's position in society and not on one's racial group. Therefore, some slaves were Arabs, some were Persian, and some were Roman and other slaves from other racial backgrounds.

Siddeeq Hasan Khan in *Fath ul-'Allām li Sharh Bulugh il-Marām*, vol.2, p.332 relays a benefit from *an-Najm ul-Wahhāj* that:

---

199 See Imām al-Hāfidh Ahmad bin 'Ali bin Hajar al-'Asqalānī, *Fath ul-Bārī bi Sharh Saheeh il-Imām Abī 'Abdillāh Muhammad bin Ismā'īl ul-Bukhārī*, vol.11, p.611, *hadeeth* nos. 6721-6722. Edited and checked by Shaykhs Bin Bāz and Muhibbuddeen al-Khateeb and arranged by Muhammad Fu'ad 'AbdulBāqī. Maktabah as-Salafiyyah.

> The Prophet Muhammad (*sallallāhu alayhi wassallam*) freed 63 slaves, A'ishah freed 69 and lived the same number of years. Abū Bakr as-Siddeeq (*radi Allāhu 'anhu*) freed many slaves and the Prophet's uncle 'Abbās (*radi Allāhu anhu*) freed 70 slaves as reported by al-Hākim.'Uthman freed 20 slaves while he was being besieged. Hākim ibn Hazm freed 100 slaves, loading them with silver. 'Abdullāh ibn 'Umar freed 1000 slaves, and he had made 'Umrah a thousand times and Hajj 60 times. He also had a thousand horses for the path of Allāh. Dhu'l-Khalā' al-Himyarī freed 8000 slaves in one day; while 'AbdurRahmān ibn 'Awf 30,000 slaves.[200]

This is also mentioned in the historical writings of at-Tabarī, Ibn Katheer and Ibn ul-Atheer. It is also said that when 'AbdurRahmān ibn 'Awf (*radi Allāhu 'anhu*), who was one of the wealthy companions, walked in the company of the slaves people would not know if he was a slave or not as he did not have clothes that were any different to those of slaves.[201]

Early Islām, the epoch of the Salaf, shows many examples and appeals to emancipate slaves. People were also obliged to free slaves as expiation for sins and to achieve salvation in the next life, the renowned thirteenth century West African Muslim king Mansa Mūsā is said to have emancipated a slave everyday.[202] Sylviane Diouf notes in her book *Servants of Allah* that even European travellers who were familiar with the American system of slavery expressed surprise at the leniency of the African model of slavery in the African Muslim states. For example, within the American system of slavery of black people, an article of the 'black code' regarding how to deal with African slaves, prohibits education for blacks forbidding them to read, write and in cases talk; while another article made it a felony for seven slaves to meet.

If subsequently a white person sees that they have met, the white man has the right to spit on them and give each twenty lashes. Another

200 Siddīq Hasan Khān, *Fath ul-'Allām li Sharh Bulugh il-Marām* (Dār Sādir), vol.2, p.332.

201 Saleh Abdullah Bin Humaid, *op.cit.*, p.45.

202 Mahmood Kati ibn ul-Hajj al-Mutawakkil Kati (trans. O Houdas and M. Delefosse), *Tarikh al-Fattāsh* (Paris: E. Leroux, 1913-14, Reprint Paris: Librairie d'Amérique et d'Orient Adrien-Maisonneuve, 1964), pp. 55, 115.

law during American slavery of Africans exclaimed that slaves have no souls, no wit, no intelligence and no will and that their lives are solely on account of their physical strength.[203] Even Francis Moore noted in the 1730s that many of the Gambian Muslims had house slaves which were "living so well and easy, that it is sometimes a hard matter to know slaves from their masters or mistresses."[204] In Senegal, noted another European, "slaves were treated so well, eating with their masters, working along with them, and being as well clothed…that it is impossible to distinguish them from free men."[205] A British traveller in Senegal remarked "I never saw any whip or instrument of torture used on that part of the coast, nor do I believe, from the enquiries I made, that slaves are treated with severity."[206] However, in some non-Muslim West African communities slaves and prisoners of war were killed on some occasions as human sacrifices.[207] In the West during the epoch of trans-Atlantic slavery the situation was not the same, "As the white slaves became free members of the society, conditions worsened for blacks. Since the Church taught that Christians could not be permanently enslaved, laws were passed making it a crime to teach Christianity to the blacks, on the justification that Africans did not originate with Adam and Eve, and therefore were not included in Christ's redemption."[208] As Sylviane Diouf highlights,

> The application of Islamic law concerning slavery had a profound effect on manumission. The Koran makes ample provisions for the freeing of slaves, as a mark of piety or charity or for expiation. Therefore, the manumission rate in the Islamic world was systematically higher than anywhere else.

Diouf notes that in 'New World' slavery, there was absolutely no way by which a former master could become a slave. Manumission was

203 Saleh Abdullah Bin Humaid, *op.cit.*, p.51

204 Francis Moore, *Travels into the Inland Parts of Africa* (London: E. Cave, 1738), p.30.

205 Ibid., p.50

206 Ibid.

207 Sylviane Diouf, *Servants of Allah - African Muslims Enslaved in the Americas* (New York and London: New York University Press, 1998), p.10.

208 J.B. Webster and A.A. Boahen, *The Revolutionary Years: West African States Since 1800* (London: Longman, 1967), pp.75-6.

rare and out of the question for Africans enslaved within the Americas and the Caribbean. Conversion to Catholicism was not a prerequisite for emancipation but, on the contrary, it was the justification for enslavement, with the logic that through slavery the Europeans were "civilizing" the Africans.[209]

Furthermore, the Islamic concept of slavery is very different to the new world practice of slavery. In the Islamic countries wherein slavery was practiced a slave could rise in status and could hold office. Thus, we find that a slave could become a teacher, general, leader or even royalty! Therefore, in many of the countries that used to have slaves even of late, the sons and daughters of slaves have become royalty which has not happened in the context of 400 years of transatlantic 'New World' slavery. Bernard K. Freamon states:

> Muslims employed slaves in a variety of functions and, unlike the Hindu system, slaves in the Muslim communities could rise to extremely powerful political, military, and administrative positions in the government. Perhaps the best example of such circumstances in pre-Mughal India is the rise of the so-called "slave dynasties" in Delhi between 1206 C.E. and 1290 C.E. The Sultans in Delhi, like the "Mamluk" Sultans who ruled Egypt for three hundred years beginning at about the same time, began to employ Turkic slave soldiers in their military adventures and in professional functions around their palaces in South Delhi.[210]

Therefore, in the Muslim world there were avenues to assimilation, manumission and inclusion. In the Trans-Atlantic context there was nothing of the sort, furthermore in the West the slightest amount of 'black' in a person in many ways removes a person from the dominant culture, whereas in Islam there were no barriers to the "dominant culture". C.S. Hurgronje reported in the mid-1880s that the freed black slaves

---

209 Diouf, *op cit.*, p.13.

210 Bernard K. Freamon, *Slavery and the Slave Trades in the Indian Ocean and Arab Worlds: Global Connections and Disconnections*, p.22, see: https://glc.yale.edu/sites/default/files/files/indian-ocean/freamon.pdf Accessed March 2018. From The Gilder Lehrman Center's 10th Annual International Fall Conference Slavery and the Slave Trades in the Indian Ocean and Arab Worlds: Global Connections and Disconnections November 7-8, 2008 Luce Hall Auditorium, Yale University, New Haven, Connecticut.

in Makkah "competed with the freeborn on an equal footing of perfect equality" and were well represented among influential businessmen and rich property owners.[211] Mekuria Bulcha states: "slavery in Islam was not correlated with race, or essentialised as such."[212] Bulcha also stated that: "the sources indicate that the demand for African women in the Islamic countries increased significantly after the Russian conquest of the Caucasus in the mid-19th century that closed the last source of white concubines for the harems of the Ottoman Empire and Persia."[213]

An example of this can be seen in the year 1260 CE/659 AH, centuries before the civil rights movement or any other movement fighting for the rights of people. A black man emerged in Cairo, after the Mongols had sacked Baghdad and claimed that he was from the 'Abbasid Household, the Mamluk Sultān of Egypt at the time, himself a former (European) slave ordered the chief justice of the state to launch an enquiry into the matter. After the man's origin had been established and corroborated, he was inaugurated as the 'Ameer (leader) of the Muslims and given the title *al-Muntasir*.[214] In contrast, until the Obama Administration from 2009 to 2017, no major modern Western democracy, particularly those which were slave societies such as America, had been headed by a Blackman in the last few hundred years! This would have been intolerable in the white Western world. Even Ronald Segal, in his book *Islam's Black Slaves*, which is actually utilised as a supporting reference for the evangelists, Kemet Afrocentrics and black Orientalists, noted that Islām should be given credit as slaves were freed by their owners much more frequently than was the case in Christianity and during American slavery.[215]

211 C.S. Hurgronje, *Mekka in the Latter Part of the Nineteenth Century* (Leiden: Brill, 1931), p.13.

212 Mekuria Bulcha, 'The Red Sea Slave Trade: Captives' Treatment in the Slave Markets of North-East Africa and the Islamic Societies of the Middle East.' In Kwesi Kwā Prah (ed.), *Reflections on Arab-Led Slavery on Africans* (Cape Town: The Centre for Advanced Studies of African Society, 2005), p.129.

213 Ibid., p.121.

214 Sherman (AbdulHakim) Jackson, '*Islam and the Blackamerican*' in *Islamica Magazine*, issue no.14, Winter 2005 (USA), quoting Shāfi' b. 'Ali, *Husn al-Manāqib as-Sirrīyah al-Muntaza'ah min al-Seerah al-Zāhireeyah* ('A. Khowaytar, ed., 2nd ed., 1410 AH/1989 CE), p. 79.

215 Ronald Segal, *Islam's Black Slaves: A History of Africa's other Black Diaspora*

This may explain a phenomenon which baffles the Western mind, which was that in some cases throughout the past, individuals actually wanted to become slaves in the Islamic world due to the social mobility that it afforded them! Toledano notes:

> Sometimes, individuals would agree to be reduced to slavery in exchange for a certain amount of money offered by the slave dealers. Such was the case of seven free-born Turkish boys who had been sold to the *Vāli* of Egypt in 1853 and who later demanded their freedom back. During the famine of 1867 in Tripoli, some residents of the border areas reportedly sold themselves into slavery to escape starvation.[216]

Toledano also notes that in late March-early April 1873, W.H. Wylde, Head of the Slave Trade Department, wrote saying: "However much we have been inclined to shut our eyes to the so called Circassian and Georgian slave trade when girls were sold by their parents and thought it a great privilege to become inmates of Turkish Harems with the chance of eventually becoming the wives of Turkish Officials…"[217] Toledano also notes that:

> When still in bondage, many parents – with the consent of their masters, sought to better their children's lot, as well as their own, by selling them to harems in the big cities. Having gained their freedom, they might have become less eager to do so. In addition, we should note that under normal circumstances of settlement, free-born Circassians did not sell their children into slavery.[218]

Toledano also highlights that the Ottomans were very careful not to implicate the slave-trade in whites whenever British officials issued them orders restricting the trade in blacks. The *ferman* of 1847 which prohibited the slave trade in the Persian Gulf and the Mediterranean trade – was interpreted by the Ottomans to refer only to the trade in slaves coming from Africa.[219] Toledano further states that:

(London: Atlantic Books, 2003), p.9.

216 Ehud R Toledano, *The Ottoman Slave Trade and Its Suppression* (Princeton, New Jersey: Princeton University Press, 1982), p.19.

217 Ibid., pp.170-171.

218 Ibid., p.189.

219 Ibid., p.116.

> The general worsening economic conditions in the [Ottoman] Empire during the last decades of the nineteenth century, which also affected the wealthy and powerful classes, made the Circassian female slave, even more than before a "luxury item" which only a few could afford.[220]

So this trade ended due to economic reasons internally as opposed to any notions of Western abolitionist ideals.

Shaykh 'Abdullāh bin 'AbdurRahmān Āli Bassām on the Manumission of Slaves in Islam

Shaykh 'Abdullāh Āli Bassām (*rahimahullāh*) stated:

> *'Itq* (manumission): with a *kasra* on the *'ayn* and a *sukoon* on the *tā*, so it is said *"'ataqa'l-'abd"* ("the slave was freed"), and from the verb (*'ataqa*) is: *'itqan*, *'itāqān* and *'atāqa*.
>
> The linguistic meaning (*'itq*) is: freedom and liberation, and leaving ownership.
>
> The *shari'* meaning is: Freeing slaves and liberating them from slavery.
>
> The basis of this is in the Book, Sunnah and *ijmā'*: the evidence from the Book is such when Allāh says,
>
> ﴿فَتَحْرِيرُ رَقَبَةٍ مُّؤْمِنَةٍ﴾
>
> Freeing a believing slave...
>
> [an-Nisā (4): 92}
>
> As for the Sunnah then the evidences are many such as what is mentioned in al-Bukhārī (hadeeth no. 6715) and Muslim (*hadeeth* no. 1509) from Abū Hurayrah (*radi Allāhu 'anhu*) from the Prophet (*sallallāhu 'alayhi wassallam*) who said: "*Whoever frees a Muslim slave, Allāh will free all of his limbs from the Fire...*"[221] The Ummah has reached consensus on the accuracy of manumission. There are two matters to research here:

220 Ibid., p.191

221 The similar wording is found in Ahmad, Abū Dāwood and an-Nasā'ī, it was authenticated by Imām al-Albānī.

One. The virtue of manumitting slaves

Two. Islam's position on slavery and manumission of slaves.

As for the virtue of freeing slaves: then the following *hadeeth* is sufficient for you: the *saheeh hadeeth* reported by at-Tirmidhī (no.1547) from Abū Umāmah and other Sahābah from the Prophet (*sallallāhu 'alayhi wassallam*) who said: *"When a Muslim person frees a Muslim slave then it is as if he has saved him from the fire."* The *ahādeeth* and *āthar* which exhort to the virtue of freeing slaves are many indeed. Allāh made the first form of expiation to be the freeing of slaves due to what it contains of recompensing sins, mistakes, misdeeds and the great reward that it contains due to the amount of good that it is based on.

There is no goodness that can be shown to a Muslim greater than freeing a Muslim from the ill-feeling of slavery and being owned, by freeing a Muslim from slavery his humanity will be completed from whence he was like a beast of burden in his affairs and conduct. So whoever frees a slave has successfully attained the reward of Allāh and indeed with Allāh is the best of rewards.

Secondly, Some of the enemies of the religion of Islām criticise the Islamic religion for the Islamic Sharee'ah affirming slavery which, in their view, is a totally barbaric practice. For this reason, we wished to clarify the matter of slavery within Islām and within other systems, and to briefly clarify the Islamic position on slavery. Slavery was not particular to Islam, rather it was widespread in all parts of the earth and was to be found among the Persians, the Romans, the Babylonians, the Greeks and was also affirmed by their top thinkers such as Plato and Aristotle. Slavery according to these civilisations was via many different means: warfare, captivity, kidnap and theft, rather one would sell his own children into slavery and some would make the peasants slaves. They also used to view slaves with contempt and make them do filthy and difficult work. Aristotle was from those thinkers of the past who viewed that slaves were like animals. The Pharaohs enslaved Bani Isrā'īl to the extent that they killed their children and took their women. The Europeans, after the discovery of America, treated the (original) Americans with the worst type of treatment. So this is slavery and its reasons, effects and different forms that are found in other than Islām. Now let's look at slavery in Islām:

Firstly: Islām narrows the resource for slavery as it makes all people free and a person can only be enslaved via one reason alone: that a person is captured while fighting against the Muslims, and it is obligatory on the leader of the Muslim army to choose from those captured fighters who should be put into slavery or freed depending on the general benefit (for the Muslims). This is the only reason wherein slavery is allowed and it is the reason which is transmitted in the authentic texts, for it agrees with the correct intellect also: anyone who stands in the way of my creed and *da'wah* and thus wants to wage war against me then his reward will be for me to take him for standing in front of my way and *da'wah* in order to challenge it. This is the reason for slavery in Islām, not out of looting, robbery or selling free people and enslaving them, as is found with other nations.

Secondly: Islām is kind and loving to the slave and does not over burden or tire them, the Prophet (*sallallāhu 'alayhi wassallam*) said *"as-Salah! And what your right hands possess!"*[222] The Prophet (*sallallāhu 'alayhi wassallam*) also said: *"The slave has a right to food and clothing, do not over-burden a slave with work that he is unable to do."*[223]

Rather, Islām elevated the status of slaves to the extent that it made slaves brothers to their masters, the Prophet (*sallallāhu 'alayhi wassallam*) said: *"They are your brothers, Allāh placed them under your hands so whoever has his brother under his hand should feed him, give him drink, clothe him and not over burden them with that which will overcome them. If you over-burden them then help them."*[224] Islām elevated the status of slaves in order for them not to feel any debasement, for this reason the Prophet (*sallallāhu 'alayhi wassallam*) said *"None of you should say "my slave", rather you should say "my boy" or "my girl"."*[225]

The standard in Islām is to honour humanity in this world and the hereafter without any referral to ascriptions and origins,

﴿إِنَّ أَكْرَمَكُمْ عِندَ اللَّهِ أَتْقَاكُمْ﴾

Indeed, the most noble of you in the sight of Allāh is the most

222 Reported by Ahmad, hadeeth no.11759.

223 Reported by Muslim.

224 Reported by al-Bukhārī, hadeeth no.30 and Muslim, hadeeth no.1661.

225 Reported by al-Bukhārī, hadeeth no.3552 and Muslim hadeeth no.2249.

righteous of you."

[al-Hujurāt (49): 13]

Many great personalities were freed slaves and had virtue and status which their masters did not have, so some were leaders of armies; leaders of nations and assumed noble positions – this was the basis of their honour. Along with the Shari'ah elevating the position of slaves it also facilitated freeing slaves and releasing their burdens. As a result, the Divine legislation exhorts to this and promises salvation from the Fire and to be rewarded with Paradise for the one who does this (i.e. frees a slave), as has preceded. The *Shar'* also has many ways in which a slave can be freed some of which are by compulsion some of which are by choice. As for those means which are via compulsion: when one wounds his slave he has to free him as mentioned in the *hadeeth* of the man who cut the nose of his slave and the Prophet (*sallallāhu 'alayhi wassallam*) said to the slave: *"Go! For you are free!"* The slave said *"But O Messenger of Allāh I shall be the freed slave of whom?"* The Prophet (*sallallāhu 'alayhi wassallam*) said *"The freed slave of Allāh and His Messenger."*[226] If one owns the slave in a joint partnership with someone else then his partner has to give up his share of ownership out of compulsion as is mentioned in the *hadeeth*: *"Whoever frees a portion of a slave has to free all of him."*[227]

So the Divine Legislation, along with exhorting to free slaves, made it the first form of expiation of sins, it is also the first form of expiation for: having intercourse in the daylight hours of Ramadān, for committing *thihār*, for *aymān* and for manslaughter.

The *Dīn* is One of Honour, Nobility and Equality

So after all of this, how can the Westerners, and pseudo-Westerners, come and criticise Islām for having slavery? Claiming to have freedom and human rights, when they are the ones who enslave peoples, lower nations, take their homes, consume their wealth and occupy their lands?! Look at the equality of Islām compared to what America did with the blacks by not allowing them to enter the same schools as them and not allowing them to find work, making them like animals! Where is the merciful Islamic state which made different types of people, of different religions and races as one Ummah compared to what France did

226 Reported by Imām Ahmad, hadeeth no.6671.

227 Reported by al-Bukhārī, hadeeth no.2503 and Muslim, hadeeth no.1501.

> to Algeria on the land of Algeria?! So their claims are nothing but false propaganda![228]

This frequent and continuous practice of freeing slaves contributed to the social assimilation of slaves and their descendants into Islamic societies and they were not subject to any racial discriminatory regulations and laws, assuming equal rights in the society. However, Segel neglects elaboration on this very important aspect of freeing slaves. Webster and Boahen noted:

> When some slaves became Christian, the Bishop of London proclaimed that conversion to Christianity did not bring freedom. By the early eighteenth century slave codes (special slave laws) had been created in the West Indies and Southern States whereby Africans and their children were condemned to eternal slaves; marriages and manumission were discouraged; slaves could not give evidence in court; and their masters held the power of life and death over them. Under slave codes, Africans lost their status as persons and became the master's property, in the same relationship to him as his dog or house.[229]

This is not to justify any type of slavery but just to make a comparison between the practice in the Americas and that which developed within some Muslim societies. The major difference is that under trans-Atlantic slavery of black people, the slaves were merely property and not people as such and furthermore there were little avenues for betterment, in the Islamic world however such stigmas were not attached. Even Segal notes that under the Ottoman Empire slaves were treated in conformity with Islamic teachings and had rights. He admits that soldiers and civil servants who were slaves for the Sultān "rose to become generals and governors."[230] He even notes that free Muslims, who were protected from enslavement according to Islām, bribed or insinuated their way into becoming slaves for the Sultān due to the prospects of attaining high office! Olaudah Equiano, an African who directly knew about American slavery as he had been a slave, had visited fifteen African and

---

228 From 'Abdullāh bin 'AbdurRahmān al-Bassām, *Tawdeeh ul-Ahkām min Bulūgh il-Marām* (Makkah al-Mukarramah: Maktabah al-Asdī, 1423 AH/2003 CE), vol.7, pp.237-242.

229 Webster and Boahen, *op.cit.*, p.76

230 Segal, *op.cit.*, p.106

Caribbean countries. He believed that religion as opposed to colour and race was the decisive factor in Islamic countries. He said about the Turks, "I believe that they are fond of black people and several of them gave me pressing invitations to stay with them, although they keep the Franks (or Christians) separate and do not suffer them to dwell immediately amongst them."[231] Annemarie Schimmel stated in her book *Islam: An Introduction*:

> Slavery was not abolished by the Koran, but believers are constantly admonished to treat their slaves well. In case of illness a slave has to be looked after and well cared for. To manumit [free] a slave is highly meritorious; the slave can ransom himself by paying some of the money he has earned while conducting his own business. Only children of slaves or non-Muslim prisoners of war can become slaves, never a freeborn Muslim; therefore slavery is theoretically doomed to disappear with the expansion of Islam. The entire history of Islam proves that slaves could occupy any office, and many former military slaves, usually recruited from among the Central Asian Turks, became military leaders and often even rulers as in eastern Iran, India (the Slave Dynasty of Delhi), and medieval Egypt (the Mamluks). Eunuchs too served in important capacities, not only as the guardians of the women's quarters, but also in high administrative and military positions.[232]

The French writer Roger Du Pasquier stated in his book *Unveiling Islam*:

> To answer this question, it should first be remarked that Islam has tolerated slavery but has never approved of it, and that all its teachings and prescriptions in this regard lead to its alleviation as far as possible in the short term, and, in the longer term, conduce to its progressive suppression. To abolish it would have been impossible in a world in which it was generally practiced by all the states which bordered on the new Muslim empire, and in which the idea of challenging the principle itself had not occurred to anyone. It was the custom to enslave prisoners of war -when these were not simply massacred- and the Islamic state would

231 Paul Edwards, *Equiano's Travels* (1789; reprint, London: Heinemann, 1969), p.126.

232 Annemarie Schimmel, *Islam: An Introduction* (Albany, New York: State University Press, 1992), p.67

have put itself at a grave disadvantage vis-a-vis its enemies had it not reciprocated to some extent. By guaranteeing them humane treatment, and various possibilities of subsequently releasing themselves, it ensured that a good number of combatants in the opposing armies preferred captivity at the hands of Muslims to death on the field of battle. It should be very clearly underlined that the slavery once practiced in the Muslim world cannot be compared to the form it had assumed -for instance -in the Roman Empire. Islamic legislation subjected slave owners to a set of precise obligations, first among which was the slave's right to life, for, according to a hadith, 'Whoever kills his slave shall be killed by us'. In consequence, the murder of a slave was punished like that of a freeman. There are many other hadiths which define Islam's true attitude in this regard. The Prophet said: 'Your slaves are your brethren; therefore whoever has a brother who depends upon him must feed and clothe him in the way he feeds and clothes himself; and should not impose upon him tasks which exceed his capacity; should you ask them to do such things, then you are obliged to help them.' The Sharia takes this injunction, among many others, into account when defining the responsibilities and duties of slaveholders. There is another teaching which enjoins respect for the human dignity of slaves: 'Let none of you say, "This man, or this woman, is my slave". He must rather say: "This is my man, and this my woman."' Putting into relief the provisional character of social ties and the authority exercised by slaveowners over their slaves, the Prophet said: 'It is true that God has made you their masters, but, had He so wished, He could equally well have made you their slaves.' To manumit a slave has always been regarded as one of the most meritorious of all acts, and many passages of the Qur'an recommend or even require it, particularly as a means of expiation for serious faults. Traditional legislation lays down the methods of voluntary liberation of slaves by their masters (*itq*), and there were very many Muslims who observed these, especially at the end of their lives, so as not to die and appear before God without having given full freedom to the human beings placed in their power during their earthly lives. Additionally, slaves had the ability to enfranchise themselves at their own initiative, without waiting passively for the goodwill of their masters: the procedure known as *mukataba* allowed them to buy their own freedom with sums which they saved from their work, and which the state frequently augmented with advances- a measure which the slave-owner had

> no right to oppose. In contrast to the situation under Roman law, slaves were not deprived of the legal ability to exercise their rights and to appeal to a judge against their masters in all cases of illegal treatment. Besides domestic slavery, which was generally imbued with a patriarchal character, there also existed a form of military slavery, which was frequently employed by princes in need of recruits, especially for their personal guards. This situation had the effect of conferring an often considerable influence and power on men of servile condition or origin, and some of these became the founders of great and illustrious dynasties such as the Tulunids and Mamlukes of Egypt. The object of a prosperous commercial sector, which under the Abbasid Empire was often the speciality of non-Muslims, particularly Byzantine and Venetian Christians, and Jews, slavery gradually declined in importance until, at the beginning of the present century, it was confined to a few survivals which have now disappeared entirely. Thanks to the strict traditional controls which have always regulated the practice, it would be difficult to deny that social conditions were remarkably humane during the great periods of Muslim civilization, and that these, moreover, were in conformity with the 'egalitarian' spirit of Islam, which, in a hadith, teaches that 'the blackest of Abyssinians' is superior to the most noble of Quraishes, if he has more faith.[233]

T.W. Arnold stated:

> The injunctions on slavery in Islam have removed the severity from slavery. The slaves in Turkey were not tormented as those in North Africa, and in Turkey the slaves had rights similar to the freemen, and if a master was severe, the slave could summon him before a judge. If a slave complained to his master and he did not see eye to eye then the judge could command the master to sell him to someone else.[234]

Slavery has been an issue that the Afrocentrics and black Orientalists have attacked Islām for, yet they remain silent about slavery amongst non-Muslim Africans. Furthermore, some of the Afrocentrics, such as

233 Roger Du Pasquier, *Unveiling Islam* (Cambrdige: Islamic texts Society, 1992), pp.104-07

234 T.W.Arnold, *The Preaching of Islam: A History of the Propagation of the Muslim Faith*, (London: Westminister A. Constable & Co.1896) and (Lahore: Sh. Muhammad Ashraf, 1975), p.194.

the anti-Islamic writer John Henrik Clarke, emphasise ancient Egypt and claim that this should be the model for black people to look to, this argument demonstrates the excessiveness that some will go to all in order to praise ancient Egypt and its power structures. Ancient Egypt itself was entrenched in a slave trade, enslaving its enemies and forcing them to work on state-building projects such as the pyramids. Is this really a model for black people to look to? Are the Afrocentrics actually condoning slavery? As if they are extolling ancient Egypt, by extension they would also have to justify slavery, and within the slave-system that was implemented in ancient Egypt there was a rigid caste system and little in terms of guidelines and limits, slaves were also dedicated to the false gods that the ancient Egyptians used to worship.[235] The Qur'ān mentions,

إِنَّ فِرْعَوْنَ
عَلَا فِي الْأَرْضِ وَجَعَلَ أَهْلَهَا شِيَعًا يَسْتَضْعِفُ طَائِفَةً مِّنْهُمْ يُذَبِّحُ
أَبْنَاءَهُمْ وَيَسْتَحْيِي نِسَاءَهُمْ إِنَّهُ كَانَ مِنَ الْمُفْسِدِينَ ۝

Indeed, Pharaoh exalted himself in the land and made its people into castes, oppressing a group among them, slaughtering their sons and keeping their women alive. Indeed, he was one of the corruptors.

---

235 There is one collective noun in ancient Egyptian which is written with the hoe-sign hieroglyphic that refers to groups of people who belonged to individuals and institutions. As early as the Old Kingdom of ancient Egypt, such groups were mentioned along with land and cattle. Another similar term, written with the canal-sign hieroglyphic, denotes another group of people assigned to individuals and institutions, but who were not directly connected with land and cattle. The Middle Kingdom used slaves mainly from Asia and this became a quite large source of slaves for the ancient Egyptians. Slavery increased during the New Kingdom when the Pharaohs were committed to a policy of foreign involvement and conquests in the ancient lands of Nubia, Canān and Syria and took many prisoners of war (*seqer-ankh*), these slaves were branded with the sign *ki*. In ancient Egypt slaves were branded in order to signify their status as slaves. Slaves in ancient Egypt were also sent to work in the horrific gold and copper of Nubia and Sinai, where great numbers of people died from exhaustion and dehydration in the desert heat. Some slaves in ancient Egypt did manage to rise to high positions.

[al-Qasas (28): 4]

As usual they cite the examples of ignorant Muslims as assumed examples of Islamic teachings. Slavery in Islām is not about race, the famed West African Muslim king Mansa Mūsā had Turkish and Ethiopian slaves in his entourage according to historical sources.[236]

For example, many of the powerful West African Muslim rulers had slaves that were Turkish and Caucasian. Dinesh D'Souza notes, based upon the historical records of Muslim geographers and travellers such as al-Maqrizi:

> ...Slavery was widespread in Africa from antiquity. The three powerful medieval kingdoms of Ghana, Songhai and Mali all relied on slave labor. Nor were these slaves exclusively black Africans: the emperor Mansa Musa, for example, purchased Turkish slaves for his court in Mali. White Europeans who were shipwrecked off the west coast of Africa were also enslaved. The Ashanti of West Africa customarily enslaved all foreigners.[237]

Shaykh Sālih bin 'Abdullāh bin Humayd (Imām of Masjid al-Harām, Makkah and a former Professor of Islamic Law at *Umm ul-Qurā'* University in Makkah), stated:

> In the first clash between Muslims and their enemies, the Battle of Badr, the Muslims won, and a number of the noblest Arabs fell captives in the hands of the Muslims.[238]

This also refutes any notions of Islām being intrinsically Arab-nationalist as if this was the case then disbelieving "noble Arabs" would not be enslaved by Muslims from non-Arab origins. An authentic *hadeeth* in *Saheeh Bukhārī* reported on the authority of Ibn Muhayreez (*radi Allāhu 'anhu*) who said: I saw Abū Sa'eed (*radi Allāhu 'anhu*) and I asked him. He said: We went out with the Messenger of Allāh (*sallallāhu 'alayhi wassallam*) on the campaign of Banu al-Mustaliq, and we captured some prisoners from among the Arabs. The version in *Saheeh Muslim* states:

---

236 This was noted by al-Maqrīzī, an Arab historian who died in 1442 CE. See N.Levtzion and J.F.P. Hopkins (eds.), *Corpus of Early Arabic Sources for West African History* (Cambridge: Cambridge University Press, 1981), p.351.

237 See Dinesh D'Souza, *The End of Racism*, (New York: Free Press, 1995).

238 Saleh Abdullah Bin Humaid, *op.cit.*, p.40

"We captured some women from the Arabs..." Clearly indicating that all were captured regardless of origin, Clarence-Smith highlights that:

> Ethnicity and race have stirred much interest among scholars investigating slave systems, but they appear to have been marginal in Islam. In part, this was because Muslims took people from so many origins, including the noble Arabs themselves. However, credit should also be given to the Ulama's unyielding refusal to take such factors into consideration, whatever the prejudices of secular elites and the general practice.[239]

An example of this will be demonstrated shortly, this is not to deny that Islām allows "slavery", as Islām clearly allows the indentured servitude of war captives with rights for the captives, yet Islām does not allow the enslavement of free-people of whatever religion and does not allow the enslavement of Muslims. This is important as many who criticize Islām for slavery are unaware that many gluttonous Muslims who traded and kept slaves also enslaved Muslims and this is forbidden in Islām. Therefore, the comments by Mark Perry who stated "the Qur'an permitted the enslavement of converts"[240] are absolute nonsense and also the overly simplistic arguments that are mentioned by the likes of Serge Trifkovic.[241] Suffice to say that Perry did not cite this supposed

---

239 William Gervase Clarence-Smith, *Islam and the Abolition of Slavery* (London: Hurst and Co., 2006), pp.83-4.

240 Mark Perry, *Perceptions of Race in the Arab World.* This is a bizarre claim by Perry, in fact during the peak of what is termed as 'Barbary' slavery (the slavery of white European Christians by North African Muslim corsairs/pirates) those who were responsible for much of the enslavement were white European converts to Islām who were termed as being 'renegades'!? These Muslims had came into North Africa in order to better themselves, looking for a new life and in order to seek fortunes, they may have been disaffected sailors or soldiers, peasants oppressed by feudal lords or may have started out slaves at one point. Also during Ottoman rule, some of the sailors of Otoman fleets were Greeks who had fled Greek Christiandom for a bette· life under the rule of the Ottoman Muslims as there was upward mobility and ι meritocracy within the Ottoman navy and Ottoman society at large. Whereas v·ithin Greek society one was trapped within a certain position and could not move up. For example, Murād Ra'ees was a Scotsman who became an admiral within the Ottoman navy, as a Scotsman or Irishman could not move up within English society unless one was an aristocrat.

241 Serge Trifkovic, *"Islam's Wretched Record in Slavery"* in *Frontpage Magazine,*

verse wherein the Qur'ān is alleged to make this injunction!? Perry and others have to make a more thorough study of the Qur'ān and Sunnah before they give their own uninformed opinions about Islām. As a result Perry makes a number of comments which are clearly refuted from the Qur'ān and the words of the Prophet Muhammad (*sallallāhu 'alayhi wassallam*). He does not even quote from the authentic and verified *hadeeth*, choosing to refer to strange and weak *hadeeth* and referring to scholars that are not experts in *hadeeth* science.

Castration and Slavery in the Muslim World

The huge 'trading,' kidnapping,[242] castration and enslavement of free people outside of warfare with Muslims has nothing to do with Islām at all. Nadia Maria El-Cheikh (2005)[243] notes, in quoting from Hilal as-Sābī':

> It is generally believed that in the days of al-Muqtadir billaah... the residence contained 11,000 eunuch (*khaadim*) – 7000 blacks and 4000 white Slavs – 4000 free and slave girls and thousands

November 20 2002. Serge Trifkovic is a Serbo-Croatian academic who also compares Islām to fascism and questions the massacres of Muslims in Bosnia!? He is the author of *Sword of the Prophet* (Boston: Regina Orthodox Press, 2002) and *Defeating Jihad*. He testified for the defence team of a Serb politician who was later found guilty of war crimes and crimes against humanity at the *International Criminal Tribunal for the Former Yugoslavia*!!?

242 An example of this is in 1961 CE when the former editor of the Arabic *al-Ahrām* newspaper (of Cairo) was present at a conference in Casablanca when Libya's Minister of Foreign Affairs and Shaykh Muhammad Mahdi from the Malian delegation who were pressing for the extradiction of a Malian citizen who was then living in Libya. The editor of *al-Ahrām* heard Shaykh Muhammad Mahdi say: "The man in question is wanted in my country, he was the chief of a Mali tribe. A little before my country's independence (in 1960), he called upon the members of his tribe to undertake the pilgrimage to Makkah. Many listened to him, among them were men and a large number of women accompanied by their children. After much excitement they arrived at Makkah, and they were sold to many slave-traders. After having gained money by selling his own people, this man left Makkah, and instead of returning to Mali, he went to Libya where he opened a business." (*al-Ahrām* newspaper, January 27, 1961 CE)

243 Nadia Maria El-Cheikh, 'Servants at the Gate: Eunuchs at the Court of Al-Muqtadir,' *JESHO*, 48, 2, p.1.

of chamber servants.

This would suggest that 4th century AH/10th century CE already eunuchs were being used in huge number. Nicolini (1999) states:

> Another 'speciality' was the eunuch, especially appreciated in the Ottoman Empire. The organ mutilation was carried out in totally unhygienic conditions, resulting in a survival rate of one in ten of those eunuchs transported from Africa.[244]

Cheney (2006) stated in *A Brief History of Castration*:

> Eunuchs were employed not only in the palace, but in more common residences. In fact, they were found throughout Ottoman society. It has been noted that the Ottomans preferred black eunuchs who had been "castrated completely and who were physically ugly." And black eunuchs generally remained in the majority. "By the force of the circumstances, the white eunuchs were always less numerous than the blacks, and from the 16th century, they became more rare at the Ottoman court; the supply ceased completely with the annexation of the Caucasian regions by the Russians at the beginning of the 19th century." Black eunuchs were imported from Egypt, usually between the ages of eight and 11. The mortality rate was very low for young boys castrated before puberty, but rose to high levels for those castrated after maturity. As noted previously, most of the operations were done in Upper Egypt, although a group of professionals worked in Egypt during the 17th century *djerrah-i djellabis*, because "a private person had no legal right in the empire to castrate his slave."[245]

Cheney then states that the Ottomans issued a *firman* [royal decree][246] in 1857 outlawing the practice, however questions can be raised about some of Cheney's statements in his book, though he was writing in 1955. Middleton (2005) states in *World Monarchies and Dynasties* under 'eunuchs, royal':

---

244 Beatrice Nicolini, 'Religion and Trade in the Indian Ocean: Zanzibar in the 1800s', *ISIM Newsletter* (Leiden), no.3, vol.1, 1999, p.28.

245 Victor T. Cheney, *A Brief History of Castration* (Bloomington, Indiana: Author House, 2006, 2nd Edn.), p.55.

246 A *'farman'* (also *firman*), is a word of Persian origin meaning "edict" or "directive".

> Castrated men who served as advisors and top officials for monarchs and in many countries and periods. The cruel practice of castrating men in order to provide pliable slaves or loyal servants for royal masters occurred in many civilisations. Many died during the painful and unsanitary removal of the testicles (and sometimes the penis as well), and most of the rest lived miserable lives. But oddly, small numbers of royal eunuchs were able to use their peculiar status to amass and wield great power, even controlling the destiny of empires.

Middleton continues under 'Slave Eunuchs in Turkey':

> In contrast, the eunuchs of the Ottoman Empire were generally of slave origin; by the sixteenth century, most Ottoman eunuchs were black Africans. Neither their race nor their legal status prevented some of these eunuchs from rising to positions of great power. The Chief Black Eunuch was often one of the most powerful officials at the Ottoman court. In fact, the only blacks ever to rise in the Ottoman imperial service were eunuchs. In the early nineteenth century, European observers reported on castration "factories" in southern Egypt, where several hundred young black boys were prepared each year for sale as eunuchs. When castration was banned in Egypt around 1860, the operation moved south to the Sudan. According to informants, a large majority of the boys (from 97 to 99 percent) survived...[247]

Somel (2003) stated in *Historical Dictionary of the Ottoman Empire* under 'Eunuchs':

> In Ottoman Turkish, *hadim ağast* (castrated *agha*). Eunuchs were castrated male slaves of the sultan's palace who acted as functionaries in the inner part of the palace. Eunuchs were divided into white and black. White eunuchs were mostly of Caucasian origin; one of their functions was to educate and drill slave boys levied from Christian villages. The head of the white eunuchs (*kapt ağast*) was the supervisor of the whole palace. Black eunuchs were usually brought from the region around the Sudan and acted as functionaries in the imperial harem. The head of the black eunuchs (*dârüssaâde ağast*) was under the command of the *vâlide sultan* (mother of the sultan). When, after the 16th

247 John Middleton, *World Monarchies and Dynasties* (London and New York: Routledge, 2005), pp.291-292.

> century, sultans increasingly ascended to the throne as minors, the *valide sultan* and the chief black eunuch emerged as major political figures. In the political conflicts that dominated the central administration, the chief black eunuch often represented the "palace party". Though their power faded in the 19th century, black eunuchs continued to exist until the dissolution of the empire.

Hathaway and Barbir (2014) also state in *The Arab Lands Under Ottoman Rule: 1516-1800*:

> Early in the seventeenth century, eunuchs of the imperial harem, the overwhelming majority of whom were African, began to be exiled to Egypt when they were removed from office...By the middle of the century, even the Chief Harem Eunuch, one of the most influential figures in the entire empire, was routinely exiled to Cairo upon his deposition...An exiled Chief Eunuch received a stipend and, furthermore, would have planned ahead for his last years in Cairo, so that by the time he arrived in Egypt he would have a large, comfortable house waiting for him, along with a number of agents and followers. In Egypt, he could amass property, endow pious foundations, and even purchase his own elite slaves from the Caucasus, creating the curious phenomenon of a castrated African ex-slave who owned uncastrated Caucasian slaves. He might also purchase his own eunuchs or cultivate ties of patronage with lower-ranking harem eunuchs already in Egypt.[248]

In some of the Muslim Empires, slaves were linked to race in that some of the slaves were of a different race of the host empire and its majority. Tougher (2009) states in *The Eunuch in Byzantine History and Society*:

> Less well known, perhaps, is that the Ottoman court also employed white eunuchs. The Ottoman case exemplifies the fact that in Islamic states court eunuchs tended to be ethnic outsiders.[249]

This indicates that there came to be a racial association in some parts of the Muslim world in regards to slavery and that racism in some instances may have played a role in how different races were perceived.

248 Jane Hathaway and Karl Barbir, *The Arab Lands Under Ottoman Rule: 1516-1800* (London and New York: Routledge, 2014), p.103.

249 Shaun Tougher, *The Eunuch in Byzantine History and Society* (London and New York: Routledge, 2009), p.45.

Therefore racism set in along with practices which were contrary to the teachings of Islam. Michael Winter (2003) states in *Egyptian Society Under Ottoman Rule, 1517-1798*:

> The black aghas, eunuchs, sent from the sultan's palace to Egypt to act as directors of *waqf* were a special group that was paid salaries and pensions in Egypt. The Egyptian soldiers resented them bitterly and were jealous of the strength of their high income and connections in Istanbul. It was primarily from Egypt and through Egypt that the black aghas were sent to the imperial harem in Istanbul. Since the beginning of Ottoman rule, the pasha of Egypt was required to send 'black, nice-looking foreign (*'ajemi*) aghas who do not understand Turkish.' At least twice in the eighteenth century the Porte sent out strongly worded circulars forbidding the mutilation of young boys destined to become eunuchs in the harems. In 1127/1715 an imperial edict was sent to the *vali* and the *qadi* of Egypt declaring that castrating young boys to turn them into eunuchs was inhuman and violated the Shari'a law and the sultan's orders. The decree stated that the boys were castrated in 'terrible places, resembling slaughterhouses, in Jirja, Fayyum and Cairo itself.' The edict cited the fatwa issued by Sheyhül-Islam 'Abdürrahim, the Grand Mufti of Istanbul, who declared this kind of mutilation a forbidden innovation (*bid'a*). He said that many of the unfortunate boys died after castration; the survivors were doomed to be deprived of progeny and had to spend their lives in the company of women. The edict should be made public and the original kept in the Citadel of Cairo. This impressive edict would have been more convincing had the Porte not kept demanding a fresh supply of eunuchs from Egypt a short time before and after the document was issued. We have at least three edicts, dated 1124/1712, 1133/1722 and 1150/1737 addressed to the governor of Egypt urgently requesting aghas for the sultan's harem.[250]

Toledano (1998) states in *Slavery and Abolition in the Ottoman Middle East*:

> I could not find any specific indication that during the second half of the nineteenth century, young boys were being made into eunuchs on Ottoman territory. The fact that the anti-slave trade

250 Michael Winter, *Egyptian Society Under Ottoman Rule, 1517-1798* (London and New York: Routledge, 2003), pp.41-42.

> conventions signed between Britain and both Egypt (1877) and the Porte (1880) included clauses prohibiting castration is not sufficient proof that such operations were actually still being performed within the empire.[251]

McMahon stated in *Women Shall Not Rule: Imperial Wives and Concubines in China from Han to Liao*:

> The Ottoman Empire supposedly took eunuchs only from foreign lands, especially Africa but also border regions inhabited by Caucasians, and only took boys, who as in China and elsewhere were castrated involuntarily (Islamic law prohibited castration).[252]

Favazza (1996) stated in *Bodies Under Siege: Self-Mutilation and Body Modification in Culture and Psychiatry*:

> The early Arabs did, however, purchase castrated slaves, who were employed as harem keepers. Beginning with the mid-thirteenth century Mameluke period in Egypt and with the fourteenth-century Ottoman Empire in Turkey, eunuchism flourished. Eunuchs not only served in harems but also married and held the highest political positions. The Muslims did not perform the castration themselves but rather purchased eunuchs. Some monasteries in Egypt supported themselves by becoming "eunuch factories." Another center for the production of eunuchs was Khartoum, where slave raiders brought their captives to barbers, monks and physicians to undergo castration. The trade in eunuchs was brisk and extremely profitable, fully castrated slaves being the most desirable harem employees.[253]

Kia states in *Daily Life in the Ottoman Empire:*

> The white eunuchs were mostly white men imported from the Balkans and the Caucasus and served the recruits at the palace

---

251 Ehud R. Toledano, *Slavery and Abolition in the Ottoman Middle East* (Seattle and London: University of Washington Press, 1998, 2012), p.45

252 Keith McMahon, *Women Shall Not Rule: Imperial Wives and Concubines in China from Han to Liao* (Lanham, Maryland and Plymouth, UK: Rowman and Littlefield Publishers, 2013), p.45.

253 Armando R. Favazza, *Bodies Under Siege: Self-Mutilation and Body Modification in Culture and Psychiatry* (Baltimore and London: The John Hopkins University Press, 1996), p.182

> school. The black eunuchs "underwent the so-called radical castration, in which both the testicles and the penis were removed," whereas in the case of eunuchs from the Balkans and the Caucasus, "only the testicles were removed."[254]

Hathaway and Barbir (2014) state:

> By 1800, the majority of African slaves entering the Ottoman domains came from what are now Sudan and Ethiopia, and a majority of these were women.

They then state:

> As noted above, a portion of the African slaves incorporated into ayan households were eunuchs. In Egypt, however, eunuchs delivered to the province by the trans-Saharan slave caravans or by Red Sea ships were augmented by eunuchs exiled from the Ottoman imperial harem in Istanbul. These two groups of eunuchs, in point of fact, represented different stages of the eunuch career. Because castration is against Islamic law, young male slaves from Ethiopia, Somalia, Sudan and Nubia were castrated in Coptic Christian villages in Upper Egypt, then transported to Cairo for sale in the slave markets.[255]

Abbott (2001) states in *A History of Celibacy* in the chapter entitled 'Coerced Celibacy':

> Later, eunuchs were brought into households as servants and into the Ottoman sultan's palace, despite Islamic law's proscription of castration. At first, the Ottoman eunuchs were white, bought from European dealers. Vienne, in France, was the center for the actual surgery. Later, most eunuchs were either Ethiopians or black Africans, enslaved and mutilated outside the boundaries of the empire to avoid legal problems. By the reign of Suleiman (1520-66), black eunuchs were more powerful than white. The African eunuchs' behaviour could be peculiar, petulant, and socially inept, and they were known as eccentrics.

Well, maybe Abbott should have added that undergoing such a brutal and savage procedure involving the removal of their genitalia may have

254 Mehrdad Kia, *Daily Life in the Ottoman Empire* (Santa Barbara, California and Oxford, England: ABC-CLIO, 2011), p.42.

255Hathaway and Barbir, *op.cit.*, p.102.

had a slight impact on their behaviour, somewhat. Abbott continues however and does note, in evoking what has also been stated by Toledano (1998: 43):

> Young boys were usually the victims. They were the most valued eunuchs because they had not already had, and could never have, any offspring to dilute their loyalty to their owners. In the early nineteenth century, these children were taken to Egyptian villages for castration, often performed by Coptic priests. Frequently, the surgeries were fatal, thanks to incompetent castrators and unhygienic conditions. Pus often clogged the urethra, killing the wounded boy. Scores of contemporary accounts testify that throughout their lives, surviving eunuchs suffered hormonal and psychological disorders, and many were intensely bitter about their deformity, about which, unlike their Chinese counterparts, they had no consultation and over which they had no control. The eunuchs who emerged alive from the ordeal, however, were precious commodities, expensive, rare and difficult to obtain. What better gift to impress and ingratiate oneself with the sultan, the man with everything else? So the palace seldom needed to purchase eunuchs as the vast majority were given as gifts. Once "manufactured," the young eunuchs were sent to a highly regimented school where strict, elderly, castrated instructors taught them Turkish high-court culture, the etiquette of the palace and how to perform their duties there. [256]

Toledano (1998: 44) states in *Slavery and Abolition in the Ottoman Middle East*:

> Dr Louis Frank, in a report written in 1802, states that these operations were performed in the Upper Egyptian village of Abu Tig. The Swiss Arabist J.L. Burckhardt adds the village of Zawiyat al-Dayr near Asyūt in Upper Egypt, where Coptic monks regularly "manufactured" eunuchs at the time of his travels in 1813 and 1814. He also mentions a place west of Darfur whence some eunuchs were being imported into Egypt, but most were sent to the Holy Cities in the Hijaz...Sultan Ahmet III ordered the governor of Egypt in 1715 to put an end to the castration of Ethiopians in Egypt and the surrounding area. However, the vezir died a while later and his order was never implemented.

256 Elizabeth Abbott, *A History of Celibacy* (James Clarke and Co., 2001), p.326-327.

Rodriguez (1997) states in *The Historical Encyclopedia of World Slavery*:

> Since castration violated Muslim law, eunuchs destined for Islamic lands were occasionally castrated by non-Muslims outside Islamic territory. Castration could entail removing only the testicles, or it could mean removing the entire genitalia, as was the case for Chinese eunuchs and African eunuchs in the Ottoman Empire. In the latter method, the threat of death from blood loss or infection was proportionally greater, and even if the eunuch survived, he often suffered painful complications, most commonly urinary tract infections. Nonetheless, many eunuchs lived to quite advanced ages: some Chinese and Ottoman eunuchs died in their nineties.[257]

Rodriguez also notes, as does Hathaway (2002: 139),[258] that East Africans were utilised more as due to them coming from a dense disease pool they would have more likely survived the castration operation more so than Caucasian slaves. Also they were regarded as physically unattractive and as a result of that it would have reduced opportunities for infidelity with women. Thus, eunuchs were neither a sexual nor a political threat and this also explains why they were given political position within the imperial courts.

This grotesque description reveals how far from Islam this barbaric savagery, child mutilation and slavery was and that it was in total opposition to the teachings of the Prophet Muhammad *(sallallāhu 'alayhi wassallam).* Moreover, it also demonstrates that it is folly to merely regard any black Muslim who brings these abuses of Allāh's Divine Legislation as in someway being "an Afrocentric". As history has shown that black people were often specifically targeted for slavery and the interior of Africa, mainly East and Central Africa, was also viewed as being a reserve for slaves, ripe, in some cases, to be mutilated. Although the al-Murābitūn in North-West Africa may have used military slaves this system itself was far different to that which affected East Africa and there was no concept of castration of slaves, which appears to have been rife from the 16th century CE in the East.

257 Junius P. Rodriguez, *The Historical Encyclopedia of World Slavery* (Santa Barbara, California and Oxford, England: ABC-CLIO, 1997), vol.1, p.261.

258 Jane Hathaway, *The Politics of Households in Ottoman Egypt: The Rise of the Qazdaglis* (Cambridge and New York: Cambridge University Press, 1997, 2002).

West Africa was not affected by Middle Eastern slavery and this was largely due to having strong and established Muslim Empires which were powerful way before the Ottoman Empire or the Mamluk Empire were even established. Empires such as the Ashanti Empire, Dahomey, Sokoto Caliphate, Songhai, Ancient Ghana, the Yoruba and others. These were highly efficient and organised empires which had a military tradition which would not have tolerated outside encroachment. The only instance where this happened in West African medieval history was in the case of the Songhay Empire. In 1591 CE, Morocco, under the order of the tyrannical ruler, Ahmad al-Mansūr as-Sā'dī, sacked the Songhay Empire (modern-day Mali), an African Islamic empire, and then began enslaving the population (Sikainga, 1998: 57).

In a hadeeth Qudsī the Prophet Muhammad *(sallallāhu alayhi wassallam)* stated that Allāh said: *"Three types of people will stand apart on the Day of Resurrection as My enemies, and an enemy of Mine will be doomed. A man who vowed in My name then betrayed; a man who sold a free person as a slave and gained a price for selling him and a man who employed a worker and had him do the assigned work then failed to pay him his wages."*[259] As

259 Bukhārī on the authority of Abū Hurayrah (*radi Allāhu'anhu*) and also reported by Ibn Mājah and Imām Ahmad in his *Musnad.* There is another *hadeeth* wherein the Prophet Muhammad (*sallallāhu alayhi wassallam*) stated: *"Three types of people will not have rewards for their prayer: a man who forces himself as an Imām on a group of people; a man who postpones prayer until its time has gone and a man who enslaves a free person."* This *hadeeth* is reported by Abū Dāwūd and Ibn Mājah, however both on the authority of 'AbdurRahmān bin Zayd bin Aslam al-Ifrīqī who is very weak due to his fabrication of narrations attributed to his father, as mentioned by al-Hākim in his book of weak narrators entitled *ad-Du'afā.* Imām al-Bukhārī stated about 'AbdurRahmān ibn Zayd that "his *hadeeth* are not authentic" as relayed in *at-Tārīkh al-Kabeer*, vol.1, p.618; Ibn Hibbān stated about 'AbdurRahmān ibn Zayd that "he deserves to be abandoned" as stated in *al-Majrūheen min al-Muhaditheen wa Du'afā wa'l-Matrūkeen*, edited by Mahmood Ibrāheem Zāyid (Halab: Dār ul-Wa'ī, 1396 AH, 1st Edition and 1402 AH for the 2nd Edition), vol.2, p.57; Ibn Sa'd stated that 'AbdurRahmān ibn Zayd "reported many hadeeth and was very weak" as found in *at-Tabaqāt al-Kubrā*, vol.5, p.413; al-Fasawī noted in *al-Ma'rifah wa't-Tāreekh*, vol.3, p.43 placed 'AbdurRahmān ibn Zayd amongst those who should not be narrated from; Abū Hātim stated that "he is not strong in *hadeeth* but was righteous". The only scholar who graded 'AbdurRahmān bin Zayd as above the level of *da'eef* (weak) was Ibn 'Adī who stated that "there are

for castrating slaves in order for them to be eunuchs, then this is totally against the teaching of the Prophet Muhammad (*sallallāhu 'alayhi wassallam*), for he said in a *hadeeth* which has been reported in Abū Dāwūd, "*whoever castrates his slave, we will castrate him.*"[260] Ibn 'Abbās stated: "Allāh's Messenger (*salallāhu 'alayhi wassallam*) absolutely forbade castrating animals" and in this narration are the words '*Nahyan shadeed*' [i.e. 'with a severe prohibition'].[261] Muslim scholars mentioned this, such as Ibn Hajar, an-Nawawī and as-San'ānī. Ibn Hajar al-'Asqalānī stated in *Fath ul-Bārī*:

> It is prohibited, therefore it is *haram*, and there is no difference of opinion concerning that in the case of the sons of Adam [i.e. humans].

Ibn Hajar also said:

> The wisdom behind the prohibition of castration is that it is contrary to what the Lawgiver wants of increasing reproduction to ensure continuation of jihad against the disbelievers. Otherwise, if permission had been given for that then many people would have done that and reproduction would have ceased and the numbers of Muslims would have become less as a result and the numbers of disbelievers would have increased, and that is contrary to the purpose for which the Prophet (*sallallāhu 'alayhi wassallam*) was sent. It also has a number of negative consequences: self-injury, deformity and causing harm which may lead to death. It also eliminates the quality of masculinity that Allāh created in the

---

hasan (good) *hadeeth* from him and some of them (i.e. scholars) attested to his truthfulness, and he was from those who they recorded *hadeeth* from." For more see Ibn Hajar al-'Asqalānī, *Tahtheeb at-Tahtheeb*, vol.6, p.178. Ibn Taymiyyah has also highlighted his weakness in narration.

260 The *hadeeth* is also reported by an-Nasā'ī but with some additions to it and al-Hākim authenticated it, as mentioned in *Subul us-Salām*, vol.3. However, Imām al-Albānī graded it as weak in *Silsilah ad-Da'eefah*.

261 Ash-Shawkānī, *Nayl ul-Awtār* and also relayed by Imām Ahmad. Ash-Shawkānī said the narration has an authentic chain of transmission however al-Albānī stated that this wording is not authentic however there are supporting narrations which raise it to the level of *hasan*. Bin 'Umar stated that Allāh's Messenger (*sallallāhu 'alayhi wassallam*) prohibited the castration of horses and cattle. It is reported by Ahmad in his *Musnad* and Ibn 'Adiyy in *al-Kāmil* though this is weak.

> man, and it is changing the creation of Allāh and it is a kind of ingratitude for blessings. Moreover, it is imitation of women and finally it is choosing that which is imperfect over that which is perfect.[262]

Ibn Muflih in his book *al-Ādāb ash-Shar'iyyah wa'l-Minh al-Mar'iyyah* stated in vol.3, p.129-130 under the sub-heading of 'Castration of Cattle and Humans':

> Imām Ahmad said: "It does not please me that a man castrates anything."
>
> Qādī [Abū Ya'la] stated in *Ahkām us-Sultāniyyah*: "it is prohibited to castrate humans and cattle and one is to be punished for doing so"...ash-Shāfi'ī prohibited the castration of humans and animals...[263]

The *Lajna ad-Dā'imah* (*Permanent Committee for Islamic Research*) of the top Islamic scholars in Saudi Arabia issued a *fatwa* wherein they were asked about the issue of slavery and why does not Islām outlaw slavery, from their reply:

> By this it is known that the basis of slavery is only through prisoners-of-war or captives obtained when fighting Jihad against the disbelievers. Its purpose is to reform those enslaved by removing them from an evil environment and allowing them to live in a Muslim society, who will guide them to the path of goodness, save them from the clutches of evil, purify them from the filth of disbelief and misguidance, and make them deserving of a life of freedom in which they enjoy security and peace.

They further stated:

> And if there are no lawful Islamic wars, then it is not permissible to establish or institute slavery.[264]

They also noted with regards to slavery that:

262 Ibn Hajar al-'Asqalānī, *Fath ul-Bārī*, vol.9, p.119

263 Al-Imām al-Faqeeh al-Muhaddith Abū 'Abdullāh Muhammad ibn Muflih al-Maqdisī, *al-Ādāb ash-Shar'iyyah wa'l-Minah al-Mar'iyyah* (Beirut: Mu'assisat ur-Risālah, 1419/1999, 3rd Edn., eds. Shu'ayb al-Arna'ūt and 'Umar al-Qayyām), vol.3, p.129-130.

264 *Fatawa Islamiyah, Islamic Verdicts, Vol. 5* (Darussalam: 2002), pp.96-99.

> ...it was a worldwide system operated in all countries. Therefore, Islam laid down a system which ensured the gradual eradication of the system of slavery and its progressive abolition. While it continued, Islam was to ensure the rights of slaves.[265]

An honest Christian missionary, Cardinal Charles Lavigerie, noted in 1888 CE:

> The Qur'an does not enjoin slavery, but merely permits it. Indeed, the Qur'an goes further, because it places the liberation of captives at the top of the list of merciful deeds, through which believers may be worthy of heaven. Strictly speaking, nothing would prick the consciousness of Muslims in the abolition of slavery. However, habits are there, and have acquired a sacred character through their very antiquity, so that one will not be able to get rid of them at once.[266]

In 1935 CE, Prince Faisal bin 'Abdul'Azeez expressed a distaste for slavery and never had any; he told a Western journalist that some two thirds of the slaves in Saudi Arabia had probably lost their freedom in non-scriptural ways (i.e. via kidnapping).[267] Saudi Arabia is often frowned upon for only abolishing the slave trade in 1962, forgetting that Saudi Arabia was only fully established as a nation in 1932. So it took them 30 years and they did not have to go through a civil war to abolish it. In an article in the *Arab News* newspaper on 14th Ramadān 1424 AH corresponding to Friday 7th November 2003, Reem Mohammed al-Faisal, a Jeddah-based photographer wrote:

> As for the first accusation, I do not deny that Arab slave traders sold Africans as well as Europeans, Caucasians, Indians, Malays and any other race they could lay their hands on. The Africans too traded in slaves, as did every other race since the beginning of history. However, my point in reference to slave trading in America is that since its inception slavery has been a social phenomenon resulting from economic upheavals and wars. But it became a racial phenomenon creating a first among many firsts for that country, whereby if you were of Negroid extraction then

---

265 *Al-Dāwah Islamic Monthly Magazine*, no.50, Shawwal 1426 AH/November 2005 (Riyadh), p.29 – *fatawā* answered by the *Permanent Committee for IFTA*.

266 Quoted in Clarence-Smith, *op.cit.*, p.17

267 Mohamed Awad, *Report on Slavery* (New York: UN, 1966), p.121.

you automatically became a slave. A Negro was born for only one reason — to serve, to be a beast of burden. He was to live and die a slave, marry only a slave and breed a race of slaves. It didn't matter who you were or where you came from. If you were black then you were a slave in the eyes of the Americans.

Slaves in other civilizations could be white, black or Chinese. They could be scientists or government functionaries. In the Muslim countries slaves were poets and scholars producing great literary and scientific works. They were mystics and saints, sultans and pashas. Nearly all the Ottoman sultans were born of mothers who were slaves, and these women themselves wielded great powers in the state. The mothers of the Muslim sultans came from all races. The mother of the Ottoman Mahmoud the Reformer was French. The mothers of the Fatimid caliphs were black. Egypt was ruled by slaves for six centuries. As for Saudi Arabia's slaves, they shared the same food, clothes and homes as their owners and many of them became rulers of vast regions in the land and were active in the running of the state. Now, we come to the second accusation, which is Saudi Arabia's late abolition of slavery. Slavery in Saudi Arabia was abolished in 1962.

I personally would love it if slavery had never existed, but it did and still does in many parts of the world both in its classic and its modern form, but that is a subject for another article. If slavery in Saudi Arabia was abolished in 1962, that is because Saudi Arabia did not exist as a modern state before 1932, which means it took thirty years after its creation to end slavery, and that without a civil war. Even though at the time Saudi Arabia was suffering economically, it still went ahead with the eradication of slavery, which must have added to its economic troubles. After the end of slavery in Saudi Arabia its slave population became an integral part of Saudi society, benefiting as fully from all the rights of citizenship as other Saudis. They went to the same schools and universities. They lived and traded in the same neighbourhoods without the discrimination the blacks had suffered in America. The American experience was different. In order for the Americans to abolish slavery they had to go though a civil war which remains until this day the bloodiest war America has fought and the one in which it suffered the most casualties.

Even after the success of the abolitionists in America, the suffering of the blacks didn't end. They were discriminated against in every

> way, barred from living in the same neighbourhood as the whites, prevented from attending the same schools and universities or sharing the same seat on a bus or a water fountain with white Americans, until they ended up imprisoned in ghettos in their own country. Up until the sixties the blacks in America were still living on the sufferance of the whites, and were it not for the inevitable explosion of the black population in America they might still have been suffering from this apartheid life. Even today the blacks are victims of a more subtle discrimination in America. When the blacks constitute only 20 percent of the American population yet make up 90 percent of the prison population there, doesn't this beg the question: When will the blacks be truly free and equal in America?[268]

Moreover, aside from castration there were other aspects of the slave trade in the Muslim world which were in total opposition to the teachings of Islam in regards to humility, honour, dignity, decency and modesty. This will be discussed in the section below.

Nudity of Slaves in Slave Markets in the Muslim World

Although there are many Orientalist depictions of Arab slave traders 'inspecting' and 'checking' slaves, it appears that some of these depictions may not have been far from the reality of what was occurring in the Muslim world. Barker (2016: 2-3) states in this regard:

> The physical inspection of slaves' bodies was deeply humiliating. This humiliation was not incidental. It served to reinforce the powerlessness and dishonor of slaves through the profanation (*ibtidāl*) of their bodies in contrast to the inviolability (*ḥurmah*) of the free body. The humiliation was made especially acute by examining the naked bodies of slaves in public places. Thus by the time a slave changed hands from the old master to the new, a relationship of power and subjection, honor and dishonor, had already been established through the process of inspection. Humiliating displays of power during the inspection also inhibited the slave's unique ability as a human commodity to interfere with his or her own sale. Individual slaves could choose to

268 http://www.arabnews.com/node/239985

> cooperate with, acquiesce to, or resist the entire inspection process; confirm or deny the claims of sellers about their health and character; encourage or discourage particular buyers; and in some cases give or withhold consent in contracts for their own sale. Such manoeuvring occurred within very narrow constraints and could be dangerous for the slave. Yet buyers and sellers could not afford to ignore the ability of slaves to exercise their own will in the midst of sale. Humiliating them helped to forestall and overcome their resistance. For these reasons, inspecting a slave was a complex undertaking and difficult to carry out effectively. It is not surprising that some prospective slave owners sought advice before attempting to buy a new slave. Much of this advice was probably shared in person, but there was also a written genre of slave-buying advice.[269]

All of this shows that slavery and the slave trade was still entrenched in the Muslim world and was far from the teachings of the Prophet (*sallAllāhu 'alayhi wassallam*). Barker notes that a slave traders medical inspection manual was written by a physician named Ibn al-Akfānī, which again indicates that those who wrote about the slave trade were not connected to Islamic knowledge as Ibn al-Akfānī was a medical physician. Barker notes (2016: 5):

> The author of The Book of Observation, Muhammad ibn Ibrāhīm ibn Sā'id ibn al-Akfānī al-Ansārī, was born in Sinjār in northern Iraq in the 1280s.He moved to Syria and then to Cairo in the course of his studies, settling down as a physician at the Mansūrī hospital in Cairo by the 1320s. He was also a prolific writer and composed dozens of treatises on a wide variety of topics from ophthalmology to astronomy. His most famous work was an encyclopedia that covered sixty branches of knowledge gathered under the headings of literature, logic, theology, physics, geometry, astronomy, mathematics, and the practical sciences (such as politics). He died in 1348 at the age of sixty, a casualty of the first outbreak of the Black Death in Cairo. Therefore, although the text of The Book of Observation is not dated, it

269 Hannah Barker, "Purchasing a Slave in Fourteenth Century Cairo: Ibn al-Afkhānī's Book of Observation and Inspection in the Examination of Slaves." *Mamluk Studies Review 19* (2016), 1-24.

> was probably composed in Cairo in the second quarter of the fourteenth century. Ibn al-Akfānī applied his medical knowledge to the purchase of slaves in practice as well as in theory. Slave traders and brokers frequently consulted him about the health of their slaves.

As a result, what occurred was a full nude inspection of the genitalia of both male and female slaves, and this was often done in public. Moreover, the genitalia would also be handled and prodded and breasts felt – such a humiliating experience is utter contrast to the teachings of Islam yet was apparently widespread in the slave markets of the Muslim world and carried out by Muslims in a manner which would make Guantanamo Bay sound like a holiday resort!

Slavery Through Haram and Prohibited Kidnapping of Free People

Therefore, in order for slaves to be taken in Islām there must have been a legitimate war between Muslims and their non-Muslim enemies. In this case, the horrific slave trading, which in reality was through kidnapping Muslims and other free people, was totally against Islam. As seen in Mauritania, Morocco, the Ottoman Empire,[270] the brutal Barbary Coast slavery of white European Christians by North African Muslims[271] and raids into the Congo by the client associates and allies

---

270 For more on how slaves were acquired within the Ottoman Empire, kidnapping was just one method utilised, refer to Ehud R Toledano, *The Ottoman Slave Trade and Its Suppression* (Princeton, New Jersey: Princeton University Press, 1982), pp.15-19.

271 This form of slavery was particularly brutal due to the historical context in which it took place. It developed after 1492 CE after the expulsion of the Muslims from Spain which thus increased polarisation between Muslims and Christians who were living in close proximity to each other. The Muslim kingdoms and states of Morocco, Algiers and Tunis all consciously and passionately, in order to settle the score, began building galleys, attacking European merchant shipping adventures, raiding European coastal communities (of Italy, Greece and Spain) and taking slaves. This state of war led to some gross transgressions of the Divine Legislation of Islām as Muslim pirates began attacking peaceful coastal towns, burning towns, destroying livestock, demolishing churches in Southern Europe etc. In Europe however, this history is played down and there is not much admittance that Muslims took slaves, they are termed as being 'captives' rather than slaves, some writers for example constantly refers to 'captives' and not slaves

of the 'sultāns' of Omān in Zanzibār. Thus, throughout history there are numerous examples of how these formerly great Islamic countries strayed from the correct understandings of Islām. This straying from the correct Islamic understandings contributed to these countries only to be later destroyed themselves by the superior fire-power of the Europeans, leaving their own Islamic societies and traces of Islamic culture totally destroyed up until today. Indeed, the Prophet Muhammad (*sallallāhu 'alayhi wassallam*) stated in an authentic hadeeth that:

« وإني سألت ربي لأمتي أن لا يهلكها بِسَنَةٍ بعامة ، وأن لا يسلط عليهم عدواً من سوى أنفسهم فيستبيح بَيْضَتَهُم ، وإن ربي قال : يا محمد إني إذا قضيت قضاءً فإنه لا يُرَدّ ، وإني أعطيتك لأمتك ألا أهلكهم بِسَنَةٍ بعامة ، وألا أسلط عليهم عدواً من سوى أنفسهم فيستبيح بيضتهم ، ولو اجتمع عليهم من بأقطارها حتى يكون بعضهم يُهلك بعضًا ويَسْبِي بعضهم بعضًا »

I asked my Lord that my ummah not be destroyed by drought, and that it not be overcome by enemies outside of them. My Lord said: "O Muhammad! When I issue a decree it is not reversed. I have granted for your ummah that they will not be destroyed by universal drought. And that they not be overcome by enemies outside themselves even if they gather against them in droves, but some of them will destroy each other, and some will capture (and enslave) each other."[272]

as if to deny the fact that they were slaves and to pander to the European reader.

272 An authentic hadeeth collected by Muslim and narrated from Thawbān (*radi Allāh 'anhu*). Also collected by Tirmidhī, Ahmad, Ibn Mājah, Abū Dāwūd and Ibn Hibbān. At-Tirmidhī said "it is *hasan saheeh*". Al-Albānī deemed it as *saheeh* in *Saheeh Sunan at-Tirmidhī, Saheeh Sunan Abī Dāwūd, Saheeh Sunan Ibn Mājah* and *Saheeh al-Jāmi'*. Al-Arna'ūt in his verification of *Saheeh Ibn Hibbān* with the arrangement of Ibn Balbān said "its chain of transmission is *saheeh* according to the conditions of Muslim". Al-Hākim said "the hadeeth is *saheeh* according to the conditions of Shaykhayn." Al-Baghawī in *Sharh us-Sunnah* said "this hadeeth is *saheeh*". Ibn Katheer in his *tafseer* said "the hadeeth is good and strong". Ibn Hajar in *Fath ul-Bārī* from the narration of at-Tabarī said: "with an authentic chain of transmission". While al-Haythamī said in *Majma' uz-Zawā'id*: "the narrators of

There is no doubt that such tolerance of oppression, with slavery and entrenchment in a slave trade being an example, led to the downfall of Muslim states as Allāh states in the Qur'ān:

وَمَا كَانَ رَبُّكَ لِيُهْلِكَ الْقُرَى بِظُلْمٍ وَأَهْلُهَا مُصْلِحُونَ۝

> And your Lord would not have destroyed the cities unjustly while their people were reformers.
>
> [Hūd (11): 117]

And the *Mufassireen* mention in regards to this noble *ayah* that oppression is a cause for the destruction of countries. Ibn Taymiyyah:

أن الله يقيم الدولة العادلة و أن كانت كافرة ولا يقيم الظالمة وان كانت مسلمة

> Allāh will establish a just state, even if it is disbelieving and will not establish an oppressive state, even if it is Muslim.[273]

Slavery in the Ottoman Empire

Although slavery within the Ottoman Empire had the feature of social mobility, which as noted earlier could not be found in the Trans-Atlantic Slave system for example, there were still some troubling aspects of slavery there. Namely, the frequent and abundant usage of castrated slaves, which has been discussed in depth in the section above. Although such castration procedures did not occur within Ottoman territories the eunuchs were seen as rare oddities which could be presented to Ottoman princes and sultans. As noted earlier, this is a complete anathema to Islam as the Prophet Muhammad (*sallallāhu 'alayhi wassallam*) forbade this, so how on earth a wholesale trade based on such male genital

---

Ahmad are those of the *Saheeh*".

273 Shaykh ul-Islām Ahmad Ibn Taymiyyah, *Majmū' al-Fatāwā* (Madeenah al-Munawwarah, KSA: Majma' Malik Fahd, 1415 AH, 1425 AH/2004 CE. Eds. 'AbduRahmān bin Muhammad bin Qāsim and his son Muhammad) vol.28, p.146; *al-Istiqāmah*, vol.2, p.248.

mutilation could thrive demonstrates just how distant Muslims were from Islām for generations. Toledano notes in his book *The Ottoman Slave Trade and Its Suppression* that:

> When war failed to satisfy the demand for slaves, slave-raids were organised to supply the markets. In the late 1850s, raids were still launched from the *Vilāyet* of Tripoli into the areas of Kavar and Aïr in order to produce slaves for the northern markets. Acting as agents for Savana kings, the Touareg and supra-tribal kingdoms "made raiding and capturing of slaves a regular enterprise and fed the victims into a complex trading system." In the Upper Nile, Bahr al-Ghazal, and the White Nile areas, the activity of the European and Ottoman ivory traders quickly developed in the 1850s into a massive slave-raiding and slave-trading operation. The nature of the merchant camps, or *Zarības*, and their aggressive trading practices soon created a need for slave labor and slave troops, which was satisfied through extensive slave dealing. The raids were led by "northern traders" or Syrian, Egyptian, and north-Sudanese merchants, most of whom were Ottoman subjects. In Ethiopia, slave-raiding expeditions were carried out into the southwestern regions and even to the negroid areas surrounding the country. Here, the marauders came from Kaffa and the Galla principalities. The Ottoman governor of Massawa reported in 1860 on slave raids into Hubāba, some fifty hours ride from town. The raids were organised by "five or ten" merchants from Massawa with the cooperation of the tribal shaykhs in the area.
>
> To this mode of acquisition we should add kidnapping, a practice prevalent both at the supply sources and in the Ottoman Empire. Kidnapping differed from raiding in that it was not organised as an aggressive, large-scale operation, but was conducted on a small scale, often on an individual basis. Also, it was aimed at unprotected persons in an isolated position, rather than at whole villages ready to defend themselves against potential marauders. Kidnapping was commonplace in Ethiopia and the regions around Lake Chad. It occurred frequently on the eastern borders of Anatolia among the people of the Caucasus. The Lâz were accused of abducting Georgian women and children while the men were serving in the Sultan's armies. The Ottoman vice-consul in Potide had to intercede with the Russian authorities in 1865 in order to obtain the release of Ottoman subjects who had been

> kidnapped by Abaza tribesmen and taken to Russian territory. After their migration to the Ottoman Empire in the early 1860s, Circassians were often implicated in the abduction of free-born Muslim children; in Bulgaria they were accused of kidnapping Bulgarian, Greek, and Tatar girls. The Ottoman Penal Code of 1858 imposed a penalty of one year's imprisonment on abductors of children, and the relevant articles were expanded in 1860 and again in 1867.[274]

In the late seventeenth century, many Islamic scholars condemned the slave trade and the racism that began to be associated with it, which brings us on to our second instance of slavery among Muslims within Islamic history, which is the case of Morocco.

Slavery in Morocco

Morocco began enslaving from the epoch of Yūsuf ibn Tashfeen (1061-1106 CE) who used military slaves from the sub-Saharan regions south of Morocco. Rodriguez (1997: 305) noted, basing this on Levtzion (1973), in regards to Ancient Ghana and its trade that:

> Gold remained the primary commodity in this trade from Ghana, but slaves, destined for faraway markets in North Africa and elsewhere, were also sold. Ancient Ghana obtained slaves through purchase and by raiding neighbouring peoples and states. The Arab scholar al-Idrisi, writing in the twelfth century, confirmed that "the people of Barisa, Silla, Takrur and Ghana raid the country of Lamlam, capture its inhabitants, and bring them to their own countries, where they sell them to merchants who come there. The latter export them to other countries".

Then again in 1591 CE, Morocco, under the order of the tyrannical ruler, Ahmad al-Mansūr as-Sā'dī, sacked the Songhay Empire, an African Islamic empire and then began enslaving the population. The Moroccan ruler Mulay Ismā'īl, the second 'Alawī Sultān (1672-1727 CE), whose mother was a slave from sub-Saharan Africa, also began an unjust program of forced conscription and enslavement of black Moroccans. When black children reached the age of ten, they were forced to join the army. Under the rule of Mulay Ismā'īl many white European Christians were also enslaved along what is known in the

274 Toledano, *op.cit.*, pp.16-17.

West as the 'Barbary coast', the North African coastal ports. The main difference in the slavery that occurred in 16th-18th century Morocco however, than what occurred in the Middle East and Ottoman Empire, was that the savage and brutal act of castration was not utilised. Also there is the fact that they still remained within Africa and hence still connected to Africa. Shaykh Sidi 'AbdusSalām bin Jāsūs of Fās (Fez, Morocco) objected to the slavery system in later seventeenth century Morocco as free Muslims were enslaved purely due to the fact that they were black. He stated:

> This is unashamed enslavement of freemen and reducing them to servitude with no Divinely Legislated justification. The Harateen of Fes are free like all other free born Muslims. Their free status is unquestionable. Therefore, any admission by them that they are slaves of named or unnamed persons, or any testimony given by others accusing them of being slaves, irrespective of why such testimony was presented, is indeed the result of pressure and coercion. This is witnessed and seen and there is no lack of evidence to support it. Their admission to slavery, even if it was of their own volition and not forced on them, is invalid. According to the Divine Legislation they cannot be subjected to slavery nor bound by their own admission. Their freedom is a right Allāh bestowed on them. Therefore, they have no right to choose to be slaves.[275]

In regards to the term 'Haratin', then Badran (1985: 4) suggests that it is shrouded in mystery but that generally the term refers to a people who were dark skinned original inhabitants of north Saharan oases and were a cultural mix of ancient north African black populations and light-skin Berbers. Though they were free they were considered by other Berbers and Arabs who displaced them as being inferior and of lowly status. They were farmworkers and not landowners and received a fifth from Arab and Berber landlords. They were therefore in a quite vulnerable position on account of their black features, non-tribal affiliation and blind loyalty to their patrons. Badran says that by the second half of the 17th century Haratin communities could be found in all of the major Moroccan towns. By 1690 they were urbanised and shared in

275 Adapted from A.A. Batran, "*The Ulamā of Fez, M. Ismail and the Issue of the Harātīn of Fas*" in John Ralph Willis (ed.) *Slaves and Slavery in Muslim Africa*, vol.2 (London: Frank Cass, 1985) pp.9-13

the economic prosperity of cities such as Fez and became prominent citizens. This explains why the 'Ulama of Fez were particularly troubled by the forced conscription policy of Mulay Ismā'īl.

Ibn Jāsūs noted that the enslavement of free Muslims was tantamount to rejection of the Islamic Sharee'ah or at least bringing it into disrepute. Ibn Jāsūs was arrested and imprisoned in Meknes for three months (4th June – 8th September 1708) and many other scholars fled the city. He was released on the condition that he pay a large fine but he could neither pay nor did he remain silent on the issue. The governor of Fez, Bu 'Ali ar-Rūsī, re-imprisoned Ibn Jāsūs, tortured him. Ibn Jāsūs was later executed by strangulation on 4th July 1709 by the Sultān for sticking to the truth and evidence and not blindly following the erroneous ruling.

Another Muslim scholar Abu'l-'Abbās Ahmad bin Khālid an-Nāsirī[276]

---

276 He is Abu'l-'Abbās Ahmad bin Khālid bin Muhammad bin Muhammad bin Ahmad bin Muhammad an-Nāsirī and his lineage goes back to 'Abdullāh bin Ja'far bin Abī Tālib, husband of the sister of Hasan and Husayn (*radi Allāhu 'anhum*). An-Nāsirī was from a family that was known for virtue and knowledge which had migrated to the city of Salā (Salè), near Rabat in Morocco in 1220 AH/1805 CE. He was born on Saturday 22 Dhu'l-Hijjah 1250 AH/March 1835 CE in Salā, which at that time was a city that was known for Islamic sciences, Arabīc language and the study of Islamic texts.

He studied the Qur'ān (*Warsh 'an Nāfi'*) with al-Hajj Muhammad 'Alawī as-Salāwī and Muhammad bin Jīlānī al-Hāmidī. He also studied the works of ash-Shātibī, Ibn 'AbdulBarr, Ibn Mālik and Ibn Subkī with his cousin 'AbdusSalām bin Talhah. An-Nāsirī studied the sciences of the Arabīc language with his teacher 'Allāmah Muhammad bin 'Abdul'Azeez as-Salāwī and studied a number of works on grammar, *balāghā* (rhetoric), logic, *fiqh* and *usool ud-deen*. He was pivotal in disseminating knowledge, conducting research and benefiting the general masses of people in Morocco, excelling in historical works. He was also concerned with socio-religious issues moreso than most scholars of the time. He was very eloquent and as a result his lessons would be full and would have an effect on those present. He was strongly influenced by the *sunnah* in all affairs and strongly opposed the people of innovation and refuted them, exhorting them to refer back to the Qur'ān and *sunnah*. He opposed the leaders and sects of desires who had entered into the *deen* that which was not from it, "He also strongly safeguarded waking the Muslims from their heedlessness to the clear *manhaj*", (Biography by Ja'far and Muhammad an-Nāsirī, *Kitāb ul-Istiqsā' li-Akhbār Duwal al-Maghrib al-'Aqsā* (Dār

condemned the erroneous, invalid and racist practice of enslaving Muslims from sub-Saharan Africa as it contradicted the Islamic *Sharee'ah* and was an incorrect belief regarding slavery. In his book *Kitāb ul-Istiqsā*[277] he notes:

---

ul-Baydā [Casablanca]: Dār ul-Kitāb, 1954), vol.1, pp.14-15).

From his most correct and authentic books in particular are his historical *magnum opus*, *Tārikh ul-Istiqsā'* and *Ta'dheem ul-Minnah bi'n-Nusrati's-Sunnah* which according to Ja'far and Muhammad an-Nāsirī in their biography of him in the first volume of *Kitāb ul-Istiqsā'*, "are filled with warning against this disease and these (false) opinions by paying attention to spreading authentic Islamic knowledge amongst the ummah and referring people to study from the books of the Salaf." He advised a number of governors in Morocco during his era on issues related to governance, economics and the *deen*, he thus travelled to the cities of Tanger, al-'A'rāish (Larache), Marrākush (Marrakech), Dār ul-Baydā' (Casablanca), Salā (Sale), Tetwān (Tetoun), Ghumārah etc. initially he refused the posts as he thought that they would avert him from his scholastic efforts. He died on Thursday 16 Jumadā Ulā 1325 AH/12 October 1897 CE. He authored over thirty books (see ibid. pp.27-34) and his two main students were the jurist and author of Salā, al-Hajj Tayyib 'Awād and the historian Abū 'Abdullāh Muhammad bin 'Ali ad-Dakālī as-Salāwī. From the titles of the works that he authored, there is nothing whatsoever that shows that he was *Sūfī* and in fact in the lengthy biography of him by Ja'far and Muhammad an-Nāsirī, there is no reference made whatsoever to Sufism. Furthermore, from the thirty works that he authored, none of the books have anything to do with Sufism, the contrary in fact, in the form of his book *Ta'dheem ul-Minnah bi'n-Nasrati's-Sunnah*. There may have been some members of his extended family and clan that were *Sūfīs*, but as for Abu'l-'Abbās there is nothing to suggest that he was. Kurt S. Vikør in his book *Sufi and Scholar on the Desert Edge: Muhammd bin 'Ali al-Sanusi and his Brotherhood* (London: Hurst & Co., 1995) refers to Ahmad bin Khālid an-Nāsirī as being an historian and no where mentions him as being a *Sūfī*, and refers to others from the Nāsirī family as clearly being *Sūfīs*. An-Nāsirī died on 16 Jumadā al-Ulā 1315 AH/October 12 1897 CE, *rahimahullāh*.

277 There is also a new annotated edition by M. Hajji, B. Boutaleb & A. Tawfiq (Dār ul-Baydā' [Casablanca]: Mansurat Wizarat al-Taqafa wa-l-Ittisal, 2001-2005 CE) in 8 volumes. The oldest edition is the 1949 CE edition which is in nine volumes. A summarized edition was also published into three volumes in 1418 AH/1997 CE again by Dār ul-Kitāb in Casablanca. An-Nāsirī himself published it himself in four volumes in Cairo in 1894 CE which was translated into French by the Orientalists Grauille in 1906 CE, G.S. Colin in 1923-25 CE and Fumey

It will be clear to you from what we have related of the history of the Sudān (Black lands, i.e. sub-Saharan Africa) how far the people of these lands had taken to Islām from ancient times. It will also be clear that they are among the best peoples in regard to Islām, the most religiously upright, the most avid for learning and they have love for the people of (Islamic) knowledge. This state of affairs is found in most of their kingdoms bordering on the Maghrib, as you know. Thus, will be apparent to you the severity of the affliction which has beset the lands of the Maghrib since ancient times in regard to the indiscriminate enslaving of the people of the Sudān (the black lands) and the importation of droves of them every year to be sold in the market places in towns and countries where men trade in them as one would trade in beasts or way worse than that. People have become so inured that generation after generation, even the common people believe that the reason for being enslaved according to the Divine Legislation is merely that a man should be black in colour and come from those regions. This, by Allāh, is one of the foulest (*afshahu*) and gravest evils perpetrated upon Allāh's religion, as the people of the Sudan (the black lands, i.e. Africa) are Muslims who have the same rights and responsibilities as ourselves. Even if you assume that some of them are pagans or belong to a religion other than Islām, nevertheless the majority of them today, as in former times, are Muslims, and judgement is made according to the majority and that Islām and kufr (unbelief) claim equal members there, who among us can tell whether those brought here are Muslims or unbelievers. To sum up: as we have said, the innate condition of humankind is freedom and lack of any cause for being enslaved, whoever maintains the opposite is denying the basic conditions. And since it has known from time before that the people of the Sudan who border us are mostly or wholly Muslims, and since men of integrity and others have frequently made the point that they wage war against each other and kidnap each other's children and sell them unjustly. And we see that those who enslave them are those with no manners and no deen, the time is as you know and its people are as you see. We should therefore have no hesitation in declaring that anyone who enters into a transaction of this forbidden nature in hindering

---

in 1934-36 CE. This 1954-5 edition which is used for these quotes is available from the library at *SOAS, University of London* and the fifth volume discusses sub-Saharan Africa.

> his salvation. As for the claim that the slave-traders have laid their hands upon them, this is not sufficient reason in the Divine Legislation to allow one to buy slaves from them, since it is a weak evidence which amounts to a lie.[278]

He concludes his condemnation of the slavery of Muslims on racial grounds by saying:

> ...we ask Allāh to grant success to whom He has charged with the affairs of His servants, in order to bring an end to this corruption; as the reasons for Divinely Legislated slavery which was prevalent during the period of the Prophet (*sallallāhu 'alayhi wassallam*) and the righteous forefathers (*Salaf us-Sālih*) has been lost today. The main reason being *jihād* to establish the Word of Allāh as the most high and guiding the people to the *deen* which Allāh has chosen for His servants. This is our *deen* which our Prophet (*sallallāhu alayhi wassallam*) has legislated for us. Opposing it, is opposing the *deen* and other than this is not legislated, and success is in the Hand of Allāh.[279]

Shaykh Ahmad Bābā at-Timbuktī (*rahimahullāh*)[280] a Muslim scholar of Berber origin from Mali wrote a book on slavery in 1614 CE called *Mi'rāj us-Sūd illa Nayl Hukm Majlūb us-Sūd*[281] in which he condemned the enslavement of Muslims. Furthermore, a Moroccan Islamic scholar, Muhammad as-Sanūsī bin Ibrāheem al-Jārimī, wrote a treatise attacking Moroccans who considered black Africans to be intrinsically slaves. The treatise was entitled *Tanbih Ahl ut-Tughyān 'alā Hurriyyat is-Sudān* [Alerting the People of Tyranny to the Free Status of the People of the Black Lands], which was written between 1312 AH/1894-95 CE and 1316 AH/1898 CE. He quotes from an-Nāsirī for example whose work was only available around the latter date indicating that it was probably written around the latter date. Al-Jārimī says:

---

278 Shaykh Abu'l-'Abbās Ahmad bin Khālid an-Nāsirī, *Kitāb ul-Istiqsā' li-Akhbār Duwal al-Maghrib al-'Aqsā* (Dār ul-Baydā' [Casablanca]: Dār ul-Kitāb, 1955. Eds. Ja'far and Muhammad an-Nāsirī), Vol.5, abridged from pp.131-134.

279 Ibid.

280 1556 – 1627 CE

281 Also known as *al-Kashf wa'l-Bayān lī Ansāf Majlūb us-Sudān* [An Explanation and Clarification of the Types of People that can be Enslaved from the Black Lands].

> When I travelled to the land of the Further Maghrib I found some of the uncouth Moroccans claiming that all blacks without exception were slaves who did not deserve to be free. For how should they deserve that, being black of skin? On this matter they relate fantasies that have no foundation to them in the Legislation or the natural order. As for the Divine Legislation, nothing came down from the Lawgiver (Allāh) that would explain why among all peoples they should be enslaved rather than others. With regard to nature, (such an argument is unacceptable) because the natural order rejects blacks being slaves without a compelling legally justified reason.[282]

This clearly indicates that the Muslim scholars condemned the racist brand of slavery that linked race to slavery as it had no Islamic basis to it. Thus, we do not find a bona-fide Islamic scholar in history trying to bring proofs from the Qur'ān and Sunnah that such a racist form of slavery is justified, as opposed to other religions wherein they actually twisted, quoted and utilised their religious books as source references to justify slavery. Al-Jārimī then reaffirms this by concluding that:

> This contradicts the view of the mass (*jumhūr*) of the Islamic scholars to the effect that the innate condition of people is freedom; indeed, some have stated that there is consensus over this…the one who denies something over which there is consensus and which is known by necessity, is certainly a disbeliever.[283]

Interestingly, in modern day Morocco this entire history is effectively either unknown or denied, yet it is more than likely that due to a lack of education generally, not to mention of history specifically, this aspect of Morocco's history has effectively been erased from the modern Moroccan psyche. To the extent that Morocco is considered one of the most racially tolerant North African country today.

---

282 J. Hunwick, *"Islamic Law and Polemics over Race and Slavery in North Africa (16-19th Centuries)"* in Shaun E. Marmon (ed.), *Interdisciplinary Journal of Middle Eastern Studies: Slavery in the Islamic Middle-East*, vol.7, (Princeton: Markus Wiener Publishers, 1999), p.62. The copy of this manuscript of al-Jārimī is preserved in the *Centre de Documentation et de Recherches Historiques Ahmed Baba*, Timbuktu (Mali), ms no.1575.

283 Ibid.

Basra and Iraq: the Zanj Slave Rebellion

The Arabic term '*Zanj*' ('black skinned'), may in fact be derived from the Persian '*Zangh*' ['black'] was used classically to largely refer to East Africans, and hence the name of the country 'Zanzibar'. In fact, it has also been said (Rosenberg, 2017: 96) that the term may have arrived into Arabic from the Roman 'Azania' for the South-East African coast, Kenya down, and from which 'Tanzania' has derived. Pliny the Elder (23-79 BCE), the Roman author and natural philosopher, referred to the 'Azanian Sea' that stretched around the south coast of Africa. Talhami (1977) suggests that the term is vague and its meaning unclear.

It is also used rarely to apply to West Africans, yet even among the Arabs it appears that the meaning and application are somewhat confused. Tolmacheva (1986) notes that the earliest mention of the term '*Zanj*' in the Arabic sources is that of the astronomer al-Fazarī in the 780s wherein the term was used to denote one of the countries within Africa.[284] It was asserted that the term was used in a poem after the Alid massacre in 680 CE, however it may have been interpolated later. Then al-Jāhiz (d.869) utilised the term in his writings, while the botanist al-Birūnī used the term '*Zanji*' to refer to the mineral hematite and al-Baytār used the term to refer to black rhubarb.

The slaves taken to Southern Iraq in the 9th century CE were largely from the East African coast and were brought to work in the salt marshes and removed earth to plant crops. They were in regular conflict with their overloads as a result of the harsh and brutal conditions in which their diet was also lacking (Ingram, 2015: 45). Prior to the 869 Rebellion there were in fact two other uprisings by the Zanj in Iraq, in 70 AH (689-90 CE) and in 694 CE and it has been argued by historians that these revolts effectively did away with experiments of plantation slavery in the Middle East and agricultural labour-intensive servitude which would later be utilised to the industrial level practice seen during the Trans-Atlantic experience in the Americas. However Harms (2013: 4) argues that in Bahrain in the mid-10th century Bahraini princes had 30,000 Ethiopian slaves working in agriculture.

The first uprising occurred during the rule of Umayyad Dynasty

284 Marina Tolmacheva, "Towards a Definition of the Term Zanj", *Azania 21* (1986).

under Khalid Mus'ab ibn az-Zubayr and involved small gangs that were involved in rioting and pillaging and was easily dispersed by the Umayyad troops. Zanj prisoners were beheaded and their corpses hanged publicly (Ingram, 2015: 46). During the second revolt, their leader was known as 'Shir Zanj' ['the lion of the Zanj'] and the Umayyad governor of the time, Hajjāj bin Yūsuf ath-Thaqafī sent troops on two different occasions to quash the rebellion.

In regards to the main and third Zanj rebellion itself, which occurred from 869-883 (CE), then it had an impact on the stability of the Abbasid empire and its financial and military security as it coincided at a time when the empire was both in political crisis and facing off a number of challenges. The Caliph Mu'tazz was struggling to meet the needs of his Turkish military men who demanded reforms of the Iqta' system and conflicts arose between him and his non-Arab inner circle.

It was documented quite extensively by the historians at the time such as at-Tabarī (d.923 CE) and others.[285] It was begun by a man called 'Ali bin Muhammad who claimed to be a descendent of Ali ibn Abī Tālib (*radi Allāhu 'anhu*). In order to further his aims of power he rallied the oppressed slaves, which could have been a cynical move to merely rally troops and an army of his own, and asserted to be the saviour and aider of the black slaves and offered them wealth, property and slaves of their own in return. He had tried to revolt prior and would even later declare himself as the Mahdi. Some commentators have maintained that he was a stalwart defender of justice and fairness for the oppressed slaves.

The Zanj used sophisticated guerrilla tactics, seized boats, killed entre crews and took prisoners of war. When Ali bin Muhammad was eventually captured he was beheaded and his head impaled on a lance as an example and a warning to his followers from the Zanj. The remaining Zanj either accepted Muwaffaq's offers to join his government forces or fled to the desert were they either died of thirst of were taken as slaves by Bedouins (Ingram, 2015: 50).

Various theories have been posited as to the *raison d'etre* of the revolt ranging from a class struggle to a race war to an early instance of civil

285 Translated by David Waines, *The History of al-Tabari (Ta'rikh al-rusul wa'l-muluk), Volume XXXVI, The Revolt of the Zanj.* (Albany: State University of New York Press, 1992).

rights to mere pillaging. Massignon (1934) argues that violent guerrilla warfare tactics were adopted by the Zanj which resulted in mosques being burned down, buildings ransacked and the inhabitants of Basra massacred. At-Tabarī discusses more about the military aspects of the revolt and how the Abbasids were able to put down the rebellion. This account is what Popovic (1999) relies upon in his modern account of the Zanj revolt.

Talhami (1977: 452) argued, like Popovic who followed her in this, that Arab Bedouins, Bahranis and some enslaved Africans contributed to the rebellion and that the majority were not those regarded as 'Zanj'. She argued, citing the historian G.S.P Freeman-Grenville (1975) that large numbers of slaves transported from the East African coast is unsubstantiated. Talhami cites Persian and Arab geographers, such as Ibn Hawqal, al-'Umarī and al-Mas'ūdī, asserting that there is little to indicate that there was a thriving slave trade from East Africa before the 10th century. Popovic however suggests that the revolt had little socio-economic impact and there was no change whatsoever in terms of irrigation and agriculture in Iraq. Segal (2001) however argues that there were and reduced black agricultural slave labour in the Middle East.

Nicolas McLeod (2016) wrote an MA thesis on the Zanj rebellion wherein he contends that "racial ideologies" and a "racialised social structure" was at play. Despite setting out to assess the situation of the Zanj revolt in Iraq, McLeod also attempts to look at what he considers to be Islam's stance on race. Yet McLeod neither quotes from classical Qur'anic exegesis nor does he refer to any *ahadith* from the Prophet (*sallallāhu 'alayhi wassallam*) regarding race and brotherhood! This is exacerbated by McLeod repeatedly referring to what he calls an "Arab-Islamic Slave Trade", as if such a trade was 'Islamic'.

Oman and Zanzibar

The slave trade conducted by Oman was rampant and interestingly in terms of the history and religious context, Oman is an Ibadite-Kharijite sect. This may explain why there has been little in the way of any Omani religious scholarly discussion or condemnation of slavery. Moreover, out of all the Gulf states, Oman profited the most from slavery and its trading, with Zanzibar being the main port for acquisition of slaves from the East African interior. In the mid-14th century CE, the traveller Ibn Batūta, claimed to have visited the East African coast and noted that the region had become prosperous due to the trade in ivory, gold and slaves. The Portuguese conquest of the coast in the 16th century aimed to seize control of resources for themselves.

Zanzibar became a Sultanate in 1840 when the ruler of Oman, Said bin Sultan, moved his capital from Muscat in Oman to Stone Town, Zanzibar after defeating the Portuguese at Mombasa, Kenya. Said bin Sultan viewed Zanzibar as being conducive for clove growth and clove plantations, to be worked by slaves. When he died in 1856, his son Majid assumed control and consolidated his power on the slave trade while his successor Barghash bin Said helped to abolish the slave trade and established Zanzibar's infrastructure. This was done through a treaty with the British in 1873 that aimed to replace slave revenue with legitimate economic activities such as the trade in coir, coconuts, rice, rubber and ivory. In 1886 both the British and the Germans sought to gain control over Zanzibar's trade routes and agreed on dividing the territories. Both countries leased coastal territory from Zanzibar and established trading stations which they later used to take over mainland possessions.

In 1890 the United Kingdom and the German Empire signed the Helioglan-Zanzibar Treaty which made Zanzibar a British protectorate which lasted for several decades, during which time the power and authority of the Sultan was greatly diminished and the country's slave trade curtailed. Most of the sultans were aligned with the British except for Khalid bin Barghash and in 1896 when he seized power over that of the British-supported candidate, Hamood bin Muhammad, he was given a choice to either give up power or go to war against the British. He opted for war and this ignited the Anglo-Zanzibar War which has been dubbed as "the shortest war in history", lasting less than hour before his forces surrendered!

The British Protectorate ended on 10 December 1963 through the 1963 Zanzibar Act which made provision for full self-government in Zanzibar as an independent country within the British Commonwealth. When the British Protectorate ceased, Zanzibar became a constitutional monarchy under Sultan Jamshid bin 'Abdullāh, who would be overthrown a month later in the Zanzibar Revolution. Not long after in April 1964, Zanzibar united with Tanganyika to become Tanzania. An interesting paper by an Omani academic, Yusuf A. al-Ghailani, has been written on the topic of the slavery in Oman entitled *British Early Intervention in the Slave Trade, 1822-1873.*[286] Al-Ghailani states:

> In fact the traffic in this business was considered illegal by most of the people who were involved in it. It was certainly not favored by Islamic law, which encourages a belief in freedom, justice, and equality. However, those who were involved in the trade were illiterate in Islamic thinking and as a result of the harsh circumstances of their lives, the demands of their societies, and the small size of the population; they found themselves in absolute need to have these people to help them either in overseas trade or working on the land. A proportion of the slaves were brought from their original lands for the purpose of trading in them. There was another fact which persuaded the Arabs to become involved in this illegal trade, which was that slaves had been brought to the markets of East Africa by the black people themselves, who sold them either for money or goods to the Arab traders.
>
> The trade in black people from the East African Coast was mainly considered as a form of trade between Zanzibar and its dominions on one hand and the coasts of Arabia and the Persian Gulf on the other hand; and by far the largest portion of the traffic was taken to the Arabian Peninsula through three different stages, before it reached its final destination. These were the land journey from their original homes inland to the coast; secondly a short trip across the sea to Zanzibar, where the main open slave market was held; and thirdly the final sea journey from Zanzibar to Arabia or any other part of Asia. In fact this was the case with the traffic in Zanzibar, where these three stages were sometimes reduced to two only, when slaves passed from Mozambique, Pemba, Dar-es-Salaam, Kilwa, and Mombasa to Zanzibar. Kilwa was the principal port of shipment for Zanzibar and its dominions, but sometimes they could be shipped directly from Kilwa to the northern Po.

Al-Ghailani therefore notes that those involved in the trade were devoid of both Islamic knowledge and understanding. However, his assertion

286 Yusuf A. Al-Ghailani, 'British Early Intervention in the Slave Trade, 1822-1873' in *History Research*, Oct.-Dec., 2015, Vol. 5, No. 4, 225-238.

that Africans, possibly as a result of intra-tribal warfare, delivered captives to Omani traders, with neither Omani raiding nor demand is questionable. As Al-Ghailani makes no referral whatsoever to the likes of Tippu Tip who was of mixed Omani and Black East African origin. Tippu Tip (1832-1905) was the one who embarked on slave raids in to the interior of East Africa as far in as Congo and is well known. Tip was an Ibadi-Khārijī who was totally ignorant of Islam and motivated by wealth, status and position. His whole life, from even a young age, had revolved around slave raiding and trading and also the ivory trade. He had met European travellers such as David Livingstone (the Scottish reverend, explorer and British missionary) and Henry Morton Stanley (who in 1887 proposed that Tip be made governor of the Stanley Falls District, Leopold II and Barghash bin Said both agreed to this).

In 1886 Tip organised resistance against Leopold II's Congo Free State and enlisted the help of Gongo Lutete, himself an individual who had been enslaved by the Swahili and Omani slave traders and then had gained freedom and aligned himself with the Batetela and Bakussu tribes of Congo. The Congo-Arab War, largely between the Belgians and Swahili slave traders, saw the death of Tip's son, Sefu in October 1893, meanwhile Lutete had betrayed Sefu and joined the Belgians. Sefu crossed the Lomani River with 10,000 men, only 500 of these were Zanzibari officers while all the rest were Congolese. He set up two forts there which were attacked and forced Sefu to retreat. The war itself was a proxy war and a farce in that most of those actually doing the fighting were Congolese on both sides.

Rumaliza (born circa 1855), a Qādirī-Sūfī, was another figure during the Congo-Arab War and was on the side of Tip, having formed trading alliances with him. Rumaliza was another slave and ivory trader who dominated Tanganyika from his base at Ujiji, where he was also proclaimed 'sultan' and led a Swahili community, on an old slave route that led from Stanley Falls up the Lualaba River to Nyangwe. He was defeated by the Belgian forces led by Baron Francis Dhanis in January 1894. It was during both Tip's and Rumaliza's watch that slave traders massacred 400 women of the Manyueme tribe in Nyangwe (modern-day Maniema in Eastern Democratic Republic of Congo) which was a slave trading centre in eastern Congo controlled by the Zanzibari/ Omani Arabs and Swahili peoples according to David Livingstone's diaries on July 15 1871, Arab slavers massacred 400 women and children within a couple of hours.

East African slaves were therefore from Mozambique, Pemba, Dar es-Salaam, Kilwa (was the main port town on the coast between Mozambique and Zanzibar, from which slaves could be transported directly to Zanzibar) and Mombasa. The British pressure to reduce this traffic continued effectively and was demonstrated by the Political Resident in the Gulf, Lewis Pelly who forced Sayyid Majid of Zanzibar to be more active in his opposition to the activities of the trade. In 1822 the Moresby Treaty was signed between the British and the Sultan of Zanzibar and by its terms the British had the right to stop the trade in slaves between East Africa and the European countries, mainly France and Portugal. In October 1863, Sultan Majid issued an order to prohibit the export of slaves from Kilwa. In January 1864, this order was extended to all of his dominions in Africa. The British attempts to stop the trade had become an essential feature of their policy, and traders' dhows sailing under the Sultan's flags were considered an easy target for search and detention.

However, the trade actually remained in existence, as measured by British success in the capture of slaves and slavers on the high seas; capture was undoubtedly the major threat to those who still carried on the trade. The number of slaves who reached the Arabian and Persian Coast after the 1850s was considerably decreased compared with that during the 1830s and 1840s, but the smugglers managed to escape capture and deliver small numbers to their territories on the African Coasts. Though it is difficult to give a reliable or exact estimate of the number of slaves who reached their final destination during the 1840s and 1850s, the yearly figures could reach between 10,000 and 20,000 persons. Slaves were destined to India, where they were used on sugar and tea plantations. In 1840 there was a slave revolt in Zanzibar and existing Arab trading families, distinct from the Omanis who had in fact their own policy of introducing more Omanis into Zanzibar to supersede the already existing Arab trading families, began to rely on the centralised armed forces of the Omani colonial state (Barghat and Othman).[287] The 1840 Zanzibar Slave revolt proved to be difficult for the Omanis to control when slaves from the Zigua tribe hailing from a few miles inland from

287 Barghat and Othman, *Colonialism*

the coast opposite Zanzibar. They marched to the coast, captured a few dhows and resisted for a few months until troop reinforcements from Hadramaut arrived to suppress the revolt.

In 1851, the American Consul at Zanzibar, Charles Ward, estimated the annual rate of importation of slaves to Zanzibar to be between 8,000 and 10,000, the majority of them arriving from Kilwa. At Zanzibar the slaves could be sold either in the open market or direct to the slave-traders, and then shipped to Arabia and the Persian Gulf, where a ready market was found for slaves, the total export of slaves not smuggled from Kilwa in the five years 1862-1867 was about 97,302 (Al-Ghailani, 2015: 230).

The Barbary Coast and Galley Slavery

Up to 1, 250, 000 white European Christian captives entered the Maghrib from 1530-1780 CE as slaves, while Algeria imported about 625,000 from 1520-1830 CE.[288] Between 1500-1800 CE corsairs sanctioned by the North African governments of Tunis (Tunisia), Tripoli (in present-day Libya), Algiers and Morocco attacked European ships in the Mediterranean and raised European shores, capturing thousands of 'captives' as European writers generally refer to them, but were slaves in reality. North African Muslims took European slaves from as far as Iceland! But most were taken from southern Italy.

Giles Milton in his work *White Gold: The Extraordinary Story of Thomas Pellow and Islam's One Million White Slaves*,[289] notes that in the early 1700s the trade in white European slaves was booming throughout North Africa, even though in size it did not compare to Europe's profitable transatlantic slave trade. Most European slaves taken into North Africa passed through Salè. Milton's *White Gold* however does not seriously or critically analyse the sources and seems very Orientalist, as it exaggerates tales and stories which Milton merely accepts unquestioningly. The title of Milton's book, like Segal's, is rather sensationalist in its vocabulary and it would have been better to title the book '*North Africa's One*

288 Ibid., p.13 quoting John B. Wolf, *The Barbary Coast: Algiers Under the Turks, 1500-1830* (New York: London, 1979), p.151.

289 London: Hodder and Stoughton Ltd, 2004 and Farrar, Straus and Giroux: 2005, 2nd edition

Million White Slaves'.

The problem with Segal and Milton's works is that they never refer to anything like a "Christian black slave trade" yet frequently mention an "Islamic black slave trade" or an "Islamic white slave trade"!? In any case, Europeans were also taken as slaves and this has only been an arena which has attracted research interest recently, some note that European historians before ignored this slave trade as Europeans did not want to present themselves as being victims or were embarrassed by it. Some have even watered down the enslavement of Europeans by pandering to the European reader by referring to 'captives' as opposed to using 'slave', which in Islamic law is in fact a slave in any case. Lands to the north of the Black Sea probably yielded the most slaves to the Ottomans from 1450 CE.

A compilation of estimates indicates that Crimean Tartars seized about 1,750,000 Ukranians, Poles and Russians from 1468-1694 CE.[290] The densely populated Caucasus was also a major source of white slaves for the Middle-East[291] and from 1800-1909 CE, the Ottomans imported some 200,000 slaves from the Caucasus, mainly Circassians, with another 100,000 slaves arriving with their Circassian masters in the 1850s and 1860s. The Mamluks[292] served the Abbasid Caliphs in 9th century Baghdad and were recruited from Turkic non-Muslim slaves in areas north of the Black Sea, the steppes of modern-day south-western Russia and the Caucasus. The *Saqālibah* (sg. *Siqlabi*) were the slavs of Eastern Europe ('slav' is actually what the term 'slave' originates from, as they were a major source of slaves) and the historian Ibn Hawqal noted that these peoples were brought as slaves to Muslim Spain via

290 Clarence-Smith, op.cit., p.13. Quoting Alan B. Fisher, *"Muscovy and the Black Sea Slave Trade" in Canadian-American Slavic Studies, 6/4* (1972): pp.577-83, 592-3.

291 Clarence-Smith, *op.cit.*, p.13

292 The Mamluk sultanate of Egypt originates with the Ayyūbī ('Ayyubid') dynasty that Salahuddeen founded in 1174 CE. The Mamluks were originally European slave soldiers from Circassia, Georgia and the regions north of the Black Sea. They were either sold into slavery by impoverished steppe families or kidnapped by slave-traders. The Mamluks defeated the Mongols in Homs in 1260 CE, firstly at the Battle of 'Ayn Jālūt. The Mamluk sultanate was later conquered in 1517 CE by the Ottomans and thus came under their rule.

Galicia, Frankia, the Lombard Kingdom and Calabria in southern Italy. Shatzmiller (1993: 327) highlights that white slaves that were later freed formed the backbone of the Middle eastern armies to the extent that the Arab solider had moreorless disappeared.

Robert C. Davis emphasises that in the seventeenth century slavery was not something which white Europeans did to other people but was rather a reality which could even happen to them, due to the North African slave trade of Europeans. As a result, even though many contemporaries try to play it down, at the time it was something which was very serious and was circulated in diplomatic reports, popular broadsheets, word-of-mouth accounts throughout Europe and via narratives of those who had been enslaved in chains to be set to work in the galleys of Morocco, Algiers, Tunis or Tripoli.

The Mediterranean was a sea of fear for many southern Europeans which had many social and psychological effects upon the southern Italian coastal regions which were attacked frequently by pirates from Muslim countries. Throughout the first half of the seventeenth century theses pirates regularly went up into the Channel and even into the Thames estuary, plundering local shipping and coastal towns. The pirates from Algeria were said to have taken around 350 British ships between 1672 and 1682 CE and took between 290 and 430 British slaves per year.[293]

Galley slavery was widespread in the early modern Mediterranean and the victims were not only the enslaved but also prisoners of war, convicts and a small number of paid workers. By the sixteenth century, both the Christian powers and the Turkish Empire were capable of organising huge fleets of hundreds of galleys which each required between 150 and 300 oarsmen. Davis notes that it was a labour force which reached its maximum at the time of the Battle of Lepanto, in 1571, when an estimated 80,000 rowers were sent into action against each other,

> …most of them slaves, and not just on the Muslim side: in the galleys of Spain, France, Malta, and some Italian states one could find thousands of Moors, Turks, catholic converts, and not a few Protestants condemned to the oars. Still, by the later 1600s,

293 Robert C. Davis, *Christian Slaves, Muslim Masters: White Slavery in the Mediterranean, the Barbary Coast and Italy, 1500-1800* (Basingstoke and New York: Palgrave Macmillan, 2004), p.4

> galley slavery can be considered primarily an Islamic rather than a Christian institution, in part because the Barbary corsairs were more successful in capturing slaves, but also because the Christian powers were quicker to convert to fully-rigged sailing ships that could cruise the Mediterranean without recourse to oarsmen. In the Barbary regencies, the peak of corsairing activity – and thus the peak of demand for galley slaves – came between the late 1580s and the 1640s, a period in which the re'is of Algiers, Tunis, and Tripoli, with their 50-60 galleys, would have required 10,000-15,000 slave rowers to man the fleets. It was only towards the end of the seventeenth century, as corsairs themselves finally made the change from oared galleys to sail, that the need for slave muscle finally slackened.[294]

In Spain in the seventeenth century CE, capital crimes were punished with servitude in the galleys, a policy introduced by Ferdinand and Queen Isabella who needed to support their powerful state with labour.[295] Spain needed a standing galley fleet to protect its interests along its southern coast and in the Mediterranean using a slave-rowing force rather than use free employed oarsmen. Galleys were the main way of exploiting male convicts in Spain in the seventeenth century CE. As Christians could not serve on galleys, slaves were North African Muslims who had been captured in war and also Muslims from sub-Saharan Africa.

Coastal slaving expeditions became famous and even legendary in parts of Europe due to the terror and pillage which was associated with it, much of which totally contradicted the teachings of the Prophet Muhammad (*sallallāhu 'alayhi wassallam*).[296] These Muslim pirates not only laid

294 Ibid., pp.74-75

295 For more on this see Ruth Pike, *Penal Servitude in Early Modern Spain* (Madison: University of Wisconsin Press, 1983)

296 Indeed, the slavery of white Europeans in the Barbary regencies was quite brutal and included a number of inhumane practices which were in total opposition to the teachings of the Prophet Muhammad. For example, in Algiers slaves were kept in what were known as 'Bagnos' which were like prisons and featured regular and random beatings of captives, degrading clothing, mistreatment, enforced celibacy and other abuses of these slaves. In the galleys, slaves would number three to five to an oar and oarsmen would be chained by their wrists to the oar itself and also by their ankles, which left them with restricted movement. When slaves

their hands on as much loot and booty as they could but it is said that they also laid waste to villages and towns that they came across, they destroyed important settlements, demolished towns, burned boats and food stores and killed livestock. Pirates from Algeria took 7000 captives in the Bay of Naples in 1544 CE, 6000 were taken when they sacked Vieste in Calabria in 1554 CE, 4000 men, women and children were taken when Granada was attacked in 1566 CE, yet these rates decreased in the seventeenth century. Davis notes that the Sicilian archives also provide evidence about these slave-raids in the form of the hundreds of ransom requests sent to Palermo by Sicilian slaves and their relatives, which indicates that the island was attacked at least 136 times between 1570 and 1606 CE.[297] By the 1580s, Haëdo asserted that "Thus it is, as you know, that they have ravaged and ruined Sardinia, Corsica, Sicily, Calabria, the coasts of Naples, Rome and Genoa, the Balearics, and all the coats of Spain."[298]

The slavery of white Europeans was so abundant that a quarter of the population of Algiers were slaves, as the city was based on this form of slavery. The proportion of European slaves in Tunis and Tripoli was smaller than that of Algiers, around 10-20 percent, but in all three regencies, white slaves were both a significant and highly visible presence.[299] These high numbers of white European slaves influenced the make-up of Algiers as Algiers was described by J. Billoud as being a "white city" in terms of blood and race like European coastal ports, as opposed to reflecting a typical Moorish or Turkish city according to Billoud.[300] Also there were European reverts to Islām who were present

---

wanted to relieve themselves they would have to climb over others to go to the toilet area and those who were too exhausted would foul themselves where they sat. This resulted in a disgusting stench along with the slaves being tormented by rats, fleas, bugs and other parasites. See Davis, *op.cit*, pp.76, 134.

The allowance of this environment by Muslims goes to show how far these pirates were from applying Islām and also indicates that the corsairs/pirates of North Africa at this time were totally ignorant of Islamic standards and were more concerned with their own interests.

297 Ibid., pp.7-8

298 Ibid., p.35

299 Ibid., p.103

300 Ibid., p.205, ff.116

in Algiers at this time, who were referred to as "renegades" by the white European slaves, and also contingents of Albanians and Bulgarians serving in the militia.

There were obvious differences between Barbary (North African coastal areas) slavery and trans-Atlantic such as the fact that white Christian slaves in North Africa were able to try to pay for their freedom and return to their lands however this was rare and very difficult. Another difference was the fact that European slave traders in Africa wanted to meet market demands for labour production on the plantations. The North African slavery of white Christians who were taken as captives however was not really done so as a systematic trade as such.

Therefore, in the vast history of Islām Muslims have taken slaves, yet their actions in many cases had nothing to do with Islām as such but rather related to their own economic or political interests. Furthermore, it is important to demonstrate that slavery does not equal 'black Africans'! This in itself is one of the main errors of the likes of Segal, Azumah, black Orientalists, Afrocentrics and the missionaries. They apply slavery as meaning 'black Africans' and this is false, and in fact during the epoch of Barbary slavery it has been suggested that the white European slaves may have experienced racism. Francis Brooks, who was enslaved in Morocco, highlights that in the racial hierarchy of things, the white slaves were at the bottom receiving regular beatings from black task-masters. Brooks stated:

> The poor Christians were grievously hurried and punished by those Hellish Negroes...and had scarce any time to take any nourishment, or eat any of their bad Bread that was allowed them, but with a great many Threats, Stripes and Blows by the Negroes, bidding them turn Moors.[301]

A similar image occurs in the 1655 narrative of Abraham Browne (a white slave in Barbary) in Morocco. The black foreman overseeing Browne refuses to drink out of the same water pot as Browne which Browne was forced to carry from a well.[302] In a sermon written to commemorate the redemption of several Barbary captives, Cotton Mather, who had also

301 Francis Brooks, *Barbarian Cruelty* (London, 1693), p.12

302 Paul Baepler, "*The Barbary Captivity Narrative in American Culture*", in the journal *Early American Literature*, vol.39, no.2, January 2004, p.217.

helped to disseminate Indian captivity narratives, included accounts of the captive's plight in Africa and how black slave-drivers ordered them about and over-saw them.[303]

Mauritania

There has been much talk about Mauritania of late with talk of young boys being kidnapped from Senegalese border villages and taken into Mauritania to discussion about their own complex social structure which revolves around a caste system. Sir Thomas Fowell Buxton in 1839 authored a book on the trans-Saharan slave trade entitled *The African Slave Trade* in which he promoted the abolitionist discourse by introducing trans-Saharan slavery to the British public. Buxton however, referred to "cruel Moors", "merciless" individuals and "barbarians" and McDougall (2002) suggests that Buxton merely drew upon Orientalist discourse and the 19th century European context wherein the Ottomans were viewed as 'despotic'.

In Mauritania, this "slave" system, aka descent-based slavery, is found among the Moors and not the African tribes of Mauritania and the Moors comprise both 'black' and 'light-skinned' (of Berber and Arab-origin) peoples. Not all of the "slaves" are black, but the majority are and it is not based upon coercion as many prefer that master-slave relationship. However, in the 1980s there did appear to be some very racist policies emanating from Mauritania such as the expulsion of 70,000 black Mauritanians. Although slavery was abolished in Mauritania in 1980 in which ownership was made illegal and punishable with a fine or a prison sentence of up to ten years, it was not fully criminalised in the country until 8 August 2007. However, there have been concerns in the country over the last 25 years that 'slavery', though more of a caste system, is still entrenched in their society as an off the radar custom. David Hecht in an interesting report for the BBC on February 14 1998 entitled *'"Slavery" African Style'* stated:

> That's one reason they still call themselves 'Haratan' or slaves. Another is it has become part of their Moorish heritage. The slave/master relationship is a form of kinship. Though slaves are mostly black Africans and masters or "Bidan" have more Arab Berber blood in them, they are all members of the same clans

303 Ibid., p.219

and in some cases the blacks are the chiefs. Furthermore today there are slaves who are in fact richer than their masters. While others say they are slaves but have never been owned by anyone. Haratin are in the minority but they are well represented in the government. One is a former UN Representative to Mauritania at the UN. Clearly, when people say they are 'Haratin' it doesn't mean they are not free, and yet it's the reason the US Congress has blocked aid to Mauritania.

The interviews that I made, which Jacobs refers to, was in the poorest section of the desert town of Bootilimit where Haratin and Bidan live together, often in the same raggedy old tents in the sand. They reminded me of impoverished whites and blacks living together in the US, only of course much poorer. I later went to a slightly wealthier part of town, where I was invited to the home of a local businessmen which consisted of a larger, more colorful tent in the sand. We lay on mats and were served traditional green tea by a woman who said the businessmen in French was his 'esclave'. It turned out she was also his wife. Haratin and Bidan often intermarry and it's not an issue. There are, in fact, other castes amongst the Moors of Mauritania who are worse off than the Haratin such as the 'Znaga' or shepherd caste. And there has been terrible persecution of non-Moor ethnic minorities from the south, such as the Hal-Pulār. But, as no one can say these people are enslaved, their plight gets little international attention.

Mauritania is not an easy society to understand but what is simply, despite the misinformation of Jacobs and his anti-slavery group, is that there is not the kind of slavery here that existed in the Americas a hundred or so years ago. To claim there is, is to deny the uniquely dehumanizing experience that African Americans suffered. Even in the Hollywood version of American slavery that Steven Spielberg paints in his latest film the Amistad, one evil character argues that enslaving Africans is acceptable because Africans enslave each other. The reason this argument is wrong, we learn, is because slavery in Africa is not the same thing. In Mauritania there are no plantations, no big mansions on top of the hill. If Americans are still finding it hard to get beyond their own historical experience of slavery, maybe they are not yet in the best position to judge others.

Modern Slavery in Libya

Recently there have been reports of modern-day slavery occurring in Libya in the aftermath of its civil war. This is exacerbated by the civil war which has led to the rise of various militias who, when not fighting and butchering each other, have participated in a range of illegal and illicit activities including human trafficking of vulnerable illegal immigrants largely from various parts of Africa and apparently selling them in markets.[304]

Before we assess this matter, it would be noteworthy to initially provide some background as to the context in Libya in regards to anti-black racism and Libya's internal tribal and ethnic groups. Firstly, Libya has its own black communities, the largest and most significant being the Toubou (or 'Tebu') peoples who are based in the Kufra District of the southeastern Cyrenaica Region in southern Libya near the border with Chad. Toubou peoples are also found in Northern Chad, Niger and Sudan. The Toubou peoples of Libya during the time of Gaddafi had also complained of marginalisation and disenfranchisement, and during the 2011 Libyan Civil War were involved in the fight against Gaddafi. However, Toubou peoples of Libya have often noted that other Arab Libyan tribes have attempted to claim that they are from Chad and "not from Libya", hereby trying to assert that they are not from the country. See map below:[305]

---

304 See: https://www.thesouthafrican.com/north-african-migrants-trying-to-reach-europe-via-libya-are-being-captured-sold-into-slavery/

305 From "Libya: The Importance of Managing Southern Tribal Conflicts", 4th December 2012, *Stratfor-WorldView:* https://worldview.stratfor.com/article/libya-importance-managing-southern-tribal-conflicts Accessed 8th January 2019.

LIBYA'S TRIBES

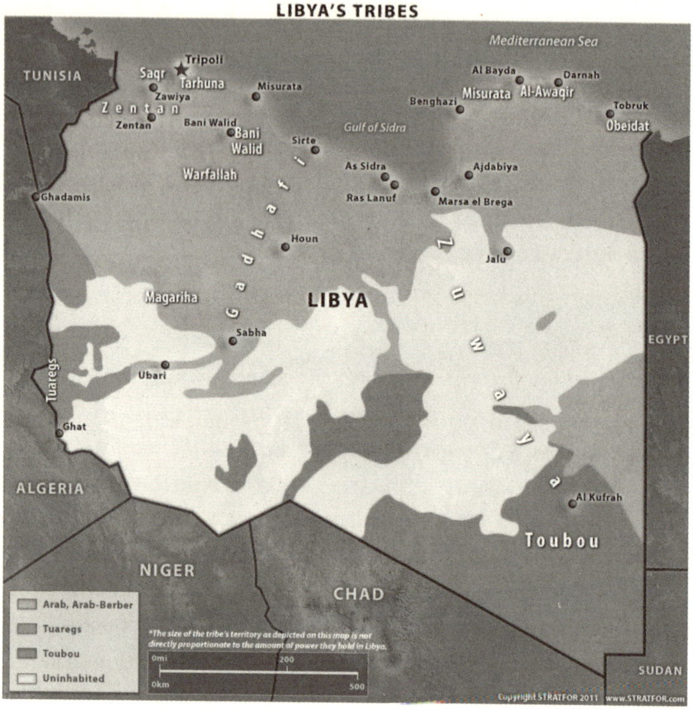

In the city of Sabha southwestern Libya in the Fezzan Region in February 2012 the Toubou asserted that they were being ethnically cleansed from the city by Arab tribes, namely the Abu Sayf tribe, and the Toubou set up their own militia, as did the Tuareg and also Arab tribes, along with competition over the scant resources in the region. A ceasefire was reached on 1 April 2012. The chaos in the country following the removal of Gaddafi saw about 4 different governments established in the country. There are also Toureg communities in Libya, who often cooperate with the Toubou due to their cultural similarities and have often. However, since the 2011 Libyan Civil War disputes occurred between the Tuareg and the Toubou, the Tripoli government backed the Tuareg and the Tobruk government backing the Toubou in the city of Ubari. In November 2015 Toubou and Tuareg representatives signed a peace accord in Doha, Qatar.[306] While in Rome on 29th March

306 See "Peace agreement between warring Libyan tribes brokered in Qatar", 24 November 2015 in *The New Arab*: https://www.alaraby.co.uk/english/news/2015/11/24/peace-agreement-between-warring-libyan-tribes-brokered-in-doha Accessed Online 8th January 2019.

2017 representatives from the Toubou tribe and the Awlad Suleiman tribe signed a permanent Peace and Reconciliation Agreement, a Tuareg delegation was also present.[307] The Italian Ministry of Interior supported the accord, and the interests of the Italians in supporting such Libyan negotiations will be discussed further shortly.

Then there is the town of Tawergha in northern Libya, 38 kilometres from Misrata, which is a predominantly black town. Misrata, known also as 'Misurata', was an Ottoman trade town and there were slaves there in the 18th century CE. It however still remains unclear as to how a large black community came to set up in Tawergha, 38 kilometres from Misrata, but it may have been after slaves were freed in the northern Libyan towns and cities of Tripoli, Benghazi and Misrata.[308] Libya was the destination of slaves from the interior of Central and Western Africa on the trans-Saharan slave trade routes and the trade was an integral part of the socio-economic fiscal revenue. It was a booming trade in the eighteenth century for Ottoman regencies such as Libya. As the northern coastal part of Libya was an Ottoman regency from 1551-1864 CE, known as the 'Wilāyat Tarāblus al-Gharb'. Interestingly, John Wright in his book *The Trans-Saharan Slave Trade* suggests that the trans-Saharan trade was not coordinated by Arabs but rather by 'Ibādī-Khārijī Berbers, Wright states:

> …the evidence suggests that not Arabs, but Berber merchants of the heretical 'Ibadi sect, managed the medieval trans-Saharan

Also see "Rival Libyan tribes sign peace deal in Qatar" in the *Middle East Eye*, Wednesday 25th November 2015 https://www.middleeasteye.net/news/rival-libyan-tribes-sign-peace-deal-qatar-state-media-413275471 Accessed Online 8th January 2019

307 Stephen Ogongo, "Two Libyan tribes Awlad Sueliam and Tebu sign a permanent Peace and Reconciliation Agreement", *Ara Pacis Initiative*, March 30 2017, see: http://arapacisinitiative.org/news/two-libyan-tribes-awlad-suleiman-and-tebu-sign-a-permanent-peace-and-reconciliation-agreement/ Accessed Online 9th January 2019

Also see "Tebu, Tuareg and Awlad Suleiman make peace in Rome", 30th March 2017 in the *Libya Herald*: https://www.libyaherald.com/2017/03/30/tebu-tuareg-and-awlad-suleiman-make-peace-in-rome/

308 John Wright, *The Trans-Saharan Slave Trade* (Abingdon, OXON and New York, NY: Routledge, 2007), pp.54, 122

> trade in black slaves, either because they had started it in the first place, or because they took it further, expanded and regulated an existing but small and random traffic.[309]

As we had noted earlier in regards to the Omani-Zanzibari slave trade, heretical 'Ibādī-Khawārij were also the main people involved in it, this may be a factor for why within these peoples there was little to no condemnation of it, a possible field for further study and research.

In August 2011 the city was besieged by anti-Gaddafi forces and accused of crimes and of supporting Gaddafi, as some of his forces were garrisoned there during their attacks on Misrata the 35,000 Tawerghans fled the city to the extent that it is now a ghost town. Thousands were displaced, some going into hiding in Sabha, some taking to the desert or staying with associates. Some Tawerghans are at unsatisfactory and unhygienic refugees camps in Benghazi, and children of Tawergha face discrimination and schools will not accept them.[310]

More recently, Libya has come to attention as a result of stories depicting modern slavery with people apparently being sold in markets. Though this appears to be more of an illicit type of human trafficking rather than "slavery" as such, and also included the capture and selling of Moroccan illegal immigrants who were in Libya, indicating that it is not a race-based issue more of a criminal human trafficking issue. Some of these traffickers are also working with elements in Ghana and Nigeria according to some reports.[311] In December 2017 the Moroccan government airlifted around 4000 sub-Saharan African migrants in Libya to repatriate them to their countries.[312] In an article for Morocco World News by Sanae Elouazi, dated 21 November 2017:[313]

---

309 Ibid., p.24

310 John Oakes, "Misuratans and the Black Tribe of Tawergha" in *Berenice Stories*, 27th January 2018: https://libyastories.com/2012/11/15/misuratans-and-the-black-tribe-of-tawergha-a-fourth-in-the-libyan-tribes-series/ Accessed Online 8th January 2019

311 See: https://www.alaraby.co.uk/english/Comment/2017/11/27/Who-is-really-responsible-for-Libyas-slave-trade

312 See: http://northafricapost.com/21008-morocco-airlift-sub-saharan-migrants-stranded-libya.html

313 The article can be accessed here: https://www.moroccoworldnews.

> The dream of reaching the "European Eldorado" through Libya has turned into a nightmare for more than 200 Moroccans, who say they were the subject of human trafficking by smugglers before being detained by Libyan forces in Tripoli and the center of Zoura near the Tunisian border. The families of Moroccans detained in Libya told the media outlet that their relatives had to pay an average of MAD 40,000 to intermediaries who were supposed to help them reach Italy. These families are also in continuous contact with the smugglers in Libya.

While Safaa Kasraoui reporting for the German online African news website *The African Courier* reported that the Moroccan Royal Gendarmerie smashed a trafficking ring based in Beni Mellal, a city located in central Morocco and arrested five people.[314] Some of the smugglers and traffickers on the southern Libyan side are actually the black Libyan tribes who earn money from transporting people from West and Central Africa into Libya and southern cities such as Sabha. An article in September 2017 by Rose-Anne Clermont and other reporters for the Online European news website *The Local* interviewed a people smuggler from the Toubou. According to METE (Multiculturalism, Earth, Territory and Education) a Palermo-based humanitarian charity organisation that helps refugees that end up in Sicily stated that the number of migrants which have landed in Italy in July 2017 was half that of 2016. There are a few reasons for this, such as EU funding into Libyan naval forces to prevent illegal immigration and also the fact that in April 2017 Italy struck a deal with the Toubou, Tuareg and Awlad Suleiman tribes of southern Libya, who profit from human trafficking at the initial stages, to create a southern Libyan border control, effectively paying off smugglers to not engage in smuggling.[315] For the southern Libyan tribes in such a marginalised and impoverished region, human trafficking is a lucrative business for those who have no other income. Italy, with other EU states, and also heads of Niger, Chad and Libya

com/2017/11/234429/moroccan-migrants-european-libya-slavery/

314 Article can be accessed here: http://www.theafricancourier.de/migration/morocco-smashes-international-migrant-smuggling-ring/

315 Rose-Anne Clermont, "Exclusive: Libyan smuggler says human trafficking will continue despite Italian deal" *The Local*, 13 September 2017: https://www.thelocal.it/20170913/exclusive-libyan-smuggler-says-human-trafficking-will-continue-despite-italian-deal Accessed 9th January 2019

came to an agreement in April 2017 to create a border patrol in southern Libya. In 2017 the EU gave Libya 180 million Euros ($215 million) to stop migrant boats in its territorial waters and to also build safe refugee camps.

Slavery and Racism in Tunisia

Tunisia presents a very interesting example as despite its attempts over the last few decades to present itself as some sort of modern liberal secular country, it is a country riddled with anti-black racism with even towns segregated along racial lines. Only just recently, October 2018, the Tunisian parliament even had to issue a law outlawing racism?![316] Black Tunisians account for 15% of the Tunisian population, as well as sub-Saharan expats and economic migrants.

It is also important to note from the outset that in the Tunisian context Islam cannot be held accountable for their own internal ignorance and racism as the nation was under the iron fist of virulent secularism for decades. Only recently in Tunisia, 2011, were Muslim women allowed to wear the Islamic attire in public places as in 1981 women wearing the hijab were banned from schools and government buildings and women wearing the hijab often lost their jobs. The Tunisian authorities at the time claimed that this was all done in order to avoid "sectarianism"?! In 2006 police were instructed to stop women in the streets and ask them to remove their hijabs!? And there was also a drive in the country to assert that the hijab was "not from Tunisian culture and came into the country uninvited"!?

Tunisia also has a record of having rulers that the major scholars have had to advise over the decades. Imām Bin Bāz *(rahimahullāh)* wrote a letter advising the former leader of Tunisia, Habeeb Bourguiba[317] over his appearance on TV during Ramadān in 1960 CE wherein Bourguiba

316 Sharan Grewal, "In another first, Tunisia criminalizes racism". *Brookings Institute*, Monday 15th October 2018. See: https://www.brookings.edu/blog/order-from-chaos/2018/10/15/in-another-first-tunisia-criminalizes-racism/ Accessed 6th January 2019

317 The name "Bourguiba" is spelt in Arabic as "Borqeebah" derived from "Boo Raqeebah" which itself is a name which is originally derived from the fus-ha "Abū Raqeebah", the name of one of his ancestors.

openly drank on TV during Ramadān saying that the economy is doing too well for the workforce to fast!? He stated on Tunisian TV on 5 February 1960:

> At a time when we are doing everything possible to increase our production, how can we resign ourselves to give up our efforts and permit the production level to descend to the zero mark? I do not believe that Islam should be able to impose such a sacrifice... this is an abusive interpretation of Islam. When fasting, man's physical forces are so depleted that he is obliged to cease all activity. No dogma is justification for such a rhythm...all practices of this religion are issues of logical intentions. But when they become incompatible with the necessary struggles of this life, Islam must be corrected.[318]

One of the ministers wrote to Imām Bin Bāz *(rahimahullāh)* thanking him for the advice saying that Islam is the religion of the state, Imām Bin Bāz said that this is not enough and Bourguiba has to openly proclaim his *tawbah* and Islam, as he openly and boldly opposed Islam. This correspondence between Imām Bin Bāz and Bourguiba and his aides was published and widely circulated. Bourguiba had also made heretical statements about the Qur'an.[319] Other scholars wrote to him requesting him to make *tawbah* and pronounce his Islam again. All of this clearly indicates to us that Tunisia over the years has not had an Islamic cultivation whatsoever, and had rather tried to pander to France, Europe and the West –all of whom did nothing to address racism in the land.

Tunisia was the first Muslim country to ban slavery in 1846 on the order of the tenth Husanid ruler Ahmad I (1805-1855),[320] while it was

---

318 See Clement Henry Moore, *Tunisia Since Independence: The Dynamics of One-Party Government* (Berkeley and Los Angeles: University of California Press, 1965), pp.56-57.

319 Refer to *Majmū' al-Fatāwā Shaykh Bin Bāz*, vol.1, p.84.

320 The Husainid Dynasty were of Cretan Turkish origin and they came into power in Tunisia in 1705 when al-Husain bin Ali defeated the Ottoman Deys. In 1881 with the Treaty of Bardo, Tunisia became a French protectorate. Prior to the Husainid Dynasty the Muradid Dynasty controlled Tunisia, and they ruled from 1613-1705 and it was founded by Murad Bey (Jacques Senti) a Janissary of Corsican origin, he was captured as a slave by Tunisian corsairs at the age of

abolished in 1884 in Egypt, 1922 in Morocco, 1951 in Libya, 1962 in Saudi Arabia and 1984 in Mauritania – we have discussed the reasons as to these dates and contexts prior, which will be worth highlighting again briefly here:

One. These Muslim states cannot be compared to the European powers of the day, the Muslim countries were not stable and often had periods of warfare, conflict, infighting and turmoil.

Two. A lot of ignorance was prevalent within the Muslim world during that period, and there was a distance from Islam generally and from Islamic knowledge particularly. This is why the main people within the Muslim world to condemn slavery within their societies and many of its injustices were the *'Ulama* [Muslim scholars].

Three. There were some legal tricks which were conducted in order to circumvent the Islamic guidelines related to slavery, such as has been seen with the issue of castration. As it was *harām*, some Muslim states, such as the Ottoman Empire and the vassal Ottoman state of Egypt under Muhammad Ali Pasha, still in theory supported and financed non-Muslim Coptic Christian monks who would perform castration operations. So although Muslims did not participate in the process, they still benefited from the people who went through the process and for which the process was conducted in the first instance. As there was a demand for slave eunuchs in the Muslim domains in the first place and hence the operations were conducted. The same is the case when it comes to manumission. It is evident that although there are clear instructions on freeing slaves within the Prophetic *ahādeeth*, as has been outlined earlier, this was seldom practiced as it was during the time of the Salaf. As during the times of the early Muslims are examples of slaves who were freed and then went on to live their lives independently rather than being viewed as little more than family pets – which appears to have occurred in the Muslim World in more recent centuries.

Four. An abolition movement may not have been deemed as necessary as Islam already had its own in-built system of abolition, via manumission contracts which were encouraged. This was unheard of in antiquity

nine and then taken to Tunis where he was purchased by the Mamluk First Bey of Tunis and later rose to become a military general and official. Modern Tunisian nationalists have framed the Husainid Dynasty as being 'Greek'.

and the medieval period, let alone cases of mass slave redemptions as occurred with the Companions of the Prophet Muhammad. Moreover, Muslim history was replete with examples of ex-slaves rising to positions of authority in government and other positions. There was therefore a meritocracy regardless of whether one came from a slave background, this aspect of 'Muslim slavery' baffles many as slavery is usually seen as synonymous with the form which occurred in the Americas and its oppression, racism, brutality and injustice. Islam was therefore not pleased with slavery, yet cooperated with it as it was a system in operation prior to Islam's spread. Islam in the first few generations was therefore seen as emancipatory, this egalitarian trend however in later generations was lost.

Five. The slave system in the Muslim World was generally not the same as that of Trans-Atlantic slavery, and hence there were instances when slaves rose to positions of authority, as has been outlined in this chapter. This could not occur within Trans-Atlantic slavery as indulged in by the European powers and in the Americas. Hence, the Trans-Atlantic slave trade was something which the European powers wanted to get rid of due to its injustices, racism and oppression. This was done with a degree of sanctimony and cynicism I opine, as the European powers had already cashed in on slavery for centuries and then after they did, had the audacity to then turn to the Muslim World and encourage them to abolish slavery.

Six. Moreover, in the Muslim World, as in the case of the Ottomans, there were slaves who were white as well and so it may not have been seen as a purely black phenomenon. This is why in some cases, as noted earlier, the Ottomans turned a blind eye to white slavery of Circassians for decades, which they benefitted from, as the European powers seemed more focused on the abolition of slavery of Africans.

In 1847 it was declared that the children of those born into slavery in Tunisia would be deemed free.[321] From an Islamic scholarly perspective, the main Tunisian scholars at the time fully agreed with Ahmad Bey's

321 Ines Mrad-Dali, "From Forgetting to Remembrance: Slavery and Forced Labour in Tunisia" in Nicola Frith and Kate Hogdson (eds.), *At the Limits of Memory: Legacies of Slavery in the Francophone World* (Oxford: Oxford University Press, 2015), p.191.

decision and one of them made reference to the works of Ahmad Baba at-Timbuktī that during that period many free black people had been enslaved.[322]

From a political perspective Ahmad Bey I also had to present liberal and modernising reforms to Britain and France who were promoting abolition at the time. Ahmad Bey I's inner circle included like-minded individuals some of whom were former Mamluks, and there was a reforming zeitgeist in tandem with the Ottoman *Tandhimāt* ['Tanzimat'] reforms. The Muslim World, as discussed earlier, were under pressure from the French to end slavery, the British themselves were under pressure from the slave abolitionist movement. In 1842 the Sultan of Morocco at the time 'AbdurRahmān bin Hishām (1822-59) was approached by the British consul to take measures to end slavery.

As a result, anti-slavery became the *zeitgeist* at the time among the British and by the mid-19th century when they wanted to abolish it for others in the Muslim World they themselves had already made a tidy profit from slavery in any case. The Muslim World also had economic interests in the 19th century slave trade. Elisabeth C. Van der Haven (2006: 43) noted that by the end of the eighteenth, begin nineteenth century a yearly amount of approximately 1000 to 1300 slaves were imported in Tunisia, according to information found in the correspondence of the English consul with Whitehall in the late years of the eighteenth century.[323]

In 1841 no more than twenty to thirty slaves, most of them women, were bought or sold in the Sūq al-Birka, where the weekly slave market in Tunis was held every Friday. The buying and selling procedure of slaves was regulated by a governor (*qā'id*) from his so called *qafa* (cage), on an elevated platform in the middle of the market. On one side of the platform were seated together – on a rug – the sellers and the official clerks to witness the sale (*udūl*), on the other side the slaves for whom a bidding was not yet made.[324] On the 17th May 1793 a delegation of

322 Elisabeth Cornelia Van der Haven, "The Abolition of Slavery in Tunisia", p.66 see: https://openaccess.leidenuniv.nl/bitstream/handle/1887/4968/second%20chapter%20dissertatie.pdf Accessed 5 January 2019

323 Ibid.

324 Ibid., p.44

black slaves from the French colony of Saint Domingo (Haiti) sailed to France and addressed the National Convention in Paris demanding the liberation of all slaves in the French colonies in America. In 1794 the French did just that.

However, though slavery was abolished in Tunisia in a legal sense, in a social sense it was still prevalent. Ahmad Bey I freed many slaves he had and they went on to become paid employees, for many however their societal position remained absolutely the same and they were kept within family bonds, whereas those who did not have any sort of familial protection were resigned to the margins of Tunisian society with some falling into crime, prostitution, peddling or menial employment.

In 1890 there was a second 'abolition' enacted by the French protectorate authorities in Tunisia who may have merely been trying to repair their tarnished global image at the time as it was believed that the French resident minister Justin Massicault who governed Tunisia from 1886-92 had made use of slave labour himself. Moreover, Mrad-Dali notes that by 1890 women and children were still being illegally enslaved in Tunisia, men were able to leave their former master more easily.[325] While Hamli (2011) reveals that Tunisian courts answerable to the Bey did not recognise crimes committed against 'Sudanese' (i.e. black) slaves, this was taken to mean that slavery was still accepted in the country by 1890 even after the supposed abolition. While some French courts were not sanctioning French slave-traders by this time, despite French sanctimony at the time about the abolition of the trade.[326] For more on the topic of slavery in Tunisia refer to Ismael Montana's *The Abolition of Slavery in Ottoman Tunisia*.[327]

The repercussions of slavery in Tunisia are still felt today by modern black Tunisians as on the birth certificates of some black Tunisians the words 'owned by' (in Tunisian dialect '*chouchane*') are written on some

325 Ibid., p. 200.

326 For more on this refer to Mohen Hamli, "The 1890 legal wrangles over Sudanese slaves in Tunisia." *The Journal of North African Studies*, vol.16, issue 3, July 2011, pp.421-429

327 Ismael Musah Montana, *The Abolition of Slavery in Ottoman Tunisia* (Gainsville: University Press of Florida, 2013).

birth certificates in the country (Mrad-Dali, 2015).[328] Many of the black Tunisians are descendants of former slaves known as the "'Abid Ghbonton." The Tunisian city of Djerba even has segregated cemeteries according to colour,[329] and intermarriage is also frowned upon. It has even been relayed that when a black Tunisian rights activist from the organisation known as Mnemty presented an example of this to Abdel-Bari Atwan, a Palestinian journalist based in London and famed for media appearances, he at first said that he would address the matter. Instead, he has merely sufficed with saying that the matter has been "exaggerated" and that there is no racism against black Tunisians[330] – hereby indicating a tangible example of the playing down of anti-black racism which is prevalent among many Arabs, which I have alluded to earlier in this study. The surnames of some black Tunisians, those who are of slave origin, highlight that they were the property of some prominent Tunisian families.

In regards to segregation in Tunisia in certain southeastern Tunisian towns in the Gabes and Medenine regions, such as in the village of Gosbah and Sidi Makhlouf in Medenine, to the extent that there are separate buses for black Tunisians, Atwan is reported to have stated "they are lucky to have two buses"?![331] Demonstrating the ignorance and low priority surrounding race within the Middle East and among some modern Arabs. Yet some Arabs express sanctimony over Israeli aggression and expect the entire Muslim Ummah to rally around to point out Zionist oppression, and at the same time will sweep under the carpet discrimination within their own countries against black Arab

---

328 For more on this see the research of Ines Mrad-Dali, "From Forgetting to Remembrance: Slavery and Forced Labour in Tunisia" in Nicola Frith and Kate Hogdson (eds.), *At the Limits of Memory: Legacies of Slavery in the Francophone World* (Oxford: Oxford University Press,2015), pp.191-208

329 See Eileen Byrne, "Black citizens say racism still an issue in the new Tunisia" in the online *The National*, 18th February 2014: https://www.thenational.ae/world/black-citizens-say-racism-is-still-an-issue-in-the-new-tunisia-1.256661 Accessed Online 8th January 2019

330 Conor McCormick-Cavanagh, "Tunisia's dark history of racial discrimination" in the online *The New Arab*, 10th June 2016. See: https://www.alaraby.co.uk/english/comment/2016/6/10/tunisias-dark-history-of-racial-discrimination Accessed 5th January 2019

331 Ibid.

communities, south Asian workers and African and Filipino maids.

An al-Jazeera documentary entitled *Tunisia's Dirty Secret* reveals that such discrimination against black Tunisians are not "exaggerated" or isolated, as the likes of the political commentator Atwan asserts. In the documentary a black Tunisian can be seen being referred to by derogatory names while walking in the streets.[332] On 26 December 2016, three Congolese students were stabbed at a train station in the capital Tunis.

Modern-day Slavery in Europe and Contemporary Sexual Slavery in Europe, America, Japan and Israel

The UK Home Office according to research it conducted in July 2018 noted that modern-day slavery costs the UK £4.3bn a year! In an article by Jamie Grierson for *The Guardian* newspaper (of London), dated Monday 30th July 2018, it was noted that the Home Office report outlined that each instance of the crime costs around £330,000 including support, lost earnings and law enforcement. As a result of the 2018 report the UK Home Office said it would review Modern Slavery Act 2015.[333] While Hannah Wheatley also writing in the *The Guardian*, on the same date, stated in an article entitled *Slavery still exists in modern Britain: My campaign aims to end that*:

> The estimate of the number of suspected victims of trafficking and modern slavery in Britain has risen tenfold from 13,000 in 2013, to 136,000 in 2018. Last year, there were 5145 cases reported in the UK – the highest on record – and 41% involved children under 18. Thousands of victims are trafficked into slavery in the UK and kept hidden in plain sight, often working seven days a week for little or no pay in nail salons, car washes, building sites, kitchens, factories and farms. They are trapped, abused and exploited, with no hope of returning to their loved ones.[334]

332 *Tunisia's Dirty Secret*, al-Jazeera, see: https://www.youtube.com/watch?v=cy-f9G6MrLY&feature=youtu.be

333 Article can be accessed here: https://www.theguardian.com/world/2018/jul/30/modern-day-slavery-costs-uk-up-to-43bn-a-year-says-home-office

334 Article accessed here: https://www.theguardian.com/commentisfree/2018/jul/30/slaves-britain-human-trafficking

In another article in *The Guardian* by Annie Kelly, dated Thursday 19th July 2018 she noted:

> Billions of pounds worth of laptops, mobile phones and clothing likely to have been made using slave labour are being bought by UK consumers every year, researchers have said. The global slavery index, which attempts to measure the scope and scale of slavery across the world, claims that G20 countries annually import more than £272bn of products from places with a high prevalence of modern slavery. The UK imported £14bn of "at risk" goods last year including electronics, garments, fish, chocolate and sugar, said the study. The US was found to have imported similar goods worth $144bn (£110bn), making it by far the biggest global importer of products potentially made by slaves. The authors of the index said public demand for products at low prices was allowing slavery to thrive across the world.

Then Kelly said at the end of the article:

> The authors of the study estimated that 136,000 people in the UK live as slaves, a number 12 times higher than the official government figure of 13,000. North Korea has the highest number of people living in slavery, with estimates suggesting that one in 10 North Koreans are victims of state-sponsored forced labour. Eritrea, Burundi, Central African Republic and Afghanistan were also named among countries with the largest number of slaves per capita. Last year, Walk Free along with the International Labour Organisation and the UN's International Organisation for Migration released a new global estimate of 40.3 million people thought to be in conditions of slavery. Women account for 71% of this total, with 15.4 million believed to be victims of forced marriage.[335]

All of this occurring within the vicinity of a Christian country. Now it would not be fair to pin this onto Christianity, so by the same token it can also not be fair to utilise instances of human rights abuses, human trafficking and modern slavery in the Muslim world against Islam. Furthermore, the non-Muslim 'developed' world has a huge problem with what has come to be known as a "sex slave trade", which seems to be discreetly swept under the carpet by those who like to constantly

335 Article accessed here: https://www.theguardian.com/global-development/2018/jul/19/british-public-14bn-goods-slaves-global-slavery-index

point the finger at Islām for slavery whether historical or contemporary. *The Department of Health and Human Services - Rescue and Restore Campaign* defines sex trafficking as "a modern day form of slavery in which a commercial sex act is induced by force, fraud or coercion." Europe currently has a problem with a huge "sex-slave" smuggling and trafficking trade and estimates are that as many as 120,000 women every year are smuggled into Western Europe![336] Martin Wainwright stated in an article for *The Guardian* (of London) in 2007 entitled *'Slavery returns to Britain on large scale, study say'*:

> Slavery has made a "horrific" return to modern Britain, according to the most wide-ranging study of the secret world of forced labour yet published. Shocking statistics about the country's sex trade, including an estimated 5,000 under-16s coerced into prostitution, mask equally violence-ridden and illegal practices in jobs ranging from crop picking and factory work to nursing and the catering trade. Victims are now in the tens of thousands, according to the report by researchers at Hull University, commissioned by the Joseph Rowntree Foundation. It says that parts of the economy depend on slave labour, in the same way that 18th century industries like sugar profited from the "triangular trade" between West Africa, the Caribbean and Western Europe. "We are not devaluing an emotive word," said Professor Gary Craig, associate director of the Wilberforce Institute for the study of slavery and emancipation at Hull. "The shackles may not always be physical, although I have no doubt that in some cases they are. Debt bondage, theft of passports and ID, and threats of violence are tools of slavery." The report details case after case where conditions contravene the United Nations' 10-point definition of forced labour. Prof Craig and co-author Aidan McQuade, director of Anti-Slavery International, say a large percentage also meet the three definitions of modern slavery: extreme economic exploitation, absence of human rights and actual or threatened violence. Documented instances include two Vietnamese men who paid £18,000 to an agent in Vietnam for London hotel jobs, came to Britain legally for work agreed at £4.95 an hour, but then had their passports taken by the agent's British counterpart and were given food only for two months. When they protested, their families in Vietnam were threatened with violence. A woman from Latvia had her passport confiscated by a Hull agency that

336 See *"EU 'to protect' sex slaves"*, *BBC Online*, Thursday 8 March 2001.

> forced her to work 16-hour shifts at a Barnsley factory, sleeping between them in a car. A couple from Eastern Europe paid another Yorkshire agency £250 for an "introduction to work" in the Humber port of Goole, where they were underpaid and slept in a dormitory shared with eight men. "When they said that they were going to tell the police, their savings of £200 were stolen and the woman was threatened with violence," says the report. "They estimated that there were at least another 800 people in the area living and working in the same circumstances." The findings were endorsed yesterday by Archbishop Desmond Tutu, who said he was shocked by the spread of slavery. He said: "I just didn't know about all these forms that exist. It is hidden. Generally people would not believe that it is possible under modern conditions." Prof Craig said: "That is our most important point. So many people say: 'Come on, slavery was then, and this is now. It can't possibly happen.' But it does, and on a large scale." The report calls for the government to acknowledge that most victims came to Britain legally but were then trafficked by criminals into illegal jobs. Prof Craig said: "There is still an attitude that trafficked people are illegal entrants, rather than victims, so on top of all their suffering they are then deported." It suggests improved training for employment agency and local council staff to spot potential slavery conditions, and for the government to ratify the recent Council of Europe convention against the trafficking of people, something the prime minister, Tony Blair, has promised but not yet done."[337]

A US government report published in 2002 estimated that 50,000 people a year are trafficked into the US and in 2003 said that the figures were about 18,000 to 20,000. A US *Department of Justice* report in June 2004 said that 14,500-17,000 women were smuggled into the US annually, the majority of these sex slaves from Eastern Europe and East Asia. In Italy it is estimated that there could be more than 40,000 foreign prostitutes, mostly from Albania. The former Italian MP, Carol Bebbe Tarantelli says that the women are slaves:

> They are brought here…their passports are destroyed often, usually as a matter of fact they are tortured to break down their wills. They're moved around from place to place so they don't

337 Martin Wainwright, '*Slavery returns to Britain on large scale, study say*' in *The Guardian* (of London), Monday February 26 2007

> know where they are. They don't speak the language, they're terrified and they can't escape. They're held in slavery.[338]

In the UK, *'Operation Pentameter'* was established to tackle the sexual slavery gang problems that occur in the UK. Some of these women were tricked, thinking they were coming over for employment and then enslaved for the sex slave trade.

> Many have been tempted to the UK by promises of a lucrative summer job; others have come after trafficking gangs posed as employment agencies insisted their parents sign consent forms to permit them to travel. The investigation has also shed light on what appear to be the beginnings of a shift in the landscape of the country's slave trade, police say...Most trafficked women still come from countries such as Albania, Poland, the Czech Republic, Slovakia, Romania and Lithuania; others from China, Thailand and some African states...three months ago police believed women were being sold from between £3000 and £4000.[339]

Simon Jeffrey noted with regards to Europe's sexual slaves that:

> Three quarters of them are foreign, with many smuggled into the country from Eastern Europe and Asia as sex slaves...the largest numbers were from Thailand, Russia, Brazil and Kosovo. Superintendent Chris Bradford said "It's like a slave market."

Richard Elias reported that:

> Six thousand women are being held as sex slaves in Scotland, police said yesterday. Brutal gangs imprison the terrified girls in brothels, rape them repeatedly to break their spirits and force them to have sex with up to 60 men per day...Senior cops believe that 85 per cent...are sex slaves trafficked into Britain from Eastern Europe and elsewhere.[340]

Kevin Bales, author of *Disposable People: New Slavery in the Global Economy* and president of Free the Slaves, a Washington based anti-

---

338 *"Italy's sexual slave trade"*, *BBC Onlin*e Edition, Wednesday 2 August 2000

339 See Paul Lewis, *"Nightmare world of suburban sex slaves"* in *The Guardian* (of London), Monday May 8 2006.

340 Richard Elias, *"Scotland's 6000 sex slaves"* in the *Daily Record* (of Scotland), 22 February 2006

slavery NGO, estimated that up to 250,000 sex slaves exist in the US. Donna M. Hughes, Professor of Women's Studies at the *University of Rhode Island* stated:

> Men physically travel the world to buy women and children in prostitution as a form of tourism…The methods used in trafficking for sexual exploitation comprise a modern slave trade.[341]

As for within Israel, according to Matthew Gutman, about 3000 women from Russia are bought and sold in Israel each year,[342] most of the women are from the former Soviet Union.[343] Chaim Nardi, a sociologist at *Tel Aviv University* compiled a report on the sale of women in 2000 CE and has since updated it.

As for Japan then during the Second World War imperial Japan recruited around 200,000 from non-Japanese Far-Eastern countries to be sex slaves in military brothels, these women were known as "comfort women" (*Ianfu*).[344] *Chuo University* Professor Yoshiaki Yoshimi states there were about 2,000 centers where as many as 200,000 Korean, Chinese, Japanese, Filipino, Taiwanese, Burmese, Indonesian, Dutch and Australian women were interned.[345] According to Professor Hirofumi Hayashi from Kanto Gakuin University, the majority of the women were from Japan, Korea and China. Others came from the Philippines, Taiwan, Thailand, Vietnam, Singapore, Dutch East Indies and other Japanese-occupied countries. Yuki Tanaka's book *Japan's Comfort Women: Sexual Slavery and Prostitution during World War II and the US Occupation* also documents the plight of these "comfort women"

341 Ed Vitalgliano, AFA Journal (Online Edition) April 2004

342 Matthew Gutman, *"Pressured by US, Israel Battles a Burgeoning 'White Slave' Trade"* in the weekly magazine *Forward* of New York (June 28 2002).

343 *"Israel women trafficking soars"*, *BBC Online News* (Thursday, 24 March 2005).

344 For testimonies and accounts by former comfort women, see, for example, Maria Rosa Henson, *A Filipina's Story of Prostitution and Slavery under the Japanese Military* (Lanham: Rowan & Littlefield, 1999); and Keith Howard (ed.), *Korean Council for Women Drafted for Military Sexual Slavery by Japan: True Stories of the Korean Comfort Women,* (London: Cassell Academic, 1996).

345 *Comfort Women: Sexual Slavery in the Japanese Military during World War II*, S. O'Brien, Trans. (NY: Columbia University Press, 2000). Original work published 1995.

of the Japanese.[346]

Japanese authorities hoped that by providing easily accessible prostitutes and sexual slaves, the morale and ultimately the military effectiveness of Japanese soldiers would be improved. Also, by institutionalizing brothels and placing them under official scrutiny, the government hoped to control the spread of Sexually Transmitted Diseases. In the early stages of the war, Japanese authorities recruited prostitutes through conventional means. Middlemen advertised in newspapers circulating in Japan and the Japanese colonies of China, Korea, Taiwan and other places. Many who answered the advertisements were already prostitutes and offered their services voluntarily. Others were sold by their families to the military due to economic hardship.

However, these sources soon dried up, especially from Japan. The Ministry of Foreign Affairs resisted further issuance of travel visas for Japanese prostitutes, feeling it tarnished the image of the Japanese Empire. The military turned to acquiring comfort women outside of mainland Japan, especially from Korea and occupied China. Many women were tricked or defrauded into joining the military brothels, many were also kidnapped from the rural areas as the Japanese military demanded that local leaders get women for them. Neither admission of such sex slavery has been stated nor any legal responsibility for such abuses.

Chapter Conclusion

Dr Yusuf Progler of the University of New York has noted however, that the polemic over Africans, Muslims, Arabs and slavery has an aspect that is driven by politics. In the 1960s there was a decision taken by politicized scholars to discredit Islām in the eyes of Africans and African-Americans.[347] Indeed, W.E.B. Dubois highlighted that: "In this whole story of the so-called 'Arab slave trade' the truth has been

346 London: Routledge, 2002.

347 This was due to the fact that many African-American civil rights groups were expressing their solidarity with the Palestinians as an oppressed people. The '*American-Israel Public Affairs Committee,*' a well funded and powerful Zionist lobby in Washington, monitored African-American supporters of the Palestinians such as Kwame Toure.

strangely twisted."[348] Due to the apartheid that was practiced in South Africa and likewise in occupied Palestine there was solidarity between Africans and Arabs throughout the 1960s and 70s in the West, therefore a divide was made between them. Progler notes that:

> Arab-American scholars subsequently uncovered a plan for driving a wedge between Arabs and Africans and the role of American academic institutes in achieving it. They found increasing attention to the Arab role in African slavery began in the 1970s, when the Ford Foundation funded a series of seminars at Princeton University. The choice of subject matter for the seminars provided strong evidence that political preferences resulted in the formulation and support of scholarly agendas. One of the seminars dealt with 'slavery and related institutions in Africa.' The grant proposal for the Princeton seminars emphasized a supposed African fear and resentment of Arabs and Muslims. Invited Israeli scholars tried to persuade black nationalist leaders not to rely on Arab nations, claiming that the Arab slave traders depopulated African countries. By convoluting slavery, Arabs, and Islam, the seminars were designed to destroy relations between Africans, Arabs, and Muslims. To assure the main achievement of this aim, Princeton did not invite any Muslim or Arab scholars.

Hishām Aidi, a researcher at *Columbia University*, has also noted how:

> Israel and Zionist organizations have long been interested in the issue of race and ethnicity in the Arab world. Israel has a long history of training and arming groups in Kurdistan and southern Sudan...The Zionist concern for minorities in the Arab world is strategic: by focusing on how Arab states (mis) treat their minorities, pro-Israel scholars can shift the spotlight from Palestine, highlight Arab double standards, demonstrate how the subordinate status of minorities in the Middle East necessitated a Zionist project...and show how Israel protects minority rights better than any other state in the region.[349]

There are certain Zionist websites, some of which are sites of former Israeli heads of state, which are excellent examples of this and furthermore in

---

348 W.E.B. Dubois, *The World and Africa* (New York: International Publishers Inc., 1969) p.68

349 Hishām Aidi, "Slavery, Genocide and the Politics of Outrage – Understanding the New Racial Olympics" in *Middle East Report* (Spring 2005).

2001 C.E. Rabbi Schmuley Boteach tried to organize a visit to Sudan for a number of African-Americans including the Reverend Al Sharpton, to "reconnect them with their people"!?[350] The trip would also include a trip to Israel to visit Israeli victims of terrorism. Sharpton himself caused anger to the Jewish organizers of the event when he went to visit Yasser Arafat![351] Hishām Aidi thus noted how:

> Most of those who address the subject of race in the Arab world – including Bernard Lewis himself - have a political axe to grind. They use to seek race as an ideological weapon to counter African-American claims that Islam is "better on race" than the West, or to shift attention from Palestine to Arab oppression of some minority.

Thus, they strategically and deliberately look at the Muslim-Arab world and nowhere else where oppression is taking place. Quite simply, Islām is about liberation and the Qur'ān contains many verses about equality and human dignity. Later generations of Muslims had not remained true to the teachings of Islām and thus the horrific and terrible examples of rapacious and miserly Muslims can be seen with the histories of Zanzibār, Morocco, Mauritania and 'Irāq, all attesting to this. Dr Progler also remarked that:

> The two most often cited cases of Arab involvement in African slavery were unusual moments in an otherwise mutually productive interaction. Both were in the 19th century. One involved Muhammad Ali Pasha, a Westernizing despot who

350 Maybe Rabbi Schmuley should work on reconnecting his own people in Israel to the reality of the sex slave industry which is prevalent in Israel! About 3000 women from Russia are brought and sold in Israel each year. In one particular case, eighteen men were involved in drug sales, smuggling, trafficking and prostitution of women. The women were bought for $7500 and traded in and bartered with for all sorts of goods. "They were tortured and measured and prodded in heinous ways to ensure quality of product" a central district policeman stated. See Matthew Gutman, *"Pressured by US, Israel Battles a Burgeoning 'White Slave' Trade"* in the weekly magazine *Forward* of New York (June 28 2002). Chaim Nardi, a sociologist at *Tel Aviv University* compiled a report on the sale of women in 2000 and has since updated it.

351 Ibid.

> ruled Egypt in the first half of the 19th century.[352] Just as the slave trade was being outlawed in Euro-American metropoles, Ali Pasha picked up the slack by engaging in slave expeditions to the southern Nile region, the Sudan. The other instance involved the Sultan of Oman in a similar scheme, this time to harvest spices on plantations he and his European partners ran off the coast of East Africa. But these sad moments in Arab-Muslim-African history are not representative of the thousand year contact between African and Arab cultures in the context of Islamic civilization. They are projected back in history, using selective and at times spurious evidence, to build a case for alleged centuries of Arab slavery, and for confusing them with the forms of slavery practiced by Europeans.[353]

Dr Yusuf Progler says that an example of this stereotyping of Muslims and Arabs can be seen in the anti-Islamic Afrocentric book *Black Holocaust for Beginners* which on one page depicts a turbaned Arab raping a naked African woman while his harem of wives, covered in full black Islamic attire of the *Niqāb* and *ʻAbayah* look on!! This is an image which itself is based on that of a European Orientalist fantasy. "This unlikely image is presented as the sum total of centuries of Arab-Muslim-African co-existence."[354] However, Progler seems to suggest that the slave trade on thc East African coast, orchestrated by the likes of Ali Pasha and the Omani Sultans of Zanzibar, was all coordinated in association with European powers when this was not the case. The likes of Rumaliza and Tippu Tip were not acting in conjunction with Europeans, the contrary in fact. As noted earlier, in many cases slavery on the East African coats was only brought to an end via European intervention and gunboat diplomacy. Progler also fails to note instances of slavery in the Muslim world in Mauritania, Morocco, the Zanj Rebellion, the Barbary Coast

352 The Turko-Egyptian conquest of the Sudan upset the regional balance. This new power had far greater resources at its command than any of the indigenous Sudanese kingdoms. It also made for greater demands on its subjects for slaves and tribute. The northern Sudanese peoples of Nubia, Sennar, Kordofan and the Red Sea were the first to be conquered and they were the first to be conquered into collaboration with the army in massive slave-raids into the hinterlands. See Douglas H. Johnson, *African Issues: The Root Causes of Sudan's Civil Wars* (Indiana: Indiana University Press, 2004 and Oxford: James Currey), pp.4-5.

353 Ibid.

354 Ibid.

and the Ottoman Eunuch usage; Ali Pasha and the Omani experience are but two examples.

Shaykh Sālih bin 'Abdullāh bin Humayd (Imām of *Masjid al-Harām*, Makkah and a former Professor of Islamic Law at *Umm ul-Qurā' University* in Makkah), states superbly that:

> ...it is only in this century that the Westerners have felt a touch of consciousness. It is a great injustice on their part to feel superior to Islamic legislations which were ordained more than fourteen centuries back. It is rather a case of 'projection' charging others with one's own faults.[355]

The practice of slavery in early Islām was radically different to that in the Americas, wherein the status of a slave was linked to a person's colour, slavery and colour was synonymous within this context. Diouf highlights: "Thus, freed Africans and their children, who should have been – according to their own culture and religion – fully integrated into American societies, remained the objects of humiliation, segregation, discrimination and racism, a condition that could have only damaging psychological as well as social repercussions."[356] Basil Davidson, one of the distinguished historians of Africa noted in his book on the slave trade:

> Some European writers, possibly out of an understandable but quite unhistorical conviction that 'Europe should not bear all the blame,' have tended to equate the Asian-Arab trade with the European trade, or even to portray the first as much larger than the second...This argument will not bear examination. There is not a shred of evidence that the Indian Ocean trade ever carried, or could have carried, a tithe of the slaves that were taken across the Atlantic...The clinching fact is that the eastern world...never knew an economic situation which could have used captive labor on the scale of the Caribbean and American mines and plantations.[357]

Indeed, Davidson was referring to the fact that some historians (such as

---

355 Saleh Abdullah Bin Humaid, *op.cit.*, p.52

356 Diouf, *op cit.*, p.15

357 Basil Davidson, *Black Mother – The Years of the African Slave Trade* (Boston: Little, Brown & Co., 1961 and UK: James Currey Publications, 1994), p.80.

Paul Bairoch) have claimed that the numbers of slaves that were taken across sub-Saharan Africa reached a total of 25 million slaveş against the 11 million of the trans-Atlantic slave trade!?[358] This is an example of the extravagance that many have over this issue and how some historians arrive at any array of figures with no evidence whatsoever. Ralph Austen for example, attempted to provide rough calculations on the number of slaves taken via the Sahara; however his figures are only based on meagre sources.[359] Raymond Mauvy also claims that 14 million slaves were traded in throughout the Muslim world from the seventh century up to the twentieth century. Yet again, this figure does not really reflect the demographics, as there would thus be huge communities of black people descended from slaves in Arab countries, and although there are some who would fit that background, if these conjectural figures were accurate there would be black descendants of slaves that would number the amounts of black people in the Americas for example. However, as Davidson has noted, slaves were very expensive so these high rates and figures do not add up. For example, sub-Saharan African Muslim captives which were sold in North Africa from the eleventh to fifteenth centuries CE were expensive due to the costs of trans-Saharan commerce and were only an exception rather than the rule during thirteenth and fourteenth century Portugal.[360]

Importantly, the thrust to depict Islām as an intrinsically racist entity which justified slavery of people of African origin was promoted by a variety of Zionist and pro-'Israeli' scholars. Bernard Lewis in his book that was supposed to assess 'Race and Color' in Islām in fact did not bring forth the clear evidences of the sources texts of Islām and only quoted from scholars who were not known for their Islamic knowledge. Israel Shahak in *Jewish History, Jewish Religion* states, in refutation of Lewis,

> None of the passages that Lewis mentions even approach certain

358 Paul Bairoch, *Economics and World History: Myths and World History* (Chicago: University of Chicago, 1993).

359 Ralph Austen, "*The Trans-Saharan Slave Trade: A Tentative Census,*" in H.A. Gemery and J.S. Hogendorn (eds.), *The Uncommon Market: Essays in the Economic History of the Atlantic Slave Trade* (New York: Academic Press, 1979), pp.66-68.

360 Leslie B. Rout Jr, *African Experience in Spanish America: 1502 to the Present Day* (Cambridge, England: Cambridge University Press, 1976), pp.3-12.

> Talmudic statements...without mentioning all sides, the attack on Islam is mere slander.[361]

Ronald Segal, of South African Jewish extraction, has a book entitled *'Islam's Black Slaves.'* The title is immediately quite strange and gives the impression that Islām itself promotes the slavery of 'blacks' and as a result many Kemet Afrocentrics refer to the book. Segal repeatedly refers to what he calls 'Islamic black slavery' and the 'Islamic black slave trade' (on pages 60, 197, 238 for example) and also refers to what he erroneously describes as the "slave markets of Islam" (on page 56 for example) which is all quite deceptive as it attempts to show that there was a systematic focus on black people as slaves, which was 'Islamic'.

Segal never refers to the "slave markets of the Christians in America" or to the "slave markets of the Christians in the Caribbean" or to a contemporary "European and Anglo-American Christian sex slave trade" or to a "Jewish sex slave trade"[362] but as is the case with the Orientalists, black and white, when it comes to Islām those who nominally attach themselves to it are seen as behaving in the name of Islām, while when it comes to other people the same is not ascribed. In this way, the religion of Islām is accused, indicted and charged.[363] There was never any Islamic justification given for enslaving black people exclusively or Muslims, and we do not find any scholars who even attempted to use the Qur'ān or the Sunnah to justify it.

This is in contrast to what developed in Christianity wherein many

---

361 Israel Shahak, *Jewish History, Jewish Religion: The Weight of Three Thousand Years* (London: Pluto Press, 1994), p.106.

362 These will be discussed later on in this chapter.

363 An example of how Segal's book has been applauded and heavily relied upon by the Christian fundamentalists and evangelist missionaries can be seen with the *'Christian Action'* magazine (vol.4, 2004) in a piece entitled '*The Scourge of Slavery*' where only Islām was accused, while Christianity was mentioned in the context of being a heroic American saviour! The article quotes Segal some 5 times! The article has since been placed on the 'Frontline Fellowship' website, a Christian missionary group who conduct evangelical preaching and anti-Islamic propaganda in Africa, particularly in Southern Sudan, Sudan, Chad and other parts of Africa. See an online version of the article here: http://www.frontline.org.za/index.php?option=com_content&view=article&id=312:the-scourge-of-slavery-the-rest-of-the-story&catid=20:africa-cat

Christians actually tried to justify slavery of Africans exclusively on the false story basis that the Prophet Noah cursed his son Canān to be a slave to other nations. This is important, as those who try to show that Islām was intrinsically racist cannot bring one bona fide Islamic scholar to support this. So for example, Lewis, Segal and John Alembillah Azumah (who we will discuss later) quote from racist individuals who were not known for their knowledge of the Islamic sciences at all, and this is misleading. Clarence-Smith noted that Turks, including 'Mongoloid' and 'Caucasoid' racial classifications were probably as numerous as Africans in the central lands of Islām from the ninth to the fourteenth century.[364]

There is a very interesting example from the time of the early Muslims, the *Salaf us-Sālih*, found in the book *Zuhūr ul-Basāteen Tārīkh as-Sawādeen* [Flowers in the Garden Regarding the History of the Blacks] by Shaykh Mūsā Kamara (*rahimahullāh*).[365] He quotes a passage from a book by Muhammad Ibn Mūsā Ibn 'Īsā Kamāluddeen ad-Damīrī[366]

364 William Gervase Clarence-Smith, *Islam and the Abolition of Slavery* (London: Hurst and Co., 2006), p.12.

365 He is Shaykh Mūsā Ibn Ahmad al-Habeeb Kamara of Senegal, 1864 – 1945 CE. He was born in Gouriki, Samba-Diom, in a small village in the Damga encompassed by the Futa-Toro region in Senegal. He studied Arabic and the Qur'ān at a young age in his village and he also studied with scholars of the region and Mauritania. He is regarded as an heir to the literary traditions of Timbuktu and Songhay and he lived at a period which witnessed many Islamic confrontations with the encroaching European penetration into West Africa. His book *Zuhūr ul-Basāteen* is his most voluminous work and is a massive ethno-historical study of his region in West Africa. Another historical work authored by him was a*l-Majmū' an-Nafees Sirran wa 'Alāniyya 'an ba'd as-Sādāt al-Baydāniyya wa's-Sudāniyya* [The Precious Collection, Secret and Public, on Some White and Black Notables] which is a history of the scholarly Torodbe clan in West Africa and parts of it have been translated by Constance Hilliard. Hilliard says, "His works offer the most sizeable unpublished reservoir of indigenous intellectual history and commentary existing today in West Africa." For an English translation of parts of *al-Majmū' an-Nafees* by Hilliard see the French journal/periodical *Islam Et Societies Au Sud du Sahara* (Paris: Fondation de la Maison des Sciences de l'-Homme, 1997) p. 175.

366 Muhammad Ibn Mūsā Ibn 'Īsā Ibn 'Abdul-Qādir Kamāluddeen ad-Damīrī, born in Cairo in 750 AH/ 1349 CE or 742 AH/ 1341 CE. He was from

called *Hayāt ul-Hayawān al-Kubrā*.[367] In *Hayāt ul-Hayawān*, ad-Damīrī in turn quotes the *Rihlah* of Ibn as-Salāh[368] who narrated a report from az-Zuhrī (*rahimahullāh*)[369], who related as follows:

Dameerah in Egypt and studied under numerous teachers, principally focusing on the sciences of hadeeth, *fiqh* (jurisprudence) and *sarf* (philology). He went on to lecture in Cairo and delivered sermons and exhortations in many other places in Egypt. He composed several works, mainly commentaries including a four volume work on the methodology of Imām Yahyā an-Nawawī called *an-Najm ul-Wahhāj* (*The Shining Star*), and a commentary of the *Sunan* of Ibn Mājah. He became one of the main scholars of the *al-Azhar* University and died on the 3rd of Jumadā 808 AH/ October 26 1405 CE at the age of 58 or 66.

367 *Hayāt ul-Hayawān* is probably the most important work that gained ad-Damīrī his recognition. It was the first attempt to give in a systematic form the mass of knowledge of the nature of the animal and plant kingdoms in Arabic literature. The book is mainly a para-zoological encyclopaedia but it is also full of detailed accounts from the early Muslims. It has been translated into English as *Hayat al-Hayawan – A Zoological Lexicon*, trans. ASG Jayakar of *Bombay University* (London: Luzac & Co., Bombay: Fort Printing Press, vol. 1, 1906 CE and vol. 2, 1908 CE.

368 Abū 'Amr 'Uthmān Ibn 'Abdur-Rahmān Salāhudden Ibn 'Uthmān Ibn Mūsā ash-Shahrazurī. Born in Sharkhān in 577 AH/1181 CE and he was of Kurdish descent. He was a hadeeth scholar and studied in Mosul, Baghdād, Nishapūr, Merw and in Damascus under Ibn Qudāmah al-Maqdisī. Ibn as-Salāh composed many works on *fiqh* and excelled in other areas. He taught at the *Salāhiyya* School in al-Quds ("Jerusalem") and then later went on to teach in the *Dār ul-Hadeeth* in Damascus. He died in 643 AH/ 1245 CE.

369 Muhammad Ibn Muslim Ibn 'Ubaydullāh Ibn Shihāb as-Zuhrī 50 AH – 124 AH/ 742 CE. He was one of the early hadeeth scholars and writers of Islamic literature. His grandfather, 'Abdullāh Ibn Shihāb fought on the side of the polytheists against the Prophet Muhammad and his companions at Badr and 'Uhud, and his father was on the side of 'Abdullāh Ibn az-Zubayr against the 'Umayyads. Az-Zuhrī himself along with other scholars, including al-Hasan al-Basrī, were later accused of being 'government scholars' as az-Zuhrī accepted office with the 'Umayyads. Even though az-Zuhrī was poor in wealth he was rich in knowledge having memorized the whole Qur'ān in three months and constantly engaged in searching for knowledge. He also studied the genealogies and the poetry of the Arabs, much of which he had also memorized due to his tremendous memory. Abū Zinād (*rahimahullāh*) said of az-Zuhrī, "When I would be with az-Zuhrī he used to go about with tablets and sheets of paper with him,

"I introduced myself to 'Abdul-Mālik.
"Where do you come from, Oh az-Zuhrī?" he asked me.
I responded, "From Makkah."
"Whom have you left in your place to lead (as Imāms and teachers) their inhabitants?" he asked me.
"'Atā Ibn Abī Rabāh," I answered.[370]
"Is he an Arab or a freed slave?" he asked.
"A freed slave," I said.
"How can he lead the Makkans?" he asked.
"By Deen (religion) and Sunnah," I replied.
"Certainly it is suitable that those who possess Deen and Sunnah lead men. But who then leads the people of Yemen?"

---

writing down everything that he heard, we used to laugh at him for that." A student of az-Zuhrī, Ma'mar reports that his teacher would even write on the soles of shoes when paper was not available. The first Mujaddid, 'Umar Ibn 'Abdul-'Azeez (*rahimahullāh*) admired az-Zuhrī and advised people to attend his study circles. Other scholars testify that az-Zuhrī was a major hadeeth scholar and was trustworthy. Az-Zuhrī was also very benevolent and gave much to the needy, having known poverty himself. One other early scholar, al-Layth Ibn Sa'd (*rahimahullāh*) stated that "I have not seen anyone more generous than Ibn Shihāb. He used to help anyone who came to him and if he had nothing he used to borrow." Ibn Sa'd in his *Tabaqāt* noted that az-Zuhrī collected so many *ahādeeth* that after his death his manuscripts needed several large animals to transport them. For more on az-Zuhrī and the Arabic sources where his life and achievements are recorded see: Dr. Muhammad Mustafa Azami, *Studies in Early Hadith Literature* (Indianapolis: American Trust Publications, 3rd Edition, 1992) pp. 279-293.

370 'Atā ibn Abī Rabāh (*rahimahullāh*) was described by adh-Dhahabī as being "a freed-slave, black skinned with a flat nose and curly hair." See adh-Dhahabī, *Tadhkirat ul-Huffādh* (Hyderabad, 1333 AH/1915 CE, vol. 1, p.84). He was a freed black slave of the Abū Khuthaym al-Fihrī al-Qurashī. He was a *faqeeh* of Makkah and heard directly from Jābir ibn 'Abdullāh al-Ansārī, Ibn 'Abbās, Ibn 'Umar, Abū Hurayrah, 'Abdullāh ibn Zubayr and other companions (*radi Allāhu 'anhum*). He is cited as an authority by'Amr bin Deenār, az-Zuhrī, Mālik bin Deenār, al-'A'mash, al-Awzā'ī and others (*rahimahumullāh*). During his time he was the main Muftī of Makkah who was to be referred to. See *Ibn Khallikan's Biographical Dictionary*, [*Wafayāt ul-'A'yān*] – (Paris: Oriental Translation Fund of Great Britain and Ireland, 1842), trans. Baron MacGuckin de Slane, vol.2, pp.203-205.

"Ta'ūs Ibn Kaysān," I answered.

He asked, "Is he an Arab or a freed slave?"

"A freed slave," I responded.

"How can he lead them?" he asked.

"In the same way as 'Atā," I responded.

He then said, "It is suitable that people of this kind lead men, but then who will then lead the people of Egypt?"

I replied, "Yazeed Ibn Abī Habeeb."[371]

He asked, "Is he an Arab or a freed slave?"

It was the same response as for the others. Then who will lead and command the people of Syria?" he asked.

I said "Makhūt ad-Dimishqī."

He asked, "Is he an Arab or a freed slave?"

I replied, "He is a Nubian that was a slave and released by Hadooyl."

The same discussion continued, then 'Abdul-Mālik asked, "Who will then lead (in prayer as Imāms and teachers) the people of 'Irāq?"

The response: "Maymūn Ibn Mahrām."

He asked, "Is he an Arab or a freed slave?"

[The same discussion]

Then who will lead the people of Khurasān?"

"Ad-Dakhāh Ibn Muzāhin," I replied.

He asked, "Is he an Arab or a freed slave?"

"A freed slave," I replied.

[Same discussion]

"Then who leads the people of Basrah?" 'Abdul-Mālik asked.

I responded, "al-Hasan Ibn Abi'l-Hasan."

He asked, "Is he an Arab or a freed slave?"

"A freed slave," I responded.

"And who leads the people of Kūfah? Is he an Arab or a freed slave?"

---

371 Abū Rajā' Yazeed ibn Abī Habeeb al-Azdī was an Imām of Egypt. He was born in 50 AH and was from the younger Tābi'een, he was of the illustrious scholars and was mentioned by Abū Hātim al-Bustī in his book *ath-Thiqāt*. Muhammad bin Sa'd said: "Yazeed bin Habeeb was a freed slave of 'Āmir bin Luwayy', who was from the Qurasyh. He was *thiqah* and reported many hadeeth and died in 128 AH." Others reported that he died aged 75 years of age.

> *"An Arab," I replied.*
>
> *Abdul-Mālik said, "Oh az-Zuhrī you relieve me. By Allāh the freed slaves rule the Arabs to such an extent that they preach to them from the pulpits whilst the Arabs remain beneath them."*
>
> *"Oh commander of the faithful," I responded, "such is the will of Allāh and such is the Deen. Whoever practices it is the leader and whoever ignores it shall fall."*[372]

Even though it is unlikely that this word-for-word conversation took place,[373] the scholars mentioned are an example of the historical reality of Islām as it was practiced by the early Muslims, *as-Salaf us-Sālih*. This archetype represents the veracity of how Islām liberated people from slavery to men to scholastic height and achievement. Islām took people out of the degrading servitude to men to servitude to Allāh with knowledge and scholarly endeavour. A contemporary Muslim scholar, Shaykh Mashhūr Hasan āl Salmān of Jordan notes: "The freed slaves during the Umayyad period had the highest positions and most noble status."[374]

---

372 *Hayat ul-Hayawan* (Vol.2, Part 1), pp.224-225.

373 It is also mentioned by Imām adh-Dhahabī (*rahimahullāh*) in *Siyar 'A'lam un-Nubalā*, vol.5, p.85-6 but the conversation is baseless. See Shaykh Abū 'Ubaydah Mashhūr Hasan Āl Salmān, *Kutub Hadhara minha al-'Ulama*, (Shaykh Bakr Abū Zayd, intro., Riyadh, KSA: Dār us-Samee'ī, 1426 AH/2005 CE, vol.2, 3rd Edn.), p. 76.

374 Ibid.

V

Arabs and Afrocentric/Black Orientalist Confusion

The Afrocentrics also need to study more in depth into what exactly an *'Arab'* is. The Prophet Muhammad said *"I was sent to every red and black."*[375] Ibn Hajar stated in *Fath ul-Bārī*, vol. 1, p.73:

والعرب تطلق الأخضر على كل لون ليس بأبيض ولا أحمر قال الشاعر وأنا الأخضر من يعرفني أخضر الجلدة من نسل العرب يعني أنه ليس بأحمر كالعجم والاحمر يطلقونه على كل من ليس بعربي ومنه بعثت الى الأسود والأحمر

> The Arabs apply the term 'green' to all whose colour is neither white nor red, the poet said *"I am green and whoever knows me is aware that I am green skinned from the lineage of the Arabs"*. Meaning: that he was neither red like the non-Arabs, and the term 'red' is applied to all who are not Arabs, from this aspect (the Prophet, *sallallāhu 'alayhi wassalam* said:) "*I was sent to every black and red.*"[376]

Ibn ul-Jawzī[377] a Muslim scholar of Baghdad wrote a book in the late

375 *Saheeh Muslim.*

376 Ahmad ibn 'Ali ibn Hajar al-'Asqalānī, *Fath ul-Bārī bi Sharh Saheeh ul-Bukhārī* (Cairo: Dār ur-Rayyān li't-Turāth, 1407 AH/1986 CE), vol.11, p.74.

377 Abu'l-Faraj 'Abdur-Rahmān ibn Hasan ibn ul-Jawzī (597 AH/ 1114 CE – 1200 CE). He was raised in the 'Irāqī metropolis of Baghdād where he was educated by his family who were scholars and other scholars of the Hanbalī school of Islamic *fiqh*. He became outstanding in the fields of Qur'ānic commentary, Arabic language, history and hadeeth. His works cover diverse areas and among the most notable of his published works are: *Sifah us-Safwah*, a biography of the companions of Prophet Muhammad and the early scholars of the *Salaf; Taqseem*

twelfth century CE called *Tanweer al-Ghabash fī Fadl is-Sudan wa'l-Habash* [The Illumination of the Darkness on the Merits of the Black People and the Ethiopians].[378] More on this book will be mentioned later, yet here it is worth highlighting that in his book he notes that some of the Qurayshīs were black and that blackness is found among them, largely as a result of inter-marrying with Ethiopian women. And it has been noted that the Arabs during the pre-Islamic times of ignorance wanted black women in order to strengthen their lineages. Dr Jawād Ali (1907-87), an Iraqi historian, stated in chapter 45 under *'al-'Ajam'* ['the non-Arabs'] in his book *al-Mufassal fī't-Tārīkh ul-'Arab Qabl Islām* [The Detail Regarding the History of the Arabs Before Islām] that:

> Some black people and Arabs were famed for their courage and precedence and were known as the "crows of the Arabs" and the "coyotes of the Arabs".

Then he said:

> There are tribes whose colour is predominantly black to the extent that they were termed *'adlam'* to indicate if a man was intensely black. They had blackness as they were originally from Africa as is apparent and they had established themselves in the Arabian Peninsula and became Arabised to the extent that they were included among the Arabs, while some individuals had blackness as the Arabs had married black women and some of the Quraysh inclined to marrying black concubines.[379]

---

ul-Lisān, in Arabic language and linguistics; *Zād al-Maseer fī 'Ilm ut-Tafseer*, commentary on the Qur'ān; *al-Mawdū'āt, in hadeeth; Talbees Iblees*, about extreme and heretical understandings and practices; *Rūh ul-Arwāh* and *Sayd ul-Khātir*.

378 It has been edited by Mohamed Barakat (Sudan: Omdurman Islamic University Printing and Publishing House, 1412 AH/1993 CE). It has also been translated into English as a Ph.D degree thesis at the *School of Oriental and African Studies, University of London*, by 'Imran Hamza Alawiye. It was translated by Dr. Alawiye as *Ibn al-Jawzi's Apologia on Behalf of the Black People & Their Status in Islam: A Critical Edition and Translation of Kitab Tanwir al-Ghabash fi Fadl as-Sudan wa'l-Habash* (August 1985). It is in the *SOAS* library thesis section.

Note that 'Sudan' refers to 'black people' and not the modern country of Sudan. As classically, the Arabs utilised the terms '*Baydān*' to refer to the brown and light brown Arab peoples and 'Sudan' to refer to black people.

379 Jawād 'Ali, *al-Mufassal fī't-Tārīkh ul-'Arab Qabl Islām* [The Detail Regarding

Imām Ahmad reports from the hadeeth of Dhī Mikhbar, the nephew of an-Najāshī,[380] from the Prophet Muhammad (*sallallāhu alayhi wassallam*) that he said, "*This matter used to be amongst the red-skinned people but Allāh removed it from them and placed it amongst the Quraysh but it shall return to them.*" Its chain of narration is good and shows that the term 'red-skinned' applied to al-Qahtān, one of the early and well-known Arab tribes.[381] Ibn Mandhūr in *Lisān ul-'Arab* transmitted from al-Mubarrid that he said:

«يقال لولد العربي من غير العربية: هجين؛ لأن الغالب على ألوان العرب الأدمة، وكانت العرب تسمي العجم الحمراء لغلبة البياض على ألوانهم، ويقولون لِمَن علاَ لونه البياض: أحمر، ولذلك قال النبي ﷺ لعائشة: ((يا حميراء)) لغلبة البياض على لونها، وقال ﷺ: ((بُعِثت إلى الأحمر والأسود))، فأسودهم العرب، وأحمرهم العجم، وقالت العرب لأولادها من العجميات اللاتي يغلب على ألوانهن البياض: هجن وهجناء لغلبة البياض على ألوانهم وإشباههم أمهاتهم» انتهى.

The child born to an Arab man from a non-Arab woman is referred to as 'Hajeen' because the predominant colour of the Arabs is al-Udmah [dark brown] and the Arabs used to refer to the non-Arabs as "Humrā' [red-skinned] due to white being predominant in their colour. They [i.e. the Arabs] say to the one who has more white in his colour "Ahmar" ['red-skin'] and for this reason the Prophet said to 'Ā'ishah "Humayrā'" ["Oh red one"], due to the predominance of white in her complexion. For this reason the Prophet (*sallallāhu 'alayhi wassallam*) said: "I was sent to the red and the black", "the black" refers to the Arabs and "the white" refers to the non-Arabs. The Arabs refer to their children who are born of non-Arab women who have mostly white in their complexion as 'Hajn' or 'Hujanā'', due to the predominance

---

the History of the Arabs Before Islām].

380 See pp. 40-43 for more on an-Najāshī (*rahimahullāh*).

381 Ibn Hajar mentions this in Fath al-Bārī during the course of his discussion over this hadeeth of Mu'āwiyah (*radi allāhu 'anhu*) in *Saheeh al-Bukhārī* about the statement of 'Abdullāh ibn 'Amr and there being a leader from Qahtān.

of white in their complexion and resembling their mothers.[382]

The Arabic word 'Adam' is utilized to describe dark brown and black and this is noted in the classical Arabic linguistic works. Abū Mansūr 'AbdulMālik an-Naysabūrī ath-Tha'labī (d. 1038 CE) stated in his dictionary of synonyms *Fiqh ul-Lughah wa's-Sirr ul-'Arabiyyah* [Jurisprudence of the Language and the Secret of Arabic] p.348: "'Adam' in regards to people refers to blackness, and whiteness in regards to camels." Al-Jawharī in *as-Sihhāh*, vol.1, pp.7-8 stated: "al-Ādam in regards to people refers to 'brownness'." Abu'l-Hasan 'Ali bin Ismā'eel ibn Sīdah al-Mursī, aka Ibn Sīdah stated in *Muhkam wa'l-Muhīt al-A'dham fi'l-Lughah*, vol.3, p.215 : "'*as-sahmu*', '*as-suhāmu*' and '*as-suhmatu*' refers to: blackness, and every '*aswad*' is '*as-hamu*' and '*al-ishāmu*' is intense brownness [*shadīd ul-udmah*]... for they are the Arabs, as their colours are *ādam* [dark brown], *asmar* (brown) and *aswad* (black)."[383] This meaning of '*as-hamu*' referring to '*aswad*' [blackness] was also noted by al-Mutarrizī (d.1213 CE) in his book *al-Mughrib fī Tarteeb il-Mu'rib*, Zaynuddeen ar-Rāzī (d. 1266 CE) in *Mukhtār us-Sihhāh*, az-Zabīdī (d. 1790 CE) in *Tāj ul-'Arūs fī Jawāhir il-Qāmūs* and many others.

In Sudan for example, it is clear that many in the north are 'black,' if we mean by this dark brown skin complexion. Northern Sudan has many different tribes, yet it should be noted that '*Arab*' does not exclude having a dark brown skin complexion, i.e. 'black' as understood in the West. In Sudan itself for example, the people describe themselves with a variety of colours such as yellow, green, brown and blue! There are Arabs from Saudi Arabia, Yemen, Palestine and North Africa that are just as '*black*' as the average '*black person,*' in a Western context and frame of reference. An '*Arab*' however, is maybe better defined as a linguistic group as opposed to a race.[384] Abū 'Uthmān 'Amr ibn Bahr al-Fuqaymī

382 Imām al-'Allamah Abu'l-Fadl Jamaluddeen Muhammad bin Mukrim Ibn Mandhur al-Afriqi al-Misrī, *Lisan ul-Arab* (Beirut: Dar us-Sadir, 1300 AH/1882 CE), vol.13, p.431.

383 Abu'l-Hasan 'Ali bin Ismā'eel Ibn Sidah al-Mursi, al-Muhkam wa'l-Muhīt al-A'dham (Beirut: Dar ul-Kutub al-'Ilmiyyah, 1421 AH/2000 CE, ed. Dr AbdulHameed al-Hindawi), vol.2, p.209.

384 Sudan for example is composed of many tribes, some of these tribes mixed with Arabs in the past and some of the tribes are originally from the various tribes

al-Basrī al-Jāhiz (160 AH – 225 AH/ 776 CE – 869)[385] wrote one of the earliest books in Arabic against Arab nationalism and racism entitled *Risālah Fakhrus-Sudan 'Alā al-Baythān* [Treatise of the Pride of Black People Over the White People]. In the book, al-Jāhiz has a chapter called "Arabs Are Amongst the Black People," he notes:

> There are black tribes amongst the Arabs, such as the Banu Sulaym ibn Mansūr. All who dwell in the Harrah other than the Banu Sulaym are also black. They use Ashban slaves as shepherds, water carriers, workers and servants and take Byzantine women for wives.[386]

Al-Jāhiz was a famed scholar of mainly science and history and especially in regards to Arabic prose. In terms of defining an 'Arab' then one of the Islamic scholars of the past, Ibn Taymiyyah (*rahimahullāh*), provided some guidelines on this matter:

The Definition of an 'Arab'[387]

---

of Nubia (the name for what constitutes where southern Egypt and northern/ central Sudan is now located), for example tribes such as *Jāli, Juhayna, Baqqara* and *Kawahla*, are 'Arabs' now in the linguistic sense but not in the ethnic sense with many of the Nile Nubians speaking Arabic as a second language. Likewise, many of the north Africans are descended from people that mixed with the Arabs, so some of the north African Berbers for example are now 'Arabs' linguistically, but ethnically they are Berber, or Berber ethnically and linguistically with Arabic as a second language.

385 His grandfather was Fazārah who was black and possibly Ethiopian, a freed slave of 'Amr ibn Kila'. Al-Jāhiz was a prolific Mu'tazilī writer credited with the authorship of two hundred works in several disciplines. His early years were spent in the prosperous and culturally diverse town of Basra, where he was born. He was a Mu'tazilī influenced by rationalism as opposed to the Qur'ān and Sunnah. We quote him however here as he refers to a fact that can be assessed which also refutes the claims of non-Muslims about Islam and Muslims.

386 T. Khalidi (translator), *Fakhrus-Sudan 'Alā al-Baythān* (*The Islamic Quarterly*; Vol. 25; 1981), pp. 3-26.

387 From Shaykh ul-Islām Ahmad bin 'Abdul-Haleem bin 'Abdus-Salām Ibn Taymiyyah, edited by Dr Nāsir bin Abdil-Kareem al-'Aql, *'Iqtidā' as-Sirāt ul-Mustaqeem li-Mukhālifa Ashāb al-Jaheem* (Riyadh: Dār Ishbilia, 1419 AH/1999 CE) pp.164-166. The sub-section also contains benefits from Imām Muhammad

Ibn Taymiyyah noted that originally the name 'Arab' was a name for people of three kinds:

> Firstly: Those whose language was Arabic.
>
> Secondly: Those who were the children of Arabs.
>
> Thirdly: Those who lived in the land of the Arabs which is the Arabian peninsula from the Qulzum sea,[388] the sea of Basra and from the farthest limit of Yemen up to where Shām begins. So Yemen is included as their land but Shām is not included. This was the land of the Arabs, at the time of the awakening and dispatch of the Arabs and before it. When Islām came and spread into large cities the Arabs remained living in these lands, from the far East to the far West and to the coasts of Shām and Armenia. These lands were the dwellings of the Persians, Romans, Berbers and others.

With regards to places and locations which are to be defined as 'Arab countries' then Ibn Taymiyyah provides some interesting details:

> The lands divide into two:
>
> One. Those places that were strongly affected by the Arabic language to the extent that their people do not know anything except the Arabic language. Or the people knew Arabic and ungrammatical and colloquial Arabic that had entered the Arabic language. Such as most of Shām, 'Irāq, Egypt, Andalus etc. and

---

bin Sālih al-'Uthaymeen and Imām Muhammad Nāsirudeen al-Albānī (*rahimahumullāh*).

388 This was a former name of the Red Sea.

I think that Persia[389] and Khurasān[390] was like that in the past.

Two. The places where non-Arabs were the overwhelming majority such as the land of the Turks, Khurasān, Armenia, Azerbaijan[391] and similar countries. These places split into: those who were Arabs from the beginning to those who were Arabs by way of residence and those who are not Arabs.

---

389 Dr. Kees Versteegh notes that in Persia, during the first three or four centuries of Islām, Middle Persian, the literary language of the Sassanid Empire, disappeared. During the epoch of the Seljuk Empire, Arabic remained the language of religion and in some cases of science, but Persian was the cultural language and it remained so even when Turkish was introduced as the new language of administration. In Ottoman Turkey, the knowledge of three languages, Arabic, Persian and Turkish was part of the cultural baggage of an intellectual. This is why most Turkish loan-words from Arabic, entered via Persian. See Kees Versteegh (University of Nijmergen), *"Linguistic Contacts Between Arabic and Other Languages" in Arabica: Journal of Arabic and Islamic Studies, vol.4* (Leiden: Brill, Oct. 2001), p.494.

Later, some Shi'a scholars such as the Qajar prince Jalal od-Din Mirza (d.1871 CE) made serious attempts to replace Arabic words in Farsi (Persian) with only 'authentic' Farsi pre-Islamic words!!?

390 Khurasān is a huge province in north-eastern 'Irān stretching from 'Irāq in the west to the borders of India in the east. Its current major cities include Naysabūr (Nishapur) and Mashhad. The Muslims took Islām there during the time of the Sahābah. The older 'greater Khurasān' included parts that are now in Irān, Afghānistān, Turkmenistān and Uzbekistān. Four of the main historical cities of Persia are located in the older Khurasān: Nishapur (now in Iran), Merv (now in Turkmenistan), and Herat and Balkh (now both in Afghanistan). The Mongols conquered it in 1220 C.E. and a powerful earthquake devastated the province in 1997 C.E. See: http://www.lib.utexas.edu/maps/middle_east_and_asia/iran_pol01.jpg

Versteegh also notes that in Khurasān, the local Persian elite remained in power after the Arab Muslims conquered it and were entrusted with the levying of taxes. As a result, Arabs probably had to learn Persian there in order to communicate. Currently, as Versteegh highlights, there are few Arabic/Farsi bilingual speakers except in the province of Khuzestan which has remained Arabic-speaking. (Versteegh, *Op. Cit.*, p.491).

391 Azerbaijan is currently situated to the far north of 'Irān, one of its famous cities was Tabreez (Tabriz) currently in the extreme north of 'Irān. See: http://www.lib.utexas.edu/maps/commonwealth/caucasus_cntrl_asia_pol_00.jpg

Therefore, the origins and lineages split into three kinds:

One. People who are originally of Arab descent and maintained the Arabic language and place of origin. Or maintained the language and not the place of origin, or maintained the place of origin and not the Arabic language.[392]

Two. People who are originally of Arab descent, in fact they are from Bani Hāshim but their language and place of residence became non-Arabic, or one of the two.[393]

Three. People who are not aware of their origin and do not know if they are originally of Arabic descent or non-Arabic descent. Most of the people today are of this kind, regardless of whether they were Arabs of the place of homeland or language, or non-Arabic in one of the two.

Likewise, Arabs by way of language spilt into three categories:

One. People that speak Arabic in pronunciation, articulation and intonation.

---

392 In his explanation to *'Iqtidā' as-Sirāt ul-Mustaqeem* (Riyadh and 'Unayzah: Istiqāmah Recordings, 1416 A.H, tape no. 13), the Noble Shaykh Muhammad bin Sālih al-'Uthaymeen (*rahimahullāh*) was asked:

> "How can it be possible for a person that does not know Arabic, to be an Arab by way of residence and from the children of the Arabs, even though the person does not possess the Arabic language and tongue?"

The Shaykh responded by saying:

> Yes it is possible and this is apparent. For example, if there is a person in the Arabian peninsula but does not know the Arabic language. The workers that we have who do not know the Arabic language are spoken to by children in the languages of the workers, not in Arabic. Sometimes a translator is needed, so a child will translate from the language of the servants and workers into Arabic. They are not Arabs originally, but it is possible for them to be Arabs by way of residence and home, but not Arabs by language.

393 In his explanation of *Iqtidā' Sirāt ul-Mustaqeem*, Shaykh Muhammad bin Sālih al-'Uthaymeen (*rahimahullāh*) was asked: "What about a person who is an Arab by language and descent but loves the Western countries and the non-Arabs, is such a person an Arab?" Imām Ibn al-'Uthaymeen replied: "This is not good, such a person is an Arab by language and descent but not an Arab in thinking." Muhammad bin Sālih al- 'Uthaymeen, *Iqtidā' Sirāt ul-Mustaqeem* (Riyadh and 'Unayzah: Istiqāmah Recordings, 1416 AH), tape no. 13.

Two. People that speak Arabic in pronunciation but not with intonation. Such as those who became Arabicized (*musta'rab*) and had not studied the Arabic language from the Arabs and spoke another languages, then they studied the Arabic language later. This is the case with most of the people of knowledge that had learnt Arabic.

Three. People that no longer speak Arabic, except a little.

So the two groups of people, one of which were strongly affected by Arabic and the other that was more influenced by non-Arabic and those who had already gave in either by power or by custom and tradition. So if Arabic divides into origin, language and residence then the rulings differ due to the difference in these divisions, especially with regards to origin and language. The intent here is that what I mentioned about the disapproval of imitating the non-Arabs is just something which was of importance during the early era of Islām, from the first and foremost people (the Sahābah). As everything that was closer to their guidance is preferred, and everything that is further differs from their guidance is contradictory. Regardless of whether an opponent to that guidance today is an original Arab by descent or an Arab by language, and this has come from the Salaf. Al-Hāfidh Abū Tāhir as-Silafi in *The Virtue of the Arabs* narrated from Abū Ja'far Muhammad bin 'Ali bin al-Hasan ibn 'Ali that he said: "*Whoever is born into Islām is an Arab.*" This is narrated from Abū Ja'far. Because whoever is born into Islām is born into the homeland of the Arabs and acquired its speech, this is how the matter is.[394] Whoever contemplates on what we have mentioned in this chapter will know the intent of the Sharee'ah in what we have mentioned from the blessed agreement and the censured

394 It is mentioned in the explanation of *'Iqtidā' as-Sirāt ul-Mustaqeem* (Riyadh and 'Unayzah: Istiqāmah Recordings, 1416 A.H, tape no. 13) by Shaykh Muhammad bin Sālih al-'Uthaymeen (*rahimahullāh*) a narration from as-Silafi from Abū Qāsim al-Hallāl from Abū Muhammad al-Hasan ibn Husayn an-Nawbakhtī from 'Ali ibn 'Abdillāh al-Mubashir from Ibn Harb al-Mashā'ī from Ishāq al-Azraq from Hishām ibn Hassan from Hasan from Abū Hurayrah (*radi Allāhu 'anhu*) who said "*whoever speaks Arabic is an Arab.*" However, this is not authentic for it contains the *'an'an* of al-Hasan who is *mudallis*.

It has also been noted by Ibn Asākir, adh-Dhahabi and an-Nasā'ī that the narration, which is also found in *Tarīkh ud-Dimashq* of Ibn Asākir, is not authentic due to the presence of Salmān bin 'Abdillāh who is a weak narrator and unreliable.

opposition to it, as I began with the indications of it, its reasons and the wisdom in it.

With regards to the African context then, Veesteegh (2001) notes that in the period of the spread of Islām during the 7th century, Egypt and North Africa were superficially Arabicised. During the later Bedouin invasions of the Banu Hilāl and the Banu Sulaym (10/11th centuries CE), first in Egypt and later in North Africa, which up until then had continued to speak Coptic in south of Egypt and Berber in North Africa, were Arabicised. During later centuries the Sudan and parts of central Africa were Arabicised. Many Arabic-speaking tribes migrated to the Baqqarah belt, the Savanna region of central Africa; as a result, native speakers of Arabic are found all over this region, as far west as the Bornu region of Nigeria.[395] Therefore, indicating how people who are 'black' can be regarded as 'Arabs', as they are 'Arabs' by way of language within the definition explained by Shaykh ul-Islām Ibn Taymiyyah in the 13th century, yet in their origin they are descended from indigenous peoples of a country outside of the Arabian peninsula.

The best example of this is in Sudan, and a lack of awareness of this issue has led to considerable misunderstanding, confusion and ignorance. The tribes in the north of Sudan who are regarded as 'Arabs' are *musta'rab* (Arabicised), such as the tribes of the Ja'alieen, Shā'qiyyah, Juwaynah (of the northern Nile regions), Kabbābish,[396] Kawahlah, Kafonja and Baqqarah[397] nomadic tribes, all of whom are originally Nubian[398] with

---

395 Versteegh, p.483

396 Kabbābish territory is in northern Kordofan, in north-western Sudan at the beginning of the Libyan Desert. Their ancestors came from Arabia and intermarried with indigenous Beja and other north-African ('black') tribes. They are a nomadic tribe who herd camels and many of the Kabbābish moved out of the desert and closer to the cities. They are 'black' (in the Western term of reference), yet in Sudan the very dark skinned southern Sudanese may describe them as being 'white'?!

397 Baqqarah are found in Chad and Sudan and they are the second largest group in Western Sudan. They are a cattle-herding tribe and include the following tribes of Humr/Messiriyyah, Rizayyat, Shuwiyyah, Hawazma, Ta'isha and Habbāniyyah. Baqqarah nomads originated from the Juhayna tribe.

398 The original people of northern Sudan and southern Egypt are the Nubians and historically Nubia extended from Dongola in Northern Sudan up the Nile

some Arab mix in their lineages. They are all 'black', an issue which they never deny, let us reiterate that their country is of course known as 'the black lands' (Sudan), and in their language they became 'Arab' and in their cultural structure they also became 'Arab' and they are regarded by all other Arabs worldwide as being 'Arabs'.

This concept is difficult for some people in the West to comprehend but it has to be kept in mind that not everyone in the world shares the same concepts and ideas of race, language and identity as people living in England and America! So for example, converts to Islām, black, white and other, who then learn and speak Arabic to a high-level are sometimes mistaken for being Arabs by Arabs themselves, this indicates that being an 'Arab' is related to language. In the same way, when black people speak English as their first language in the West are not generally considered to be 'English' *ethnically* and therefore are not seen as sharing anything in common with those who are originally English. This then leads to confusion as countries debate "what is means to be a truly British citizen" for example, yet if they took this linguistic aspect into consideration it would be enough in itself to quash any notions of non-white people not being 'integrated' or 'included' within a society.

The Fur in Eastern Sudan are linked to Northern Sudan to a certain extent yet they still maintain their tribal solidarity. In the past, the old

---

to Aswan in southern Egypt. Today Nubians are concentrated in three cities, Kom Ombo in southern Egypt and Wadi Halfa and Kashm ul-Girba in northern Sudan. They have a rich history and some of the ancient Egyptian Pharaohs were Nubians (the 25th and 26th Pharaonic dynasties were Nubian as Nubia conquered and ruled over ancient Egypt. They officially accepted Christianity in 580CE and when Islām came the regions of the Nubians came under the control of the Muslims and a treaty was made between the Muslims and the Nubian king at the time. This treaty re-established trade and allowed Nubia to remain Christian, there were no forced conversions as some erroneously assert with no evidence. For the next six centuries the Nubians remained Christians and they gave way to Islām in the sixteenth century, so interestingly, West Africans became Muslims before the Nubians of East Africa did which indicates why the Islamic history of West Africa is much more extensive than that of that particular part of north-East Africa. There are two main groups, the Kenuzi and the Fedidjah; the Kenuzi speak Kenuzi-Dongalawi while the Fedidjah speak Fedidjah-Mahaj. A group of them have become *musta'rab*; yet they are all bi-lingual.

Fur sultāns derived power due to their direct and indirect control over the trade of ebony, ivory, spices, rich cloth, slaves and other goods from Darfur to Egypt via the Forty Days Road (Darb al-Arba'een). The Fur maintained their independence until the year 1916 CE when the ruling sultān was defeated by the British and the province was thus politically integrated into Sudan. The Fur are also bi-lingual and *musta'rab* but recently, as we noted earlier, they have begun to use the word 'African' in order to get their regional struggle with the central government brought into international sphere. The Beja of North-Eastern Sudan are also 'black' and many have huge Afro hairstyles and they are a nomadic people.[399] As the Arabs did not conquer Sudan, when the Beja embraced Islām in the 7th century CE they did not all take on Arabic language and as a result they have their own distinct culture from the Arab tribes of the Sudan.

Black Orientalism in Practice

Sherman ('AbdulHakim) Jackson notes in his book *Islam and the Blackamerican*:

> Black Orientalism is essentially a reaction to the newly developed relationship among Islam, Blackamericans and the Muslim world. It has followed the shift from Black Religion to historical Islam as the basis of Islamic religious authority among Blackamerican Muslims. Its ultimate aim is to challenge, if not undermine, the esteem enjoyed by Islam in the Blackamerican community by projecting onto the Muslim world a set of images, perceptions, resentments and stereotypes that are far more the product of the Black experience in the United States than they are of any direct relationship with or knowledge of Islam and the Muslim world. By highlighting the purported historical race-prejudice of the Muslim world and, in some instances, the alleged responses to it, Black Orientalism seeks to impugn the propriety of the relationship between Islam and Blackamericans and ultimately to call into question Blackamerican Muslims' status as "authentic," loyal Blackamericans.[400]

---

399 The Beja are in turn split into five tribal branches: Hadandawa, Beniamier, Amarar, Ababda and Halanga. They mainly reside in the North-Eastern region of Sudan near the broder with Eritrea.

400 Sherman Jackson, *op.cit.*, p.102

One of the defining aspects of black orientalism is its lack of source references for some of its very serious claims and assessments. This is also complemented with citations of black Muslim progress when it suits. So for example, with regards to Chancellor Williams, it can be observed that he makes a massive contradiction in his book as he flips the script and begins praising the great Islamic trade and education centre of Timbuktu in Mali!? Thus, Williams is in a dilemma, as on the one hand he cannot deny that Timbuktu was African and Islamic, wherein Arabic was studied as well as spoken, an issue that Williams discretely neglects contemplation on, yet on the other hand Williams wants to assert that the Muslims and Arabs systematically destroyed African civilization throughout the continent!?

In a TV series aired on the UK's BBC2 in July 1999 CE entitled *Into Africa (Wonders of the African World)*,[401] the Orientalist Henry Louis Gates Junior made a brief tour of Africa. Gates Jnr also made some snide comments about Islām. Yet at the same time, Gates Junior, like Chancellor Williams and others, constantly felt the need to praise what he called "the black achievement of our ancestors in Timbuktu who had knowledge of Arabic and science." The pragmatism that characterizes the black Orientalists/Afrocentrics clearly indicates that they follow their own desires and use whatever they want from African history when it suits them. Gates Junior despite his 'Afrocentric' agenda fell into the trap of applying simplistic Western concepts of racial classifications onto Africa. Dr Thomas E.R. Maguire noted that even Molefi Asante, the pioneer of Afrocentric thought, considered Henry Louis Gates Jr's TV series as a "Eurocentric enterprise."[402]

Gates views every culture, person, artefact and place that he encounters within his own vision of Africa within a Eurocentric definition of civilization. For example, when Gates Junior went to Zanzibār he asked one of the people there "are you black?" The Zanzibārī man was clearly surprised and simply replied that he was of Zanzibār. Similarly, whilst in Timbuktu, Gates Junior asked the library keeper of the old Arabic manuscripts whether the authors were "black or not." (!?) This is one

---

401 In the USA it was titled *'Wonders of the African World'* and in the UK as *'Into Africa.'*

402 Thomas E.R. Macguire, *The Islamic Simulacrum in Henry Louis Gates Jr's 'Into Africa' in West Africa Review, no.1* (2), January 2000.

of the major problems with the Afrocentrics, due to their Western experience and context, and reliance on anti-Islamic European sources, they also apply simplistic Eurocentric and Western classifications onto Africa.[403] So it confuses them when a 'black man' also regards himself as an 'Arab.' As stated before, an Arab is more of a linguistic group than a race as such and thus the skin colour demarcations are not always satisfactorily pertinent in such a context. Jackson also highlights this error of Gates Junior,

> In a word, Gates-like the Afrocentrics-embraces the concept and definition of blackness as institutionalised in the history, customs, and legal tradition of the Unites States and then seeks to impose this on East African Muslims. Any East African Muslim who does not identify with this definition of blackness is in turn cast as a self-hating Negro. No allowance and no agency at all is granted to the East Africans themselves-at least not the East African Muslims-to indulge their own definitions of blackness.[404]

At the same time it must be stated that Gates Junior whilst in East Africa did experience confusion due to the many people who claim to be 'Arab' in origin. Due to there being little or no evidence in many cases for people to prove these claims it is something that Islām actually prohibits, to falsify lineages. Sa'd and Abū Bakrah (*radi Allāhu 'anhum*) reported that the Prophet Muhammad (*sallallāhu 'alayhi wassallam*) said "*Whoever knowingly claims to belong to anyone other than his father, Paradise will be denied him.*"[405] The Prophet Muhammad (*sallallāhu 'alayhi wassallam*) also said in a *hadeeth* narrated by 'Abdullāh bin 'Amr: "*Whoever claims to belong to someone other than his father will not smell the fragrance of Paradise, even though its fragrance may be smelled from a*

---

403 Gates himself, as Thomas E.R. Maguire has noted,

> ...comes from a very traditional Western academic background (Yale, Cambridge, Harvard) and he maintains its general structures with the exception of its generally demeaning depiction of Africa. Gates continually makes comparisons between Africa and Europe through the six episodes of Into Africa, as if the two regions are distinct poles of a radical dichotomy which he intends to equalize.

404 Jackson, *op cit.*, p.118

405 Reported by al-Bukhārī, see *Fath ul-Bārī*, vol.8, p.45

distance of five hundred years."[406]

At the same time though, it has to be mentioned that this should not be seen as a problem which only affects some African Muslims as the matter is also widespread in the West wherein people of African origin from the Caribbean and the Americas will even celebrate occasions such as St. Patrick's Day claiming that they have some Irish origins! Indeed, many people of African origin in the Caribbean completely deny that they have any African blood within them whatsoever!? Some lighter skinned African-Americans even discriminate against those who are darker skinned!?[407] So much for accusing African Muslims of denying their ethnic and tribal origins, colourism is clearly prevalent to disturbing levels among the black community in the West. AbdulHakim Jackson notes:

> ...I find it hard to believe that in a world dominated by white supremacy the only Africans who have a problem with blackness are those who happen to be Muslims. And it is here that Professor Gate's Black Orientalism comes front and center...And only the Muslims are presented as evincing those disturbing complexes of apparent self-loathing. Blackness is never problematized when speaking to African Jews or Christians...And in later segments,[408] Ethiopian Jews and Christians are not asked about theirs. We never get a sense of how Ethiopian Jews reconcile their Hebrewness with their Africanness. Nor is the Ethiopian Jewish charge of racism given any attention. We are never granted any insight into how Ethiopian Christians relate to all

---

406 *Saheeh hadeeth* from Ibn Mājah, see *English Translation of Sunan Ibn Majah*, vol.3 (Darus-Salam Publishers, 2007 CE), '*Abwāb ul-Hudūd*' [Chapters on Legal Punishments], p.496.

407 See: http://www.eeoc.gov/press/8-07-03.html

"The U.S. Equal Employment Opportunity Commission (EEOC) today announced the settlement of a rare color harassment and retaliation lawsuit under Title VII of the *Civil Rights Act of 1964* against *Applebee's Neighborhood Bar & Grill*, an international restaurant chain headquartered in Overland Park, Kansas. The settlement provides $40,000 to Dwight Burch, an African American former employee who was discriminated against based on his dark skin color by a light skinned African American manager, and terminated when he complained to corporate headquarters."

408 Of the documentary

> those apparently "white" images in their icons. Nor do we get a sense of whether the Ethiopians' fine hair and pointed features place them, in their own minds, above their woolly haired, full-featured West African bretheren…In the end, the message is, again, as clear as it is subtle: Not only do Muslims in Africa have a deep aversion to blackness, only Muslims in Africa are afflicted with this disease. This double standard, along with its implicit message, is repeated throughout Wonders.[409]

Dr Thomas E.R. Maguire considered Henry Louis Gates Jnr's TV show as seriously misrepresenting Islām in Africa. Maguire notes that Gates' series added to the "arsenal of post-modern strategies to discredit Islam." Maguire also notes how Gates not only reinforces stereotypes about Islām but also shows bias and sympathy to Christianity. For example, when Gates travelled to Ethiopia, he totally ignores the Muslim presence in the country and says nothing about the Christian King Najāshī (*radi Allāhu anhu*) and how he and many of his bishops accepted Islām and gave sanctuary to the early Muslims. Rather, Gates speaks of the "Muslim invaders" and that Ethiopia was "well protected from Islamic neighbours by formidable mountain ranges." The Afrocentrist Molefi Asante has also made historical mistakes and inaccurate claims:

> The Arabs with their Jihads, or holy wars, were thorough in their destruction of much of the ancient culture. It is also as if small bands (of fleeing Egyptian priests) keeping ahead of the Islamic onslaught managed to preserve certain aspects of the traditional culture of Egypt.[410]

The claim that north Africa should not be considered part of Africa is based on the premise that it is not 'black' and this is utter nonsense as they are indigenous north African ethnic groups who are 'black'! For example, the *Harateen* in southern Morocco are believed to be descended from aboriginal black populations of the Sahara Desert. They are found in most Saharan oases, among the Arab populations of Mauritania, in the villages of southern Morocco and Algeria.[411] Dr Maguire therefore

---

409 Jackson, *op cit.*, p.119-120

410 Molefi Asante, '*Afrocentricity and Culture*' in Asante and Kariamu Welsh Asante (eds.), *African Culture – The Rhythms of Unity* (Westport, CT: Africa World Press, 1985)

411 See G. Camps, "*Recherchs sur les Origins des Cultivateurs Noirs du Sahara*" in

noted that,

> Edward Said exposes the deepest roots of Orientalism as a paranoia stemming from the conflict between European Christianity and Islam. Henry Louis Gates Junior upholds these fundamental elements of Orientalism within an Afrocentric framework.

Indeed, and this is a familiar trait of those who argue against Islām from the view of extreme Afrocentricity. Cheikh Anta Diop, an expert in African history also noted, in contrast to the idea that the Muslims violently destroyed non-Islamic African peoples and their belief systems, that:

> African religions, more or less forgotten, were in the process of atrophying[412] and being emptied of their spiritual content, their former deep metaphysics. The jumble of empty forms they had left behind could not compete with Islam on the moral or rational level. And it was on that latter level of rationality that the victory of Islam was most striking. That was the fourth cause of its success.[413]

Dr Yusuf Progler of the University of New York highlights:

> Modern Western, supposedly 'objective,' scholarship on Africa and Islam redefined and reduced the legacy of a long and mutually prosperous relationship between Arabs, Muslims and Africans by harping on the nineteenth century Arab involvement in the slave trade, which itself resulted from Western colonization. This emphasis, repeated incessantly, distorts the Islamic impact on and contribution to Africa. It was designed to obscure the memory of many centuries of peaceful Muslim trade relations, migrations, and intermarriages in Africa – not to mention the development of a vibrant local African Islamic culture.[414]

However Progler's point that "the 19th century Arab involvement in the slave trade" resulted "from Western colonialism" is inaccurate and

---

Reve de l'occident Musulman et de la Mèditerranèe, 7 (1970), pp.35-40. The *Harateen* were forcibly conscripted by Mulay Ismā'eel during the tyrannical ruler's reign.

412 I.e. dying

413 Diop, *op cit.*, p.166

414 Yusuf Progler, *Islam and the Politics of Slavery in American Academia in Muslimedia* (June 1999).

quite far off the mark. It will be assessed later in the chapter on slavery. Furthermore, Diouf splendidly notes:

> It is significant that Islam is rarely, if ever, mentioned in studies on or references to African religions. After one thousand years of continuous presence, dissemination by the sub-Saharan Africans themselves, accommodations to the local cultures, and an overall record of voluntary conversion rather than imposition, Islam is still considered a non-African religion by most American scholars. For some, to see Islam's influence on and importance to Africans in both Africa and the New World acknowledged is almost a belittling of what they think are authentic African cultures and Africans. Islamic influence is wrongly perceived as Arabization and a reflection of the supposed weakness of traditional cultures in the face of foreign entities.
>
> Interestingly, Chinese, Indonesian, and Albanian Muslims are not seen as being Arabized; only sub-Saharans are viewed as acculturated, which seems to indicate that some advocates of African cultures have internalized the anti-African prejudices they are fighting in other settings. In this mindset, to celebrate the so-called real Africa, or what is perceived as being the real Africa, Islam and the Muslims have to be denied or minimized. The reality is that traditional African religions have usually been favorably disposed toward Islam and the Muslims and have taken from them what they deemed useful to their own preservation and continuity. However, in a mythical and false reconstruction of African cultures as static, millennial, untouched, and uninfluenced except by force, Islam has no place.[415]

In this way, only black people are made out to be those who are so gullible to become 'Arab' when they embrace Islām and no other people, white people who become Muslims are not mentioned at all as being 'passive receivers' of Islām, only black people?! This therefore shows the rather dim and simplistic view that the anti-Islamic Kemet Afrocentrics and writers themselves hold of black people.

Black Orientalism and Evangelical Christian Propaganda

We have discussed the role of Chancellor Williams in promoting this

---

415 Sylviane Diouf, *Servants of Allah – African Muslims Enslaved in the Americas* (New York and London: New York University Press, 1998), p.204.

branch of black Orientalism/Afrocentricity and more recently this has also been championed by John Alembillah Azumah. Azumah is currently professor of 'World Christianity and Islam' and the director of international programs at Columbia Theological Seminary. He formerly worked at the Henry Martyn Institute and International Centre for Research, Interfaith Relations and Reconciliation in Hyderabad, India. Founded in 1930, the institute boasts on its website that it "has become a major centre for research and teaching on matters related to Islamic studies." As a result, they offer certificates, diplomas and graduate diploma programmes in Islamic studies and inter-faith relations.[416] They have an annual residential course entitled '*Islam and Interfaith Relations*' an intensive two-week programme (60 hours) every May, "the main objective is to gain a deeper and more sympathetic understanding of Islam." The Henry Martyn Institute has relations with none other than Crowther Hall-Church Mission Society, the Church of Scotland, Luther Seminary, Church of Sedar Mission, Lund University and the Middle Eastern Council of Churches.

John Azumah's book *The Legacy of Arab-Islam in Africa: A Quest for Inter-Religious Dialogue* contains a number of inaccuracies and incorrect aspersions about Islam in Africa.[417] At the outset the book appears to want to foster understanding and mutual awareness regarding Islām in Africa and related issues, yet in reality is entrenched in anti-Islamic rhetoric and steeped in European Orientalist influence, and not just romantic Orientalism, but rather radical de-mythologiser Orientalism![418]

---

416 Regarding the post-graduate diploma course, a one month course, they say it is "designed for those who seek a deeper knowledge of Islam and interfaith relations…students are not assumed to have any significant previous background in Islam. This programme can also serve as a preparation for students who wish to enrol in the Master of Technology-Islam degree under the senate of Serampre." *HMI* also collaborates with the Frije University of Amsterdam and other institutions in offering a Ph.D. in Islam in Asia and Christian-Muslim relations.

417 Azumah can be seen speaking here: https://www.youtube.com/watch?v=hV-KAyW7pI8

418 Radical de-mythologiser Orientalism is largely based on the ideas and theories of Wansborough, Patricia Crone and Michael Cook. The book *Hagarism: The Making of the Islamic World* (Cambridge: 1977) authored by the latter two is the archetypal 'demythologiser' Orientalist work. It seeks to throw doubt on the Islamic source texts whether they be hadeeth, historical compilations,

Indeed, Azumah mentions in the preface:

> However, the focus on Muslim evidence needs to be critical. All scholarly students and even more non-Muslim students of Islām should reject the temptation of treating Muslim evidence as sacrosanct or representing the whole truth.[419]

Thereby rejecting an entire corpus of history regarding Islām in Africa that has been conducted by Muslims, merely on the basis that Muslims have done it! What is important is that the accepted methodology is to use Muslim sources and not reject them. Norman Daniel commented that when Islamic evidence is rejected, the evidence which is used instead is neither evaluated at all nor is the Islamic evidence which was discounted in advance. Daniel highlights:

> There is a subsidiary but also important consideration. Far from considering statements by Muslims to be reliable even about Islam, Christians thought all Islamic statements suspect... Christian witness was presumed reliable, Islamic writers suspect.[420]

Arnold states in his book simply called *History*:

---

exegesis of the Qur'ān, and merely rejects the entire corpus of Islamic sources due to their claim that they contain doubt and are unreliable. They go further in their void theorems by only accepting non-Muslim sources for understanding the Islamic dispensation and this biased approach is false. As a result, they have been discarded by a number of established Islamic historians in the field and their works have by and large been rejected. Sadly some universities in London still blindly utilise the books of the de-mythologiser Orientalists as core reading for so-called 'Islamic history' courses!? This school of Orientalism has thus found a mass of support from evangelical Christian fundamentalists who thus endeavour to utilise de-mythologiser critiques of Islām in their missionary and propaganda tracts. Examples of this can be seen with the likes of evangelical propagandists over the last 20 years such as Robert Morey, Craig Winn, Jack Chick, Robert Spencer, Joseph Smith et al. they are both comfortable bed partners as both are based on categorically denying and rejecting Muslim sources and viewpoints. This is what the so-called "inter-religious dialogue" of Azumah is based upon.

419 John Alembillah Azumah, *The Legacy of Arab-Islam in Africa: A Quest for Inter-Religious Dialogue* (Oxford: One World, 2001), p.xiii.

420 Norman Daniel, *Islam and the West: The Making of an Image* (Oxford: One World, 1997), p.275.

> Historians must stick with what the sources make possible...They cannot invent new accounts, or suppress evidence that does not fit with their narratives.[421]

Azumah claims that his reasons for throwing doubt upon Islamic sources and Muslim writings are due to the following:

> Some individual scholars have, for various reasons, even gone beyond acknowledging the merits and achievements of the Islamic dispensation to romanticizing and idealising the Islamic past.[422]

As a result, Azumah refrains from referring back to Islamic sources, yet has no problem in referring to anti-Islamic ones! In fact he does not even bring much in the way of African sources and references. We can see the sheer arrogance of this refusal to refer back to Islamic sources and its danger when Azumah claims that the Prophet Muhammad (*sallallāhu alayhi wassallam*) made disparaging remarks about Ethiopians yet does not even quote the *hadeeth* source for this. So from where does Azumah get this claim, from none another than Bernard Lewis, regarded by some commentators as being an ardent Zionist![423]

In fact, Azumah's chapter 'Muslim Slavery and Black Africa' he relies heavily on Bernard Lewis, particular the controversial book which is full of inaccuracies *Race and Color in Islam*, throughout the sixty pages of the entire chapter. What further rebuts Azumah's claim is the fact that the Prophet Muhammad (*sallallāhu 'alayhi wassallam*) used Ethiopian words and some Arabic words, some of which are in the Qur'ān, are actually of Ethiopian origin! In one hadeeth the Prophet Muhammad (*sallallāhu 'alayhi wassallam*) mentioned one particular word '*al-Harj*' [riotous killing] which he said was of Ethiopian origin.[424]

Azumah on page 155 also accuses so-called "Arab militias" of slave-raiding in Sudan, and we have dealt with this matter in-depth in a

---

421 John H. Arnold, *History* (New York, NY: Sterling Publishing, 2009), p.160

422 Azumah, *op.cit.*, p.xiii

423 Azumah, *op.cit.*, p.131

424 This hadeeth is recorded by Imām Ahmad in his *Musnad* from Hudhayfah and also by Imām al-Bukhārī from Abū Mūsā and 'Abdullāh ibn Mas'ūd (*radi Allāhu 'anhum*).

previous chapter. On pages 156-157, he quotes a somewhat obscure 11th century CE dossier on slavery by Ibn Butlān, without mentioning who Ibn Butlān actually is and without even noting if Ibn Butlān is a Muslim or not. Ibn Butlān was an Arab Christian and not even a Muslim!![425] So from where did Azumah get this information about Ibn Butlān? From Bernard Lewis!! In fact, in the whole chapter (on 'Muslim Slavery and Black Africa') Azumah quotes from Bernard Lewis some eighteen times! Azumah only quotes from one Muslim author on the subject!? This kind of selectivity and rejection of anything authored by Muslims on the subjects at hand demonstrates the partisan methodology of Azumah in the book. As Norman Daniel stated:

> This means using remote and even more unreliable sources…this is just what medieval writers did when they hung on to poor evidence that contradicted the Muslim witness.[426]

De Baets states in his book *Responsible History*:

> It is history that can be abused, not the past. Sources from the past and facts and opinions about the past can be intentionally distorted. But the past itself cannot be affected by acts in the present. Abusive history is continuously confused with other types of history.[427]

De Baets also notes:

> Incompetent (or "bad") history – the product of error, imperfect insight, bias, and lack of training, can be heavily distorting and prejudiced, but it is not irresponsible or abusive as long as it does not transgress the moral boundary of dishonest or gross

425 Abu'l-Hasan al-Mukhtār ibn 'Abdun ibn Butlān (died circa 458 AH/1066 CE) was an Arab Christian physician and monk from Baghdad who authored *Taqweem us-Sihhah* (*Health Guidelines*) which describes in detail the beneficial and harmful properties of foods and plants. It is more of a herbal medicinal treatise which also includes sections on breathing, exercise, rest and mental health. It became popular in the European Middle Ages as '*Taccuinum*' and the modern Italian word '*taccuino*' (handbook, guide, notebook) is taken from the popularity of this Arabic book.

426 Daniel, *op.cit.*, p.325

427 Antoon de Baets, *Responsible History* (Berghahn Books, 2009), p.11

negligence.[428]

Dr Hasan 'Uthman states in his book on Islamic historiography *Manhaj ul-Bahth at-Tārīkhī* [The Method of Historical Research]:

> The historian also has to possess the talent of critique as it is not permitted for him to accept all statements and believe all documents and sources without study, testing and investigation. He should take what is truthful or what is as near to it as possible, and put aside whatever is not like that. If the historian lacks the faculty of critique then this feature is dropped from him and he becomes a person who merely relays all what he reaches him as if it is the true reality. History is neither studied nor written in this way.[429]

Dr Muhammad bin Sāmil as-Sulamī, the former head of the College of Sharee'ah and Islamic Studies at Umm ul-Qurā' University stated in his book *Manhaj Kitābat it-Tārīkh il-Islāmī* [The Methodology of Writing Islamic History] when discussing 'Principles in Source-Referencing':

> The sources in relation to the historian form the greatest importance because without maintaining the sources he will be unable to write or research history. History is transmitted knowledge which relies upon taking from sources, because history is a report about an event which happened and then finished. Imagination, guessing the unseen and experiments do not suffice as is done by the literary writer, story-teller, poet and physiologist.[430]

Furthermore, Azumah demonstrates a total misunderstanding of the *jihād* of 'Uthmān ibn Fūdī (Dan Fodio)[431] and attempts to show that

428 Ibid., p.14

429 Dr Hasan 'Uthmān, *Manhaj ul-Bahth at-Tārīkhī* [The Method of Historical Research]. Cairo: Dār ul-Ma'ārif, 1964, 8th Print. 19

430 Dr Muhammad bin Sāmil as-Sulamī, *op.cit.*, pp.235-236

431 Abū Muhammad 'Uthmān ibn Muhammad ibn Fūdī, born in Marratta in northern Nigeria in 1168 AH/ 1754 CE. The name 'Dan Fodio' is the Hausa rendition of Ibn Fūdī. He was from a family of scholars that migrated to Hausaland from Futa Toro before the 15th century CE, bringing with it the Islamic tradition of Timbuktu. He waged a jihad in 1217 AH/1802 CE against clans that had opposed Islām and the Muslims. He established the Sokoto Islamic state which

the *jihād* of 'Uthmān Dan Fodio was a virulently anti non-Muslim phenomena, which is a gross simplification of the situation. Yet as we will see upon closer inspection and with deeper investigation, Azumah's

---

ruled by *Sharee'ah* in West Africa. He is known for his *tajdeed* efforts and his stance against innovations.

A number of folkloric legends and myths surrounded the personality of Dan Fodio as some people claimed that he could "walk on water" or appear in dreams. Some people even claimed that he was the *Mahdi!* All of these ideas were refuted by Dan Fodio himself during his time. In a book entitled *Tanbeeh al-Faheem*, Dan Fodio refuted the claims of a man named Hammā who lived in Maganga, Nigeria and was claiming to be the *Mahdi*, the man was later executed for his heresy, see M.A. al-Hajj, *The Mahdist Tradition in Northern Nigeria*, A.B.U. 1973.

Dan Fodio however did make some comments in some of his works that were in line with the Ash'arīs, but at times he clearly said things in line with the *Salaf* (pious predecessors) as have been mentioned. He therefore was akin to Imām an-Nawawī and Ibn Hajar, who also had teachers that were of the Ash'arī *'aqeedah* but were not pure Ash'arīs. Dan Fodio's chain of scholars however reveals interesting facts. One of teachers was Jibreel ibn 'Umar of the Tuareg tribe who had made Hajj and thus lived in Makkah for a while. In Madeenah, Jibreel Ibn 'Umar studied with Muhammad Murtada az-Zabeedī (1145-1205 AH/ 1732-1791 CE) who was originally from India but had travelled to az-Zabeed in Yemen where he lived for a while and studied before going on to teach in Madeenah himself.

One of az-Zabeedī's teachers was Shāh Waliullāh ad-Dehlawī (1702 – 1762 CE) of Delhi in India. Dan Fodio's uncle who taught him hadeeth was Muhammad bin Rāj who had studied under Abu'l-Hasan as-Sindee also from India and a teacher of hadeeth in Madeenah. Abu'l-Hasan as-Sindī was a student of Muhammad Hayāt as-Sindee another great hadeeth scholar of India who was also teaching in Madeenah. One of Muhammad Hayāt as-Sindī's students was Muhammad ibn 'AbdulWahhāb (*rahimahumullāh*). Also see a recent study conducted in Nigeria and written in Arabic entitled *Asāneed al-Faqeer ad-Da'eef al-Mutashāfī bi'l-Mushaffa' Ahmad as-Shareef* (Ms. University of Ibadan Library 82/137: Ibadan, Centre of Islamic Documentation (CAD). This *sanad* was also mentioned by an American Muslim researcher who had graduated from *Madeenah* University.

Also see the research of a non-Muslim researcher Stefan Reichmuth in his "*Murtada al-Zabidi (d. 1791) in Biographical and Autobiographical Accounts – Glimpses of Islamic Scholarship in the 18th Century CE*" in the Islamic studies journal *Die Welt Des Islams – International Journal for the Study of Modern Islam* (Leiden, Boston and Koln: Brill, Vol. 39, No. 1, March 1999) p.70.

attempts to use the efforts of 'Uthmān Dan Fodio as supporting his claims of this violent anti-African anti-non-Muslim in fact is a proof against Azumah and not for his arguments. Azumah states:

> In fact Dan Fodio, right from the very beginning of his 'reform' movement, considered military jihad against the vast numbers of traditional communities in the region to be a top priority.[432]

This is a gross simplification of the events, as Azumah glosses over the background to 'Uthmān Dan Fodio's *jihād* in Sokoto and neglects the details of what took place, furthermore none of the historians of the Sokoto *Khilāfah* (Caliphate) have agreed with Azumah's biased and partisan argument. As a result, Azumah totally avoided referring to the fact that there was actually a detailed and systematic agenda that 'Uthmān Dan Fodio had, it was not a mere military confrontation directed at non-Muslims as Azumah claims. Not only were practicing Muslims being oppressed by the nominally Muslim Habe rulers, but they were also guilty of oppressing its subjects and thus not implementing Islām in its correct manner with regards to legislation, which is supposed to avoid transgression, corruption and suppression of Muslims. Islamically this is acceptable as 'Uthmān Dan Fodio and those with him became the dominant force. Al-Hāfidh Ibn Hajar al-'Asqalānī transmitted this in his book *Fath al-Bārī* from Imām Ibn Battāl, who has an explanation of *Saheeh Bukhārī* which has been published:

> The *fuquhā* (Islamic jurists) have reached consensus that obedience must be made to the leader who becomes dominant (*mutaghallib*)[433] and making *jihād* with him and that obeying him

432 Ibid., p.92

433 Shaykh 'Ali Hasan al-Halabī al-Atharī mentioned in regards to this in a lesson in March 2006 CE at the Imām al-Albānī Centre in 'Ammān, Jordon: "Here we must stop at this word "*mutaghallib* (the one who overpowers and becomes dominant)" for a while. In the next session it will be made apparent to us that the paths for a ruler acquiring power are numerous and from the paths are in the case of a ruler who becomes dominant and overpowers others (*al-Mutaghallib*). It is when a person opposes the Divine Legislation and revolts against the Muslim leader and thus becomes dominant, and this has happened in Islamic history and the scholars noted that this opposes the Divine Legislation. However, the one who revolted against the Muslim ruler has established and settled security and command now and is able to control the Muslim lands as he obviously is a Muslim

> is better than revolting against him due to the blood which would be spilt in that and this would not be permissible unless there was clear *kufr* from the leader.[434] [435]

In any case, in regards to 'Uthmān Dan Fodio the Habe rulers were actually committing clear *kufr* by worshipping other deities other than Allāh, slaughtering to other than Allāh, making vows to other than Allāh and the like. Furthermore, the Habe rulers at the time had made lawful a number of things which go against the Divine Legislation of Islām, such as forbidding people from accepting Islām, outlawing the *hijāb* and Islamic clothing. As Mervyn Hiskett, a non-Muslim historian of the Sokoto Islamic phenomena, who for Azumah would thus be a reliable source as he is not Muslim, highlights:

> The reformers' criticisms of the Habe administrators were various and detailed…In general, he and his associates complained of the tyrannical and arbitrary nature of the Habe government and instanced such abuses as confiscation of the peasants' cattle and beasts of burden…[436]

This is what Azumah neatly neglected to mention, that 'Uthmān Dan Fodio was fighting against an oppressive government not merely innocent 'traditional African believers' as Azumah claims! Therefore,

---

yet has opposed the consensus of the Muslims by revolting in the first place yet has seized the reins of power from the first bearers of it. The scholars have reached agreement that the leader who overpowers the reins of authority from another leader is to be obeyed and this is Divine Legislated. Why? Because it is feared that revolting against this one again will only cause a worse tribulation. For that reason, the greatest intents of the Divine Legislation is that preventing the harms takes precedence over enforcing the benefit."

434 *Sharh Ibn Battāl 'alā Sahīh al-Bukhārī* (10/8).

435 Shaykh Ali Hasan said in the above mentioned lesson: "As now the leader would have been expelled from the condition of being a Muslim due to falling into clear *kufr*. For this reason, the Prophet (*sallallāhu 'alayhi wassallam*) said: *"Until you see clear (buwāhan) kufr, for which you have with you evidence from Allāh."* Pay attention here: *"you have with you ('indakum)"* meaning that this evidence is firmly settled in you hearts and is clear in front of your eyes, not any type of *kufr* rather it must be clear, explicit and apparent!"

436 Mervyn Hiskett, *The Sword of Truth: The Life and Times of the Shehu Usuman dan Fodio* (Evanston, Illinois: Northwestern University Press, 1994), p.74.

'Uthmān Dan Fodio became dominant due to the values that he was seen to possess, the very fact that he was successful was due to the large following that he gained from the indigenous people and also due to the order and stability that he was viewed as bringing to Sokoto. Indeed, Ibraheem Sulaiman notes that the universal nature of the Shehu's appeal made it possible for a large number of non-Muslims to accept Islām.[437] Michael A. Gomez also highlights that "non-Muslim Fulbe fought under Usuman dan Fodio"[438], indicating that non-Muslims freely joined him. Abdur Rahman I. Doi also noted that 'Uthmān Dan Fodio managed to bring an end to internal feuds among the Hausa states by uniting those states under one general authority of one ruler with the sultān of Sokoto at its head.[439] At the time of the *jihād* of 'Uthmān Dan Fodio Hausaland was divided into two groups of states, the Hausa Bakwai (the seven original Hausa states: Kano, Zazzau, Gobir, Katsina, Dauro, Rano and Biram) and the Banza Bakwai (the seven non-recognised states such as Kabi, Zamfara, Nupe, Yawuri, Yoruba, Borgu and Gurma).

Zamfara for example was at the height of its power in the early eighteenth century until it was annexed by Gobir. These small kingdoms were constantly at war with each other and thus by the beginning of the nineteenth century all of them were in decline due to their mutual hatred except for Gobir.[440] Another reason for 'Uthmān Dan Fodio's popularity during his time was his stance against the extensive and indiscriminate enslavement which was legislated by those he was fighting against which was affecting not only Muslims but also non-Muslims. However, Azumah in his enthusiasm to impugn the activities of 'Uthmān Dan Fodio with anything negative, states in blatant ignorance of the historical facts:

> Muslim enslavement of traditional African believers during the wake of jihad movements is one single factor that accounts for

437 Ibraheem Sulaiman, *A Revolution in History: The Jihad of Usman Dan Fodio* (London and New York: Mansell Publishing Limited, 1986), p.106.

438 Michael A. Gomez, *Black Crescent: The Experience and Legacy of African Muslims in the Americas* (New York: Cambridge University Press, 2005), p.115.

439 Abdur Rahman I. Doi, *Islam in Nigeria* (Zaria: Gaskiya Corporation Limited, 1984), p.44.

440 Charlotte A. Quinn and Frederick Quinn, *Pride, Faith and Fear: Islam in Sub-Saharan Africa* (Oxford: OUP, 2003).

> large-scale conversion to Islam in eighteenth- and nineteenth-century Western and Central Sudan.[441]

In fact, it was the other way around! Those who Azumah calls 'traditional African believers' (by this he means the nominal Muslim ruling government during the time of Shaykh 'Uthmān Dan Fodio) were the ones active in enslaving all and sundry! Hiskett mentions:

> Shehu Usuman directly refers to the common practice of enslaving Muslims: once in an Arabic work entitled *Masa'il Muhimma* [Important Matters] written in Degel in A.H. 1217/A.D. 1802... and again in a Fulfulde poem, *Tabbat hakika* (Be Sure of That)...[442]

Therefore, the claim that Islām spread during the eighteenth and nineteenth centuries in West Africa due to slavery is absolutely false which Azumah did not support with any clear evidence whatsoever, even though he claims to bring "census reports later" to support that!? 'Uthmān Dan Fodio's efforts highlighted the abuses of Islamic legislation and the people supported him due to his call for correct and proper adherence to the Divine Legislation. Also the ruling nominal Muslim Habe authorities (who Azumah constantly refers to as being "traditional African believers"!?) were by no means the under-dogs as Azumah would have us think, they actually possessed fire-arms which made their slave-raiding easier to implement, Hiskett thus informs:

> Another reason may be that in about A.D. 1730 muskets became readily available in Habe states. The possession of fire-arms by the privileged Sarakuna- the courtiers of the Habe courts- certainly gave them superior fire power which made slave-harvesting among the ill-armed peasantry easier and more rewarding.[443]

Ibraheem Sulaiman thus highlights that 'Uthmān Dan Fodio demanded the release of prisoners, some of whom were not Muslims and Dan Fodio also called for the abolition of all unjust taxes.[444] Hiskett mentions:

---

441 Azumah, *op.cit.*, p.98

442 Hiskett, *op.cit.*, p.77

443 Ibid, p.78. Firearms were also used by Moroccan armies under the order of the tyrannical ruler, Ahmad al-Mansūr as-Sā'dī against Mali in 1591 CE and by the Ottomans against the Mamluk dynasty in 1517 CE at the Battle of Cairo.

444 Sulaiman, *op.cit.*, p.106

> At any rate, there is no doubt that enslavement threatened many people in Hausaland at the time the Shehu was preaching in their communities. It was, therefore, natural that they should try to escape the threat by seeking his protection. Thus the particular factor of slavery reinforced the general undercurrent of sympathy for Islam as an attractive alternative to the, by now, centuries' old domination of the Habe chiefs, and the animism they represented.[445]

Therefore, Azumah's claim that 'Uthmān Dan Fodio's efforts were the cause for mass enslavement of people in West Africa is a total misrepresentation of the historical facts, as mass enslavement was taking place by the enemies of Shaykh 'Uthmān during his time and was one of the reasons people fought against the enemies of Islām. If Azumah really desires "inter-faith" dialogue he should begin by presenting all historical facts and not simplifying detailed issues in order to make Muslims in Africa out to be violent anti-non-Muslim jihādists who are only concerned with fighting against "traditional African believers", as Azumah says. The real reasons for the spread of Islām in West Africa, to the frustration of the Christian evangelical missionaries, was highlighted by Norman Daniel wherein he said "Islam was making great advances in Africa, because it was spread by traders who lived lives intelligible to the African peoples, and often were themselves African."[446] This factor is something which Azumah denies and is frustrated by which makes Azumah formulate a number of erroneous arguments.

Furthermore, we also know that during the epoch of Shaykh 'Uthmān Dan Fodio (*rahimahullāh*), many people were voluntarily becoming Muslim, as one of the edicts which Nafata the ruler of the Habe authorities made against Dan Fodio was that "no more conversions to Islam were to be allowed and those who were not born Muslims should return to their former religion." Usman Bugaje notes:

> But by stopping others from preaching he must have hoped to muzzle the mass conversion that the preaching was producing, since every conversion meant a shrink in his authority and accretion of Shehu's power.[447]

---

445 Hiskett, *op.cit.*, p.79

446 Daniel, *op.cit.*, pp.326-27

447 Usman Muhammad Bugaje, *The Contents, Methods and Impact of Shehu Usman*

Therefore, people were embracing and accepting Islām of their own accord during the epoch of 'Uthmān Dan Fodio not due to having been enslaved - which is what Azumah tries to claim was the reason for so many people in West Africa becoming Muslims. Azumah then proceeds with trying to make out that 'Uthmān Dan Fodio despised African languages and had an inferiority complex! Azumah states:

> They anathematized local languages like Hausa as 'ajami, profane and eulogized Arabic as the language of God; they promoted Arabic and nomadic ways of dressing (wearing of the veil by women and turban by men) as against traditional Hausa forms.[448] (!!)

Azumah also says that:

> ...it was Africans mercilessly enforcing Arab ways of life upon fellow Africans in the name of God![449]

This is a blatant slander and falsity from Azumah, as it is well known that the Hausa of northern Nigeria, as most Muslims all over the world, have their own Islamic culture that reflects their cultural background and experience. However, Azumah, who has his own agenda of presenting Islām in West Africa as being entrenched in "pro-Arab culture", attempts to show that Muslims rebuffed anything African and this is clear deception. As for the claim with regards to dress then this is how indigenous people of the savannah regions of Africa dress anyway! In following Azumah's method of denying any voice to Islamic sources or research, let's refer to what David Robinson, a non-Muslim Western historian of Africa, has to say on this issue:

> Muslims in the different parts of Africa were eager to express their faith in concrete terms, what academics often call visual culture...they also adopted what they took to be very specific Islamic forms for their own production.[450]

Dan Fodio's Teachings, 1774-1804 (MA Dissertation, Institute of African and Asian Studies, University of Khartoum, March 1979 CE), pp.40-41.

448 Azumah, *op.cit.*, pp.98-99

449 Ibid., p.99

450 David Robinson, *Muslim Societies in African History: New Approaches to African History* (Cambridge: Cambridge University Press, 2004), p.44.

Robinson for example notes how Muslims in Africa have always applied Islām in accordance with their indigenous cultures, he further says in regards to 'Uthmān Dan Fodio and the issue of languages that he used the following accurate point:

> Uthman, his family, and his chief ministers soon began to write down their experience- how they moved from reform to revolution and the implementation of a "true" Islamic state. They wrote primarily in Arabic for scholarly consumption and primarily in the spoken languages for lay consumption. By their actions, they gave a strong boost to ajami literature. Ajami means "non-Arabic" and refers to writing of "foreign" languages in the Arabic script. There are many ajami corpuses in Africa. Uthman and his entourage wrote their ajami in Fulfulde, Hausa and Tamacheq...[451]

So according to Robinson 'Uthmān Dan Fodio gave a "strong boost" to non-Arabic literature and this is only adequate as they were communicating in the language that was spoken by the majority of common people in their lands. The fact is that 'Uthman Dan Fodio and his followers did not force people to learn Arabic clearly proves that they did not consider it to be necessary for all common people to have an in-depth knowledge of Arabic as they would have mentioned this in their writings. So again Azumah is trying to form his own ideas via denying the clear evidences, Azumah did not mention at all in his book that 'Uthmān Dan Fodio communicated in Fulfulde, Hausa[452] and Tamacheq and totally denied this factor. Robinson also says of the daughter of 'Uthmān Dan Fodio, Nana Asma'u that she:

> ...wrote extensively in the languages that were widely used in Hausaland. She made a special point of writing Fulani and Hausa ajami poetry for recitation to her teachers, families, and whoever would listen to her...[453]

So in any case there was never widespread bilingualism in West Africa

451 Ibid., p.145

452 Many Hausa speakers migrated eastwards towards Chad and Sudan especially during the nineteenth century and most of these particular Hausa speakers are bilingual in Arabic and Hausa, their Hausa dialect contains many Arabic loan-words.

453 Robinson, *op.cit.*, p.149

between Arabic and indigenous languages even though certain languages were written in Arabic script such as Hausa, Fulfulde and Yoruba. Arabic was mainly used for correspondence between various rulers of the region and Islamic scholars since the eleventh century CE when Islām reached West Africa. Therefore speakers of these languages and other major languages in the West African region such as Twi, Songhay, Bambara and Wolof all had some exposure to the use of Arabic as a religious language, but not as a widely spoken language or even lingua franca for common Muslims in the region.

Azumah is therefore guilty of viewing African Muslims as being the only Muslims on the face of the earth who blindly follow other people's ignorant cultures over Islām, as if only African Muslims are the ones susceptible to this and no one else, in fact Azumah speaks as if African Muslims are so stupid as to accept the cultures of non-African Muslims as being from Islām!? Azumah states:

> It is only on this basis that we have been critical of the universalisation of the Arab factor in Islam as 'orthodox' and therefore the only vehicle of expressing 'true' and 'pure' Islam. It is in this vein that we have been critical of the apparent double standards whereby, indigenous Persian, Indian and North African elements appropriated in Muslim practice are regarded as 'original and unmistakably Islamic' whilst African elements are indiscriminately branded as 'pagan survivals.' In short, the question raised in the work is not whether Islam in an Arab cultural garb is right or wrong but why in African cultural trappings it is at best inferior and at worst kufr.[454]

This demonstrates the falsehood of Azumah's arguments, I personally do not know of any educated and knowledgeable Muslim who regards the indigenous cultural practices of Muslims in India, Persia or North Africa as being the model for Muslims in Africa to follow?! This is blatant deception, and as for the claim of the 'Arab factor in Islam as orthodox' then this is false, as in Islām piety is based on the application of Islām in an individual not merely as blindly following the cultures of Muslims in other parts of the world. Then Azumah states that,

> It is in this vein that we have been critical of the apparent double standards whereby, indigenous Persian, Indian and North

454 Azumah, op.cit., p.239.

> African elements appropriated in Muslim practice are regarded as 'original' and unmistakably Islamic.

So where are the double standards? Azumah did not present any African Muslim who said that the ignorant indigenous cultural practices of any Muslim in India, Persia or North Africa should be the model for Islamic practice in Africa! The only "double-standards" then emanates from Azumah himself, who claims to promote "inter-faith dialogue" and "cross-religious discussion" and then rejects Islamic sources and the Muslim witness on the basis that it is not reliable and exaggerated! So it is rather quite patronising to consider African Muslims as being so empty and void and so susceptible, impressionable and gullible as to blindly accept any cultural practice, belief or custom on the basis that any ignoramus from India, Persia or North Africa does it! Azumah himself, and those who share his erroneous view, demonstrate that they in fact hold Africans and black people in contempt by viewing them as being so ignorant that they cannot distinguish or judge between foolish cultural practices from different parts of the Muslim world and Islām as taught in the Qur'ān, *sunnah* and ways of the early Muslims.

Then Azumah continues by stating "...whilst African elements are indiscriminately branded as 'pagan survivals." So according to Azumah's derogatory view of African Muslims, aspects of African culture are rejected amongst African Muslims while the cultures of India, Persia and North Africa (the rather odd list of countries which Azumah thinks African Muslims accept as authentic Islām in practice) are accepted outright!? What nonsense from Azumah! So according to this, an ignorant practice that is performed by common Indian Muslims such as kissing the fingers when hearing the *adhān* (the call to prayer) for example should have been blindly adopted by African Muslims, yet we do not find this at all amongst African Muslims or any other ignorant baseless cultural practice that is performed by Muslims from India, Persia and North Africa (the sequence of countries that Azumah refers to).

Azumah further tries to project contemporary examples of communal violence in Nigeria onto the efforts of Shaykh 'Uthmān Dan Fodio as if the efforts and example of Shaykh 'Uthmān Dan Fodio has led to current inter-religious problems in Nigeria and by extension, West Africa. As for the "jihad tradition" which Azumah speaks of, then he has grossly misunderstood it as we have demonstrated. Azumah's claims that he desires "inter-faith dialogue" are thrown into serious question considering his dubious claims about Muslims in West Africa and his inaccuracies. Yet he speaks as if he is speaking on behalf of non-Muslim Africans saying:

> The issue that concerns non-Muslims is 'Islam' as it is understood and lived by their Muslim relations and neighbours. It is this Islam, and not the so-called 'true' and 'original' Islam in textbooks, that affects non-Muslims.[455]

But this is a rather flawed argument as if certain Muslims are not following true Islām, then what are they following? And if certain Muslims are practicing Islām in ways which are causing distress to their non-Muslim neighbours (which is actually against the *sunnah* of the Prophet Muhammad, (*sallallāhu alayhi wassallam*) then they are totally opposing true Islām and thus we have to refer to 'textbooks' (as Azumah says) in order to find the correct Islamic views for them to abide by. If anyone who claims to be a Muslim rejects the Islamic texts then obviously such a person's Islām is questionable and thus cannot be viewed as acting in the name of, or according to, Islām.

However, Azumah is saying that any ignorant Muslim who does an action has to be viewed as acting in the name of Islām even if such a Muslim is an ignoramus, lacks knowledge of the Qur'ān, *sunnah* and way of the early Muslims or may even reject the Islamic sources. The 'Islam' that may be understood by many Muslims may be based on erroneous ideas, cultural practices, extremism, neglect, blind-following of ancestors and may have nothing at all to do with Islām, such as the practices of female circumcision, forced marriages, terrorism, grave-worship, suicide bombings which are all practiced in the name of Islām but have no basis in the Qur'ān, *sunnah* and way of the early Muslims. For Azumah to deny this and say "No they are acting in the name of Islām" which is simplistic and denies the solution to it - which is based in the Islamic sources. But then Azumah contradicts himself, after saying that non-Muslims are concerned about "the Islam as understood and lived by their Muslim relations and neighbours" and not "the true and original Islam that is found in textbooks" then goes on to say that Muslims conservatively follow Islām and this has led to bloody conflicts?! He

455 Azumah, *op.cit.*, p.234

says:

> To espouse a thorough-going Islamic conservatism which has no room for tolerating let alone celebrating diversity and difference can (and has proven to be) potentially bloody.[456]

So now Azumah claims that Muslims are "espousing Islamic conservatism" this is odd, as what is it based on? After Azumah has stated prior that non-Muslims are concerned with the Islām that is practiced, lived and understood by any Muslim which is not based on any rigorous conservatism or focus on the fundamental texts of Islām?! Maybe Azumah needs to refer to Islamic history and the history of Muslims in Spain which is one of the biggest proofs against the doubts of the Islamophobes and their '*dhimmitude*'[457] claims. In fact, the history

---

456 Ibid., p.236

457 The concept of '*dhimmitude*' was formulated by Bat Ye'or in her book *Islam and Dhimmitude: Where Civilisations Collide* (Cranbury, New Jersey: Associated University Presses, 2002). The name 'Bat Ye'or' is not a real name and is rather a false Hebrew pseudonym that she uses, her real name is Giselle Littman and she is an Egyptian born British Jewish author who claims to specialise in the Middle-East and Islām. It is worth highlighting some aspects of her background as it helps us to understand some of the main reasons as to why she has formulated her ideas.

Littman was born in Cairo, but her Egyptian nationality was revoked in 1955 because she was Jewish so her family had to leave Egypt for England in 1957 wherein they became stateless refugees. Littman herself has described how her life experiences influenced her research interests when she said:

> I had witnessed the destruction, in a few short years, of a vibrant Jewish community living in Egypt for over 2600 years and which had existed from the time of Jeremiah the prophet. I saw the disintegration and flight of families, dispossessed and humiliated, the destruction of their synagogues, the bombing of the Jewish quarters and the terrorizing of a peaceful population. I have personally experienced the hardships of exile, the misery of statelessness and I wanted to get to the root cause of all this. I wanted to understand why the Jews from Arab countries, nearly a million shared my experience."

She authored a book entitled *The Jews in Egypt* in 1971 and then a study on Copts in Egypt under another false pseudonym, Yahudiya Masriya (Egyptian Jew) in Arabic. Claiming to focus on the status of non-Muslims under Muslim rule she attempts to recruit Christians and other non-Muslims into supporting the Zionist

of Muslim Spain is something which the Islamophobes gloss over

project by explaining away Christian expressions of appreciation of Muslim tolerance as false consciousness inspired by an inferiority complex and self-hating hang-up due to the aftermath of *jihād*, which she terms as "*dhimmitude*."

Littman (Bat Ye'or) claims that any injustices against Muslims are mere figments of the imagination and are only referred to in order to cover up an Islamic master plan for subjugating the non-Muslim world?! In the second half of the book she vilifies anti-Zionist Christians as being '*dhimmi* pawns.' However, she does not seek to attempt to dismiss Jewish critics of Israel in the same manner, such as Israel Shahak for example. Littman (Bat Ye'or) in her simplistic assessment of Islamic history dismisses any accusations of treachery on the part of the Jewish tribe of Bani Quraydhah during the time of the Prophet Muhammad (*sallallāhu alayhi wassallam*) and she also resorts to cut-and-paste quotations, context dropping and selective quotes from scholars and historians, as a result, she omits and glosses over any other positions that refute her claims.

She claims that European persecution of Jews came about after Europeans learned these "new techniques" from the Muslims!! She also argues a similar line in her book *Eurabia: The Euro-Arab Axis*. Littman does not admit that Palestinian Christians and Muslims have shared a common cause as victims of Israeli persecution, oppression, tyranny and injustice merely claiming that Arab Christian anti-Zionists have *dhimmi* submission to Muslim masters. Even the Israeli murder of Christians is blamed on the Muslims (on pages 278, 386).

She therefore claims that Muslims are intolerant due to their ideas on *jihād* and that the Divine Legislation (*Sharee'ah*) "wages a perpetual war against non-Muslims who refuse to submit." However, academics and professors in the field have raised questions concerning Littman's arguments. Esther Benbassa, director of religious studies in modern Judaism at the *Sorbonne University* in France said in an interview for the French weekly *Le Point* that Littman (Bat Ye'or) "is not a professional historian and that, though restrictions on Jews in Arab countries existed, they were more symbolic than practical, with non-Muslim minorities enjoying protection, autonomy and freedom."

Sidney H. Griffith in the *International Journal of Middle East Studies* writes in regards to Littman's book *The Decline of Eastern Christianity under Islam*:

> The problems one has with the book are basically twofold: the theoretical inadequacy of the interpretive concepts jihad and dhimmitude as they are employed here; and the want of historical method in the deployment of the documents which serve as evidence for the conclusions reached in the study. There is also an unfortunate polemical tone in the work.

and do not assess in depth due to the implications it has against their anti-Islamic agendas. In Muslim Spain, and for eight hundred years of Muslim rule there, Jews and Christians were tolerated and many Christians actually travelled from France, England and other medieval European countries in order to study, learn and live in the high culture of Muslim Spain. Regarding Azumah's statement:

> ...blacks are stereotyped and demonised in Muslim sources as sub-human, at best, non-human at worst.[458]

The following chapter will totally rebut this absurd point raised by Azumah so we will not go too in-depth into it now as it is dealt with subsequently. Yet it is important to note that the above claim is very serious and considering the fact that Azumah quoted a Christian, who he believed was a Muslim (!), demonstrates the lack of meticulous research that Azumah has undertaken in this issue.

In assessing these claims, it is noteworthy to mention that Henry Stubbs (a contemporary of Hobbes) who was an expert in Ottoman policies of tolerance highlighted that if the Europeans adopted Ottoman policies of tolerance it would solve the problems of religious hatred and communal violence. Interestingly, after Hobbes, Locke wrote a famous treatise on tolerance which became the basis for American freedom of religion acts and policies, based on the Ottoman model. Littman's work is utilised and referred to by the likes of Daniel Pipes, Oriana Fallaci, 'Jack Chick', Robert Spencer, Craig Winn, far-right groups in Britain and others.

458 Azumah, *op.cit.*, p.233

VI

Does Islām Teach Racism?

It should also be noted, in order to refute the Afrocentrics, Zionists, Orientalists and Christian missionaries, that throughout the history of Islām, Muslim scholars have written monumental works to do with slavery, racism and equality. These issues were never even discussed by any of the world's religions and civilisations until the last two hundred years or so, let alone books written on such issues. At times when ignorance was rife, it was only the Muslims who carried the light of knowledge and some of the examples that will be presented here should indicate to people that Islām has to be judged upon the Qur'ān and *Sunnah*, not on ignorant Muslims.

Ibn ul-Jawzī (*rahimahullāh*)[459] a Muslim scholar of Baghdad wrote a book in the late twelfth century CE called *Tanweer al-Ghabash fī Fadl is-Sudan wa'l-Habash* [The Illumination of the Darkness on the Merits of the Black People and the Ethiopians].[460] It is a historical summary of

---

459 Abu'l-Faraj 'Abdur-Rahmān ibn Hasan ibn ul-Jawzī (597 AH/ 1114 CE – 1200 CE). He was raised in the 'Irāqī metropolis of Baghdād where he was educated by his family who were scholars and other scholars of the Hanbalī school of Islamic fiqh. He became outstanding in the fields of Qur'ānic commentary, Arabic language, history and hadeeth. His works cover diverse areas and among the most notable of his published works are: *Sifah us-Safwah*, a biography of the companions of Prophet Muhammad and the early scholars of the *Salaf; Taqseem ul-Lisān*, in Arabic language and linguistics; *Zād al-Maseer fī 'Ilm ut-Tafseer*, commentary on the Qur'ān; *al-Mawdū'āt*, in *hadeeth*; *Talbees Iblees*, about extreme and heretical understandings and practices; *Rūh ul-Arwāh* and *Sayd ul-Khātir*.

460 It has been edited by Mohamed Barakat (Sudan: Omdurman Islamic University Printing and Publishing House, 1412 AH/1993 CE). It has also been translated into English as a Ph.D degree thesis at the School of Oriental and

the social history of sub-Saharan Africa and the meritorious deeds of some well-known persons of African origin in the Islamic world. At the time of writing this book, Baghdad was becoming colour conscious and racism was beginning to set in, deviating from the justice and equality that Islām emphasizes.

Before the contents of the book are looked at, it must be noted that Ibn ul-Jawzī was not just any simple Muslim scholar writing a book out of sanctimony, rather he was one of the most prolific writers and erudite scholars to have existed in Islamic history. He was a specialist in *hadeeth*, jurisprudence (*fiqh*), and history. He was also famed for his *da'wah* activities (calling to Islām), teaching and writing. In 1965 CE, 'Abdul-Hameed al-'Ajūlī produced a comprehensive account of Ibn ul-Jawzī's works, wherein he classified them and stated where they could also be found, he listed 384 books to Ibn ul-Jawzī's name.[461] Shaykh ul-Islām Ahmad Taqiyyuddeen Ibn 'Abdul-Hameed Ibn Taymiyyah (*rahimahullāh*) said that Ibn ul-Jawzī wrote over one thousand books.[462]

Ibn ul-Jawzī in *Tanweer* tried to restore the purity of Islām and raise the morale of some of the black community in Baghdād at that time by reminding of their role in history. The contents of the book, as per Alawiye's translation, are as follows:

(a) Those Who Belong to the Sudan

(b) The Cause of Their Dark-skin

(c) The Enlivening of Shem, the Son of Noah, by Jesus the Son of Mary

(d) The Kingdoms of the Black People and Their Extent

(e) The Collective Moral Excellence of the Character of the Black People

---

African Studies, University of London, by 'Imran Hamza Alawiye. It was translated by Dr. Alawiye as *Ibn al-Jawzi's Apologia on Behalf of the Black People & Their Status in Islam: A Critical Edition and Translation of Kitab Tanwir al-Ghabash fi Fadl as-Sudan wa'l-Habash* (August 1985). It is in the SOAS library thesis section.

Note that 'Sudan' refers to 'black people' and not the modern country of Sudan. As classically, the Arabs utilised the terms 'Baydān' to refer to the brown and light brown Arab peoples and 'Sudan' to refer to black people.

461 Arabic text entitled *Mu'allafāt Ibn ul-Jawzī* [A Study of the Works of Ibn ul-Jawzī], 1965.

462 Ibn Rajab al-Hanbalī, *Kitāb ad-Dayhl 'Alā Tabaqāt ul-Hanabilah*

(f) Things Distinguished by Darkness from Amongst Animals, Trees and Plants

(g) The Obviousness that there is no Preference for Light-Skinned Peoples Over Dark-Skinned People Based Upon Colour; Indeed Preference is Based Upon Piety

(h) The Companions Who Migrated to Ethiopia

(i) The Deputation of Quraysh to the Negus (Najāshi) to Retrieve the Companions of the Messenger of Allāh

(j) The Correspondence of the Prophet with the Negus (Najāshi)

(k) The Arrival of the Ethiopians to the Messenger of Allāh...And Their Play With Hirāb (Lances) in the Mosque During His Presence

(l) Qur'ānic Words of Ethiopian Origin

(m) What the Messenger Heard of the Ethiopian Language That Pleased Him

(n) The Assignment of the Call to the Ethiopians

(o) The Prophets Who Were Black

(p) The Eminent King of Ethiopia

(q) The Distinguished Black Males Amongst the Companions of the Prophet Muhammad

(r) The Distinguished Black Females Amongst the Companions of the Prophet Muhammad

(s) Prominent Learned Black People

(t) Poets and Those Who Composed Poetry Amongst the Black People

(u) Groups of Clever, Intelligent and Generous Black Males and Females

(v) The Pious and Ascetic of the Black People

(w) The Famous Black Females

(x) Those Who Preferred Black Concubines to Light-Skinned Ones and Who Loved and Died From Their Love of Them

(y) Qurayshīs Who Were Sons of Ethiopian Women

(z) Some Exhortations and Injunctions

(ā) Some Invocations and Glorifications of Allāh, Mighty and Majestic

(bb) Some Transmitted Supplications

All of this from a Muslim scholar writing in the 12th century C.E. and by the contents one could assume that Ibn ul-Jawzī is even more

'Afrocentric' than the Afrocentrics, without even once having to refer to European Christians, Freemasons and other Eurocentric sources!! Rather, Ibn ul-Jawzī was writing from Islamic sources, thus the incredulous statement of Azumah which we mentioned earlier is totally untrue, that: "...blacks are stereotyped and demonised in Muslim sources as sub-human, at best, non-human at worst."[463] While Rosenberg in his 2017 book *Black and Slave: The Origins and History of the Curse of Ham* also goes to great lengths (pp. 96-102) to suggest that the "association between black and slave can be seen in Arabia as early as the time of the Prophet of Islam."

Indeed, the scholar Muhammad al-Ameen ash-Shanqītī (*rahimahullāh*)[464] in his *Adwā' ul-Bayān* refutes the opinion that mixed-race marriages are not permitted by highlighting that such a position goes against the practice of the Prophet Muhammad who married his freed-slave Zayd ibn Hārithah (who was a black Arab) to Barakah Umm Usāmah who was a black woman from Ethiopia. Also the Prophet Muhammad (*sallallāhu alayhi wassallam*) married Usāmah ibn Zayd (*radi Allāhu 'anhu*) who was black to Fātimah Bint Qays, who was a woman from the Quraysh. Also Bilāl the black Ethiopian married the sister of 'AbdurRahmān ibn 'Awf who was from the tribe of Banī Zahra bin Kilāb. Imām ash-Shanqītī also mentioned in the context of refuting racist rulings that were made by some Mālikī scholars based on *shādh* [irregular] views which have been attributed to early scholars such as Tawūs about allowing black women to marry without a guardian as they are intrinsically ugly and lowly, he noted the fact that there are black women who are noble and beautiful and as a result some Arab literary authors and poets extolled the virtues of the black women that they loved, Imām ash-Shanqītī mentions these lines of poetry in '*Adwā ul-Bayān*.[465] The poetry that

463 Azumah, *op.cit.*, p.233

464 Shaykh Muhammad al-Ameen bin Muhammad al-Mukthār al-Jaknī ash-Shanqītī al-Mauritānī al-Mālikī al-Afrīqī (1320-1393 AH/d. 1974 CE), *rahimahullāh*, a famous scholar and Mālikī jurist in his homeland, Mauritania. He taught *tafseer* in the Prophet's Mosque in Madeenah and *usūl ul-fiqh* in Riyādh and Madeenah. His books are used in the College of Sharee'ah in Saudi Arabia. The most notable of his works is *Adwā' ul-Bayān li-Tafseer al-Qur'ān bi'l-Qur'ān*.

465 Muhammad al-Ameen bin Muhammad al-Mukthār al-Jaknī ash-Shanqītī al-Mauritānī al-Mālikī al-Afrīqī, *Adwā' ul-Bayān fī Īdāh al-Qur'ān bi'l-Qur'ān*, vol.1 (Beirut: Ihyā Turāth al-Arabī, First Ed., 1996 CE/1417 AH), p.247.

Imām Shanqītī brings are the poetry and stanzas which Ibn ul-Jawzī also mentioned in his *Tanweer al-Ghabash*, which was transmitted in the works of poets such as Ibn Marzubān.[466]

Other Muslim scholars who wrote similar books include Jalāluddeen as-Suyūtī (*rahimahullāh*)[467] who wrote three books about black people which were: *Raf' Sha'n al-Hubshān* [*Raising the Status of the Ethiopians*], *Azhār ul-'Urūsh fī Akhbār ul-Hubūsh* [*The Flowers of the Thrones Concerning Information About the Ethiopians*] and *Nuzhat ul-'Umr fi't-Tafdeel Bayna al-Bid wa's-Sūd wa's-Sumr* [*The Promenade of a Lifetime Concerning Preference for Light-Skinned, Dark Skinned and Brown Skinned Peoples*].[468] These scholars were arguing and writing as Muslims using the Qur'ān and *Sunnah* as their main sources. J.A. Rogers thus mentions in his book *Sex and Race*:

466 See Mohamed Barakat (ed.), *Tanweer ul-Ghabash*, pp.185-195; quoting from works of Arabic poetry such as *al-Aghānī* by Abu'l-Farj al-Asbahānī, edited by 'AbdusSatār Ahmad Farrāj (Beirut: Dār uth-Thaqāthah, 1401 AH/1981 CE, Fifth Edition). Muhammad Ibn Khalaf Ibn Marzubān also authored a work which today is very pertinent entitled *The Superiority of Dogs Over Many of Those Who Wear Clothes!* Translated and edited by GR Smith and MAS 'AbdulHaleem (Warminster, UK: Aris and Philips, 1978).

467 'AbdurRahmān ibn Abī Bakr, known as Jalāluddeen as-Suyūtī (1145 CE – 1505 C.E./ 911 A.H.) was a hadeeth scholar, historian, linguist and *faqeeh* (jurist). He was born in Asyūt (Assiut) in Upper Egypt and was of Persian and Circassian origin. He flourished in Cairo during the declining years of the Mamluk dynasty. In that city, as-Suyūtī was taught by some of the most prominent scholars of his time and he became known for his erudition at an early age, later becoming a teacher of high repute himself. At the age of forty he was a leading scholar in all of the various Islamic sciences, secluding himself and devoting his time to writing. About 400 works are attributed to him the most notable are his Qur'ānic commentary that he wrote along with Jalāluddeen al-Mahālī, the famous commentary known as *al-Jalālayn*. As-Suyūtī's other noted works are *al-Itqān fī 'Ulūm il-Qur'ān, Tadreeb ur-Rāwī, al-Jāmi's-Sagheer* and *ad-Durr al-Manthūr fi't-Tafseer bi'l-Ma'thūr*.

468 For more information on these works see: Akbar Muhammad, "The Image of Africans in Arabic Literature – Some Unpublished Manuscripts," in John Ralph Willis (ed.) *Slaves and Slavery in Muslim Africa, Volume 1 – Islam and the Ideology of Enslavement* (London and New York: Frank Cass & Co. Ltd, 1985), pp.67-65.

> In short, the Negro[469] was discriminated against in no phase of Mohammedan life on the ground of color alone. Islam was the greatest and freest of all great melting pots.[470]

Other Arab scholars who made racist and so called 'rationalist,' comments were not basing their foolish claims on the Qur'ān and Sunnah, but rather upon the ideas and methods of Hippocrates,[471] Herodotus,[472] Tacitus,[473] Galen,[474] Strabo[475] and Ptolemy[476] and their notions related to the climes and how this supposedly impacted temperaments. Medieval Arabic geographical, historical and medical texts, with Ibn Khaldun being the most prominent, described the world as comprising seven latitudinal climes and the 'median clime' was portrayed as being the Middle East, while Africans, Turks and Europeans were framed as all residing in harsh and extreme climes which impacted their thinking,

---

469 During the time J.A. Rogers was writing, the Spanish word '*Negro*' was used to describe people of African origin in the West.

470 J.A. Rogers, *Sex and Race* (New York, 1967), p.108.

471 An ancient Greek doctor and medical expert, he has many works attributed to him that were written circa 400 BCE.

472 The ancient Greek historian who was born in Halicarnassus (modern-day Bodrum in Turkey) lived in the fifth century CE, 484-425 BCE. He was a contemporary of the philosopher Socrates (470-399 BCE), Thucydides (460-400 BCE), often dubbed as "the father of scientific history" and "the father of political realism", and Euripedes (480-406 BCE), the Greek tragedian. Cicero conferred upon Herodotus the title "the father of history". He is seen as being the first historian to have broken from Homeric tradition in that he treated historical subjects as a method of investigation and critically assessing his materials and then arranging them in to a historiographical narrative. The *Histories* is the only book which he is known to have authored in which he also studies the origins of the Greco-Persian Wars and assesses the lives of Darius, Xerses, and the Battles of Marathon, Thermopylae, Artemisium, Salamis, Plataea and Mycale.

473 In his book *Germania*, authored in 98 CE, the Roman historian Tacitus (56-120 CE) refers to the cold environment impacting the Germanic tribes and their temperament. The surviving portions of his two major works, *Annals* and *Histories*, examine the reigns of Roman Emperors Tiberius, Claudius and Nero.

474 An ancient Greek physician who died circa 199 CE

475 A famous ancient Greek geographer and traveller, died circa 24 CE.

476 Greco-Egyptian geographer, astronomer and mathematician of the 2nd century CE

bodies and sexuality. This Greek notion would also later impact on environmental determinism a discredited precursor to the Darwinian theory of natural selection. Humoral pathology was also linked to this,[477] however Muslim scholars would mention humoral pathology in their writings, such as Ibn ul-Qayyim Jawziyyah (*rahimahullāh*), did not mention anything about climatic theory and race as they were aware that it was in full contradiction to the teachings of Islam about racial brotherhood. It may also have been the case that Ibn Khaldun influenced European thought, such as that of the French enlightenment political philosopher Montesquieu (1689-1755) during the 18th century who himself was impressed by the ideas of the French traveller Jean Chardin who had been in Persia and had begun to also utilise climatic determinism.

Similarly, some scholars and writers relied heavily on the *Isrā'īliyat* (Jewish sources) and they thus regurgitated distorted ideas from the Biblical and Talmudic sources.[478] Thus, we find that scholars who lived in the Muslim world in the past and relied on Greek and biblical-Talmudic sources echoed racism in their writings like the unacceptable statements found in works such as *Murūj adh-Dhahab wa Ma'ādin al-Jawhar* [*Meadows of Gold and Mines of Gems*] by al-Mas'ūdī[479] and *al-*

---

477 Humoral pathology, also referred to as Humorism or Humoralism, is based on the idea that the human body has four important fluids or humors: blood, phlegm, black bile and yellow bile. It is also referred to as the 'Hippocratic doctrine of the four humors'. After Hippocrates the theory was adopted by ancient Greek, Roman, Muslim and then European physicians.

478 For example, scholars such as Ibn Khaldūn, al-Mas'ūdī (in *Murūj ul-Dhahab*), Ibn Qutaybah (died 276 AH/ 889 CE), Avicenna/Ibn Sīnā (died 1037 CE), al-Ya'qcbī (died circa 284 AH/ 897 CE) contain many unacceptable stories and analysis. This was due to their over-use of non-Islamic sources in order to understand certain phenomena.

479 The author of *Murūj adh-Dhahab* is 'Alī bin al-Husayn al-Mas'ūdī (d.346 AH) who was born in Baghdad and died in Cairo. According to al-Mamqānī in *Tanqeeh al-Maqāl*, vol.2, pp. 282-283 he was a *Shī'ī* of a somewhat extreme nature who used to accept the infallibility of the Shi'ite Imāms. Adh-Dhahabī stated about al-Mas'ūdī in *Siyar 'A'lam un-Nubalā*, vol.15, p.569: "He was a reporter and a person of strange and odd reports and arts, he was a Mu'tazilī." He also spoke against the four righteous Caliphs as well as against the Umayyads and the Abbasids, as indicated to by Dr Sulaymān 'Abdullāh al-Madeed as-Suwaykat in

'Iqd al-Fareed of Ibn 'AbdurRabbih. But this racism could not have been justified from the Qur'ān and Sunnah. It is odd that some scholars rely on works such as *al-'Iqd al-Fareed* and *Murūj adh-Dhahab* to try and prove that Islām teaches racism when these two particular works have been rejected as unreliable by Muslim scholars in any case![480]

John Hunwick also notes that racist prejudice did not formulate into a systematic doctrine amongst the Arabs as it did in Europe. Neither was there any Muslim to come and use the Qur'ān as the basis of inferiority of races and peoples, as happened with the Bible and the '*Hamitic myth*' in which Ham is cursed and thus made black. Abū Mūsā al-Ash'arī (*radi Allāhu 'anhu*) said that he heard the Prophet Muhammad (*sallallāhu 'alayhi wassallam*) say, "*Allāh created Ādam from a handful which He gathered from throughout the earth, so the sons of Ādam vary as the earth varies; some are red, some are white, some are black, and some are of colours in between. Some are easy-going, some are harsh, some are evil and some are good.*"[481]

A factual study by Ephraim Issac examines the relevant Judaic commentaries and reveals that the Jewish sources contain no link between the Biblical 'curse of Noah on Ham' and the changing of skin colour.[482] Furthermore, Issac indicates that the Rabbinical literature

---

his book *Manhaj al-Mas'ūdī fī Kitābihi at-Tārīkh* [*The Methodology of al-Mas'ūdī in his Book of History*]. Also Ibn Hajar al-'Asqalānī in *al-Lisān al-Mīzān* (vol.4, p.225) stated about al-Mas'ūdı that:

> His book of history is full of foolish and insignificant things because he was a Mu'tazilī Shī'ī! To the extent that he claimed that Ibn 'Umar (*radi Allāhu 'anhu*) refused to pledge allegiance to 'Alī and then pledged allegiance to Yazeed ibn Mu'awiyah, al-Hajjāj and 'AbdulMālik ibn Marwān instead.

480 See for example Shaykh Abū 'Ubaydah Mashhūr Hasan Āl Salmān, Shaykh Bakr Abū Zayd, intro., *Kutub Hadhara minha al-'Ulama* [*Books Which the Scholars Have Warned Against*], vol.2, 3rd Edn. (Riyadh, KSA: Dār us-Sumay'ī', 1426 AH/2005 CE), pp. 44-5; 53-7 for a critique of the "historical" writing of al-Ya'qūbī, Ibn 'AbduRabbih and al-Mas'ūdī.

481 *Musnad Ahmad, Tirmidhī* and *Abū Dāwūd* (*Mishkāt ul-Masābīh*, vol.1, p.36, hadeeth no. 100)

482 Ephraim Issac, "*Genesis, Judaism and the 'Sons of Ham',*" in John Ralph Willis (ed.), *Slaves and Slavery in Muslim Africa, Vol.1 – Islam and the Ideology of*

mentions that Canān not Ham was cursed as was thought by many Jewish, Christian and Arab ignoramuses throughout history in order to justify slavery, racial superiority and colonialism. Issac demonstrates that Cush is the traditionally accepted father of African peoples in the Jewish scriptures. The blackness of Cush was associated with purity and beauty with no racial stigmas attached. Thus, we find in some Jewish sources descriptions of the Children of Shem (which includes the Israelites) as being "*black and beautiful.*" Though the description of Canān as being "black and ugly" is puzzling, yet it is clear from this passage that 'ugly' and not 'black' is the pejorative word. This is demonstrated by the fact that the ancestors of the Israelites are also described as being black, with many Rabbis recognizing this.

Even though there are racist statements from certain Muslims these have nothing at all do to with Islām. Racist poems and proverbs do exist in some Arab literature, these statements are not exactly from good practicing and knowledgeable Muslims and contradict what the Prophet Muhammad (*sallallāhu alayhi wassallam*) taught, for example, such racist Arab proverbs were collected by writers such as al-Maydānī (d.1124 CE) in his *Majma' al-Amthāl*,[483] Ibn 'Abdur-Rabbih (d.940 CE) in '*Iqd ul-Fareed* and al-Askārī (d.1005 CE). Yet it should also be known that these compilers in some cases were relaying what others said and not necessarily their own beliefs or ideas.

Today the Islamic world displays how Islām unites people from all over the world and an example of this can be seen at the Islamic University of Madeenah. Being one of the sacred places on the Earth for Muslims, Madeenah itself is a centre for the Muslims. The Islamic University of Madeenah includes Islamic scholars from all over the world such as Ghana, Nigeria, Algeria, Mali, Mauritania, India, Bukhāra in central Asia, China, Afghanistan and many other countries. It is a learning centre that demonstrates how Islamic knowledge has been spread across the world and not exclusive to any particular group of people.[484] Prejudice and injustice maybe prevalent in some Muslim countries, therefore such prejudice should be abandoned, dealing with people with the fair dealing and justice that Islām demands. Moreover, Muslims

Enslavement (London and New York: Frank Cass and Co. Ltd., 1985) pp.75-91.

483 Published in Egypt in two volumes in 1352 AH

484 See the biographies of such scholars at www.fatwa-online.com

themselves must return to true Islām in order to achieve the blessings that Allāh gave the Muslims during the epoch of the Salaf.[485] Regarding this Imām al-Albānī (*rahimahullāh*) said in *Silsilatul-Ahadeeth ad-Da'eefah*, commenting on a fabricated *hadeeth* that praises the Arabs:

> For Islam's glory, its repute and its honour is not dependent on the power and strength of the Arabs. That can be achieved without them also, as it happened during the Ottoman period, especially at the beginning of their reign when Allāh (*subhānahu wa ta'ala*) gave glory to Islām through them so that Islām penetrated right up to the heart of Europe. But when the Ottomans began to leave Islamic laws replacing them with those of the European ones, (exchanging the lowly for the lofty), their power and influence declined in those areas, until they lost political power in their own country. Today all that remains is but a little of those appearances that show their Islām of the past! With their fall, all of the Ummah suffered great humiliation. The enemies of this Ummah entered into their lands and colonized them all, except for small patches of lands here and there. Now the situation is that although they have been able to get rid of the colonizers, they remain their slaves in many ways. In any case, the point is that Islām gains or loses its glory, repute and honour with that of its adherents, be they Arabs or non-Arabs, and as a hadeeth states "there is no superiority of the Arabs over the non-Arabs except by *Taqwā*."

Such national pride belongs to the Jāhiliyyah days which the

485 For example, many Muslims complain about the actions of the occupiers of Palestine and the injustice that is being meted out against the Muslims. However, many of these same Muslims have the same complexes as the occupiers themselves?! So how do they expect Allāh to give the Muslims victory with this current trend of thought?! Some modern Arabs will be quick to condemn Israeli atrocities and discrimination with an element of sanctimony, especially when their adherence to the Sunnah, Manhaj and intelligence is questionable, yet turn a complete blind eye to rampant anti-black racism and anti-Asian discrimination within their own societies, coupled with utter ignorance of racist injustices and slavery, in some cases of Muslims, which occurred in history.

There is no doubt that this arrogance that is exhibited by some Muslims is the reason for the weak state of the Muslims and their currently being slaves themselves, to the West. This was also noted by the great Islamic scholars of this era such as Shaykh al-Albānī and Shaykh Muhammad bin Sālih al-'Uthaymeen.

Prophet (*sallallāhu 'alayhi wassallam*) destroyed. Nor should the Arabs forget the fact that it was their intelligence, language and character that led to their choice as the first bearers of the message of Islām. If an Arab realizes this today then he is more likely to guard those qualities and take it upon himself as a duty to spread the word of Islām. But if he abandons them, then he has no superiority over anyone. In fact, a non-Arab who bears the same qualities is, without any doubt whatsoever, superior to an Arab. True superiority then comes from following the guidance the Prophet (*sallallāhu 'alayhi wassallam*) brought, and can be gained by anyone who qualifies himself with the qualities approved by Islām such as *īmān*, virtue, righteous living, Ihsān etc. The Prophet (*sallallāhu 'alayhi wassallam*) said, "He who was left behind by his actions will not be brought forward by his lineage." In short, true merit is in adorning oneself with certain qualities. When those qualities are lost, the merit is lost: "There is no superiority of an Arab over a non-Arab except by *Taqwā*." And this should show the fallacy of the one who calls to Arab nationalism while he is devoid of those qualities that should go with it (being an Arab). Rather such a person is a Westerner both in appearance and in soul![486]

486 Imām al-Albānī, *Silsilat ul-Hadeeth ad-Da'eefah*, commentary upon a weak hadeeth no.161. The weak *hadeeth* being *"I am Arab, the Qur'ān is Arab and the language of the people of Jannah is Arab."*

VII

A Response to 'An African Asks Some Disturbing Questions of Islam'[487]

This is a response to one of the tracts distributed by the 'Pharisee' Joseph Smith[488] al-Kadhāb[489]: '*An African Asks Some Disturbing Questions of Islam.*' This pamphlet is just one example of the hypocrisy, lies and

---

487 Originally written in 1997 by Abū 'Abdullāh 'Abdur-Raheem Ibn Green, a Muslim *da'ee* (caller to Islam) noted for his talks at Hyde Park Speaker's Corner in London during the last decade wherein many people embraced Islām. He is currently in charge of Islamic propagation at *Central Mosque* Regents Park. The original work '*An African Asks Some Disturbing Questions of Islam*' was by an evangelical Christian pamphleteer by the name of '*Brother Banda.*' 'Banda' utilized many Afrocentric arguments mainly borrowed from Chancellor Williams and the leaflet was distributed at *Hyde Park Speaker's Corner*. This particular work also indicates the unity of Islām as 'Abdur-Raheem, though neither a scholar nor student of Islamic knowledge, being a white English Muslim that follows the Qur'ān and Sunnah took it upon himself to refute the simplistic allegations that Islām was an 'intrinsically racist religion.' My notes on this chapter will be indicated by [AH] at the end of the footnote.

488 Joseph 'Jay' Smith is an 'arch-deacon' and senior Christian missionary polemicist against Islām in the UK. He is an Anglo-American born in India from a radical Evangelical background and has a variety of degrees and diplomas. He has studied 'divinity theology' in America and also studies at the *School of Oriental and African Studies, University of London*. Smith however is not even regarded highly by the de-mythologiser orientalists at *SOAS*. When asked in 1998, a former lecturer of Smith's, G. Hawting, described Smith as being: "A Christian missionary with his own agenda, obviously extreme in his theories, too radical in his claims to be accepted at a scholarly level and a trouble maker." Enough said! [AH]

489 An Arabic term for a compulsive liar [AH]

falsehood of the Christian missionaries and in particular the infidel Smith, whose papers are rampant with such falsehoods. We pray that Allāh allows us to expose every single one of their lies to the world, and especially to those who innocently trust their slanderous writings, so the truth of the reality of the worst of created beings can be known. The Bible says a lot of nice things, but it also contains some horrifyingly brutal and racist comments as well. The fact is that Western Christianity has often used the Bible to support its racist ideals. Indeed, the God of the Old Testament often seems to be portrayed as an exclusive God of the Israelites:

> There is no god in all earth, but in Israel.
>
> [Kings 5: 15]

> You (Children of Israel) are a holy people unto the Lord your God. The Lord has chosen you to be a special people that are upon the face of the earth.
>
> [Deuteronomy 7: 6]

Some of the sayings attributed to Jesus seem to reflect this attitude. When a non-Jew Samaritan asks him for help he refers to them as dogs. Jesus also stated that he was only sent to the lost sheep of the *Children of Israel.* Interestingly, the passage where he is supposed to have told his disciples to "*go unto the nations,*" is not found in any of the most ancient manuscripts and is now considered spurious. Furthermore, the concept that Jesus was the acclaimed "*Son of God,*" and so called "*manifestation of God*" does have some racist overtones, i.e. that '*God made flesh*' was a Jew. Now concerning the Cushite wife of Moses mentioned in Numbers, without trying to dismiss entirely the proposition that "the God of the Bible hates racism," the context seems to be more suggestive that God's anger was for their upsetting Moses than any hatred of racism. Not that I believe the Bible is inherently racist (God's favour to the Israelites has other acceptable explanations) but there has been a history of racism associated with Christianity that has caused many to flee, and often in numbers, to Islām.

What follows in *A Disturbing Question Concerning the Muslim Qu'ran* is illustrative of the idiotic type of problems these missionaries use in their desperate attempts to slander God's final revelation, the Qur'ān. The verse quoted (Sūrah 3 (Āl Imrān) 106-107) clearly has nothing to do with skin colour or race. If a white man was thrown into a fire, what colour would he become? And if a dark-skinned person were to be put under an intense light his skin would shine with that light. What's racist about that? Interesting enough, there is another passage in the Qur'ān which the Black Nationalist '*Nation of Islam*,' another group of perverters of the true meanings of God's word, use to support their racist ideals that all white people are damned. This verse describes the unbelievers on the Day of Judgement as being blue-eyed![490] In fact, the words are only common Arabic idiomatic usage to describe terror, as in the English term '*green with envy*.' Only misguided fools would use such passages to support claims of racism. It becomes all the more incredible in light of the clear verse of the Qur'ān that states:

وَجَعَلْنَاكُمْ شُعُوبًا وَقَبَائِلَ
لِتَعَارَفُوا إِنَّ أَكْرَمَكُمْ عِندَ اللَّهِ أَتْقَاكُمْ إِنَّ اللَّهَ عَلِيمٌ خَبِيرٌ ۝

> We made you into tribes and nations that you may get to know one another (not that you should hate each other) And the best of you in the sight of Allāh are those who are most conscious of Allāh.
>
> [*al-Hujūrāt* (49): 13]

And the well known authenticated statement of the Prophet Muhammad:

---

490 This is the verse in the Qur'ān wherein Allāh, Most Wise, says,

يَوْمَ يُنفَخُ فِي الصُّورِ وَنَحْشُرُ الْمُجْرِمِينَ يَوْمَئِذٍ زُرْقًا ۝

> The Day when the Trumpet shall be blown, and We shall gather the criminals (sinners), blue-eyed.
>
> [*Tā Hā (20)*: 102]

The Arabic word here '*Zurq*' is a plural form of '*Azraq*.' This verse has been interpreted by some commentators of the Qur'ān to mean that out of fear all human beings on the Day of Judgement will turn blue. Because of fear, their blood would dry up and it would seem as if there was no blood left in their veins making them look bluish-white. The other, and much stronger opinion, is that the horror of the Day of Judgement will turn eyes bluish-white, the sense of horror will seize them causing their eyes to petrify. The verse has never been understood by the early Muslims to mean 'white blue eyed Europeans' will only be punished and gathered on the Day of Judgement!! [AH]

"*There is no difference between the white and the black, the Arab and non-Arab, except in Taqwā (God-consciousness).*"[491] Also the verses in the Qur'ān that clearly state that it is a revelation for all mankind, that all mankind is descended from Adam and Eve, and Adam was made from dust are more than sufficient proof to dispel concerns of racism in the Qur'ān or the religion of Islām. Furthermore, the lack of racism is something found practically manifested amongst the Muslim nations, as epitomized in the *Hajj*, where pilgrims from all over the world join together in the worship of the One True God, Allāh, dressed in the same two pieces of seamless white cloth. The sight was enough to change Malcolm X from a racist black nationalist to a true Sunnī Muslim.[492]

How could this Christian be blind to these facts, when even the scholars amongst his co-religionists have recognized the distinctive non-racial quality of Islām?

> The extinction of race consciousness between Muslims is one of the outstanding achievements of Islam, and in the contemporary world there is a crying need for the propagation of this Islamic virtue.[493]

> No other society has such a record of success in uniting in an equality of status, or opportunity and endeavour so many and so varied races of mankind. The great Muslim communities of Africa, India and Indonesia, perhaps also the small community in Japan, show that Islam has still the power to reconcile apparently irreconcilable elements of race and tradition.[494]

It seems to me that Banda is either wilfully blind, or merely trying to slander Islām with anything he can lay his hands on, and if he can't find anything he'll happily lie and invent it! We need to ask if this is truly the way of one who claims to be a follower of the '*Prince of Peace*' the one who praised meekness, humility, honesty and justice, and condemned the lying hypocrisy of the Scribes and the Pharisees? This Christian writer reeks of that very same type of lying hypocrisy that Jesus, peace be upon him, was so vocal in condemning.

491 *Musnad Ahmad.*

492 Refer to Alex Haley, The Autobiography of Malcolm X.

493 AJ Toynbee, *Civilization on Trial* (New York, 1948), p. 205.

494 HAR Gibb, *Whither Islam* (London: Victor Gollancz, 1932)

In the light of what we have discovered so far, can we trust those comments that follow? In the next section *'A Disturbing Question Concerning African History,'*[495] Banda is puzzled about the lack of unbiased historical research by Muslims concerning the African people. We have already witnessed how 'unbiased' Banda has proved to be, and his own complete lack of objectivity will become even more apparent when we further examine his claims. The first lie we find is in his accusation that Islām destroyed the African churches. If he means by that Islām destroyed them because when Islām came people voluntarily left Christianity in droves and embraced Islām through their own realization that it is indeed the true religion, then emphatically "YES!" And no Muslim would fail to be proud of that. But this is not what Banda means, as he clearly shows further on when he gives his reasons for the disappearance of the Christian Church as forced conversion and slaughter at the hands of the Muslims. This, you guessed it, is another complete lie. De Lacy O' Leary wrote in his book on Islām:

> History makes it clear, however, that the legend of fanatical Muslims sweeping through the world and forcing Islām at the point of the sword upon conquered races is one of the most fantastically absurd myths that historians have ever repeated.[496]

The Qur'ānic verse that Banda quotes are, of course, quoted out of context, and the correct understand is established by reference to other Qur'ānic verses and the sayings of the Prophet Muhammad. Without a

495 Banda stated: "As an African I am very puzzled at the lack of balanced historical research by Muslims concerning the African people." This statement displays the clear lack of any real historiographical knowledge that individuals like Banda have. If Banda knew 'African historical research' himself he would have known that there is a mass of literature in Africa written in Arabic by African Muslims. Such as *Tarīkh as-Sudan* written in 1653 by 'Abdur-Rahmān as-Sa'dī at-Timbuktī, *Tarīkh al-Fattāsh* written in the 18th century CE by Mahmood al-Kāti, and also the work of Ahmad Bābā at-Timbuktī and Mūsā Kamarah. Not to mention other scholars such as Ibn ul-Jawzī and as-Suyūtī and Muslim historians, travellers and geographers such as Ibn Munabbah, Abu'l-Fida, Ibn ul-Mukhtār, Ibn Fadhlallāh al-'Umarī and al-Bakrī. This basic evidence can be found in any concise West African history book regarding Islām, so Banda has little excuse to make this erroneous claim. [AH]

496 De Lacy O'Leary, *Islam at the Crossroads – A Brief Survey of the Present Position and Problems of the World of Islam* (London: 1923), p.8.

doubt Islām calls upon Muslims to fight against the forces of disbelief, oppression and tyranny. This is nothing new in fact, Banda could find some even more brutal verses in his own book if only he had eyes to see:

> And the Lord said, "Go through the city, and smite; let not your eye spare, neither have you pity. Slay utterly the old and young, both maids and little children, and women".
>
> [Ezekiel 9: 5]

And as for not taking friends those who have insulted Allāh by saying that he has a "Son" and committed the crime of ascribing divinity to His creation, the ultimate evil, then does Paul not say something similar?

> Do not be yoked together with the unbelievers. For what do righteousness and wickedness have in common? Or what fellowship can light have with darkness?[497]

What becomes even more laughable is when he quotes the names of so-called '*African*' Christians, such as Augustine of Hippo (whose mother's name was Monica and father Patricius), Tertullian, Clement and Athanasius. Now do they sound like African names to you? A little 'unbiased' historical research will show the origins of these names and the racial origins of these 'Great thinkers.' They are Greek and Roman colonialists, which is rather like quoting Pit Bota or Cecil Rhodes as founders of 'African' civilisation.

Now for a real 'African' church we might turn our attention to Ethiopia, but the Christian would rather ignore that, since Negus, the King of Ethiopia at the time of the Prophet Muhammad (*may the peace and blessings of Allāh be upon him*) and a good number of his bishops, as well as many of the Ethiopians, became Muslims, voluntarily, recognizing Muhammad as a true Prophet. Indeed, large numbers of the Muslim armies that liberated North Africa from the tyranny of the Christian Byzantine empire were Ethiopians. The very same Roman colonialist stock that Banda quotes as examples of '*African*' Christianity actually complained to the Muslim '*Ameer* about the large numbers of blacks in his army and asked him to keep them well away because they were frightening them. "Take away that black man, I can have no distinction with him," exclaimed the Christian Archbishop Cyrus when the "Arab

497 Corinthians 6:17.

conquerors" had sent a deputation of their ablest men to discuss terms of surrender of the capital of Egypt, headed by the companion of the Prophet Muhammad, 'Ubādah Ibn as-Sāmit, *may Allāh be pleased with him*, as the most ablest of them all, 'Ubādah Ibn as-Sāmit was black.[498] To the sacred archbishop's astonishment, he was told that this man was commissioned by the General, 'Amr Ibn al-'Ās; that the Muslims held blacks and whites in equal respect, judging a man by his character not his colour. "Well if the black man must lead, then he must speak gently," ordered the prelate, "so as not to frighten his white auditors."[499]

Furthermore, Banda and his evangelical brethren must be walking with blinkers on their eyes and cotton wool in their ears when he asks,

---

498 More on this is discussed in the chapter 'The Afrocentic Assault on Islam'. Some historians suggest that al-Muqawqis, who made this remark, is not to be identified with Cyrus, the Patriarch of Alexandria but rather with a Sassanid governor of Egypt at that time. The term 'Muqawqis' is the Arabic-derived name of the Coptic 'Pikaukasos' which means 'Caucasian', as the Sassanid Empire reached up to the Caucasus. The term 'al-Muqawqis' came to be applied to all Egyptian Patriarchs by Muslim historians. However, due to the close role in treaty arrangements between Cyrus and the Sahābah as noted in the historical record, 'Muqawqis' most likely refers to him than anyone else. Allāh knows best.

In any case, these facts refute the mass of Afrocentric and Orientalist literature that mention "Arab" invasions, conquests and 'rises,' in North Africa, when the main leaders and many of those fighting to spread Islām were in fact black. Usāmah bin Zayd (*radi Allāhu anhu*) who was one of the young commanders of the companions of Muhammad (*sallallāhu 'alayhi wassallam*) was of African origin, 'Ubādah Ibn as-Sāmit (*radi Allāh anhu*) for example, the commander of the Muslims that went into Egypt, was a 'black' (dark-skinned) Arab and Tāriq bin Ziyād (*radi Allāhu anhu*) who was the commander of the Muslims that went into Spain was also originally from one of the north African tribes. When Shām (Greater Syria) was conquered by the Muslims, Halab's conquest owed much to a freed black slave by the name of Dāmmis who was affiliated to the tribe of Banu Tārif, the ruling family of Kindah. Dāmis lead the reinforcements which went to the aid of Abū Ubaydah ibn ul-Jarrāh (*radi Allāhu 'anhu*). See Abdul Aziz al-Shinnawy, *The Islamic Openings* (*al-Fatuhat al-Islamiyah*), trans. Heba Samir Hendawi, revised by A.A. Mischler (al-Mansura, Egypt: Umm al-Qura, 2002). [AH]

499 SS Leeder, *Veiled Mysteries of Egypt* (London, 1912), p.332

> So why do we not hear of this African church, and why do we not see any remnants of it today?

I lived in Egypt for ten years. One third of the population, after one thousand and four hundred years of Muslim rule, is still Coptic, which is one of the oldest Christian Churches. I passed their Churches many times and visited their monasteries in the desert. The Ethiopian Church is still existing, as are the Catholic, Orthodox, Syriac, Maronite and numerous other Churches still exist all over the lands liberated by the Muslims.[500] Historical records show that Christian Churches actually wrote to the Muslims inviting them to come and liberate them from the tyranny of their Christian brethren – the Byzantines!

Banda goes as far as to expose himself with a blatant contradiction when he mentions the three Christian mini-sates of Sudan having their own written language, centres of learning etc from 350 CE to 1500 CE, yet claims that it was all destroyed by Muslim invaders in 1275 CE? As for the present war, we ask all inquiring minds to ponder what "peace-loving, turn-the-other-cheek, resist-not-your-enemies" Christians are doing fighting a civil war against the legitimate government of Sudan, and what the "peace-loving, turn-the-other-cheek, resist-not-your-enemies" European and American Evangelists are doing funding these rebels. It is also noteworthy that over half of the deaths in that civil war, and much of the destruction, has been caused by the rival Christian groups fighting each other!

I suggest anyone who is interested in reading a truly unbiased account of the treatment of Christians by the Muslims get hold of *The Preaching of Islam* by TW Arnold.[501] E. Alexander Powell says in his book *The Struggle for Power in Muslim Asia*,

> In their wars of conquest, however, the Muslims exhibited a degree of toleration which puts many Christian nations to shame.[502]

---

500 For example in Muslim Spain, Egypt, Syria, Jordan, Yemen, Tunisia, Morocco, with these last three countries still home to large communities of Jews. [AH]

501 T.W. Arnold, *The Preaching of Islam: A History of the Propagation of the Muslim Faith*, (London: Westminster A. Constable & Co.1896) and (Lahore: Sh. Muhammad Ashraf, 1975), p. 80.

502 E. Alexander Powell, *The Struggle for Power in Moslem Asia* (New York and London: The Century Co.1923).

Through my reading of Joseph Smith's papers, I have developed a method for predicting Evangelical Christian lies about Islām. When you read, "*The Muslims say...*" or "*The Muslims believe...*" or something similar, then there is about an 85% chance that what will follow will either be a complete lie or gross distortion. The section on slavery is an excellent example. In the second line he states that, concerning slavery, wait for it, "Muslims say it was only a Christian phenomena." Do they? Which Muslims is he talking about? I don't think that there are any Muslims that say slavery was only a Christian phenomenon, since slavery existed before Christianity came along. The facts are that the Bible, both the Old and New Testaments approve of slavery and there is not one single Biblical verse condemning it. The only verse that comes within a hundred miles is Paul's recommendation to Christians to try and free themselves if they are slaves because they should be slaves to Christ alone. In fact Biblical teachings approve of slavery and even enjoin it. If the hypocrite Banda condemns Islām because of slavery, then he also condemns his own book. Let's browse through a few examples:

> And the Lord said unto Moses, "Avenge the children of the Midianites,"They warred against the Midianites, as the Lord commanded Moses, and they killed the males. And they took all of the women as captives, and their children, and took the spoil of their cattle, and took all of their flocks, and all of their goods. And they burnt all their cities wherein they dwelt, and all their goodly castles with fire. Moses said, "Have you kept all of the women alive? Now kill every male among the children, and kill every woman that has known a man by lying with him, but keep all of the young girls for yourselves".
>
> [Numbers 31: 1]

> When you draw near to a city fight against it, offer terms of peace to it, and if its answer to you is peace and it opens to you, then all of the people that are found within it shall do forced labour for you and shall serve you. But if the city does not make peace with you, then you shall besiege it... you shall put all its males to the sword, but the women and the children, the cattle and everything else in the city, all its spoil, you shall take as booty for yourselves; and you shall enjoy the spoil of your enemies."
>
> [Deuteronomy 20: 10-17]

"Oh no! That's the Old Testament," cries the Christian! "The New Testament has replaced all that!" Not so. Paul actually instructs the flock on how to behave as slaves:

> Slaves, obey your earthly masters with respect and fear, and with sincerity of heart, just as you would Christ...Serve wholeheartedly...And masters, treat your slaves in the same way. Do not threaten them...
>
> [Ephesians 6: 5]

Nota Bene: Paul does not order Christian masters to release their Christian slaves, just to be nice to them! What reeks even more of hypocrisy is that Banda tries to use the secular Western nations condemnation of slavery to show how "*Christianity*" condemned slavery. Yet this very liberal, non-literal, non-Biblical based form of "*Christianity*," - followed by the likes of Livingstone and Wilberforce[503] – is the very same type of Christianity these evangelicals, like Banda and his bunch, so vehemently attack for their understandable refusal to believe the Bible is the Word of God, and their readiness to accept the modern scientific criticisms of the Biblical texts. When one shows the short-comings and corruption of Imperialism and the Western consumer societies they cry "this is not Christianity and they are not true Christians." But when, as in this article, they wish to condemn Islām, or any other religion, they produce statistics to show how much better "*Christian*" Europe is. They want to have their cake and eat it too. Now let us not forget that the USA fought a civil war against the Southern *'Bible Belt'* States just over one hundred years ago, and partly over the issue of slavery (Southern white American Christians approved of it and found support in the Bible).[504]

---

503 William Wilberforce of Hull was active in the 19th century CE abolition of slavery movement and called for the ending of New World Slavery and British involvement in it. [AH]

504 W.E. Lecky notes

> The Church did not condemn slavery. Orthodox and heretic, Roman and barbarian alike assumed the institution to be natural and in-destructible. Pagan laws condemned to slavery any free woman who married a slave; the laws of Constantine [a Christian emperor] ordered the woman to be executed, and the slave to be burned alive. The Emperor Gratian decreed that a slave who accused his master of any offence except high treason to the state should be burned alive at once, without inquiring into the justice of the charge.

Islām does not encourage slavery, nor does it forbid it. It does however, encourage the freeing and kind treatment of slaves. A slave in Islām is treated as a member of the household, and must be fed with the same food and clothed with the same clothes as the master or mistress. It is forbidden to overwork a slave and the slave has the right to buy his or her freedom and the owner does not have the right to refuse. In fact, the way slaves are treated in Islām, as one European writer commented, was better than the way servants were treated in Europe. Slavery in Islām has never been a racial issue. In fact, North African black Muslims,[505] as well as Turks and Mongols, had Caucasian slaves. Those are the facts. As for slavery being a means of people coming to the true religion, then I swear by Allāh, on the Day of Judgement, Banda will wish that he had been enslaved and become a Muslim than meet Allāh as a Christian.

Culture and Conclusion

Banda's "*Truth Tract*" proudly points out that Moses was married to a Cushite "*African*," according to the Bible. Muslims also believe, and in fact the Prophet Muhammad, *may the peace and blessings of Allāh be upon him*, described Moses as being "*Black with curly hair.*"[506] Furthermore,

---

William Edward Hartpole Lecky, *History of European Morals from Augustus to Charlemagne*, vol.2 (New York: D. Appleton and Co., 1877/1975 Reprint), p.61, as quoted by Will Durant, *The Story of Civilization*, vol. 4, p.77.

505 For example, many of the powerful West African Muslim rulers had slaves that were Turkish and Caucasian. Dinesh D'Souza notes, based upon the historical records of Muslim geographers and travellers such as al-Maqrizi:

> …slavery was widespread in Africa from antiquity. The three powerful medieval kingdoms of Ghana, Songhai and Mail all relied on slave labor. Nor were these slaves exclusively black Africans: the emperor Mansa Musa, for example, purchased Turkish slaves for his court in Mali. White Europeans who were shipwrecked off the west coast of Africa were also enslaved. The Ashanti of West Africa customarily enslaved all foreigners.

See Dinesh D'Souza, *The End of Racism*, (New York: Free Press, 1995). Also refer to the chapter on slavery and in particular the discussion regarding slavery of white Europeans in North Africa. [AH]

506 These *ahādeeth* are in Bukhārī and Muslim. In *Kitāb ul-Īmān* in *Saheeh Muslim* for example, it is narrated from Ibn 'Abbās, referring to the miraculous

this same "*Truth Tract*" completely fails to point out that Abraham was also married to an "*African*," Haggar,[507] whose son Ishmael, is descended. Joseph 'Jay' Smith, one of the Evangelicals responsible for other "truth tracts," is in love with a book called *The Haggareenes*,[508] which was another name for the Arabs – who were therefore named after an African. This title "*Haggareenes*" was used by the Christians as a derogatory term against the descendants of a son and daughter of Africa, as was the term "*Saracens*" (the term that the Crusaders used for the Muslims), which means "*Those rejected by Sarah.*"

Now a closer look at Christian/Pauline theology concerning Abraham, Haggar and Ishmael, would have left one wondering why Sarah's racism went unpunished? Islām teaches the true history, corrupted by the Jews[509]

Night Journey (*al-'Isrā wa'l-Mi'rāj*) of the Prophet Muhammad (*sallallāhu 'alayhi wassallam*), that the Prophet met Prophet Mūsā. About Mūsā's appearance Muhammad said: *"Mūsā was Ādam (dark brown) and he had curly hair, like the men of Zūt."* In another narration from Ibn 'Abbās also in Bukhārī and Muslim and in al-Bayhaqī *"like the men of Shānū'ah" (one of the old tribes in Yemen)."* [AH]

507 In Islām, her Arabic name, *peace be upon her*, is Hājār. [AH]

508 What 'Abdur-Raheem meant here was the book *Hagarism: The Making of the Islamic World* (Cambridge University Press, 1977) by Patricia Crone and Michael Cook. 'Abdur-Raheem forgot the exact name as he wrote this refutation from memory. The book argues that the Arabs invented Islām and that Islām was not fully solidified until two hundred years after the death of the Prophet Muhammad (*sallallāhu 'alayhi wassallam*). Additionally, the book claims that in inventing their new religion and culture, the Arabs took bits from other established and past civilizations to help them in building their own new 'Islamic civilisation.' The book is a popular reference work for ignorant and anti-Islamic Jews and Christians who wish to further their futile and vain polemic against Islām. The book is even studied on the '*Origins of Islam*' course at the School of Oriental and African Studies, University of London! Furthermore, in 'Abdur-Raheem's devastating 73 page refutation of Joseph Smith's writings, 'Abdur-Raheem collected the statements of 16 other non-Muslim scholars of Islamic history that have strongly rejected the claims of the book *Hagarism*. The book is not even recognised by their own Orientalists! [AH]

509 For example a contemporary and popular orthodox Jewish Rabbi has verified this. Rabbi Schmeul Botech, or "*Schmuelee*," of Oxford, former head of the Jewish L'Chaim Society of Oxford University, who is popular in the West as a Rabbi up-to-date with modernity, recognized by his New York accent, wrote an article in

and Christians, of Abraham and Ishmael. It was Ishmael, the half-African, who was the first son of Abraham. It was both Abraham and his half African son Ishmael that were tested and favoured by Allāh. It was Abraham, the Friend of God, and his half-African son Ishmael that raised the foundations and built the first house, the *Ka'bah*, for the worship of the One True God, Allāh. Muhammad *may the peace and blessings of Allāh be upon him*, a descendent of Ishmael, returned the *Ka'bah* and the world to the pure monotheism of Abraham. In this same city, Makkah, whenever anyone visits, they must circumambulate the *Ka'bah*, and make "*Sai'ee*," that is running between the two hills of Saffā' and Marwah in remembrance of Haggar, daughter of Africa, who ran from one hill to the other looking for help, as Ishmael lay crying in the sand. It is from the well of *Zamzam* that every pilgrim drinks, where none other than the Angel Gabriel dug with his wing and the water started to flow, and Haggar and Ishmael drank. What better reason can one think of for the sons of Africa to turn up there to pray?

As for the "Arab dress" which Banda complains that has to be worn (another lie!)[510], it is no different from that which was worn by Jesus, and most of the people of North Africa and Ethiopia. In fact Nigerian and East African Muslims have their own, immediately identifiable, African dress.

As for Banda's other idiotic statements,[511] then the Qur'ān is also

---

the *Guardian Newspaper's* religion column in 1998 stating: "Ishmael had already gone off the path." [AH]

510 Banda stated in his leaflet: "Yet why is it that we are obliged to start wearing 7th century Arab dress once Islām is taken on? What's wrong with my good African cultural dress?" In addition to what 'Abdur-Raheem has stated about this foolish comment, it is also noteworthy to mention that none of the former *Hyde Park Christian Fellowship "Africans"* of the 1990s (in fact only about three of the main *Speaker's Corner* Evangelicals are "African" anyway) ever wore "good African cultural dress." Rather they paraded about Hyde Park in Western suits, cowboy hats and some not even bothered about their appearance! [AH]

511 Banda said:

> Furthermore, why are we required to read God's word and only speak to Him only in Arabic? Does God only speak Arabic? Is He not capable of understanding my African language? Thank God that the Holy Bible is now in over 2000 known languages around the world. Because I know

translated into many languages, and no Muslim doubts that Allāh can communicate in and understand every language also, but Allāh, in His infinite wisdom, chose to reveal His final revelation in the Arabic tongue, and he has preserved that language. Banda talks about his Bible, but compare some of these translations with their "most ancient manuscripts" which are in Greek (not an African language I think) which itself was not the original language of Jesus and the Prophets, you will see how they have fulfilled exactly God's accusation in the Qur'ān of changing and perverting God's word. Now if Banda and his like have so little regard for God that they feel free to pervert His message, then do you think they will feel shy to lie to you and me?

Banda and his Evangelical bunch do not love the truth, nor do they love you. They love only their father, the father of lies, the Devil, who wants to misled you from the true religion, the pure monotheism of Abraham and Ishmael and Muhammad, may Allāh's peace and blessings be upon them all. As for Banda's final question,[512] I will let some unbiased non-Muslims answer:

> Truly if the question must be put, whether it is Mohammadan[513] or Christian nations that have done most for Africa, the answer must be that it is not the Christian. Christian travellers, with every wish to think otherwise have remarked that the Negro who accepts Mohammadanism acquires at once a sense of dignity of human nature not commonly found even among those who have been brought to accept Christianity. Here we find in central Africa, the use of decent clothing, the arts of reading and writing and, what is more, which had forbidden and to a great extent, has abolished immodest dancing and gambling and drinking,

---

> my God is able to speak every language. It's not a problem for Him.

Suffice to say that Banda did not mention what "African language" he understands?! [AH]

512 Banda's final remark in his petite leaflet was:

> Now that I have asked my questions, you too ask yours. Who indeed has helped me as an African the most: Islam or Christianity? You need to choose wisely, because your life depends on it.

513 At the time Reverend Bosworth-Smith was writing in England, the ignorant term '*Mohammadan*' was used to describe a Muslim and '*Mohammadanism*' for Islām. [AH]

which inculcated upon the whole a pure morality, and sets forth a sublime and at the same time, a simple theology, is surely deserving of other feelings than the hatred and the contempt which some portions of our religion's press habitually pour onto it.[514]

As a religion the Mohammadan religion, it must be confessed, is more suited to Africa than is the Christian religion; indeed, I would even say that it is suited to the world as a whole.[515]

Wa'al-Hamdulillahi Rabbil al-Ameen
And all praise is due to Allāh, Lord of the Worlds

514 Reverend Bosworth-Smith, *Mohammad and Mohammadanism* (London, 1874), p.92
515 Lancelot Lawton, *The Sphere.*

VIII
Edward Blyden

One of the most important Pan-Africanist thinkers of the 19th century was Edward Blyden (1832 – 1912 CE). Born in Saint Thomas in the Danish West Indies (now the US Virgin Islands), he spent most of his life on the African continent. He was an accomplished linguist, writer, educator and world traveller who strongly defended Africa and its cultural and social heritage. Blyden was far from the modern day armchair black historians who merely theorise and talk, as he had a practical involvement in Africa and the empowerment of black people. Most important here though is the fact that Blyden had positive attitudes towards Islām and viewed Islām as a major vehicle for regenerating Africa, despite the fact that Blyden was recognized as being a Christian. Blyden believed that Islām gave Africans, and black people in general, more of an identity as opposed to Christianity. Blyden had experience himself of the hypocrisy of Christianity as he was refused entry as a student to enrol at the Rutger's Theological College by fellow white Christians because he was West Indian.[516]

Blyden's book *Christianity, Islam and the Negro Race*[517] is a collection of his writings on race, culture and the African personality. Blyden mentions that under Christianity, "African avenues to intellectual improvement were closed," and thus "Africans were doomed to perpetual ignorance."[518] Blyden also notes that,

---

516 Richard Brent Turner, *Islam in the African American Experience* (Bloomington: Indiana University Press, 1997), p.48.

517 This book was first published in 1888 CE and then re-published in 1994 by *Black Classic Press.*

518 Ibid, p.15

> The Negro[519] in Christian lands, where he has been under the training of the white man, exhibits a cringing and servile spirit.[520]

Further, Blyden's research and eyewitness accounts refute the simplistic arguments put forward by the anti-Islamic and Islamophobic Afrocentrics and Christians. For example, Blyden states,

> The political and social institutions of the Arabs had already been tried and found suitable to the wants and tastes of the Negro tribes. Indeed, the two peoples, if not of cognate origin, have protracted inter-communications, and by the similarity of the physical influences which have, for ages, operated upon them, become similar in tastes. And it was not difficult for the Arabs to conform to a great extent to the social and domestic customs of the Africans, by their teaching, by their intelligence, by their intermarriages with the natives, by the trade and generosity of their merchants, they enlisted so many interests and such deep sympathies that they rapidly took root in the country.[521]

Blyden further stated in *Christianity, Islam and the Negro Race*:

> Every traveller who enters the Muslim regions of West and Central Africa with sufficient basis of information is forced to admit that the man makes a great mistake who approaches the Negro Muslims with the idea that they are "benighted Africans." Islam in Africa, instead of being treated in the offhand and contemptuous manner adopted by some, who seem to have gathered all their knowledge of Islam from the Arabian Nights, ought to be approached with earnestness and respect; for there is much in Islam which Christians may profitably study, and from which Christians might learn important lessons.[522]

From Blyden's positive remarks about Islām are:

> It is certain that many of these West African tribes have received the religion of Islam without it being forced upon them by the

519 During the time that Blyden was writing, the Spanish word '*Negro*' was used in the English language to describe people of dark skinned African descent.

520 *Christianity, Islam and the Negro Race*, p.2

521 Ibid, p.23

522 Ibid, p.73

> overpowering arms of victorious invaders.[523]

Blyden also mentioned:

> The introduction of Islam into Central and West Africa has been the most important, if not the sole, preservative against the desolations of the slave trade. Islam furnished a protection to the tribes who embraced it by effectively binding them together in one strong religious fraternity and enabling them by their united efforts to baffle the attempts of powerful pagan slave hunters. Enjoying this comparative immunity from sudden hostile incursions, industry was stimulated among them…Large towns and cities have grown under Islam's energy and industry. Dr Barth[524] was surprised to find such towns or cities such as Kano and Sokoto in the centre of Africa – to discover the focus of a complex and widely ramified commerce, and a bust hive of manufacturing industry, in a region which most people believed to have been a desert.[525]

Blyden opined, contrary to the outbursts of writers such as John Azumah:

> Islam extinguishes all distinctions founded upon race, colour or nationality, "I admonish you to fear Allah" said the Prophet Muhammad to his companions, "And yield obedience to my successors, even if he is a black Ethiopian slave."[526] And therefore, throughout the history of Islam, in all countries, race or "previous condition" has been no barrier to elevation.[527]

Blyden then gives the example of the former slave Kāfūr[528] who governed and ruled Egypt and Syria after proving to be a great soldier

523 Ibid, p.199

524 Heinrich Barth was one of the early European Saharan and West African travelers. His published works include the five volume *Travels and Discoveries in North and Central Africa – A Journal of an Expedition Undertaken Under the Auspices of H.B.M's Government in the Years 1849-1855.*

525 *Christianity, Islam and the Negro Race*, p. 215

526 *Christianity, Islam and the Negro Race,* p. 215.

527 This *hadeeth* is found in *Mishkāt al-Masābih* of at-Tabrīzī.

528 Abu'l-Misk Kāfūr al-Ikhshīdī ruled Egypt from 334 AH/ 945 CE – 356 AH/ 966 CE.

and statesman.[529]

> An American missionary, residing in Egypt, calls attention to the entire absence of all colour and race prejudice in the country, which seems to have struck him the more from his experience of the unreasonable and superstitious caste prejudices in the land of his birth.[530] Ibn Khaldoon, a celebrated Muslim author, makes the following observations: It is a curious circumstance that the majority of learned amongst the Muslims belonged to a foreign race, very few persons of Arab descent having obtained distinction in the sciences connected with the law, or in those based on human reason. And yet the promulgator of the law was an Arab and the Qur'an, that source of so many sciences, an Arabic book.[531]

Blyden also opined:

> The "religion of the Jews," after 800 years, nowhere furnishes such practical evidence of cosmopolitan adaptation and power.[532]

Blyden stated about Islam however:

> There is nothing in the original teachings of Islam that requires hostility to Christians. There are, no doubt, bigots and fanatics among Muslims, as there have been and are now, bigots and fanatics among Christians; but the spirit of Islam, as taught by in its original records, is tolerant.[533]

All of these remarks from an African centred scholar writing in the 19th century refute the modern radical Christian and Afrocentric tale of events about Islām in Africa put forward by many. Therefore, rather than seeing Islām as a threat to Africa it has been considered in a positive light for development by pan-Africanists such as Blyden, Nkrumah, Fanon, Walter Rodney, Dubois and others. Diop noted about the spread of Islām in Africa:

529 *Ibn Khallilkan's Biographical Dictionary*, trans. Baron MacGuckin de Slane, (Paris: Oriental Translation Fund of Great Britain and Ireland, 1842) vol.2, p. 524.

530 Lansing, *Egypt's Princes*

531 *Christianity, Islam and the Negro Race*, p.282.

532 Ibid., p.283

533 Ibid., p.297

> The Arabs in these areas, who became great religious leaders, arrived as everywhere else individually and settled in peacefully, they owe their influence and latter acceptance to spiritual and religious virtues.[534]

However, Blyden did view Islām as something which would merely prepare the way for Christianity within Africa. He considered both religions as contributing to Africa but in the long term, he envisaged Christianity to take over in Africa.

In addition, Islām has played a major role in African-American and African-Caribbean history, from the Muslim slaves who made up ten percent of the West Africans introduced in the Americas between 1711–1808 CE.

534 *Precolonial Black Africa*, p.102

IX
African Muslims Enslaved in the Americas and the Caribbean

During the peak of European mercantilism and trade, the Europeans were opposed to the Muslims who did not conduct slave raids against their own people in West Africa and were organized enough to resist European encroachment. Although Muslims were enslaved and also faced colonization, Islām became associated with resistance to foreign rule and protection of peasants, a distinction that it acquired during the centuries of the slave trade. Diouf notes: "In the end, Islam became the dominant religion of west Africa. The trans-Atlantic slave trade played its part in its success."[535]

The beginnings of this can be found with the so-called discovery of the "New World" and slaves imported into Seville, second to Lisbon as a slave port and the first enslaved West Africans that entered the Americas came from Seville, some of whom were born there. These captives had become Christians by name, but in reality still allied themselves with Islām. Furthermore the Spanish did not want to turn the so-called "New World" into another stage for a Christian-Muslim battle and thus in 1501 CE a decree was issued which banned Jews, Moors, heretics and "New Christians" (i.e. former Muslims) from entering the Americas.[536] The Spanish also refrained from slave trafficking directly from Africa as they feared that non-Christian Africans would affect the so-called "New World" yet this still did not prevent a slave revolt in 1522 in Santa Domingo. The Spanish wanted:

535 Diouf, *op.cit.*, p.41

536 Michael A. Gomez, *Black Crescent: The Experience and Legacy of African Muslims in the Americas* (New York: Cambridge University Press, 2005), p.13.

> To exclude slaves suspected of Islamic leanings, such as the notorious *esclavos Gelofes* (Wolofs) of the guinea area, many of whom not only were infidels but were prone to insubordination as well.[537]

Therefore, as Gomez notes, "the Muslim element was important in the resistance of the enslaved in Hispaniola."[538] By the late seventeenth century Puerto Rico and Colombia were just two countries which were importing West African Muslim slaves from Senegambia, referred to as being "Mandingos."[539]

Between 1662 and 1867 CE, around 37 percent of all Africans imported into the Americas arrived into the Caribbean.[540] Between 1700 and 1807 CE, Senegambia and Sierra Leone, the regions where most African Muslim slaves would have come from, supplied 6.2 percent and 15.5 percent of the total British trade respectively.[541]

---

537 Frederick P. Browser, *The African Slave in Colonial Peru, 1524-1650* (Stanfrod, CA: Stanford University Press, 1974), pp.27-28.

538 Gomez, *op.cit.*, p.16

539 Mandingas, or Mande-speakers, were mainly Muslims and were descended from the ancient empire of Mali which began in the thirteenth century CE. By this time the Spanish did not mention the Wolof Muslims as Islām came to be associated with the Mandingas from the late seventeenth century onwards and that the Jolof kingdom had faded. The Mande were part of Senegambia and there were also Mande-speaking populations in the upper Niger valley. The non-Muslim Susu and Bambara tribes of Segu and Kaara were found in the upper Niger valley in the early nineteenth century CE and they eventually embraced Islām. Mande were also in what is today Guinea, Guinea-Bissau, Sierra Leone and parts of Liberia.

540 The English spread to Jamaica in 1655 after having established their presence in St. Kitts (St. Christopher) in 1624, Barbados in 1627, Nevis in 1628 and Montserrat and Antigua in the 1630s. Jamaica had an abundance of arable flat land which fascinated the early English occupiers along with the mountains and rivers. The Spanish had maintained a minimal presence for 150 years in Jamaica before the English took it over from them in 1655 CE in a bloody seizure by a gang of soldiers which according to some historians renders Jamaica to have been "founded in blood."

541 Gomez, *op.cit*, p.47

Jamaica

Jamaica became the main port for English buccaneering operations against the Spanish until the end of the seventeenth century CE, by which time the island became a base for large-scale plantation. Due to this increase in the plantations, the amount of slaves needed grew, increasing from only 514 slaves in 1661 to 9504 in 1673; doubling between 1730 and 1762 to 146,805 and reaching a total of 291,000 by 1795.[542] By 1817 CE there were some 345,252 Africans enslaved in Jamaica, the largest amount of slaves in the British Caribbean. African Muslims enslaved in Jamaica were mentioned in 1730 when *London's Society for Promoting Christian Knowledge* received a letter from Reverend William May of Kingston that included Arabic writings by a Mandingo.

At the turn of the nineteenth century there were a series of events that led to the increase of slaves across the Atlantic. One was a conflict in the Gold Coast (modern day Ghana) that led to the Muslims to challenge the fetishist idol-worshiping Ashanti state. The king of Ashanti, the Asantehene Osei Kwame who ruled from 1777, had been chased from power and strangled to death in 1803 because it was feared that he intended to establish the Qur'ānic legislation for the civil code of the empire and thus gold and kola trades would be out of Ashanti control.[543]

542 For more on this refer to B.W. Higman, *Slave Populations of the British Caribbean, 1807-1834* (Baltimore, MD: John Hopkins University Press, 1984) and B.W. Higman, *Slave Population and Economy in Jamaica, 1807-1834* (Cambridge, England: Cambridge University Press, 1976).

543 Joseph Dupuis, *Journal of Residence in Ashantee* (London: Henry Colburn, 1824), part 2, chap. 8, p.14.

There is evidence to suggest that between 1816 and 1823 Muslims did not only perform scribal duties, but also when the Asantehene required political advice, Muslims were consulted. The Muslims seem to have provided the Ashanti authorities with information on how to judge European intentions. Boit in his commentary on Bowdich's visit to Kumasi in 1817 notes how Muslim advisors to the Asantehene questioned Bowdich on British policy in India, to the surprise of Bowdich who did not realise that there was knowledge of events in places outside of the Ashanti kingdom within the kingdom itself. See David Owusu-Ansah, *Islamic Talismanic Tradition in Nineteenth-Century Asante* (New York: Edwin Mellen Press, 1991), pp.142, 144

The Muslims of the northwest region rebelled and were assisted by other Muslims from Kong and Mouna. They were defeated and this led to the enslavement of a fifteen year old named Abū Bakr as-Siddeeq,[544] he was taken first to Kumasi and then to Lago port (then including east of Accra and west of Cape Coast) where he was sold to an English slaver in around 1805 CE. He was eventually shipped to Jamaica where he spent his next thirty years as a slave.[545]

When Madden came across Abū Bakr in 1834, he had already been "owned" by three different persons. He was initially "owned" by a stonemason named Donellan, from whom he was purchased by Haynes who baptized Abū Bakr as "Edward Donellan" (or Donlan or Doulan). In 1823 he was purchased by Alexander Anderson, who came to recognise Abū Bakr's literary skills and used him as his record keeper, which Abū

Boit's commentary on Bowdich's experience in Kumasi points to an important function of the Muslims in the Ashanti kingdom, outside the mere realm of manufacturing charms, talismans and amulets. The screening procedure of Europeans was extended to the Qur'ān itself, with Europeans challenged to swear upon it to prove that they had come to Ashanti with good intentions. The Ashanti rulers no doubt thought of the Qur'ān as a powerful administrative force and the acceptance of it had great significance in determining the status of Muslims within the Ashanti political culture. Dupuis notes that Asantehene Osei Tutu Kwame placed so much trust in the Muslims that he: "consulted them upon many important occasions, where the interests of their nation were concerned" and above all, the king "never engaged in any warfare without their society." Dupuis, *op.cit,* p.98

Owusu-Ansah notes that the influence of the Muslims in the Ashanti commercial and political spheres was particularly strong during the reign of Osei Kwame (Owusu-Ansah, *op.cit*, p.165) in 1777 and Dupuis stated that he had been destooled because Islām would cause rulers to lose any ascendancy that they may enjoy. The Ashanti rulers of Ghana had Muslims to thank for much of the stability and prosperity of their empire.

544 See Ivor Wilks, "Abū Bakr al-Siddīq of Timbuktu" in Philip D. Curtin (ed.), *Africa Remembered: Narratives by West Africans from the Era of the Slave Trade* (Madison: University of Wisconsin Press, 1967). Also see Yacine Daddi Addoun and Paul Lovejoy, "The Arabic Manuscript of Muhammad Kabā Saghanughu of Jamaica, c.1823," available online at http://yorku.ca/nhp/shadd/kaba/index.asp

545 Richard Robert Madden, *A Twelve Months' Residence in the West Indies* (Philadelphia: Carey, Lea and Blanchard, 1835), pp.126-30

Bakr conducted in Arabic. Madden was so impressed by the level of Islamic education and manners of Abū Bakr that Madden negotiated Abū Bakr's freedom with Anderson. Anderson was initially reluctant as Abū Bakr was the one who kept all the records and accounts of his business, yet several weeks later Anderson agreed to manumit Abū Bakr (describing Abū Bakr as "a good and faithful negro").

When Madden returned to England in 1835, he appealed to the Royal Geographic Society to consider Abū Bakr for a voyage to West Africa, yet this was initially refused as Abū Bakr was considered unsuitable due to his time away from Africa. Abū Bakr was brought to England in 1835 by another special magistrate Captain Oldrey and then Madden persuaded John Davidson to take Abū Bakr with him to Timbuktu. However, after leaving for Morocco in September 1835, Davidson was killed in a raid in November 1836 whilst travelling to Timbuktu. Communication with Abū Bakr was lost until 1841, when the British vice-consul at Morocco discovered that Abū Bakr had arrived safely in Jenne and was thus one of the few to actually return back to Africa and leave the life of slavery.[546] He was patient, stayed firm on his religion and all praise is due to Allāh, he was freed and was even able to return to his land.

Abū Bakr is also known for his autobiography of which three versions were written, the first was completed for Madden in 1834 while both were still in Jamaica. The second was written on passage from Jamaica to England; and the third and final version was completed in England in 1835. All three versions were written in Arabic and the first was translated orally for Madden and the last two were given to G.C. Renouard, the first and final translations exist but all of the Arabic originals have disappeared.[547] There is also evidence to suggest that the enslaved African Muslim maintained contact and communication with each other and this existence of a *watheeqah* in Jamaica indicates this.[548]

546 Gomez, *op.cit,* pp.57-58

547 See Ivor Wilks, "Abū Bakr al-Siddīq of Timbuktu" in Philip D. Curtin (ed.), *Africa Remembered: Narratives by West Africans from the Era of the Slave Trade* (Madison: University of Wisconsin Press, 1967).

548 It has been stated that the *watheeqah* was composed by African Muslim slaves themselves in the Americas to exhort the Muslims to stay on their religion and be strong in *īmān* (faith), while others hold that it was directed to Muslims within

Trinidad

In Trinidad, there is even evidence that a sizable Muslim community, under the leadership of an Imām, attempted to live independently and govern their affairs by the Shari'ah. By 1838 there were 140 Muslims living in the Port of Spain area. Their leader was Muhammad Bath, also known as "Leonas Bath" and "Jonas Bath" who arrived in Trinidad around 1804-05 after being captured in Africa by non-Muslims, there is no biography of him however. The Muslims of the Port of Spain saved collectively in order to buy each other's freedom and they also borrowed from each other to fund commercial and agricultural enterprises.

As Muhammad Bath was said to have knowledge of Arabic and Islām he may have held the role as an Islamic judge between the Muslims that had been enslaved in Trinidad.[549] Due to the organisational skills of these African Muslims enslaved in Trinidad they petitioned the British government several times to return them to Africa. At least three separate petitions were sent between 1831[550] and 1838. The 1833 petition is signed in Arabic "Ana Yūnus ibn Ibrāheem" (lit. "I am Yūnus, the son of Ibrāheem"), which therefore indicates that the Muslims of the Port of Spain did not hide their Islām and pretend to be Christians. As for Muhammad Bath, it was said of him that "he always appeared in

---

Africa and was then smuggled into the Americas. Muhammad Kaba was given a copy in 1831 however his wife destroyed it in 1832 as possessing it may have been dangerous due to the "Baptist War" of 1831-1832. This rebellion was under the leadership of Baptist missionaries and independent ministers, yet was not embraced by the Manchester branch, where Muhammad Kaba lived, this may explain his opposition to the revolt, a number of other plantations also refrained from participating in the revolt. Sultana Afroz has described the rebellion as an armed *jihād* in her article "The Jihad of 1831-1832: The Misunderstood Baptist Rebellion in Jamaica," in the *Journal of Muslim Minority Affairs 21* (2000), pp.227-43.

549 Gomez, *op.cit.*, p.71

550 The fact that a petition was drafted in 1831 before apprenticeship was instituted for slaves in the Americas indicated that their main aim was to return back to Africa. Gomez notes that with their subsequent petitions it could be argued that they were writing as property owners who were concerned about their investments.

public in the dress of a Moslem priest."[551]

The 1938 petition had twelve signatures in Arabic however, like the previous petitions it was unsuccessful.

The Mande-speaking (Mandinga) Muslims were viewed in a better light than they were in the Portuguese and Spanish American and Caribbean colonies and one of the reasons for this is that they were not seen as being subversive or rebellious, they respected authority and were also seen as being reliable. In return these slaves were often rewarded with vocationally skilled positions or placed in positions of responsibility over other slaves. Furthermore, the Portuguese and Spanish colonies were very anti-Islamic and Muslims were seen as the main threat to Spanish imperial control and dominance. In Jamaica however, the Muslims, such as Muhammad Kaba did not support slave uprisings.

There is also the case of an African Muslim slave by the name of Muhammad who was bought in 1798 from a slaver by Daniel Hill in Antigua. Similar to what happened with Abū Bakr of Jamaica, Hill found out that Muhammad had "a considerable share of Arabic literature." Muhammad lived his life openly as a Muslim which Hill respected saying he "paid the utmost attention to the religious scruples of his slave" which shows that Muhammad clung to his Islām, even whilst in slavery. After a short while, the slave holder Hill granted Muhammad his freedom and the means to begin his return to West Africa. After a three month stay in Liverpool in 1811, Muhammad obtained money from the Director of the African Institution in London to sail for Goree Island which was the nearest point to the home of his family. Muhammad thus returned back to Africa after being enslaved.[552] Gomez noted here is another example of "a gifted (literate) Muslim who is deemed above enslavement by the slaveholder and therefore sent back to Africa."[553]

551 Carl Campbell, *"John Mohammad Bath and the Free Mandingoes in Trinidad: The Question of Their Repatriation of Africa, 1831-38"* in *Journal of African Studies 2* (1975-76), p.467-68.

552 Folarin Shyllon, *Black People in Britain, 1555-1833* (London, New York and Ibadan: Oxford University Press, for the Institute of Race Relations, 1977), p.60.

553 Gomez, *op.cit,* p.81

Brazil

From the beginning of the seventeenth century up to the nineteenth, most of the enslaved Muslims in Brazil were Mande-speakers, again referred to as "Mandingoes" in Bahia and were thus largely from Senegambia, Sierra Leone and some from the Gold Coast (present day Ghana).[554] Muslims were only a very small minority out of all the slaves, accounting for as little as 2.5 percent of the entire slave population in Brazil according to some accounts yet they achieved renown even with their small numbers.

Muslim rebellion in nineteenth century CE Brazil had roots in Bahia, whose capital and port of Salvador was surrounded by fertile, well-drained wetlands known as the Recõncavo and it was thus one of the main producers of sugar in the Americas in the 1820s. In the city of Salvador, the enslaved population increased between 1808 and 1835 and thus the enslaved population was larger than the free population. African Muslims enslaved in Bahia regarded slavery as an indignity and for this reason it should not come as a surprise that Muslims who had their own enclaves and worked together to increase their economic prospects would rebel and fight for their interests against their slave captors and owners. They also distanced themselves from the free blacks who were also non-Muslims and it is said that the literate Muslims in Bahia who took part in the 1835 insurrection would not shake hands with those they viewed as being outsiders.[555]

The presence of Islām in Bahia was also evident due to the number of documents written in Arabic which were taken from those who had been killed in the slave revolt in 1835 CE or taken from those who were suspected of participating. Much of the writing were verses of the Qur'ān written in Maghribi script which is found in North and West Africa. Other materials which were confiscated after the rebellion reveal dozens of wooden writing boards or slates, upon which students would write.[556] The French consul also complained that Muslims were calling

---

554 João José Reis, *Slave Rebellion in Brazil: The Muslim Uprising of 1835 in Bahia*, trans. Arthur Brakel (Baltimore and London: Johns Hopkins University Press, 1993), p.93.

555 Gomez, *op.cit*, p.104; Reis, *op.cit*, pp.116-21

556 These were called '*wala*' or '*patako*' in Yoruba and '*allo*' in Hausa, it is also

other non-Muslims to Islām and to thus participate in the revolt. During the revolt itself, Muslims came out fighting in Islamic dress and head-wear. The purpose of the revolt is not completely clear, however the dominant view is that it was engaged in as an armed *jihād*.[557]

'AbdurRahman al-Baghdādī

A rare insight into the lives of the African Muslims enslaved in the Brazilian cities of Rio, Salvador and Pernambuco is provided by 'AbdurRahmān al-Baghdādī. He was educated in Damascus and in 1865 he was commissioned to travel to Basra in a steamship. However, the winds misdirected the fleet to Rio instead wherein he would meet Muslims that had been enslaved and teach them Islām, as their practice had become so corrupted due to slavery.[558]

The Muslims in Brazil respected al-Baghdādī due to his distinct Muslim appearance. There were some difficulties communicating with them yet there was a translator, who happened to be Jewish, who explained that they were sold into slavery due to being war captives of wars that had taken place in West Africa. Al-Baghdādī visited the homes of some of them and found that many of them were not praying properly. Al-Baghdādī learned some Portuguese and then stayed in the Muslim areas teaching the Muslims the fundamentals and basics of Islām.

After spending some time in Rio, al-Baghdādī went to Salvador (Bahia) where he found a much larger Muslim community however the Muslims there were not as eager to learn as the Muslims in Rio. After Salvador, al-Baghdādī visited Pernambuco where he found the Muslims more active than those in Rio, even though there was still the same amount of ignorance. He also found the Muslims had some corrupted beliefs and practices such as magic, divination and geomancy. He remained in Pernambuco for six months and the Muslims paid for his journey back

---

known as a '*Lawh*' in other parts of West Africa. The term originates from the Arabic word '*Lawh*' which is a 'slate', 'board' or a 'tablet'.

557 For more on the discussion of this see Gomez, *op.cit*,. pp.109-10.

558 See Abd al-Rahmān al-Bagdādī, *The Amusement of the Foreigner*, trans. Yacine Daddi Addoun and Renée Soulodre-La France (Toronto: Nigerian Hinterland project, York University, 2001). Available online: www.yorku.ca/nhp/shadd/baghdadi.pdf

to Constantinople as he had stayed in Brazil longer.

Origins of African Muslim Slaves in the Americas and Caribbean

In 1819, six Hausa and Nupe individuals interviewed in Bahia by d'Andrada all attributed their enslavement to armed *jihād.* Other conflicts among Muslims produced slaves according to interviews with Muslims in Bahia in the late 1840s by Francis de Castelnau. Some Kanuris in Borno were captured and enslaved by fellow Hausa Muslim soldiers, another example of 'Muslim-on-Muslim' hostility. Indeed, the Prophet Muhammad (*sallallāhu alayhi wassallam*) noted in an authentic *hadeeth* that: *"I asked my Lord that my ummah not be destroyed by drought, and that it not be overcome by enemies outside of them. My Lord said: 'O Muhammad! When I issue a decree it is not reversed. I have granted for your ummah that they will not be destroyed by universal drought. And that they not be overcome by enemies outside themselves even if they gather against them in droves, but some of them will destroy each other, and some will capture (and enslave) each other.'"*[559]

Another reason for the enslavement of Muslims to the Americas was due to combat in the Muslim region of Futa Jallon (in present-day Guinea or eastern Senegal/Western Mali), a mountainous area where migrations of Fulbe pastoralists from Māsina in the 15th, 16th, 17th and 18th centuries led to conflicts with the Jallonke, Mande-speaking agriculturalists. By the early eighteenth century, tensions between the Muslim Fulbe and the mostly non-Muslim Jallonke led to a war between 1725 and 1728 and fighting led to Muhammad Kaba, the most famous African Muslim enslaved in Jamaica to be taken as a captive. He was born around 1756 in Futa Jallon and was possibly from the Jakhanke community, a Mande community of related families engaged in commerce and Islamic scholarship in Senegambia[560] and he also grew up in a time when Islamic reform was gaining a foothold in West Africa.[561]

---

559 An authentic hadeeth collected by Muslim and narrated from Thawbān (*radi Allāh 'anhu*). Also collected by Tirmidhī, Ahmad, Ibn Mājah and Abū Dāwūd

560 See Lamin O. Sanneh, *The Jakhanke: The History of an Islamic Clerical People of the Senegambia* (London: International African Institute, 1979).

561 According to R.R. Madden, an Irish special magistrate sent to Jamaica to facilitate the *1833 Emancipation Act* whereby the enslaved in British territories

The war in Futa Jallon was due to internal divisions among the Muslims, after having founded a Muslim state which ruled by Sharī'ah in 1747, the Fulbe and Jallonke became opposed to each other. Another factor was due to non-Muslim forces, such as the campaigns of Kundi Burama of Wassulu, who attacked Muslim territories from the 1760s to the 1780s. This twenty year period is the most violent phase of Futa Jallon's war and was responsible for an increase of more than 100 percent of slave exports from the coasts of Sierra Leone.[562]

Indeed, Walter Rodney estimated that 75 percent of all Africans sold from the region in the second half of the eighteenth century came from the interior. Muhammad Kaba himself noted that in around 1777-78 he fell into the hands of robbers and was carried off to the coast to be sold. Other African Muslim slaves in Jamaica included the two slaves of Bryan Edwards. Edwards mentioned that his servant was a Mandingo and was brought to Jamaica as a youth, the other servant "could write, with great beauty and exactness, the Arabic alphabet and some pages from the Alcoran."[563]

The Yoruba were organised into autonomous towns like the Hausa were, but they were urban peoples who maintained their own dialects and

---

were able to enter a four-year apprenticeship period prior to acquiring their full freedom. Muhammad Kaba came from a privileged background in Africa and his father Abū Bakr al-Qādirī owned slaves, land and cattle. Muhammad Kaba was 78 years old in 1834 and he had spent some 56 years in Jamaican slavery on a coffee-producing plantation in Manchester.

He was renamed "Robert Tuffit" or "Robert Pearl" yet he probably feigned Christianity and remained a Muslim. The evidence for this is the fact that he wrote a letter in Arabic to Aboo Bakr as-Siddeeq which was mentioned by Madden and within the letter Muhammad Kaba mentions the *Shahādah*, the first pillar of Islām. As a result, even Madden did not think that he had fully embraced Christianity, nevertheless, he was baptized and became a member of the Moravian Mission at Carmel [R.R. Madden, *Twelve Months Residence in the West Indies*, vol.2 (Philadelphia: Carey, Lea and Blanchard, 1837), pp.133-137].

562 Paul Lovejoy, *Transformations in Slavery: A History of Slavery in Africa* (Cambridge, England: Cambridge University Press, 1983), p.59.

563 Bryan Edwards, *The History, Civil and Commercial, of the British Colonies in the West Indies, in Two Volumes, 2nd edition* (London: John Stockdale, Piccadilly, 1794), vol.2, pp.61-63.

localised traditions. Islām became widespread throughout Yorubaland during the seventeenth century and by the end of the eighteenth century Yoruba Muslims were taking Islām to other areas such as Dahomey in the west and also along the coast. By this time, there were Muslim communities thriving in Owu, Badagry, Iseyin, Ikoyi, Igboho, Ogbomoso and Ketu.[564] Muslims had the greatest influence in Oyo even though they were not huge in number and the important Islamic communities were located in the Oyo Empire, these communities included Yoruba, Hausa, Kanuri and Nupe. The Muslim presence in Oyo, Igboho, Ogbomoso and Osogbo was so substantial that there was a special office, known as the *Parakoyi*, which aimed at regulating the affairs of the Muslims and lead them in war.[565]

A struggle developed in 1797 when Afonja revolted against the Alafin of Oyo and joined forces with a leading Muslim scholar named as-Sālih. By 1823, Muslim Ilorin brought the imperial rule of Oyo to an end after having been inspired to a certain degree by events in Sokoto. As a result, Muslim Yoruba fled to Ilorin for security and safety from persecution by Yoruba traditionalists in other parts of Yorubaland. Between 1831 and 1833 Muslim Ilorin destroyed or defeated the Oyo Empire's major towns. The final battle between Oyo and Ilorin lead to the destruction of Oyo however the victory was short-lived, as the Muslims became entangled in factional fighting between supporters of local control and those supporting Sokoto. This in-fighting lasted from 1837 to 1878, with Ibadan emerging as victor, as it had defeated Ilorin at the Battle of Osogbo in 1840.[566]

Yoruba and Hausa captives that were exported out of the Bight of Benin during the first three decades of the nineteenth century were familiar with war and included Muslims and non-Muslims from both groups (Yoruba and Hausa) as well as others. The majority were non-Muslims but Muslims were included amongst the captives that would later find themselves enslaved. Between 1801 and 1825, some 113,839 captives left the Bight of Benin and possibly as many as 35 percent landed in Bahia which was the main destination in the so-called 'New World' of captives from the Bight of Benin and many of them could

564 Gomez, *op.cit*, p.112

565 Ibid.

566 Ibid

have been caught up in the *jihāds* of Sokoto or Ilorin.[567] Two separate slave testimonies in nineteenth century Brazil highlight the *jihāds* of West Africa.

Conclusions

African Muslims that were enslaved in the Americas, despite the fact that they spoke different languages and came from different countries shared the same religion, had a lingua-franca to refer to, a writing system via which they could correspond and their Islamic belief that bound them together. European and American observers noted this Muslim communality and cohesiveness. One of the first to mention it was Father Sandoval, a Catholic priest who wrote in 1620 C.E. that the Wolof, Mandingo and Fulani of Cartagena, Columbia had different languages and were of different countries yet still communicated with one another because they all belong, to what he described as, "the cursed sect of Mahomet." A traveller to Brazil in the mid-1800s observed the same phenomena and stressed that the Muslims were "more united among themselves than the other nations."[568]

African Muslims that were enslaved in the Americas also managed to maintain their dignity as much as they could. Mungo Park realised that the African Muslims did not hold European Christian traders in high esteem. Whilst the slave dealer Nicholas Owen noted "Our religion has made no impression in the least otherwise than a matter of ridicule or laughter in so many years as they have had us among them..." The Muslim slaves resented being the slaves of Christians and looked down upon the whites as Christians.[569] Father Etienne Ignace, a professor at the seminary of Bahia had a low opinion of Muslims that he had met. These Muslims obviously challenged the Christianity that he was trying to preach to them, he whinged:

> With their thick intellect full of nonsense, they are swollen full of pride. They are full of hate for the whites and the Christians... they cling with fanaticism to bland and exterior practices.[570]

567 Ibid

568 Edwards, *op.cit.*, p.72

569 Diouf, *op.cit.,* p.94-95

570 Ibid., p.100

Clearly, the Muslims were quite happy with their Islām considering it superior to whatever European Christians were trying to preach to them in the plantations. As a result, African Muslims were seen by white English-speakers as superior to other Africans who were enslaved, due to their literacy skills and religious beliefs and morals, Madden and Edwards for example reflect this in their work.

Islām was clearly a galvanizing force amongst the African Muslims that were enslaved in the Americas. It gave them self worth in a brutal and humiliating environment, it also instilled a feeling of superiority over the European Christians, considering themselves and their way of life as morally above others. Their daily interactions with the European Christian slaveowners could only reinforce this line of reasoning. Diouf superbly notes in her book *Servants of Allah*:

> Furthermore, to be a Muslim was prestigious because of the literacy Islam emphasized, and because it gave personal power to men and women who chose to impose a discipline on themselves rather than to submit to another people's discipline. To be a Muslim meant to be part of a close-knit, upwardly mobile community that looked after its members, offered them diverse activities and services, and was charitable and organized. It was a world in itself, with its own particular sets of beliefs that did not depend on the slaveholders' view of the world. To be light skinned had no value, to be a house slave or a field slave meant nothing. A free man in this context was not superior to a slave. Learned slaves were the teachers of free men; enslaved and jailed clerics were the spiritual leaders of the community. Islam was democratic and progressive in a society that was despotic, repressive, tyrannical, and racist.[571]

Many slaveholders in the Americas and the Caribbean showed hostility to the literate African Muslims who were enslaved. Thomas Dwight of the *American Ethnological Society* attempted to conduct a study of the slaves that were literate however noted that he experienced difficulties due to jealous slave masters. Dwight also mentioned that writer and ethnologist William Hodgson, who had lived in North Africa, tried to make inquiries about the literate Muslims in the American South but had to abandon the project "in despair" due to the hostility of their

---

571 Ibid., p.162

masters.[572] In the eyes of the slaveholders African literacy was a threat to white Christian intellectual domination. African literacy as influenced by Islām refuted the fact that Africans were supposedly inherently inferior and not sufficiently expert in intellectual studies and activities. Diouf notes:

> The Africans' skills constituted a proof of humanity and civilization that did not owe anything to the Christians' supposed civilizing influence. If these men and women could read and write, if they were not the blank slates or the primitive savages they had been portrayed to be in order to justify their enslavement, then the very foundation of the system had to be questioned.[573]

Dr Walter Rodney[574] in his famous book *How Europe Underdeveloped Africa* mentions:

> As in other parts of the world, literacy in Africa was connected with religion, so that in Islamic countries it was a Koranic education...Moslem education was particularly extensive at the primary level, and it was also available at the secondary and university levels. In Egypt there was the Al-Azhar University, in Morocco the university of Fez, and in Mali the University of Timbuktu - all testimony to the standard of education achieved in Africa before the colonial intrusion.[575]

As can be seen here Dr Walter Rodney, a hard-nosed Pan-Africanist and activist, throughout all of his valued research on how Africa came to be underdeveloped in some regions of the continent, and after gaining a Ph.D in history, did not come to conclusion that Islām had anything to do with it. Walter Rodney praised Islām for its role in Africa and its emphasis on education throughout the continent. He further notes:

---

572 Ibid., p.108

573 Ibid

574 He was a famous African-American scholar and activist killed during political friction in Guyana. He graduated from the University of the West Indies in Jamaica and also from the University of London where he gained a Ph.D in History. Despite being a Marxist, he praised Islām for its role in Africa and its emphasis on education throughout the continent.

575 Walter Rodney, *How Europe Underdeveloped Africa* (Washington D.C.: Howard University Press, 1974), p.240.

Christianity tried sporadically and ambivalently to make an impact on some parts of the continent. But most of the few missionaries in places like the Congo, Angola, and Upper Guinea concentrated on blessing Africans as they were about to be launched across the Atlantic into slavery...Elsewhere, there flourished Islam and other religions which had nothing to do with European trade.[576]

576 Ibid., p.114

Conclusion

This work has attempted to re-assess many of the anti-Islamic tendencies that have arisen within Afrocentric thought and has presented strong arguments rebutting many of their popular misconceptions. The origin and movement of *Islamophobia* amongst certain Afrocentrists has been investigated and their claims have been tackled in a comprehensive manner. As a result, it should become visible to the reader that the claims of Islam being an "Arab religion" and therefore not for those of African origin is not only a false and simplistic line of thought but also hugely inaccurate in light of what has been shown in this work.

Furthermore, such an argument should therefore lead the claimants of it to therefore abandon all of their own luxuries and fancies that they are steeped in within their own homes, considering the fact that their cars, clothes, electrical goods and many other aspects of their lives that they are engulfed in are also not "invented by black people"!? Therefore, what is observable is that due to the pervasiveness of Western culture in the current era, it has become unbeknown to those who argue that Islām is an "Arab religion" that they themselves are absolutely entrenched in a Western culture and adhering to its popular myths about Islām.

Moreover, *Defining Legends* has indicated that the majority of African-centred scholars that have written about Islām in Africa have not reached the same opinions as are propounded by the anti-Islām Afrocentrics. The reasons for this are manifold, one cause is due to those writing against Islām having their own biases and agendas whether it be in order to call to Christianity and thus gain some kind of imagined religious lead over Islām or due to a personal hatred of Islām owing to its popularity and rapid spread in the UK and the US. This hatred against Islām has led to many irrational theories in the form of fringe scholarship and fostered the kind of outbursts that are a common feature of many website forums supposedly catering for black communities in the west.

Those who write against Islām refuse to contemplate upon the likes of Franz Fanon, Cheikh Anta Diop, Kwame Nkrumah, Malcolm X, W.E.B. Dubois, Edward Blyden, and the many other historians and academics of African origin that had actually spent time in Africa who did not agree with the evangelical and Christian missionary inspired bias about Islām as espoused by Chancellor Williams in his *Destruction of Black Civilisation* or the snide comments of John Henrik Clarke. Therefore, it is upon those who write against Islām to consider a fair appraisal of Islām and its spread all over the world as opposed to regurgitating the age-old arguments that "Islām was spread by the sword."

Appendices

Appendix One

Tawheed, Pharaoh Akhenaten and the Kemet Afrocentrics

Islam is based upon *Tawheed*, singling out Allāh alone for worship, with a monotheism which is distinct from all over faiths. Allāh Says in the Qur'ān,

﴿إِنَّ اللَّهَ لَا يَغْفِرُ أَن يُشْرَكَ بِهِ وَيَغْفِرُ مَا دُونَ ذَٰلِكَ لِمَن يَشَاءُ﴾

> Indeed Allāh does not forgive that He be associated with in worship, but He forgives whatever is less than that to whomsoever He wills.
>
> [an-Nisā' (4): 116]

And Allāh Says,

﴿وَاعْبُدُوا اللَّهَ وَلَا تُشْرِكُوا بِهِ شَيْئًا﴾

> Worship your Lord and do not associate anything [in worship] with Him.
>
> [an-Nisā' (4): 36]

However, some of the Afrocentric Kemet thinkers have asserted that Islam has merely adopted *Tawheed* from the ancient Egyptian pharaoh Akhenaten. Molefi K. Asante for example stated in his book *From Imhotep to Akhenaten: An Introduction to the Egyptian Philosophers* (Menaibuc 2004), p.60: "Nevertheless, like the names of the Supreme Deity in Yoruba, Akan, Ibo, Christianity, Islam, and Judaism, the functions and roles of the Deity in Kemet remained the same through these various transformations." Herein attempting to portray Islam as a mere adapted version of the credo of the ancient Egyptian Pharaohs.

Yosef Ben-Jochannan also argues similar in his book *Black Man of the Nile and His Family* (Baltimore: Black Classic Press, 1972), p.365.

A modern writer from Egypt, Ahmed Osman, claimed in his book *Moses: Pharaoh of Egypt, The Mystery of Akhenaten Resolved* (1990) that the Pharaoh Akhenaten was in fact the Prophet Mūsā!? Yet as shall be seen in the information presented herein, such a claim is totally inaccurate. While in his 2005 book *Christianity: An Ancient Egyptian Religion* he asserts that Christianity is an offshoot of an ancient Egyptian mystery cult. The Kemet movement also shares many similarities with a white European freemasonic obsession with ancient Egypt and viewing it as one of the 'seven wonderous' places of the world. 'Kemet' is the ancient Egyptian name for ancient Egypt which they used to call it, and it means "the black lands" in reference to the black soil which was deposited along the banks of the River Nile by the annual inundation which broke its banks and enhanced their agriculture.

Many high street bookstores are filled with a peculiar and amusing array of books which attempt to "unlock hieroglyphic codes", "unravel hidden mysteries" and "delve into the understandings" of the magicians of ancient Egypt!? These theories serve as a basis of New Age and occult theology in the West. So for example, Satanist writers such as Aleister Crowley exalt ancient Egyptian religion and magic. In Crowley's book *The New Law of Man* he vainly claims that his book will replace the Qur'ān as the most universal law for humanity. Indeed, Allāh says in the Qur'ān,

﴿وَاعْبُدُواْ اللّهَ وَلاَ تُشْرِكُواْ بِهِ شَيْئًا﴾

Worship your Lord and do not associate anything [in worship] with Him.

[an-Nisā' (4): 36]

﴿قَالَ لَهُم مُّوسَى وَيْلَكُمْ

لَا تَفْتَرُوا عَلَى اللَّهِ كَذِبًا فَيُسْحِتَكُم بِعَذَابٍ وَقَدْ خَابَ مَنِ افْتَرَى﴾

Mūsā said to them (the magicians of Pharoah): "Woe to you! Do not invent a lie against Allāh or He will exterminate you with a punishment, and he has failed who invents such falsehood."

[Tā Hā (20): 61]

Other Europeans who looked to ancient Egypt for 'divine guidance' included Charles Piazzi Smyth who influenced John G. Jackson, the Afrocentric who also had a passion for ancient Egyptian occultism. There is also the argument that is popular with many in the Kemet movement that the teachings of Mūsā (*alayhi salām*) were merely taken from the ancient Egyptian *Book of Coming Forth by Day*, the 125th chapter in particular. Not only do little of the laws given to Mūsā overlap but also this ancient Egyptian magic spell book contains clear polytheism and idol-worship, so how could the Prophet Mūsā derive knowledge from this when it contravenes the pure worship of Allāh?! Allāh Says,

وَلَقَدْ بَعَثْنَا فِي كُلِّ أُمَّةٍ رَّسُولاً أَنِ اعْبُدُواْ اللهَ وَاجْتَنِبُواْ الطَّاغُوتَ۝

> We sent Messengers to every nation [saying to the people] worship Allāh and avoid Tāghūt (false deities).
>
> [an-Nahl (16): 36]

In ancient Egypt all number of paraphernalia was worshipped including dogs, cats, beetles and even the male penis! Jennings in his book *Phallicism: Celestial and Terrestrial, Heathen and Christian and its Connection with the Rosicrucians and Gnostics* stated:

> The Egyptians, among whom of ancient nations the Obelisk and the Pyramids were the most frequently employed as significant objects, held that there were two opposite powers in the world perpetually acting and reacting against each other…the obelisk meant the male instrument, while the pyramid signified the female corresponding tumefactive.[577]

Akhenaten and His Supposed 'Monotheism'

The Afrocentrics and Kemet Movement claim that Islam derived its concept of *Tawheed* and monotheism from the ancient Egyptian Pharaoh Akhenaten. John Henrik Clarke states in *Notes for an African World Revolution: Africans at the Crossroads*:

577 Hargreave Jennings and George Redway, *Phallicism: Celestial and Terrestrial, Heathen and Christian and its Connection with the Rosicrucians and Gnostics* (London: George Redway, 1884 and Reprint: Health Research, 1982), p.73

> An African king, Akhenaton, preached that concept from the throne 1300 years before the birth of Christ. That was over 3000 years ago. This man, who thought so much of life that he would not crush a flower, gave to the world the concept of monotheism or the oneness of God...[578]

Yosef Ben Jochannan states in *Black man of the Nile and his Family*:

> Even the theory of "monotheism", the belief in One God above others, was taught in Ta-Nehesi [Nubia], Ta-Merry [Egypt] and Itiopi [Ethiopia] before the birth of Moses by the Pharaoh Akhenaton [Amen-hotep IV]...[579]

Maulana Karenga stated in his essay "Black Religion": "Akhenaton stressed the worship of one God.".[580] Due to this common misconception, it will be necessary to assess this claim. Ross and Steadman (2017: 110) state in their book *Ancient Complex Societies*:

> These strong royal ties to Amun were broken just once during the New Kingdom: during the late Eighteenth Dynasty, when Akhenaten (formerly Amenhotep IV) shuttered the state temples of Egypt and instituted sole worship of Aten, the solar disk, who could be approached only through the royal family.[581]

How can the worship of the sun be conflated with the worship of the Creator of the sun!? And even here the worship of the sun cannot be direct but through the Pharaohs, combing *Shirk* in *Rubūbiyyah* with *Shirk* in *Ulūhiyyah*! The Qur'an says:

وَمِنْ آيَاتِهِ اللَّيْلُ

وَالنَّهَارُ وَالشَّمْسُ وَالْقَمَرُ لَا تَسْجُدُوا لِلشَّمْسِ وَلَا لِلْقَمَرِ وَاسْجُدُوا

578 John Henrik Clarke, *Notes for an African World Revolution: Africans at the Crossroads* (Trenton, New Jersey: Africa World Press, 1991), p.34

579 Yosef Ben Jochannan, *Black man of the Nile and his Family* (Baltimore, MD: Black Classic Press, 1972), p.104

580 Maulana Karenga, "Black Religion." In Gayraud S. Wilmore (ed.), *African American Religious Studies: An Interdisciplinary Anthology* (Durham and London: Duke University Press, 1989), p.282.

581 Jennifer C. Ross and Sharon R. Steadman, *Ancient Complex Societies* (London: Routledge, 2017).

لِلَّـهِ الَّذِي خَلَقَهُنَّ إِن كُنتُمْ إِيَّاهُ تَعْبُدُونَ﴿

> And of His signs are the night and day and the sun and the moon. Do not prostrate to the sun or to the moon, but prostrate to Allāh, which created them, if it should be Him that you worship.
>
> [Fussilat (41): 37]

Darnell and Manassa (2007: 12) state in *Tutankhamun's Armies: Battle and Conquest During Ancient Egypt's Late Eighteenth Century*:

> Although Akhenaten is sometimes characterised as a pacifist and a monotheist, both designations are simplistically false.[582]

They then stated (p.22)

> ...Akhenaten, who promoted the Aten to the most important-and indeed the only-deity of the Egyptian pantheon, with the exception of himself and his chief queen, Nefertiti.

So Akhenaten also called to the worship of himself and his wife, this is not *Tawheed* of the Prophets and the Messengers, indeed, Allāh Says,

﴿وما يؤمن أكثرهم بالله إلا وهم مشركون﴾

> Most of them do not believe in Allāh, except that they associate partners [in worship with Him].
>
> [Yūsuf (12): 106]

Darnell and Manassa also state (p.40):

> In the art of the age, Akhenaten and Nefertiti are androgynous, for they are the first male-female pairs, the Amarna counterparts of the Ogdoads deities. The thighs, belly and buttocks of the Atenist rulers are those of fecundity and pregnancy...

In the book *Holy People of the World: a Cross-Cultural Encyclopedia* Kevin McGeough mentions under 'Akhenaten':

> Akhenaten was a pharaoh of New Kingdom Egypt (eighteenth

---

582 John Coleman Darnell and Colleen Manassa, *Tutankhamun's Armies: Battle and Conquest During Ancient Egypt's Late Eighteenth Century* (Hoboken, New Jersey: John Wiley and Sons, 2007).

> dynasty, ruling from 1372 to 1355 B.C.E.) who broke with Egyptian traditions by focusing on the state cult on the worship of the sun disc Aten to the exclusion of other Egyptian gods. He has often been labelled the world's first monotheist. Although this description is likely not an accurate characterization of the belief system he imposed...[583]

McGeough then states under his entry:

> The theology of Atenism was expressed in a composition that modern scholars call "The Hymn to the Aten." The object of veneration in this is the physical disc of the sun.

Hardly sounds like a prayer to the Creator of the universe?! Allāh Says in the Qur'ān,

﴿ولا تدع من دون ا لله ما لا ينفعك ولا يضرك﴾

> Do not invoke other than Allāh that which neither benefits nor harms you.
>
> [Yūnus (10): 106]

And

﴿وَالَّذِينَ تَدْعُونَ مِن دُونِهِ مَا يَمْلِكُونَ مِن قِطْمِيرٍ﴾

> And those whom you invoke other than Him do not possess [so much as] the membrane of a date seed.
>
> [Fātir (35): 13]

Egyptian Old Kingdom Pyramid Texts contained such odd beliefs that it is clear that such idolatry and polytheism is the antithesis of Islam. For instance, the Old Kingdom Pyramid Texts make reference to the sun god Re creating himself and then other gods subsequently!?[584] Is this the *Tawheed* of the Prophets and Messengers relayed in the Qur'ān?! Allāh Says,

---

583 Phyllis G. Jestice (ed.), *Holy People of the World: A Cross-Cultural Encyclopedia, Vol.1, Entries A-G* (Santa Barbara, California, Denver Colorado and Oxford, England: ABC-CLIO, 2004), p.28.

584 See James Karl Hoffmeier, *Akhenaten and the Origins of Monotheism* (Oxford and New York: Oxford University Press, 2015), p.10

﴿تِلْكَ إِذاً قِسْمَةٌ ضِيزَى﴾

That then, is an unjust division.

[an-Najm (53): 22]

Patricia Spencer stated in *The Egyptian Temple: A Lexicographical Study*:

> Outside the precincts near the east gate Akhenaten built a place of worship for the Aten and himself.[585]

Simson Najovits states in *Egypt, Trunk of the Tree, A Modern Survey of an Ancient Land*:

> The "westerners", the dead, were supposed to worship both Akhenaten and Nefertiti. Osiris' role was eliminated.[586]

Then Najovits states:

> More correctly, Aten was a personal god only for Akhenaten and to a lesser extent for his family. The personal god for the people, the god whom they were supposed to pray to, was Akhenaten himself.[587]

Thus, Akhenaten called the people to worship himself, where's the Tawheed [Islamic Monotheism] here!? This is rather the same old practice of other Pharaohs before Akhenaten as Allāh Says about another Pharaoh:

﴿فَكَذَّبَ وَعَصَى﴾

﴿ثُمَّ أَدْبَرَ يَسْعَى﴾ ﴿فَحَشَرَ فَنَادَى﴾ ﴿فَقَالَ أَنَا رَبُّكُمُ الْأَعْلَى﴾ ﴿فَأَخَذَهُ اللَّهُ نَكَالَ الْآخِرَةِ وَالْأُولَى﴾ ﴿إِنَّ فِي ذَلِكَ لَعِبْرَةً لِّمَن يَخْشَى﴾

But Pharaoh denied and disobeyed. Then he turned his back, striving. And he gathered [his people] and called

585 Patricia Spencer, *The Egyptian Temple: A Lexicographical Study* (Abingdon, Oxon and New York, NY: Routledge, 2004), p.107.

586 Simson Najovits, *Egypt, Trunk of the Tree, A Modern Survey of an Ancient Land: Vol.II: The Consequences, How Egypt Became the Trunk of the Tree* (New York: Algora Publishing, 2004), p.138

587 Ibid.

> out...And said "I am your most exalted lord". So Allāh seized him in exemplary punishment for the last and the first [transgression]. Indeed in that is a warning for whoever would fear [Allāh].
>
> [an-Nāzi'āt (79): 21-26]

Peter Roberts states in HSC *Ancient History*:

> According to the Tutankhamun Stele, Akhenaten also closed the temples of the other gods, banishing the old burial gods. Akhenaten himself became the god of the dead as well as the living.[588]

Tamara L. Siuda, herself a white-Kemet high priestess (!), states in *The Ancient Egyptian Prayerbook*:

> During Akhenaten's reign, for reasons not entirely clear in the historic record, Akhenaten declared other gods invalid and their priests useless, and ordered all of Kemet to worship Akhenaten himself as "Sole One of Aten" who would then take the people's prayers to his Father. He did not actually order them to worship the Aten; texts state that only Akhenaten was qualified to do so, as the Disk's personal intermediary. It is important to realise that Akhenaten's religious reforms did not represent a shift towards monotheism, another common but incorrect assumption. Akhenaten, like all other kings before and after him, offers an image of the goddess ma'at in friezes, and his own hymns refer to the sun-disk by the full name of *Ra-Heruakhety in His Name of Shu Who is in the Aten*, indicating Akhenaten's "destruction" of other gods was selective, and that his intent seems more to have been to create a cult of personality than to negate other religious cults. The people were not ordered to worship the Aten, but to worship Akhenaten and his family as the embodiment of Aten and his family on earth. A number of ancient images and artifacts confirm Akhenaten's true heresy: replacing the religious traditions with himself as the focal point of worship and limiting the personal interaction between everyone else and their own god(s). He deifies himself as Shu and his Great Royal Wife Nefertiti as Tefnut, the twin children of the Self-Created One in

588 Peter Roberts, *HSC Ancient History* (Glebe, New South Wales: Pascal Press, 2006), 187

traditional Kemetic mythology. [589]

El-Shahawy and al-Misri state in *The Egyptian Museum in Cairo*:

> According to the new religion, people could only have contact with Aten and worship him through Akhenaten himself.[590]

Charlotte Booth stated in *The Myth of Ancient Egypt*:

> The only person capable of communicating with Aten was Akhenaten, who, as discussed, raised himself to the same status as the god by placing the insignia of kingship upon the god. When the artistic representations are studied closely, Akhenaten and the royal family worshipped Aten directly, standing outside with their arms raised in adoration on behalf of themselves and the people. However, all non-royals are shown as worshipping Akhenaten, as if he were a god. Akhenaten even invaded the personal worship of ordinary people, with images of the royal family in their household shrines.[591]

Charles Aling states:

> But the biggest change Akhenaten brought about was in the area of religion. First, let it be said that some of the popular conclusions that have been reached about the Amarna religious beliefs are not true. Akhenaten's new religion was not "monotheism". While it is true that he reduced the number of gods receiving official government support, he by no means reduced the number to one. The king himself remained a god, who was to receive worship from the people. In turn, Akhenaten would then worship Aton.[592]

Is this the *tawheed* of the Prophets and Messengers that Islam teaches

---

589 Tamara L. Siuda, *The Ancient Egyptian Prayerbook* (New Lenox, IL: Stargazer Design, 2009), pp.36-37.

590 Abeer El-Shahawy and Mattah al-Misri, *The Egyptian Museum in Cairo A Walk through the Alleys of Ancient Egypt* (Cairo: American University in Cairo Press, 2005), p.199

591 Charlotte Booth, *The Myth of Ancient Egypt* (Stroud, Gloucestershire: Amberley Publishing, 2011), p.ixx

592 Dr Charles Aling, "The Prelude to Amarna", in Glenn A. Carnagey Sr, Glenn Carnagey Jr and Keith N. Schoville (eds.), *Beyond the Jordan: Studies in Honor of W. Harold Mare* (Eugene, OR: Wipf and Stock Publishers, 2005), p.146.

according to the Kemet "Hotep" Afrocentrics? Allāh Says,

> وَمِنَ النَّاسِ مَن يَتَّخِذُ مِن دُونِ اللَّهِ أَندَادًا يُحِبُّونَهُمْ كَحُبِّ اللَّهِ ۞
>
> And [yet], among the people are those who take other than Allāh as equals [to Him]. They love them as they [should] love Allāh.
>
> [al-Baqarah (2): 165]

Egyptologist A. Rosalie David states in the *Who's Who of World Religions* under the entry for 'Akhenaten':

> Akhenaten worshipped the life-giving power of the sun, symbolized by the Aten; he regarded himself as the god's sole earthly representative and he and his deity became virtually interchangeable in concept.[593]

Some of the new-age London Black Kemet Cultists took issue with some of the sources which I quoted from in the 2017 leaflet on this topic, yet these sources, as has been seen in this section, did not come from AbdulHaq al-Ashanti but rather from Kemet writers themselves, as we can see here:

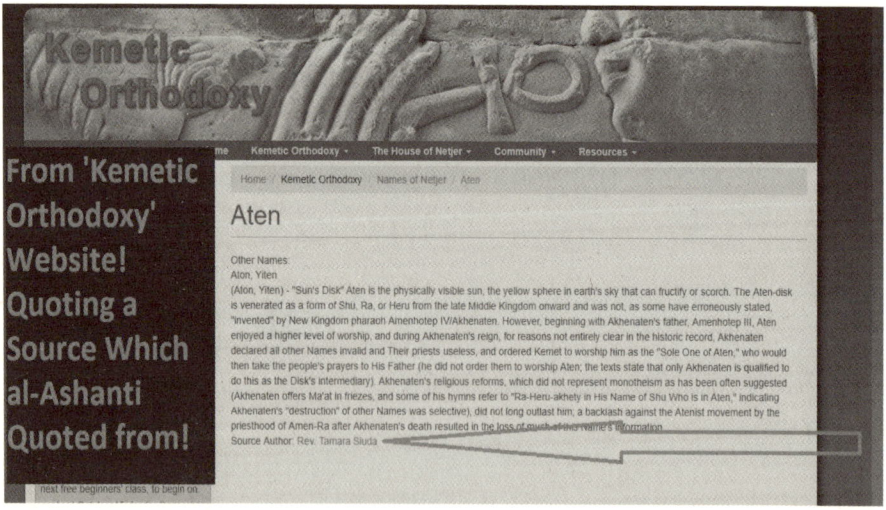

The above is from the 'Kemetic Orthodoxy' website ran by hardcore

---

593 A. Rosalie David, "Akhenaten" in John R. Hinnells (ed.), *Who's Who of World Religions* (London and Basingstoke: The Macmillan Press, 1993 Reprint), p.15.

Kemet preachers in America, led by Tamara Siuda, a white American female 'high priestess' of the Kemet Orthodox Movement!? This reveal has been met with a deathly silence on the part of the UK's new-age Black Kemet cult followers. Here is a screenshot from another Kemet Afrocentric site, 'Kemetic History of Afrika', which asserts that Akhenaton began monotheism:

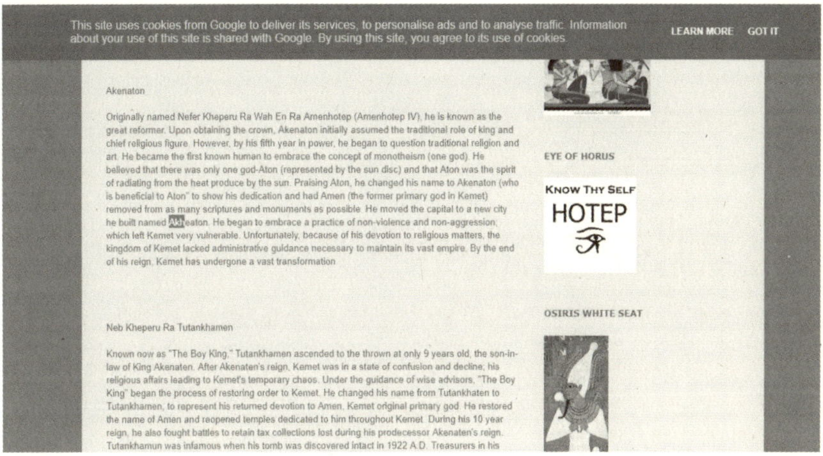

This site uses cookies from Google to deliver its services, to personalise ads and to analyse traffic. Information about your use of this site is shared with Google. By using this site, you agree to its use of cookies. LEARN MORE GOT IT

Akenaton

Originally named Nefer Kheperu Ra Wah En Ra Amenhotep (Amenhotep IV), he is known as the great reformer. Upon obtaining the crown, Akenaton initially assumed the traditional role of king and chief religious figure. However, by his fifth year in power, he began to question traditional religion and art. He became the first known human to embrace the concept of monotheism (one god). He believed that there was only one god-Aton (represented by the sun disc) and that Aton was the spirit of radiating from the heat produce by the sun. Praising Aton, he changed his name to Akenaton (who is beneficial to Aton" to show his dedication and had Amen (the former primary god in Kemet) removed from as many scriptures and monuments as possible. He moved the capital to a new city he built named Akheaton. He began to embrace a practice of non-violence and non-aggression; which left Kemet very vulnerable. Unfortunately, because of his devotion to religious matters, the kingdom of Kemet lacked administrative guidance necessary to maintain its vast empire. By the end of his reign, Kemet has undergone a vast transformation

Neb Kheperu Ra Tutankhamen

Known now as "The Boy King," Tutankhamen ascended to the thrown at only 9 years old, the son-in-law of King Akenaten. After Akenaten's reign, Kemet was in a state of confusion and decline; his religious affairs leading to Kemet's temporary chaos. Under the guidance of wise advisors, "The Boy King" began the process of restoring order to Kemet. He changed his name from Tutankhaten to Tutankhamen, to represent his returned devotion to Amen, Kemet original primary god. He restored the name of Amen and reopened temples dedicated to him throughout Kemet. During his 10 year reign, he also fought battles to retain tax collections lost during his prodecessor Akenaten's reign. Tutankhamun was infamous when his tomb was discovered intact in 1922 A.D. Treasurers in his

EYE OF HORUS

KNOW THY SELF

HOTEP

OSIRIS WHITE SEAT

So be careful of this and other incorrect aspersions against Islām which are spread by the Kemet preachers and writers, Allāh Says,

وَمَا لَهُم بِهِ مِنْ عِلْمٍ

إِن يَتَّبِعُونَ إِلَّا الظَّنَّ وَإِنَّ الظَّنَّ لَا يُغْنِي مِنَ الْحَقِّ شَيْئًا ۝ فَأَعْرِضْ

عَن مَّن تَوَلَّىٰ عَن ذِكْرِنَا وَلَمْ يُرِدْ إِلَّا الْحَيَاةَ الدُّنْيَا ۝

And they have thereof no knowledge. They follow except assumption, and indeed, assumption avails not against truth at all. So turn away from whoever turns his back on Our message and desires not except the worldly life.

[an-Najm (53): 28]

Appendix Two

The New-Age Hebrew Israelites Cult

Introduction

Black Judaism has been found in America since the 19th century, as will be outlined. However, it was in the 1960s that splinters from Black Judaism began to split further and resemble cults. The new-age Hebrew Israelite Cult in the West is a reflection of the wider black American experiment with Afrocentric cults. The cult, as represented by ISUPK, also have plans to become, as per their own words "the biggest black radical organisation on the face of this earth", hence they have incorporated precepts, ideas and eschatology of other American-born black nationalist cults.[594] The cult, especially its more extreme splinter chapters such as ISUPK, are renowned for their blind following of the Bible, uncritical reading of the Bible, babbling parrot-fashion from the Bible and nothing else, ignorance of the Hebrew language, reliance on the English language, vile manners, ignorant mentality which they have not ditched, shouting people down,[595] self-promotion, entertainment without any tangible or practical change for communities,[596] emphasis

594 There is a link between many of the late 19th century black nationalists and their core concepts related to white people and the end of the world, more on this will be discussed later.

595 According to the Bible, 2 Chr.7:14:

> If My people, who call me by my name, shall humble themselves and pray, and seek my face, and turn away from their wicked ways, then will I hear from heaven, will forgive their sins and heal their land.

596 Indeed, Andre Key states:

> The closest any Hebrew Israelite movement has come, however, to

on racial discussion mainly, colourism, hate preaching,[597] inability to adequately discuss, blind following of their various leaders and their extreme methods of preaching – all of which are far from the exemplary ways of preaching of the Prophets. Their core tenets are:

1. That black Americans, and the black diaspora, are the true descendants of the biblical Israelites. They assert that there is biblical evidence to indicate that the original Hebrews were dark-skinned – an issue which we will address later in this study. For instance they note that when the Hebrews were in Egypt, who are deemed as the biblical descendants of Ham, they were unrecognisable from the Egyptians and were thus able to hide out among them.
2. That the modern European Jewry are imposters and not the real descendants of the children of Israel.
3. That the King James Version of the Bible is wholly authoritative, while some accept it as Apocrypha.
4. That the biblical reference to "the time of the gentiles" actually means 'the time of the white man'. As a result of this, the white man's world will come to an end. In the mid to late 1990s the Hebrew Israelites fanatically promoted the false prophecy that "in the year 2000 America will be destroyed by thermo-nuclear destruction"!!!?
5. That salvation is achieved by keeping the law of the Sabbath.
6. Jesus was a black man.
7. That white people cannot be saved and as a result are to be the slaves of the Black Hebrew Israelites. As a result, you can find bizarre footage on Youtube of Hebrew Israelites demanding white people to bow down to them and even kiss their feet!? In what are perverted and disturbing instances of what is nothing short of a

---

addressing the needs of the African American community as a whole, is the "African Hebrew Israelites of Jerusalem", whose veganism program addresses the health issues of the Black community.

Hardly an exhaustive blueprint to aid the tangible real world concerns of the black community!?

See Andre Key, "If Thou do not harken unto the Voice of the Lord thy God: A Critique of Theodicy in Black Judaism", *Black Theology*, vol.12, no.3, November 2014, p.286.

597 According to Proverbs 6:16-19 God hates pride.

fetishized foolery.

8. That heaven and hell are not real and are mere "states of mind".
9. That God is to be referred to as 'Yah'.
10. That their message, to be spread solely among black people in the diaspora, they are helping the "scattered Israelites" who are ignorant of their true ancestry and heritage.

One of the more commonly quoted definitions of 'cult' was articulated at an *AFF/UCLA Conference on Cults* in 1985: "Cult (totalist type): A group or movement exhibiting a great or excessive devotion or dedication to some person, idea or thing and employing unethically manipulative techniques of persuasion and control."[598]

They further stated:

> They use special methods to heighten suggestibility and subservience, powerful group pressures, information management, suspension of individuality or critical judgement, promotion of total dependency on the group and fear of leaving it, etc. all designed to advance the goals of the group's leaders, to the actual, or possible, detriment of members, their families and the community.

Their extreme methods, harshness and fanaticism is not only a clear indication that their way is not the true teaching of the Prophets but also demonstrates that they are lacking in terms of cultivation, education and morals as is common with cults. In America they resort to the 'First Amendment Right' rather than the teachings of God whenever their avenues to preach are challenged. This also shows that the cult is very much restricted to America and its racial history and hence the cult can hardly survive anywhere else, as we shall see the cult is very much a product of the American historical and racial experience and hence steeped in Afrocentricity.

Due to their popularity in the cities of London and Birmingham at present, particularly among black communities, and their attempts to try to confuse a few Muslims, the need to refute this cult along with their false theology and pseudo-history has become all the more necessary.

---

598 L.J. West and M.D. Langone, "Cultism – A Conference for Scholars and Policy-Makers" in *Cultic Studies Journal*, Vol.3, pp.117-134. Also see *AFF* webpage.

Background and History

The Hebrew Israelite Cult is based on Black Judaism which itself was a belief system which originated with black Christians in the 1800s within the American South Pentecostal Holiness movement. They claimed that they received a revelation that American blacks were in fact the true Hebrews and hence the chosen people, effectively appropriating the Jewish racial origin story as a form of self-pride and empowerment. In doing so, they held that identification with Israel rather than Africa as a racial point of origin was a sound source of self-determination for the black American community. Fernheimer states in her Phd thesis:

> During the Middle Passage from Africa to America, Africans were stripped of their ancestral languages, cultures, and customs. Though Southern slave owners held a variety of views concerning slaves and Christianity, upon their arrival in America many slaves were often forcibly converted to Christianity. In spite of this "Christian" affiliation, it was the Jewish history of the Old Testament and the concepts of "chosenness, exile, suffering, and redemption" that proved most compelling to American blacks. In "African American Religious Encounters with Judaism, 1790-1930, an Overview" Chireau argues that "enslaved black Christians selected those parts of the Hebrew Bible that affirmed their experiences both as persons of faith and as an oppressed race" (Chireau 18). In The Black Jews of Harlem: Negro Nationalism and the Dilemmas of Negro Leadership, Harold Brotz also notes that one of the Black Jews' central beliefs is the "inward dignity that he [the black slave] was able to acquire by conceiving of himself as a descendant of the patriarchs". He links this interpretation that the "Negroes are really the Hebrews of the Bible" with the radical, Protestant religious tradition to which many African Americans had been exposed during slavery. He attributes this development in part as a response to the need for blacks to find a mode of positive identity construction in the face of the increased racism that Jim Crow laws and disenfranchisement effected. Like the Protestants who came before them, the slaves "believed themselves to be another Israel, a people who toiled in the 'Egypt' of North America but who were providentially guided by the same God who had led the Jews into the Promised Land" (Chireau 18). Confronted with the dehumanizing conditions of slavery where families were often separated and the basic humanity of individuals was denied, it is not surprising that

> the Exodus narrative proved to be so compelling. It promised hope for liberation and redemption from their present, persistent suffering. This strong identification is expressed in many of the minstrels and slave songs. Featuring Moses and Joshua, these songs exemplify the extent to which Old Testament themes and characters had been absorbed into slave culture and provided a source of resistance.[599]

This credo of the Hebrew Israelite cult asserts that when the Kingdom of Israel was destroyed the Israelites were scattered across the African continent, specifically targeted by other African tribes and then captured, enslaved and sold to European slave traders who took them to the Americas – this they claim without a shred of credible historical evidence whatsoever. This narrative suggests that there were even specific pick-up points where European slavers took 'Black Hebrew Israelites'.[600] Hence, many Hebrew Israelite cults, such as ISUPK, condemn West Africans whom they hold responsible for selling "the Israelites" (!?) into slavery. The role of Joseph J. Williams is also relevant in the history of Hebrew Israelite theology and ideas. Joseph J. Williams (1875-1940) was a white American Jesuit missionary and ethnographer who wrote for the *Catholic Review* and also for the American Geographical Society.

Williams was based in Jamaica in 1912 for five years and established a good relationship with the African-Jamaicans. He was fascinated with the anthropology of Jamaica and African cultural traditions and folklore and was the first to theorise that the African-Jamaicans were largely from the Ashanti tribe in Ghana and that the Ashanti were originally Hebrew Israelites – who were not black!? No black person ever preceded Joseph J. Williams with this claim about the Ashanti and he had never been to West Africa. All of this Williams concluded with scant evidence and little in the way of historical, cultural or documentary evidence, it was a work of pure pseudo history. Williams authored *Hebrewisms of West Africa* (New York: The Dial Press, 1930) and some have argued that

599 Janice Wendy Fernheimer, *The Rhetoric of Black Jewish Identity Construction in America and Israel: 1964-1972* (Austin: University of Texas, May 2006, Phd Thesis), pp.39-40. Accessed 12 June 2017: https://www.lib.utexas.edu/etd/d/2006/fernheimerd82976/fernheimerd82976.pdf

600 Southern Poverty Law Centre, *'History of Hebrew Israelism'*, accessed 19th May 2017. See: https://www.splcenter.org/fighting-hate/intelligence-report/2015/history-hebrew-israelism

Williams' Victorian racism has been carried over by modern Hebrew Israelite cults.[601] Some modern Hebrew Israelites claim that the Ewe tribe is proof that the tribe are in facts 'Jews' originally and that the word 'Ewe' is pronounced as 'Jew' but without the 'j'. This argument demonstrates a lack of knowledge as 'Ewe' is not pronounced like that at all, but rather as if it rhymes with 'ever', but with a 'w' rather than a 'v'. Similarly, claims have also been made by some Hebrew Israelites that 'Ashanti' comes from the biblical 'Ashan' (a supposed son of Judah referred to in Josiah 15: 1, 42); Dakar (in Senegal) originates from the Biblical 'Deker (a supposed father of one of the officers of Solomon who oversaw Israel)'; that the name of the West African country Chad originates from the Biblical 'Ohad' (a supposed grandson of Simeon mentioned in Genesis 46: 10) and that 'Igbo' originates from 'Hebrew'. All of these assertions are totally false:

- 'Ashanti' or 'Asante' is not from 'Ashan' as per the bible, rather it is derived from Twi and means 'because of the war': '*nti*' means 'because of' and '*ɔsa*' refers to war. It also carries the connotation of 'being warlike'.
- 'Dakar' most likely has a Wolof origin, referring to the Tamarind tree.
- 'Chad' is pronounced locally as 'Tshade' or 'Tchade', with a single syllable and refers to a 'large space of water' in Kanuri and 'lake' in Bornu. This is nowhere near the two-syllable 'Ohad' as per the Bible!?
- As for the issue of the Igbos, then some Hebrew Israelites assert that just because some white Europeans during slavery referred to 'Heebos' then this refers to 'Hebrews', when the reality is that they mis-pronounced the word 'Igbo'. Also the new-age Hebrew Israelites pronounce 'Igbo' as 'Eeboo' and this is incorrect, as the pronunciation is actually 'E-bow' not 'Eeboo'.

There has been some discussion about the Igbo tribe of Nigeria and their supposed connection to the ancient Hebrews. The first to make this assertion was the Igbo writer and abolitionist Olaudah Equiano (1745-

601 Henry Goldschmidt, *Race and Religion Among the Chosen People of Crown Heights* (London and New Brunswick: Rutgers University Press, 2006), p.271, ftn.32.

1797) who commented that there were similarities between the Igbos and the Hebrew practice. Some of this was due to a romantic regard of his people and a biblical projection onto his people. Equiano makes reference to some Igbo practices and customs such as circumcision, seclusion of women after birth and purification and naming their children after a special event. It should be noted here that from an Islamic perspective if these practices are found among aboriginal and native peoples, this is a hallmark that they have retained what is from their natural disposition (*fitrah*) as relayed from their ancestors and from the first man and his progeny, as opposed to being from "the lost tribe of Israel". Yet those who propound the Hebrew-Igbo myth neglect the fact that Igbos, traditionally, and like many other West African tribes, eat bush pig, bush rat, dogs, hyenas, snakes, squirrels, porcupines, snails, lizards, crab, crayfish, rabbit – all of which violate any biblical dietary laws. The so-called Hebrew origin of the Igbos has been addressed by more serious Igbo historians, Afigbo states:

> Basden (1912), pointing to certain constructions found in the Igbo language and what he considered the deep religious feeling of the people, propagated the view that Igbo culture probably evolved under the Levitical Code. Impressed by what he considered the superior intelligence of the Aro Igbo and by their religious system and rituals, Palmer (1921, 1928) contended that they carried Hamitic blood in their veins and that it was under their leadership that the "higher" aspects of Igbo culture had evolved. Similarly, impressed by Igbo sunworship and by the feature of dual organization in their social structure, Jeffreys (1946, 1951, 1954, 1956) held that the Igbo at some stage in the past had come under Egyptian influence, the carriers of this influence probably being the Nri of Awka in Northern Igboland. With regards to aims, both the Igbo and the British colonial elite hoped, through the use of this "Oriental hypothesis," to unravel the mystery of the Igbo past, but beyond this the two groups were not in agreement. Thus, while the Igbo would assert that they were originally Hebrews or Egyptians (Ike 1951: 1-4; Mathews 1927), their British counterparts went no farther to assert that the Igbo had come under the influence of either the ancient Egyptians or the Jews.

Then Afigbo states:

> The pseudo-scientific racial theories prominent in the colonial period made their impact on the Igbo in two ways. In the first place, colonialism was a severe humiliation for the Igbo. It also gave them Western education, which made them capable of accepting the myths about the cultural similarities between them and the peoples of the Near East. To show that they had not always been as "despicable" as the colonialists found them, they started laying claim to an Eastern origin on the basis of such cultural similarities. Since at this time history taught that the East was the civilizer of mankind, the Igbo, through the claim to Eastern origin, came to assign themselves a higher place in the history of the world than they would assign to their British masters.
>
> Nor was that all, for the Oriental hypothesis has continued to wax strong among the Igbo. Under colonial rule, the Igbo came to see all the world as a fair field for business and spread out in large numbers as traders, mission agents, government officials, migrant farmers, and so on. The allegedly aggressive Igbo approach to business soon won them the deep-seated distrust and hatred of their more easygoing Nigerian neighbours. Consequently, they became the victims of communal riots, or threats of them, wherever they went in Nigeria. Publicists and others soon started drawing parallels between Igbo business acumen and their suffering at the hands of other Nigerian ethnic nationalities, on the one hand, and the Jewish experience throughout history, on the other. Between 1967 and 1970, embattled Biafra provided the perfect parallel to the state of Israel surrounded by hostile Arab nations. The Igbo not only made this comparison themselves, but also believed in it.

Afigbo continues:

> By the late 1930's, the Oriental hypothesis had been argued out ad nauseam and abandoned, since no amount of research, not even Mathews's *[sic]* at Arochukwu and Jeffreys's *[sic]* at Awka, could uncover solid historical or anthropological evidence in its support. C.K. Meek, the government anthropologist who had coordinated the research into this and related issues in Igboland, closed the debate as far as the government was concerned when he warned (1937: 5) that: "no purpose would be served by engaging in speculations about ancient cultural contacts, such as that the prevalence of sun-worship, of forms of mummification,

> and of dual organization points to some distant connection with Ancient Egypt. As far back as we can see within historic times, the bulk of the Igbo peoples appear to have lived an isolated experience." By 1940 then, the Oriental hypothesis was to all intents and purposes dead as a serious explanation of Igbo culture history.[602]

Molefi Asante has also made historical mistakes and inaccurate claims:

> The Arabs with their Jihads, or holy wars, were thorough in their destruction of much of the ancient culture. It is also as if small bands (of fleeing Egyptian priests) keeping ahead of the Islamic onslaught managed to preserve certain aspects of the traditional culture of Egypt.[603]

Molefi Asante thus asserts that these "aspects of ancient Egyptian culture" were kept amongst the Wolof, Yoruba, Ashanti and other West African tribes. Other characters that have axes to grind are writers such as Wole Soyinka, claiming that Islām and Arabs are responsible for "the cultural and spiritual ravaging of the continent,"[604] and all of this is noted without a shred of historical evidence from either African, Arabic or European sources, and if any sources are mentioned then they are actually white European ones!! Soyinka has even gone so far as to suggest that north Africa should not be considered part of Africa! Soyinka's deep hatred for Islām and Arabs owes a lot to his internal Nigerian political schism, though this is never openly acknowledged or admitted by Soyinka.

Mgbeafulu states:

> The tradition is considered to be more of a fable than reality. No wonder the theory have been opposed *[sic]* and even rejected by

602 A.E. Afigbo, "Prolegomena to the Study of the Culture History of the Igbo-Speaking Peoples of Nigeria" in B.K. Swartz and Raymond E. Dumett (eds.), *West African Culture Dynamics: Archaeological and Historical Perspectives* (The Hague and Paris: Mouton Publishers, 1980), pp.307-309.

603 Molefi Asante, '*Afrocentricity and Culture*' in Asante and Kariamu Welsh Asante (eds.), *African Culture – The Rhythms of Unity* (Westport, CT: Africa World Press, 1985)

604 Wole Soyinka, *The Burden of Memory, The Muse of Forgiveness* (New York: Oxford University Press, 1999), p.42.

> some indigenous writers. Afigbo has written of its proponents as victims of the 'oriental mirage' and warned that the oriental extraction should not be taken seriously. Similarly, Isichei has dismissed the theory as 'a mistaken stereotype'. To Onwuejeogwu the argument is unscientific, and only fulfils man's quest for its origin without coming close to the answer.[605]

Onunwa states:

> Some elders still claim that the Igbo are the original inhabitants of their present place of abode. Some late theories of Hebrew link are yet to be confirmed with authentic ethnographic data.[606]

Some sceptical Igbo commentators have asserted that more recently groups of Igbos in Nigeria, in order to escape poverty in the country, have claimed a Hebrew and Jewish origin in order to be shipped to Israel as occurred with the Ethiopian *Beta Israel* peoples.

It should be noted also here that Jews did find themselves in parts of West Africa, such as in Mali for instance. However, this was after 1400 and in more recent history of the last 600 years as Moroccan Jewish traders migrated south into West Africa. Prior to this there is no evidence of 'black Jewish communities' in West Africa. The 17th century West African chronicle, *Tārīkh ul-Fattāsh*, authored by Mahmood al-Kātī or his descendants, mentions that in Tindirma in Mali there was a community of 1500 people known as 'Bani Israel' however they were not local and most likely some Hebrew Israelites try to refer to the likes of the historians al-Idrīsī, Ibn Khaldun and Leo Africanus–yet there is nothing of the sort in the writings of Ibn Khaldun and al-Idrīsī. Ibn Khaldun actually expressed some anti-black sentiment in his writings, as alluded to earlier in this book,[607] and as for al-Idrīsī then the evidence is yet to be provided where he stated that he encountered black Jews

---

605 Mathias Chinonyere Mgbeafulu, *Migration and the Economy: Igbo Migrants and the Nigerian Economy 1900-1975* (Lincoln, NE and New York: iUniverse Inc., 2003), p.8

606 Udobata R. Onunwa, *A Handbook of African Religion and Culture* (Pittsburgh, Pennsylvania: Red Lead Press, 2010), p.xxi.

607 For more on this see Mahmood Mamdani, "Reading Ibn Khaldun in Kampala." *Journal of Historical Sociology*, 21 April 2017: https://onlinelibrary.wiley.com/doi/full/10.1111/johs.12148 Accessed 1 January 2019

in West Africa! It is just a claim repeated *ad nauseam* as if people will blindly follow it.

For those who claim a Hebrew origin of the West African tribes, be it the Ashanti, Igbo, Ewe, Ga or whichever, then there is a distinct lack of historical, archaeological and ethnography evidence for such claims. Where are the Hebrew artefacts?! If there was such an origin there would be troves of artefacts and historical evidence, however there is nothing. All modern Hebrew Israelite cults do is piece together bits from here and bits from there and then reach a conclusion that this is somehow proof of a 'Hebrew origin'. The first historical reference to a people known as 'Bani Isrāī'īl' was mentioned by Muslim chroniclers in *Tārīkh ul-Fattāsh* referring to a people who lived there in 1402 CE and had an army only of 1500 men. As for other West African tribes supposedly hailing from the ancient Hebrews then this was first posited by the white Christian missionary John Williams in the early 20th century when he made the claim about the Ashanti, and then in regards to the Igbos Equiano in the late 18th century merely mentioned what he felt were some similarities. The issues about place names and linguistic crossovers are not considered to be serious and are therefore quack theories.

James Tinney (1973: 52-54) classified three strands of American Black Judaism: (1) Black Jews – which refers to those groups who adopt Jewish practices and traditions while maintaining a Christological perspective; (2) Black Hebrews – who represent a more 'Orthodox' persuasion and (3) Black Israelites – who are essentially Afrocentrics and focus on preaching only to black males in the West, asserting with utter vitriol and fanaticism that black people in the West "are not African" and are in fact the original Semites. Tinney described them as being "the farthest from traditional Judaism in beliefs and practices."[608]

In 19th Century America, many African-Americans identified with the enslaved Hebrews as per the Bible, this led to an association and identification with the lost tribes of Israel.[609] Dispersion, exile and

608 James Tinney, "Black Jews: a House Divided" in *Christianity Today*, December 7th 1973, pp.52-54.

609 Yvonne Chireau, "Black Culture and Black Zion: African American Religious Encounters with Judaism, 1790-1930, An Overview" in Yvonne Chireau and

oppression, which African-Americans encountered, was seen by the early American Black Jews as having allegories within the biblical accounts of the experiences of the ancient Hebrews. Notions of being a "chosen people" and also divine favour from God was central to movements such as Marcus Garvey's Negro Improvement Association, the Nation of Islam and the Ras Tafarian Brethren in Jamaica. In this way, the Hebrew Israelite Cult offer what they view is a solution to black identity by offering an alternative and newly concocted racial identity to which black people can ascribe rather than "African", "African-American", "Caribbean", a national identity etc. Moreover, they attempt to construe that the prophecies related to the tribes of Israel only fit black people in the Americas. Then they assert that "the nations" have conspired to prevent black people from returning to their true ethno-religious identity. Thus, the complexity of the West African plurality of ethnicities is simplified to form a single black identity of "Hebrew Israelites" and thereby allowing possible liberation from oppression.[610] Herein they apply their situation on to the biblical accounts as if slavery and oppression are the only facets that shape the black global experience.

Black Judaism which developed in the Americas had a messianic cult approach yet did not condemn or attack other races although they did hold that black peoples in the Americas were the descendants of the biblical 12 lost tribes of Israel. Arnold Josiah Ford (1877-1935), a black Jew from Barbados was one of the most important early black Jewish figures of the Marcus Garvey era. Ford was the musical director of Marcus Garvey's Universal Negro Improvement Association and merged his form of black Judaism with Garveyite "Back to Africa" ideals.[611] Ford, like Garvey, proposed that blacks return to Africa as the rightful children of Israel.[612] Ford did try to convince Garvey to adopt

Nathaniel Deutsch (eds.), *Black Zion: African-American Religious Encounters with Judaism* (Oxford: Oxford University Press, 1999), p.16

610 Andre Key, "If Thou do not harken unto the Voice of the Lord thy God: A Critique of Theodicy in Black Judaism", *Black Theology*, vol.12, no.3, November 2014, p.284.

611 Bernard J. Wolfson, "African American Jews: Dispelling Myths, Bridging the Divide" in Yvonne Patricia Chireau and Nathaniel Deutsh (eds.), *Black Zion: African American Religious Encounters with Judaism* (Oxford and New York: Oxford University Press, 2000), p.47.

612 Kwaku Boafo, 'The Star in the Banner: Studies on North American Black-

Judaism as the movement's official religion but to no avail.[613]

Ford believed the original Hebrews were the Hausas of West Africa, who migrated to Egypt, and he also believed that Nigeria was the cradle of the Hebrew race and that the ancient traditions must be passed down orally.[614] The oral traditions reflected a cabalistic understanding. Since the Nigerians lacked the written Torah (due to the burning of books by Europeans), the Ten Commandments were hidden in the form of tribal markings. Ford and his followers migrated to Ethiopia where they attended the coronation of Haile Selassie. For Ford, all of Africa and Arabia was inhabited by Ethiopians at the time of Abraham. He believed there was no difference between the Semite and the Ethiopian.[615] He also acquired 800 acres of land in Ethiopia for his black Jewish movement, they also set up a school there. Some of the black Jews of America claimed that they were the Ethiopian Jews, or Falashas, whose names were taken away during trans-Atlantic slavery.[616] Ford was fluent in both Hebrew and Yiddish as he studied the Torah and Talmud under the patronage of white Jews and he was also a strong advocate of emigration since he believed the United States was not the true home of the real Jews. In fact, Ford rejected the word "Jew" and replaced it with "Hebrew" considering "Jews" to be white Europeans.[617] He eventually retired to Ethiopia as an official delegate to the coronation of Emperor Haile Selassie in 1930. He established himself in Addis Ababa and pursued efforts to secure territory in Ethiopia for black Jewish émigrés, where he died in 1934.

Ford provided the basis for "orthodox" Black Judaism by removing many Christian elements from its structure. Ford emphasized the Hebrew language, denied Jesus Christ as Saviour, and incorporated

---

Jewish Communities.' *Ottowa Journal of Religion*, vol.1, 2009, p.140. Accessed 12 June 2017: https://ruor.uottawa.ca/bitstream/10393/26047/1/Boafo_Kwaku_2009.pdf

613 Wolfson, *op.cit.*, p.47

614 James E. Landing, *Black Judaism: Story of an American Movement* (Durham, NC: Carolina Academic Press, 2002), p.135.

615 Ibid. p.133

616 George Eaton Simpson, *Black Religions in the New World* (New York: Columbia University Press, 1978), pp.268-9.

617 Ibid. p.135

Judaic symbols and dress.[618] Wentworth A. Matthew (1892-1973) was Ford's main disciple and became the most well known black-Jewish rabbi in Harlem continuing Ford's work. Matthew argued that "African Americans are Ethiopian Hebrews, a part of the original Israelites spoken of in the Bible". Matthew also taught that he and his followers were descended from the original Israelites through Menelik I, the son of King Solomon and the Queen of Sheba. Matthew taught that Menelik I was born in Ethiopia and moved to Jerusalem aged 12 and lived there with his father until he was 25. At this age, King Solomon feared a plot against his son's life so he sent him to Ethiopia.[619]

Menelik I then ascended the throne and became the first in a long line of Ethiopian Hebrew kings ending with Emperor Haile Selassie. Matthew believed Selassie was an undercover Jew and that he embraced the Coptic Christian Church under pressure from Great Britain. Matthew also taught that Solomon as well as all of the Hebrew patriarchs were black. The Commandment Keepers viewed Ethiopia as an extension of Israel and referred to them interchangeably. Matthew also claimed to have received his rabbinical ordination in Ethiopia from the chief rabbi of the Ethiopian Jews – this he claimed with no evidence! It is also disputed whether he even travelled to Ethiopia.

In the 1940s Matthew founded the Ethiopian Hebrew Rabbinical College where he ordained over 20 black rabbis. He also tried to have good relations with the Asknazi Jews and hoped to get their official recognition of his rabbinic status and applied for membership twice on the New York Board of Rabbis, but these were turned down as he was not considered as a bono fide Halakhic Jew. When Matthew died in 1973 he was succeeded by Levy Ben Levi who heads the movement of the Israelite Rabbinical Academy in Queens, New York. Capers Funnye was in turn ordained by Levi in 1985 and his Beth Shalom B'nai Zaken Ethiopian Hebrew sect is a direct descendent of Matthew's Commandment Keepers sect.[620]

Rabbi Matthew was an advocate of esoteric knowledge, especially in the "Cabbalistic Sciences", the Kabbaalah which involves magic and occult

---

618 Landing, *op.cit.*, p.129

619 Wolfson, *op.cit.*, p.48

620 Ibid.

practices. Though he led his congregation through Sabbath services where the Twelve Principles were observed, his Ethiopian Hebrew Rabbinical College (of the Royal Order of Ethiopian Hebrews and the Commandment Keepers Congregation of the Living God, Inc) offered additional biblical studies (Pinn 2006:86). The classes were given in Hebrew, Greek, Latin, and French, with the aim of studying "hidden meanings" in books on Jewish history, the Old Testament, and the Talmud. There is an obvious distinction between the Commandment Keepers of Harlem and the congregations of both William Saunders Crowdy (1847-1908) and Frank S. Cherry (d.1965). Ford and Matthew clearly endorsed a more nationalistic approach promoting a theology based on origin. The dream to create a black-Jewish community in Africa seemed to be their pinnacle of understanding. Both Crowdy and Cherry used Christianity to make sense of their current condition, however, simultaneously turned to Judaism to authenticate the experience. Crowdy referred to his congregations as "tabernacles". The modern Hebrew Israelite cults continue in the school of thought of Ford and Matthew,[621] yet some of the modern cults have more extreme positions as it relates to the entirety of black people in the West being descendants of the Israelites.

The modern Hebrew Israelite cult however effectively are the flip side of white nationalist racist hate groups like the Ku Klux Klan in that they exalt black people and degrade others as being non-human devils and degenerates who have been cursed by God – their belief system is therefore clearly based on turning the tables of oppression on to others and is restricted to this. Thus, Bruder and Parfitt in their book *African Zion: Studies in Black Judaism* state:

> African Americans' identification with Judaism was informed by the social and political orientations of black people in the United States and was often embedded in response to discrimination. In the eighteenth and nineteenth centuries, the appropriation of Jewish history by African Americans followed the path of a search for origins that gave them back a history and allowed them to overthrow American racism's hierarchy of values. The

621 Kwaku Boafo, 'The Star in the Banner: Studies on North American Black-Jewish Communities.' *Ottowa Journal of Religion*, vol.1, 2009, p.141. Accessed 12 June 2017: https://ruor.uottawa.ca/bitstream/10393/26047/1/Boafo_Kwaku_2009.pdf

> wider argument identifying the Hebrews of the bible with a black nation came to be an important strand in pan-African American movements in their formative period. Marcus Garvey, J.A. Rogers and George G.M. James, among many others, considered themselves to be the only true physical descendants of ancient Israel...[622]

Economic independence and self-empowerment was also emphasised by the Black Jews and was an early form of black nationalism which influenced other cults such as the Nation of Islam.

Frank S. Cherry (d.1965, his year of birth is unknown),[623] a black seaman and railroad worker, became a notable leader of the Black Jews in America. He claimed that he was a Prophet in 1886 and started a black Jew church in Chattanooga, Tennessee known as the 'Church of the Living God, the Pillar of Truth for all Nations'.[624] They argued that they were part of the original Israelite tribes that were chased out of Babylonia (and, they claim, into Central and Western Africa where they were later sold into slavery) by the Romans in 70 C.E. Cherry preached that based on a vision where the Lord appeared to him, the true Hebrews of the Old Testament were black. Cherry believed that even "God and biblical figures such as Adam, Eve, and Jesus were physically black" (Pinn 2006: 78). According to Cherry, all mankind was black until the births of Jacob and Esau. Cherry believed that white people were the offspring of Gehazi, a servant who Elisha cursed with skin "as white as snow" based on the account of II Kings 5:27.[625] He also held that white people were inherently evil and hated by God. Cherry regarded the 'white Jews' as frauds and interpolators and maintained that his followers were the true Israelites of the Bible.

Cherry also taught that the earth is square and that Jesus would return in the year 2000 to install blacks over whites in a race war – again demonstrating that their beliefs are entrenched in the American

622 Edith Bruder and Tudor Parfitt, *African Zion: Studies in Black Judaism* (Newcastle Upon Tyne: Cambridge Scholars Publishing, 2012) p.1.

623 In Anthony B. Pinn, Stephen C. Finley et al. (eds.), "Church of the Living God, Pillar of Truth for All Nations" in *African American Religious Cultures, Volume 1, A-R* (Oxford and Santa Barbara, California: ABC CLIO, 2009), p.167.

624 Fernheimer, *op.cit.*, p.47

625 Landing, *op.cit.*, p.58

racial context and situation, oppression begetting oppression, and also indicating that like many other black cult movements they are based on the search for a sacred identity – in this case, that blacks are in fact the "chosen people of God referred to in the Old Testament", so the cult is entirely based on racial issues. They assert that black people are "incomplete" until they realise their lost identity of being Israelites.

Cherry relocated his blind followers to Philadelphia in 1915, yet Cherry was not as popular as the non-racist black Jews of America such as Rev. William Christian and William Saunders Crowdy (1847-1908). Crowdy founded the 'Church of God and Saints of Christ' in 1896. Similar to Cherry, Crowdy also claimed that he received revelation. On September 13, 1893, Crowdy had a vision that he was in a large room where tables descended from above. Each table was stained with vomit and had the name of a church inscribed on it. According to Crowdy, the table labelled "Baptist" had the most prominent stain, which made Crowdy vow never again to attend a Baptist church. In his vision, a clean table finally descended inscribed with: Church of God and Saints of Christ. Crowdy believed this was his divine sanction to establish the true church. Crowdy received his visions in Guthrie, Oklahoma and began his preaching there.

Soon after, he moved to Chicago and converted many before returning to Lawrence, Kansas where he structured his organization and described African-Americans as the "heirs of the ten lost tribes of Israel". Crowdy adopted many Jewish rituals and symbols such as "circumcision of newborn boys, the use of the Jewish calendar, wearing of skullcaps, observance of Saturday as the Sabbath, [and the] celebration of Passover. Due to their Christian character, the congregations belonging to both Crowdy and Cherry shared many similarities. Crowdy blended Judaism with Christianity and Boafo (2009) states:

> ...the two groups assessed have all shared the commonality of a Christian base for their Jewish beliefs. ...It is fair to say that Crowdy and Cherry found their Jewish identity by means of Christianity.[626]

In the period 1919–1931 CE, at least eight black Jewish cults arose in Harlem, New York which kept on splintering off from each other,

626 Boafo, *op.cit.,* p.139.

disappearing and re-organising. After F.S. Cherry, the racist creed of his cult was carried on by Eber ben Yomin (aka "Abba Bivens", d.1973) who in the 1960s broke away from the "Commandment Keepers" which was the dominant mainstream black Jewish organisation at the time, founded by Wentworth Arthur Matthew (1892-1973) in 1919. In 1930 Matthew started the Israelite Rabbinical Academy in Brooklyn, New York. Abba Bivens claimed that he was taught that he was an Israelite in the deep American South and on his travels he passed through Native American reservations and also claimed that they too were also Israelites. Bivens started his own cult which came to be known as the Israelite School of Universal Practical Knowledge (ISUPK) and were based at this time in a Harlem apartment and then moved into a building on New York City's 125th Street.

Three of Biven's blind followers, Ahrayah, Mashah (Moshe Ben Karim) and Yaiqab (Peter Sherrod) joined with the "four high priests" Chazaaq, Lahab, Yahiya and Shar to take over the leadership of ISUPK. The seven of them were referred to as "the Seven Heads" and were the inner cabal of the Hebrew Israelite cult. Convicted paedophile and cult leader Dwight York tried to co-opt the Hebrew Israelites at one stage. In the 1980s the ISUPK changed their name to Israelite Church of Universal Practical Knowledge (ICUPK). Yaiqab (aka Peter Sherrod) claimed to have learnt that blacks were the true Israelites from an angel in a bar in the Mid-West of America who appeared as a black man with an afro. When the man left the bar, Yaiqab went after him to speak further but the angel had vanished mysteriously without a trace. Mashah claimed to have had several reincarnations as Moses, king David and Peter. While another of their leaders, Ahrayah, claimed that he was the reincarnation of John on account of Ahrayah making up most of Hebrew Israelite cult doctrine.

The ICUPK gained further fame in the 1990s by reviving F.S. Cherry's theory and "prophecy" that Jesus would return in the year 2000 to destroy the white race. This ridiculous belief was preached by Hebrew Israelite cults in the late 1990s, as many at the time will remember, and they even claimed that the whole world would be destroyed in "Thermal-Nuclear Destruction"! More on this will be mentioned later. This foolish prediction was similar to what the Nation of Islam used to also claim in the late 1990s that a "mother ship" will arrive in the year 2000 to save black people!?[627] In Brixton, London the Nation of Islam cult used to openly make this claim in their dialogues with the Sunni-Salafi Muslims. The Hebrew Israelites of New York, the ISUPK breakaway cult sect, still argue this – yet without specifying a date as they did in the 1990s with the ridiculous claim that the world would be destroyed in 2000! Such false prophecies and apocalyptic claims are common with cults.

Yet the extremism, racism and fanaticism is exemplified in the Miami-based *House of Yahweh* breakaway cult of Hebrew Israelites who in 1990 were indicted on Racketeer Influenced and Corrupt Organisations (RICO) charges that included extortion, arson and 14 counts of murder. Leader Hulon Mitchell Jr (1935-2007), aka "Yahweh ben Yahweh", went to federal prison for conspiring to kill random white people, including a beheading as initiation into his cult group. Robert Rozier, a former NFL player and blind follower of Mitchell, confessed to seven murders.

Mashah and Ahrayah eventually split and this even resulted in some ISUPK members staging a coup to remove Mashah and a hit was even put out on Mashah on the streets. Mashah then left that cult and formed another which he branded as the 'House of David'. Ex-members of the House of David cult branch accused Mashah of dabbling in magic, the occult and demonic incantations to possess his enemies. Ahrayah assumed leadership of ISUPK and then another member of the cult named "Chief High Priest Tazadaqyah" (aka Jermaine Grant) declared himself "the Holy Spirit" and "the Comforter" – some other cults also refer to them as this and one even calls himself "Comfy"!? Grant made the same claim of Jesus return, yet did not give a date, evidently to save himself from the embarrassment of the 1990s. He then formed ICGJC and Ahrayah supported Tazadaqyah in this and in his claim to be the holy spirit. General Yahanna was part of this cult branch under Ahrayah and Tazadaqyah, but then left ICGJC and re-formed, revamped and retained the ISUPK name-brand. Yahanna ("General Yahanna") revived the ISUPK for his own cult breakaway faction.[628] When 2000 came and

627 Hence, some American rappers in 1995 would have lyrics wherein they would state for instance that "there's only five years left", meaning that in 2000 the world would be destroyed.

628 "Captain Tazaryach" is part of this faction, and though he is probably the only Hebrew Israelite who presents himself as able to discuss matters in a sober

their prophecy did not occur, ICUPK changed their name again to the Israelite Church of God in Jesus Christ.

'Elder' Rawchaa left the ICGJC, after the failed prophecies of the cults did not come to pass, and also formed for himself the GOCC. The IUIC group eventually split from the House of David cult branch in 2003 and formed its own group led by Nathanya'ahlaGa ['Elder Nathanial'], they are characterised by their purple attire. Another cult member Tahar formed his own Black Israelite splinter cult sect entitled GMS (Great Millstone Israelites) after he was kicked out of the House of David due to his view, based on his understanding of Deuteronomy 22, which condoned the rape of young girls arguing that "when the Kingdom of God comes we gonna get 'em young" and "we're gonna get women when they 12 years old" and "you gotta rape 'em".[629] This vile emphasis on rape of underage girls and extreme sexual gratification is another feature which indicates that this is a cult. Now if it is said "the Prophet Muhammad married Aa'ishah when she was young" then this can be answered as follows:

- Such marriages were common practice at the time, and hence no Christian, Jew, Polytheist or philosopher condemned it at the time.
- Within the medieval and pre-modern anti-Islamic tracts and apologia against Islam, there is no mention of the marriage, as it was common. Indeed, the English King Richard the Second married Princess Isabella of Valois when she was 6 years old, in 1396.[630]
- There is no command or order from the Prophet Muhammad encouraging marriage at this age, as opposed to some of the Hebrew Israelite cults who openly and actively encourage, promote and preach this.

---

manner, he is a virulent Islamophobe. In one Youtube video, in which he debates New York Kemet Afrocentric "Shakka Ahmose", Tazaryach says, in order to gain closeness and proximity to Ahmose, "if that was a Qur'ān I would throw it", to which Ahmose agrees with him?! So both are avowed enemies of Islam, may Allāh give them both what they deserve in this life and the next if they do not repent and recant from this enmity.

629 See video here: https://www.youtube.com/watch?v=ffdWJAnzdTM

630 H. Eugene Lehman, *Lives of England's Reigning and Consort Queens* (Bloomington, IN: Authorhouse, 2011), p.171

The diagram below[631] demonstrates the splitting, divisions and newly-fangled cults which emerged from Abba Biven.

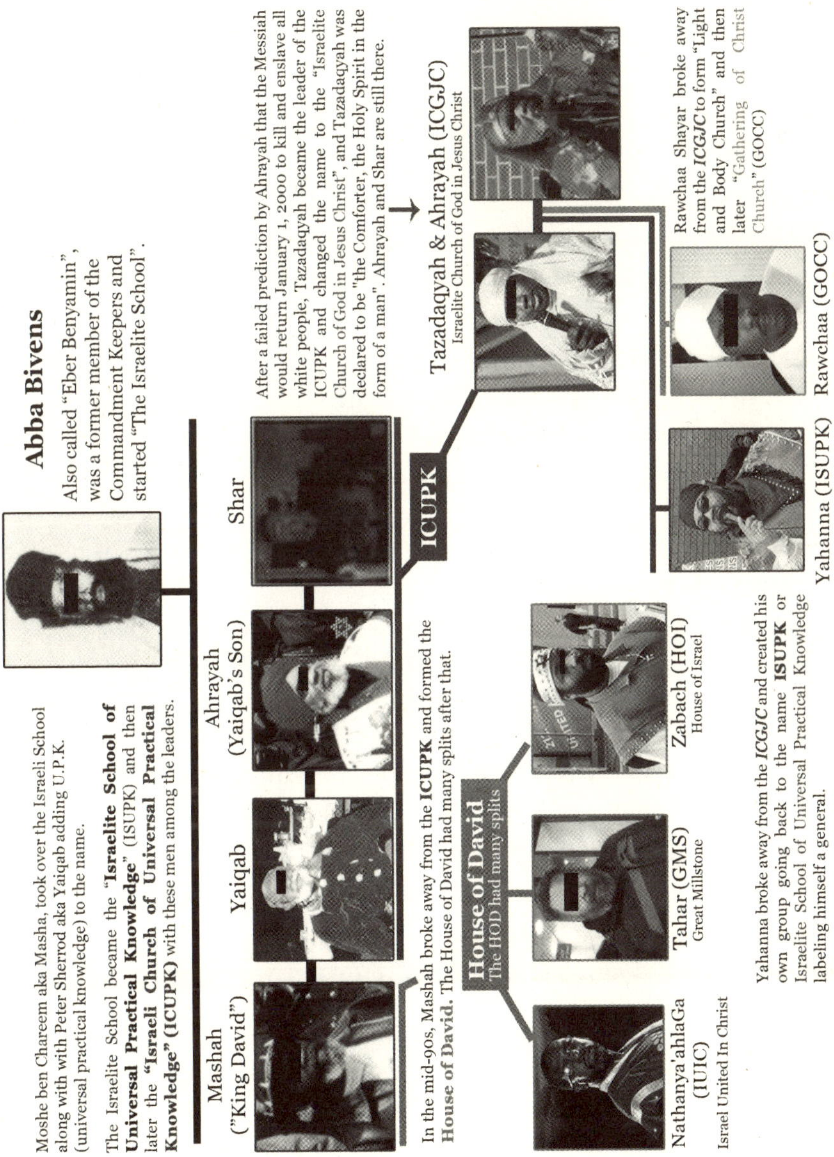

631 From: http://mrhebrew1.com/show/wp-content/uploads/2016/06/ICUPK_Chart.jpg Accessed November 2018

Main Source Texts of the Hebrew Israelite Cults

The core source books of the cult are the following, and as is the usual way with cults they restrict their follows to largely read a select few books only:

- Steven Jacobs and Rudolph Windsor, *The Hebrew Heritage of Our West African Ancestors* (Wilmington, Delaware: Rose Lee Inc., 1971).[632]
- Steven Jacobs, *The Hebrew Heritage of Black Africa* (Philadelphia: Boldlee Publishing, 1976).
- Jose V. Malcioln, *How the Hebrews Became Jews* (New York: UB Productions, 1978).
- Jose V. Malcioln, *The African Origin of Modern Judaism* (Trenton, NJ: African World Press, 1996).
- Rudolph Windsor, *From Babylon to Timbuktu: A History of Ancient Black Races Including the Black Hebrews* (New York: Exposition Press, 1969).
- Yosef Ben Jochannan, *We the Black Jews* (Baltimore, MD: Black Classic Press, 1993).
- Joseph J. Williams, *Hebrewisms of West Africa: From Nile to Niger with the Jews* (New York: The Dial Press, 1930). And he book *The Lost Tribes, A Myth: Suggestions Towards Rewriting Hebrew History* (1930)
- Ben Ammi, *God, the Black Man and Truth* (Chicago: Communicators Press, 1982).
- Ella J. Hughley, *The Truth About Black Biblical Hebrew Israelites.*
- Albert Cleage, *The Black Messiah* (New York: Sheed and Ward, 1968).
- Kelly Brown Douglas, *The Black Christ* (Maryknoll, NY: Orbis Books, 1994).
- Arthur Koestler, *The Thirteenth Tribe* (New York: Random House, 1976).

They also rely on other obscurantist and fringe works, as for the above

632 Can be downloaded here: http://www.bjpa.org/Publications/downloadFile.cfm?FileID=17218

then much can be said about them:

First of all, Windsor was born in New Jersey and later his family settled in Philadelphia where he attended Community College and studied psychology and political science. He also attended Gratz College where he majored in Hebraic studies and graduated in 1967. He was president of the Afro-Asian Israelite Cultural Center in Philadelphia, and was a member of the Black Israelite sect Adeth Emeth Israel. Windsor asserts in *From Babylon to Timbuktu* that white Jews come from blacks who turned white due to leprosy. His works are a main resource for Hebrew Israelites. Jacobs and Windsor suggest in their book that the biblical, anthropological and archaeological evidences all indicate that "from the time of Abraham, onward, Black civilisation and Hebrew civilisation were synonymous."

As for Ben Jochannan, often referred to as "Dr Ben", then he attempted to be one of the more academic writers in his works yet even with Ben Jochannan there is a mysterious shroud of mystery in terms of where he studied, the universities he claimed to have studied at and some of his highly dubious claims in regards to his scholarship. So for example, Jochannan claimed in a number of his works that he had graduated from Cambridge University in the UK. Yet upon inspection this was shown to have been utterly false and there is no record of him enrolling to study there. Indeed, his book *We the Black Jews* is quite poorly presented and very incoherent, along with cluttered presentation and it being full of articles which he comments on, this renders the book a propagation work rather than a serious academic research undertaking.

Moreover, there have been some issues as to his origins as Jochannan claimed to have a Puerto Rican mother and an Ethiopian father. It appears that he may have been influenced by the example and teachings of Ford, Matthew, Cherry and Crowdy based on his emphasis on the Falashas and Ethiopia. In his book *We the Black Jews*, on page 83 it is asserted that the Pharaoh Akhenaten was the "father of monotheism"?! He also attempts to show that ancient Egyptians were the originators of the Ten Commandments?!

Ben Ammi (born Ben Carter), according to Landing, he was the Hebrew Israelite leader and he first learned about Black Judaism from Landar Buie (who had first heard from Prophet Casey) at the age of twenty-four.[633] He attended meetings of several Black Jewish organizations including the Congregation of Ethiopian Hebrews (Landing 325). Rabbi Reuben, the congregation's leader, gave Carter the name "Ammi" which means "righteous teacher" and he then formed his own following in Chicago in the 1950s. His followers considered Ben Ammi to be the Messiah and referred to Ammi as "Adoni Rabbey" (My Lord and Master) for leading them out of the United States to the promised land of Israel. The Hebrew Israelites observe all the Jewish rituals such as Passover, Yom Kippur, and Sabbath; however, some are combined with African American Christian activities (i.e. Gospel Music).[634]

In an attempt to forge unity amongst them, the A-Beta Hebrew Israel Culture Center was founded at 4654 South Cotton Grove Avenue.[635] Regular meetings were held for Hebrew instruction, and in 1966 the center endorsed a program specifically designed to promote unity. Messenger James Stearns's Congregation of Israel; Rabbis Reuben, Lazarus and Green's Congregation of Ethiopian Hebrews; Bishop Stewart's Holy Sanctuary of Judah, and Ben Ammi's followers participated.[636]. Many of the groups had emigrationist plans, and Ben Ammi was intrigued by Greer's prediction that 1967 would be the year of the exodus.[637]

Many A-Beta members circulated leaflets predicting the destruction of America in 1970. At this time, in 1966, Ben Ammi had a vision in which the prophet Gabriel revealed to Ammi that Ammi's people should begin the exodus to the Promised Land during Passover 1967. In 1967 Ben Ammi and his followers from the 'African Hebrew Israelites' migrated from Chicago to Liberia and then to Dimona, Israel. Israel did not officially accept them as Jews and offered them the chance to convert, which they rejected, asserting that they were the original Hebrews. This sect gained media attention due to a murder case in Israel involving the sect which was related to a leadership struggle.

On January 29, 1972, three "dissident Black Hebrews" came to speak

633 Landing, *op.cit.*, p.325

634 Boafo, *op.cit.*, p.145

635 Landing, *op.cit.*, p.326

636 Ibid. p.327

637 Ibid. p.327

with their friends and relatives in the group only to be "confronted by five of Ben Ammi's supporters." A fight ensued and "one of the dissenters was killed". The Israeli court system convicted the Ben Ammi followers of manslaughter, sentencing them to 6- 24 months in prison. In 1990, after a long meeting between religious leaders Ben Ammi and Rabbi Aryeh Ben Deri, and with the help of the Illinois state legislators, the Israeli government granted the Hebrew Israelites temporary resident status.[638] This legal status allowed the Hebrew Israelites to hold jobs and receive social benefits including health and housing. They were finally granted permanent resident status in August 2003. This status enables them to vote locally and participate in civic duties—including military service—but prevents them from voting in Knesset elections. Their dream of full citizenship status has not yet been realized. [639]

One: Sons of Ham or Shem?

In keeping with common practice of cults, the Hebrew Israelites seek to confer upon their members a new identity, in this case the identity of the biblical Israelites. When a person joins a cult, they are effectively stripped of who they are and a new identity it stamped in its place, coupled with excessive detachment and distancing from their prior identity. In this way, the social support that a person had beforehand is severed and the person has to rely solely on the cult.

As for the descendants of Ham then the Bible says **"the sons of Ham were Cush, Mizraim, Put and Canaan."** (Genesis 10:6). According to the Bible Egypt is referred to as **"the land of Ham"** (Psalms 105:23, 27; 106: 22).

Cush: peoples of central and Southern Arabia. The Ethiopians are shown to have been inhabitants of both sides of the Red Sea and they also had skin of a different appearance (Jeremiah 13:23). Cush, which is the Hebrew word for black, the father of black people while Shem is the patriarch for Arabs and Jews of the Middle East.

---

638 Janice W. Fernheimer, *Stepping into Zion: Hatzaad Harishon, Black Jews, and the Remaking of Jewish Identity* (Tuscaloosa: University of Alabama Press, 2014), p,.32.

639 Ibid.; Fernheimer, *op.cit.*, p.51-53

Mizraim: refers to Upper and Lower Nile River of Egypt and its inhabitants.

Put: more associated with Libya.

Canaan: the area settled by Canaan and his sons was west of the River Jordan which was named after him Canaan was called the 'Promised Land' and was invaded by Joshua and the children of Israel (Joshua 14:1). Canaan is cursed in the Bible, not Ham, and it states **"Cursed by Canaan; a servant of servants he shall be to his brethren."** (Genesis 9:20-25). The curse of Canaan therefore does not apply to the Trans-Atlantic Slave Trade of West Africans to the Americas, the land of Canaan had never been in Africa and moreover the curse had been fulfilled when their land was conquered by the children of Israel (Joshua 9:17-27).

The story of Rahab for example, and her faith in the One True God (Hebrews 11:30-131) provides an example of how a Canaanite group eventually became part of Israel despite the injunction in Deuteronomy to kill all Canaanites and not to intermarry with them (Deuteronomy 7:1-4; 20:16-18)

According to the Bible Japeth was the father of the Caucasian people who settled in Europe and Asia. Most of Ham's descendants went into Africa, one of Ham's sons was Mizraim and he and his people settled in Egypt. Genesis 11 follows the line of Shem to Abram (before being named "Abraham" by God) and he was the first man to be called a Hebrew (Genesis 14: 13). The Bible records that Moses married an Ethiopian woman and their marriage occurred after the Exodus from Egypt (Numbers 12:1). The New Testament records that several Jews from countries in Africa came to Jerusalem for the Feast of the Pentecost (Acts 2:8-11). They may have been Jews in religion but not Semites, i.e. not descendants of Shem.

A factual study by Ephraim Issac examines the relevant Judaic commentaries and reveals that the Jewish sources contain no link between the Biblical 'curse of Noah on Ham' and the changing of skin colour.[640] Furthermore, Issac indicates that the Rabbinical literature

640 Ephraim Issac, "Genesis, Judaism and the 'Sons of Ham'," in John Ralph Willis (ed.), *Slaves and Slavery in Muslim Africa, Vol.1 – Islam and the Ideology of*

mentions that Canān not Ham was cursed as was thought by many Jewish, Christian and Arab ignoramuses throughout history in order to justify slavery, racial superiority and colonialism. Issac demonstrates that Cush is the traditionally accepted father of African peoples in the Jewish scriptures. The blackness of Cush was associated with purity and beauty with no racial stigmas attached. Thus, we find in some Jewish sources descriptions of the Children of Shem (which includes the Israelites) as being *"black and beautiful."* Though the description of Canān as being "black and ugly" is puzzling, yet it is clear from this passage that 'ugly' and not 'black' is the pejorative word. This is demonstrated by the fact that the ancestors of the Israelites are also described as being black, with many Rabbis recognizing this.

However, in saying that there is clear evidence that people who are described as "black" do not always have to come from the African continent – and the best examples of this are with the Australian Aborigines and Papa New Guineans (who though have very pronounced brow ridges which is not really found in Africa, in terms of skin colour they are "black"); the people from the Andaman Islands;[641] the 'Orang Asli' [indigenous aboriginal] Peoples of the Malay Peninsula which includes the Semang people; the Batek people who inhabit the Taman Negara National Park; the Maniq People of Thailand; the Lanoh people; the Sakai people of Indonesia; the Ati people of the Visayas which is in the central part of the Philippine archipelago; the Aeta people of

Enslavement (London and New York: Frank Cass and Co. Ltd., 1985) pp.75-91.

641 Map of the Andaman Islands:

Base 802812AI (C00213) 10-01

the Philippines,[642] Soloman Islanders (who have distinct similar broad noses), Fijians, some Sri Lankans, the Dalits of India etc.

So if we were to look at the argument from this perspective in detail,

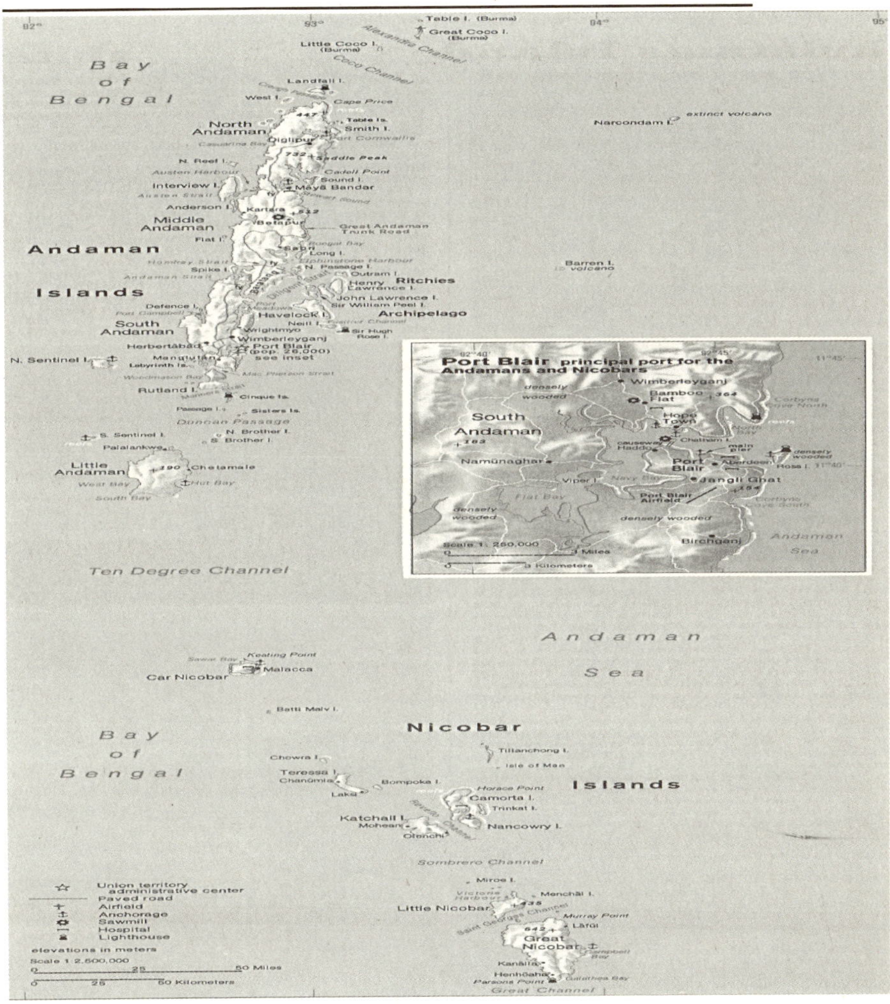

See here for images of the people from the Andaman Islands in the Indian Ocean, the Andamanese People comprise five main tribes: the Great Andamanese (who currently number about 50), the Onge (who number 100), the Jarawa (250-400), the Jangil (who are now extinct) and the Sentinelese (who number 100 to 200): http://www.leenatravels.com/indigenous-tribes-onge.php

642 Ethnic map of 'Orang Asli' [aboriginal people of Malaysia]:

which is not necessarily the nuanced perspective adopted by most of the new-age Hebrew Israelite cults, then it could argued:

1. There is some archaeological evidence from Egyptian and Assyrian art which appears to indicate that the ancient Hebrews had some physical characteristics which could be described as 'black'.
2. Some of the descendants of Ham, are also not all black.
3. There may be some historical evidence to prove that a group of ancient Hebrews migrated into Africa and took aspects of their belief and traditions with them. This occurred during the Exodus, after Assyrian captivity and after Roman persecution. This claim will be assessed in the next section.
4. Medieval authors have documented the presence of Jewish kingdoms in sub-Saharan Africa prior to the spread of Islam in Africa in the 8th century CE. This claim will be assessed in the next section.
5. Some place names in West Africa match Hebrew place names. This claim was assessed previously.
6. Some African tribes have the same genetic make up and DNA of Jews, such as the Lemba who have a higher concentration of the Cohen Modal Haplotype, more than any other Jewish population. This claim will be assessed in the next section.
7. That there is genetic evidence that all modern Jewish populations have 3-5% sub-Saharan African origin within their DNA which trace back some 72 generations.

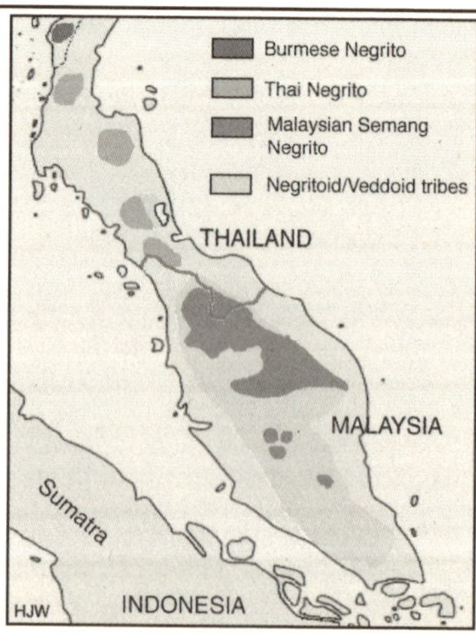

8. Deuteronomy 28 in the Bible speaks of slavery which will befall the Children of Israel.
9. A geographic argument that both Egypt and Israel were both part of the African continent and only carved into what is known as the modern 'Middle East' by European colonialists.

Based on the above, the Hebrew Israelite cults argue that black Africans have always been part of the Hebrew nation and migrated from Northeast Africa into sub-Saharan Africa over the centuries in different migration waves. They may have intermingled but they are neither the majority of the stock nor is there enough evidence to extrapolate a direct link all the way back to the ancient Hebrews.

Two: Black-Americans Solely Are "The Tribe of Judah"!? Hebrew Israelites and the "Lost Tribe" Myth

The ISUPK cult of Hebrew Israelites preach that only African-Americans from the tribe of Judah or another of the lost 12 tribes of Israel you cannot be saved. There are some differences among Hebrew Israelites and not of all them necessarily subscribe to the following chart (next page), but according to some Hebrew Israelites, of the ISUPK Cult in particular:

Ephraim and Manasseh are considered, according to the Bible, the sons of Joseph; and the northern tribes were considered a separate kingdom from the southern kingdom of Judah, a son of Leah. Only during the rule of Solomon and David were all of the tribes united and this unity lasted for 80 years. After Solomon's death in 930 BCE the kingdom split into the Kingdom of Israel in the North (the ten tribes) and the Kingdom of Judah in the South. After the Assyrian kings Tiglath

Pilesar III (732 BCE) and Sargon II (721 BCE) invaded and brought down the Northern Kingdom the Israelites were exiled in two stages to Assyria, Media and the lands neighbouring Aram-Naharaim. When the Assyrians fell to the Babylonians, the kingdom of Judah also fell and Nebechadnezzar exiled most of the Southern Kingdom of Israel to Babylon in 586 BCE. After the fall of Jerusalem, nearly 50 years later, the king of Persia Cyrus, who conquered Babylon, allowed the Judeans to return and rebuild the Temple in Jerusalem. After this period the ten tribes are not documented in the Bible and hence they are referred to as 'the Lost Tribes'. Janice Wendy Fernheimer states in her PhD thesis:

> The myth plays out in a number of different ways depending on who is claiming to be part of or have discovered "lost tribes" and to what purpose this identity or discovery is being put.[643]

There are a number of important observations about the above claims by Hebrew Israelite cults:

1. First of all, who devised this '12 Lost Tribes of Israel' chart and reached these conclusions?! There is no name ascribed to it but it has been asserted by some that the chart, which is blindly followed by Hebrew Israelite cults was formulated by Ahrayah – the same individual who claimed reincarnation and that Jesus would return in the year 2000 to kill and enslave all white people.
2. Secondly, where is the evidence, historical or otherwise, wherein this is all relayed? Where are the oral traditions, genealogical narrations or lineage records which document these Hebrew links? There is no historical evidence to suggest that the ancient Israelites from the tribe of Judah after the Babylonian captivity in the 6th century BCE and after the Jewish-Roman Wars of 70-135 CE were scattered in to West Africa.[644] The ancient Israelites mainly remained in the

643 Janice Wendy Fernheimer, *The Rhetoric of Black Jewish Identity Construction in America and Israel: 1964-1972* (Austin: University of Texas, May 2006, PhD Thesis), p.45. Accessed June 2017: https://www.lib.utexas.edu/etd/d/2006/fernheimerd82976/fernheimerd82976.pdf

644 William Hallow notes that after the Babylonian Exile, some Jews remained there while some returned back to Palestine. See William H. Hallow, "Babylon" in Bruce M. Metzger and Michael D. Coogan (eds.), *The Oxford Companion to the Bible* (Oxford: Oxford University Press, 1993), p.72.

Middle East particularly Persia, Mesopotamia, Asia Minor (i.e. Modern-day Turkey), the Balkans, Rome and the Arabian Peninsula. They were also found in North Africa and Europe.[645] There is no historical evidence from medieval historians for instance which indicate that the ancient Israelites branched off in to West Africa. By the 13th century CE waves of Hebrew descendants which were found in North Africa and other places were wiped out by famine, disease and poverty.

3. Thirdly, have the new-age Hebrew Israelite cults such as ISUPK and the others conducted any genetic studies inspecting the Y-chromosome halotypes of these peoples which indicate an origin outside of Africa and the African gene pool?! If they have conducted such research, which modal halotype did they utilise as a normative measure of ancient Hebrew descent?[646] To make such a huge claim about the so-called 'Lost Tribes' the new-age Hebrew Israelite cults need to furnish us with at least some anthropological genetics studies to back up their assertions.
4. The only one in the West to claim a huge set of black people are 'Hebrews' and possess 'Hebrewisms' was a white Christian missionary in Jamaica in the 1920s, Williams in his book! So now "an Edomite" (!?) becomes authoritative for the new-age Hebrew Israelite cult?!
5. This list is an exquisite example of how the Hebrew Israelites are America-centric as their only concern is to try to claim that peoples of the Americas represent the lost 12 tribes of Israel?! This is a clear Afrocentric political plan to focus on re-writing black history in the West. If they were really about tracing the 'Lost Tribes of the Hebrews' then why do the new-age Hebrew Israelite cults say nothing about India, Ethiopia, South Africa, Yemen or North Africa!? "Dr" Ben did in his book, *We the Black Jews*, on page 72, a book which 'Hebrew Israelites' blindly follow, and in the book Jochannan criticises what he regards as a White Jewish Ashkenazi and Sephardi hegemony. This is one of the clearest examples of

645 Maristella Botticini and Zvi Eckstein, *The Chosen Few* (Princeton University Press, 2012), p.25.

646 For more on this see Nadia Abu El-Haj, *The Genealogical Science: The Search for Jewish Origins and the Politics of Epistemology* (Chicago and London: University of Chicago Press, 2012), pp.33-41.

the incredulity of the new-age 'Hebrew Israelite' cult credo. They do not mention the Bnei Menashe of northeast India for instance who claim descent from the lost tribe of Manasseh;[647] the Bene Ephraim from southern India who claimed descent from Ephraim; the Falasha Jews of Ethiopia who claim descent from the lost tribe of Dan;[648] and the Lemba of Southern Africa.[649] A Jewish traveller in 800 CE named Eldad Hedoni visited a Jewish community in Tunisia claiming that he was from the 'Lost Tribe of Dan' and that he had knowledge of the locations of the Lost Tribes of Israel. This is all relayed in the book Sefer Eldad and in a letter that the Tunisian Jewish community whom he visited to Rabbi Zeba Gow'on. In these documents it is claimed that Dan, Napthali, Gad and Asher had migrated to the land of Cush, Ethiopia. Gerber (2011) in her entry in *The Oxford Dictionary of the Jewish Religion* corroborates Eldad's claims of being from the Ethiopian Jews and the tribe of Dan.[650] This also refutes the claim that Gad somehow got to North America, Napthali somehow got to Argentina and Chile (!!?) and Asher to Colombia and Uruguay. Eldad in his travels also claimed to have encountered the tribe of Issachar in Persia, contrary to the claims of the Hebrew Israelite cults that the tribe found itself in Mexico!? Eldad also claimed, in the 8th century CE, that he had encountered during his travels the tribe of Zebulon dwelling in the Mountains of Paran and Reuben lived opposite them behind the Mountains of Paran – Paran being the location of modern-day Western Arabia up to Sinai. Which is interesting as there were Jewish communities during early Islam who were based in Arabia.

---

647 See Hillel Halkin, *Across the Sabbath River: In Search of a Lost Tribe of Israel* (Boston: Houghton Mifflin, 2002); Nathan Katz, *Who Are the Jews of India?* (Berkeley and Los Angeles: University of California Press, 2000);

648 See Wolf Leslau, *Falasha Anthology: The Black Jews of Ethiopia* (New Haven, Conn.: Yale University Press, 1951); Zvi Ben-Dor Benite, author of *The Ten Lost Tribes: A World History* (Oxford: Oxford University Press, 2009), p.224.

649 See Magdel le Roux, *The Lemba: A Lost Tribe of Israel in Southern Africa?* (Unisa, South Africa: Unisa Press, 2003); Tudor Parfitt and Yulia Egorova, *Genetics, Mass Media and Identity: A Case Study of the Genetic Research on the Lemba and the Bene Israel* (London: Routledge, 2006); Nadia Abu El-Haj, *op.cit.*, pp.185-87.

650 Jane S. Gerber, "Eldad Da-Dani" in Adele Berlin (ed.), *The Oxford Dictionary of the Jewish Religion* (Oxford: Oxford University Press, 2011), p.236.

6. Hence, the Hebrew Israelites denounce Africans as they claim that they sold them in to slavery. Yet by extension they still have to accept that they must have therefore been in Africa in the first instance therefore?!
7. Some of the peoples above are non-black, such as the Mexicans for instance. Yet when were they taken into captivity into a land on their own, from Africa?!
8. When were the non-black peoples referred to above sent as captives to all nations and scattered in all four directions of Israel?! As per the Bible.
9. There are people in other countries who look exactly like African-Americans yet their ancestors were taken there as slaves from Africa. Mere enslavement does not make a people "Israelite".
10. The list above refers to modern countries, lands and their borders?! What sort of logic is this? Are we to deduce from this that *all* people residing in those borders, which are modern borders, are therefore "Israelites"?!
11. How on earth do the Hebrew Israelites manage to distinguish Haitians, who have West African origin, from "the so-called Negroes" (of the US) who also have West African origin?!
12. Indigenous non-black Native South Americans referred to in the above chart are not the Israelites of the Bible. Moreover, they were not brought there in mass enslavement from Africa. Though there may be Israelites mixed among them in history, as a whole they are not the Israelites of the Bible.
13. Mormons and the LDS, as did the European Pilgrims in the 17th century who were the first to adopt this method before Black American Jews and Hebrew Israelite cults, also propagate that Native Americans are Israelites, in order to preach to them to accept their beliefs. Another method therefore which new-age Hebrew Israelite Cults have taken from the "Edomites"(!?)
14. If the Hebrew Israelites claim that the above people were oppressed and therefore this alone means that they are Israelites, then all non-white peoples have been oppressed by Europeans in any case. This alone is insufficient to argue that they are therefore Israelites.
15. Moreover, possessing dark skin alone is also insufficient to claim that they were Israelites as a dark skin complexion is prevalent in

many lands which were first populated by their original inhabitants.

In regards to Native Americans being from "the tribe of Gad", the seventh born son of Ya'qūb *('alayhi-salaam)* then this not only is unsupported by any type of evidence whatsoever but also demonstrates ignorance of the religious traditions and practices of the Native Americans and their culture. Staeger mentions in his book *Native American Religions* that:

> In general, Native Americans believed that there was a divine spirit that ran through all things. Different tribes had different names for it. The Algonquin tribes called this spirit Manitou, while the Iroquois called it Orenda. To the Inuit, it was Sila. On the Great Plains, it was Wakanda. The Maya of South America called it K'ul. The basic Native American belief is known as animism. Animism is a belief system that gives divine qualities to animals and objects. To the Indians, any coyote might be the trickster god Coyote.

Deogaonkar states in *Native Americans and Native Indians*:

> In the Native American folklore there are superstitions about certain objects, animate as well as inanimate. Some objects are called fetish, meaning thereby that they are believed to be dwellings of a spirit.[651]

In *The Native American* (The Phoenix School, 1917), vol.18:

> There is a superstition existing amongst those Indians that when a mother dies at the birth of a child, the child is regarded as an evil spirit and is cast aside to die.

Varner stated in *Mysteries of Native American Myth and Religion*:

> The belief in animism appears to have been universal in scope among Native Americans and cultures elsewhere.[652]

De Lima Santos states:

> Shamanism being at the core of not only Native American

651 S.G. Deogaonkar and S.S Deogaonkar, *Native Americans and Native Indians* (New Delhi: Concept Publishing, 2002), p.58.

652 Gary A. Varner, *Mysteries of Native American Myth and Religion* (Raleigh, N.C.: Lulu Press, 2007), p.41.

> but also perhaps all religions alike, the shaman is a key figure in the understanding of Native American religion. The shaman, who also has the roles of magician, medicine man, , and poet, is someone who can get away from the earthly daily life and dive into other layers of consciousness by means of magical flight.[653]

Then de Lima Santos states:

> Such a quasi-divine understanding of the world would not be seen with the most welcoming eyes…by the defenders of monotheistic established religions…[654]

These are not the beliefs of the Prophets sent to the Children of the Israelites during the ancient times!

Hebrew Israelite Similarities With the 16-17th Century White European Pilgrims, Missionary Puritans and the Mormon Church/ So-Called "Latter-Day Saints"

The roots of claims that the Native Americans and other peoples in the Americas are of the "lost Hebrew tribes of Israel" are not with modern Hebrew Israelite cults from New York but are rather to be found in Spain, England and Holland in the mid-17th century CE.

In 1511 Pedro Martir de Anglerìa suggested that the Native Americans could be a lost tribe of Israel, and this notion was then taken up in 1580 by Juan Suárez de Peralta and Diego Durán.[655] De Peralta asserted that there were Aztec words which are in tandem with Hebrew words while Durán, a Dominican Friar, argued in his book *History of the Indies* that the Nahuas Indians of Central Mexico were a lost tribe. Bartolomé de la Casas wrote on the origins of the Native Americans in 1550 in his *Apologética Historia* which was published in 1909 and in 1559 in his *Historia de las Indias* which was published in 1876. However, he did

653 Marcel de Lima Santos, *The Ethnopoetcis of Shamanism* (New York, NY: Palgrave Macmillan, 2014), p.100.

654 Ibid.

655 William G. McLoughlin, *The Cherokees and Christianity, 1794-1870: Essays on Acculturation and Cultural Persistence* (Athens and London: University of Georgia Press, 2008), ftn.6, p.321. Also see Lee Eldridge Huddleston, *Origin of the American Indians: European Concepts, 1492-1729* (Austin: University of Texas Press, 1969), pp.33-37, 128-33.

not state that the Native Americans are descended from a "lost tribe of Israel", though that is sometimes attributed to him he makes no mention of that theory within his writings whatsoever.[656] Yates (2014: 86) for instance states that Bartolomé de la Casas advocated the theory.

These Spanish Christians wanted proximity with the Native Americans while other Spanish missionaries such as Juan Giné de Sepúlveda deemed the Native Americans as being barbaric and uncivilised. Lafaye (1987: 43) notes that there are reports that the soldiers of Cortes described Aztec temples as "Mosques" thereby assimilating all non-Christian religions as one in reviving the fervour of the Reconquista within the Americas.[657]

In 1567 in Antwerp, Joannes Fredericus Lumnius published *De Extremo Dei Indicio et Indorum vocatione* in which he argues that the Native Americans are from the lost tribes of Israel.[658] In 1607 Gregorio Garcia published *Origen de las Indios de el Nuevo Mundo* [Origin of the Indians in the New World]. In the book he reiterates the ideas of de Anglerìa, de Peralta and Durán in chapter five of the book entitled "Of the Fifth Opinion, Where it is Proved That the Indians Are the Descendants of the Hebrews of the Lost Ten Tribes".

In 1646 CE an English puritan missionary to the Native Americans in Massachusetts, John Eliot, posited that the Native Americans may be 'a lost tribe of Israel'. Eliot learnt Native American languages and had a Native American translator who was fluent in English.[659] Eliot began to preach in 1646 to the Native Americans of Nonatum, a village ten miles west of Boston.[660] He pointed out to a traditional knowledge of God, affirmation of God's Providence, giving of thanks and acknowledgement

---

656 Lee Eldridge Huddleston, *op.cit.*, pp.22-26.

657 Jacques Lafaye, *Quetzalcoati and Guadalupe: The Formation of Mexican National Consciousness, 1531-1813* (Chicago and London: University of Chicago Press, 1987, trans. Benjamin Keen), p.43.

658 Lee Eldridge Huddleston, *op.cit.*, pp.34-35.

659 Convers Francis, *Life of John Eliot, the Apostle to the Indians* (Boston: Hilliard Gray & Co and London: Richard James Kennett, 1836), pp.39-45.

660 Josiah Woodward Leeds, *A History of the United States of America: Including Some Important Facts Mostly Omitted in the Smaller Histories* (Philadelphia: J.P. Lippincott & Co.,, 1877), pp.200-202.

to God, they preserve the memories of their uncles and grandparents.[661]

This theory was also advocated by Roger Williams and in December 1635 he wrote a letter to another English minister based in Norfolk called Thomas Thorowgood. Williams asserted that the Native American language had an affinity with Hebrew and while Thorowgood was actually initially sceptical of this theory, he later adopted it after a fifteen year study and analysis of scripture, history, geography and ethnography.[662] Prior to this such ideas were unheard of, so would the Hebrew Israelites assert that "Edomites" were the first to come with this idea?!

In 1648 Thorowgood surmised that because Native Americans were easy to convert to Christianity they must be descendants from the Lost Tribes of Israel. Among his arguments were that the Native Americans wear robes and go barefoot, they anoint their heads with oil, they regularly bathe, they do not eat pork, they compute days from sunset to sunset.[663]

In 1650 Menasseh Ben Israel, a Portuguese Sephardic Rabbi whose family had moved to Holland, wrote a treatise on the subject which he presented to parliament at the time. This was during the era of the English Interregnum and as a result there was an apocalyptic sentiment as a result of the puritanism, the execution of the king, the civil war and fanatical missionary zeal unto the 'new world'.[664] Ben Israel

---

661 Nehemiah Adams, *The Life of John Eliot: With an Account of the Early Missionary Efforts Among the Indians of New England* (Boston: Massachusetts Sabbath School Society, 1847), pp.151-52

662 Nicholas Guyatt, *Providence and the Invention of the United States, 1607-1876* (Cambridge: Cambridge University Press, 2007), pp.36-7.

663 Donald Yates, *Old World Roots of the Cherokee: How DNA, Ancient Alphabets and Religion Explain the Origins of America's Largest Indian Nation* (Jefferson, North Carolina: McFarland & Co. Publishers, 2014), p. 86.

664 After the Jews had been expelled from England for 350 years after the 1290 CE edict against their presence in England, Oliver Cromwell was the one who allowed their return to England and the practice of their religion, in what came to be known as the *'Cromwellian Protectorate'* in 1695 CE. Cromwell's main reason for this was for trade and economic reasons as opposed to any notions of sharing a 'Judeo-Christian heritage.' The edict of expulsion was given by Edward the first

claimed, with scant evidence and out of political expediency at the time possibly to pander in to religious fervour which made conditions more favourable (Wolf, 2012: 24), that a band of Jews had made their way to the Americas and left their cultural mark on the Indians.[665] Ben Israel's

---

of England, which exiled them from England for 350 years. He issued writs to sheriffs of all English counties ordering them to enforce a decree to the effect that all Jews should leave England before All Saints Day. Oliver Cromwell in 1656 CE allowed the Jews to enter England and practice their religion under what came to be known as the *'Cromwellian Protectorate'*. The commercial policy which led to the *Navigation Act in October 1651*, made Cromwell try to attract the rich Jews of Amsterdam to London so that they might transfer their important trade interests with the Spanish main to England.

There were negotiations between the English and Menasseh Ben Israel of the Amsterdam community, which eventually led to Menasseh Ben Israel being allowed to enter England after the 1652-54 war between England and Holland. After the war, Menasseh Ben Israel sent his brother-in-law David Abravanel Dormido to London in order to present a petition for the readmission of the Jews. The petition was initially rejected and then Cromwell persuaded Menasseh Ben Israel to travel to London in person and present the case, which he did in 1655 CE. As a result, a national conference was summoned at Whitehall which included England's most prominent lawyers, merchants and other notables and the lawyers reached the conclusion that there was no opposition to the Jews residing in England, however the merchants and religious authorities of the day were opposed to it, thus Cromwell ended the national conference in order to prevent a decision which went against his own interests.

Even after Cromwell's concessions to the Jews, in 1664 CE an attempt was made by the Earl of Berkshire to bring about the expulsion of the Jews and in 1684 CE it was claimed that the Jews were 'alien infidels' who were perpetual enemies to 'the British crown.' In 1723 CE a special act of Parliament was passed which allowed the Jews to hold land in England on the condition that they swear an oath. In 1740 they were allowed to become naturalised British citizens if they had lived in the British colonies. The history of the Jews in England therefore, is one of a people without any status, security or safety so it is strange how some authors, such as Bat Ye'or, Oriana Fallaci, Melanie Philips, Robert Spencer et al. mention nothing of this in their writing of anti-Semitism and blame every manifestation of hatred against the Jews that has taken place in history on the Muslims.

665 Guyatt, *op.cit.*, p.37; also see Lucien Wolf (ed.), *Menasseh Ben Israel's Mission to Oliver Cromwell: Being a Reprint of the Pamphlets Published by Menasseh Ben Israel to Promote the Re-admission of the Jews to England, 1649-1656* (Cambridge:

book entitled *Mikveh Israel* was first published in Amsterdam in the mid-17th century and then translated into English as *The Hope of Israel.* Ben Israel claimed that a Portuguese Jew named Antonio Montezinos had lived in South America for 20 years and had meet Indians who had maintained their Jewish customs in Ecudor's Quinto Province, and also in Colombia.

He claimed that they were from the lost tribe of Reuben and practices among some of the Native Americans such as the belief in divine providence, the immortality of the soul, creation stories, reference to a flood, circumcision and the separation of menstruating women were taken as vestiges of these supposed Hebraic practices.[666] It should be noted again here than from an Islamic perspective if these practices are found among aboriginal and native peoples, this is a hallmark that they have retained what is from their natural disposition (*fitrah*) as relayed from their ancestors and from the first man and his progeny, as opposed to being from "the lost tribe of Israel".

Thorowgood then published his study *Jewes in America; or, Probabilities that the Americans are of that Race. With the removal of some contrary reasonings, and earnest desires for the effectual endeavours to make them Christian* (London: Printed by W.H., 1650),[667] a work published in three editions between 1650-52 and asserted that the Native Americans were not native to America but had migrated during the siege of Jerusalem in 70CE. John Dury, a Puritan minister, provided a preface to Thorowgood's work after also being somewhat sceptical and changed his mind on the basis of Thorowgood's arguments and wanted to increase Native American conversion. Parliament at the time therefore even created a committee in 1649 to propagate the work of missionaries in New England among the Native Americans and sought donations to support the work of American Ministers John Eliot and Thomas Mayhew.

Cambridge University Press, 2012), p.xxiv.

666 Richard W. Cogley, *John Eliot's Mission to the Indians before King Philips War* (Cambridge, MT and London, England: Harvard University Press, 2009), pp.85.

667 Gershon Greenberg, "American Indians, Lost Ten Tribes and Christian Eschatology" in Bryan F. LeBeau and Menahem Mor (eds.), *Religion in the Age of Exploration: The Case of Spain and New Spain* (Omaha, NB: Creighton University Press, 1996), p.143

William Penn, in the last quarter of the 17th century also adopted this view and advocated for friendly relations with the Native Americans.[668] While an Irish trader in the Americas who had lived for forty years among the Cherokees, James Adair, also posited the theory.[669] Adair published History of the American Indians in 1775, and this was then propagated by Elias Boudinot in 1816 and then Ethan Smith in 1823.

Professor Zvi Ben-Dor Benite, author of *The Ten Lost Tribes: A World History* (Oxford: Oxford University Press, 2009) and Professor of History and Middle East and Islamic Studies at New York University noted that though it was a popular theory for a while serious ethnographic and archaeological research debunked the theory as there was no plausible evidence.[670] Dor Benite also wrote an article entitled *Mormon Scripture and the Lost Tribes of Israel.* He touches on a matter which is also shared by the Hebrew Israelites Cult and shares some points which was noted by Fernheimer in her PhD thesis wherein she stated:

> The myth plays out in a number of different ways depending on who is claiming to be part of or have discovered "lost tribes" and to what purpose this identity or discovery is being put. In the American context, a confluence of forces including Puritan millenarianism, British Anglo-Israelitism and philo-Semitism, and Christian apocalypticism make Lost Tribe theories appealing. Ever since the Puritans first set foot on the "New Promised Land" of American soil the issues of Israelitism, Biblical prophecy, and millenarianism have been part of American culture.[671]

Professor Zvi Ben-Dor Benite states:

---

668 Karen Ordahl Kupperman, *Settling with the Indians: the Meeting of English and Indian Cultures in America, 1580-1640* (Totowa, NJ: Rowman and Littlefield, 1980), p.10.

669 John Ehle, *Trail of Tears: The Rise and Fall of the Cherokee Nation* (New York, NY: Anchor Books, 1989), p.1.

670 Zvi Ben-Dor Benite, *The Ten Lost Tribes: A World History* (Oxford: Oxford University Press, 2009), p.182.

671 Janice Wendy Fernheimer, *The Rhetoric of Black Jewish Identity Construction in America and Israel: 1964-1972* (Austin: University of Texas, May 2006, Phd Thesis), p.45. Accessed June 2017: https://www.lib.utexas.edu/etd/d/2006/fernheimerd82976/fernheimerd82976.pdf

> According to the Bible, the Assyrians of the eighth century B.C.E. exiled 10 of the original "twelve tribes" from their land in the northern kingdom of Israel. Many prominent Americans, such as William Penn and Elias Boudinot, believed that they ended up in America. This belief is known today among historians as the Jewish Indian theory. The theory persisted for centuries because it addressed a religious desire and theological anxiety to link the New World (America) to the Old (biblical) World. The fact that the Bible was not part of the biblical cosmography posed major theological problems for many American Christians. Simply put, if America was not mentioned in the Bible, how could it properly be "under God"? This anxiety about the biblical status of the American continent plagued many generations of US citizens. And they sought comfort in the idea that the lost tribes had come to these shores centuries ago. The idea linked both America to the Bible and accounted for the origins of America's native peoples. The theory that the 10 lost tribes of Israel had migrated to the Americas after their expulsion from ancient Israel was of course difficult to substantiate. Many went to great lengths to prove it scientifically. Numerous attempts to find linguistic or archaeological evidence in support of it failed. Eventually the theory faded away. It would most likely have been long forgotten had it not been for the work of an important figure in American religious history – Joseph Smith, the founder of Mormonism. Whereas others turned to science to prove the Jewish Indian theory, Joseph Smith appealed to supernatural revelation: a prophecy declaring that the 10 lost tribes had indeed found their way to the Americas.[672]

Thus, like the English Puritans, Spanish catholic missionaries and white American Mormons, the Hebrew Israelite Cults also:

- Try to fabricate an eschatology which can remain America-centric yet linked to the Bible.
- Concoct historical revisionism so as to place the Native Americans as "one of the lost tribes of Israel".
- Like the Mormons, seek to resolve the absence of America not being mentioned at all in the Bible and thereby formulate an America-

672 Professor Zvi Ben-Dor Benite, "Mormon Scripture and the Lost Tribes of Israel." *Bible Odyssey* website. Accessed 9th June 2017: https://www.bibleodyssey.org/en/places/related-articles/mormon-scripture-and-the-lost-tribes-of-israel

centred theology.

It thus may have been possible that the early black Israelite founders, such as Arnold Ford, and F.S. Cherry were influenced by some of these English puritan and Mormon precepts. Yet the fact remains that there is no genetic, linguistic, cultural or archaeological evidence to support the claim that Native Americans are an Israelite tribe. Moreover, there is not a shred of evidence from Native American history or tradition to demonstrate an Israelite connection, any similarities will be due to the *fitrah* [the natural disposition of humans which Muslims believe Allāh places in all peoples].

Three: Historical Denial of Black Americans Being Ethnically Associated With Africa

Although some of the founding fathers of black Hebrew Israelite sects tried to at least have some sort of connection to Africa, as in the case of Rabbi Arnold Ford who was a member of Marcus Garvey's UNIA which promoted a return back to Africa, modern Hebrew Israelite cults however have turned this flat on its head. Moreover, Wentworth Matthew, an acolyte of Arnold Ford's whom we have discussed earlier, not only asserted that some West African tribes had Hebrew roots but also had consciously associated with West Africa, Nigeria for instance in Matthew's case. Then there was Crowdy who proudly deemed himself as an Ethiopian.

The New-Age Hebrew Israelite Cults rabidly and vociferously assert that they "are not African", this they preach regularly, blindly, foolishly and stubbornly. To support this assertion Hebrew Israelite cults, such as ISUPK for example, will even display images of Animist and uncivilised tribes, who have lip plugs, elaborate and extreme body markings and decorations etc. with words such as "we are not African" above the images. Hebrew Israelite cults such as the ISUPK branch of the cult will place up pictures of tribes such as the nomadic cattle herder Mursi tribe of the Debub Omo Zone of Ethiopia which is close to the border with Sudan. It is apparent that there are not only aspects of colourism when the Hebrew Israelite cults present such images, but also an inculcation of negative stereotypical European imagery about Africa as a place of savagery, barbarism and heathenism. There are a number of points about this method of simplistic anti-African propaganda which needs to be highlighted here:

1. First of all, it is evident that blacks in the Americas and the Caribbean are of a predominantly African stock and aspects in both black diaspora language (Ebonics and Creole) and culture indicate this. Terms such as 'duppy', 'nyam', 'rara' all indicate this as they are rooted in West African speech patterns and vocabulary. In parts of South America, in Guyana and Brazil (Bahia) for instance Yoruba words and cultural connections are very much evident. If Hebrew was the key cultural trait this would be evident. Verbal games played in the Americas, such as 'the Dozens', has its roots in Igbo tradition, while stories of Anasi and the spider, as per tradition in Ghana, have connections to 'Aunt Nancy' in the US. These cultural traditions are not from 'the Hebrews'.
2. Secondly, when the new-age Hebrew Israelite cults such as ISUPK in particular, as they are the ones who champion this void argument, present images of darker skinned Africans compared to an African-American Hebrew Israelite cult follower, they are essentially regurgitating and promoting colourism, in the most ignorant of ways. It therefore appears that due to their self-hate, an inferiority complex of any association with Africa, which unfortunately is common in the black diaspora which they therefore exploit, coupled with their complete and utter ignorance of African history, heritage, culture and genetics – the new-age Hebrew Israelite cults seek to distance themselves from any connection to Africa. The reality is that they themselves, according to their own nomenclature, are in fact wholly Hamitic.[673]
3. It is absolute folly for the Hebrew Israelite cults to deem a few select tribes with ignorant practices as being representative of "Africans".
4. It is evident that the Hebrew Israelite cults, such as the ISUPK Cult, proclaim they are not African yet comfortably reside in the USA! They neither reside in any traditional environment with simple and natural living nor do they advocate this.
5. Based on the above then, it is evident that the modern Hebrew Israelite cults are very disconnected from Africa and their efforts to

673 See an example of this image, which is used in Hebrew Israelite cult propaganda material:

dissociate with their African origins represent an inferiority complex

The above image outlines precisely the problem we have here and the clear colourist and anti-dark-skin emphasis that the new-age Hebrew Israelite cults promote in their propaganda materials. Furthermore, it demonstrates that they have nothing to offer humanity except the constant discussion on race and colour – with absolutely no practical solutions or programmes to actually uplift humanity, let alone people of African origin.

Also this image here:

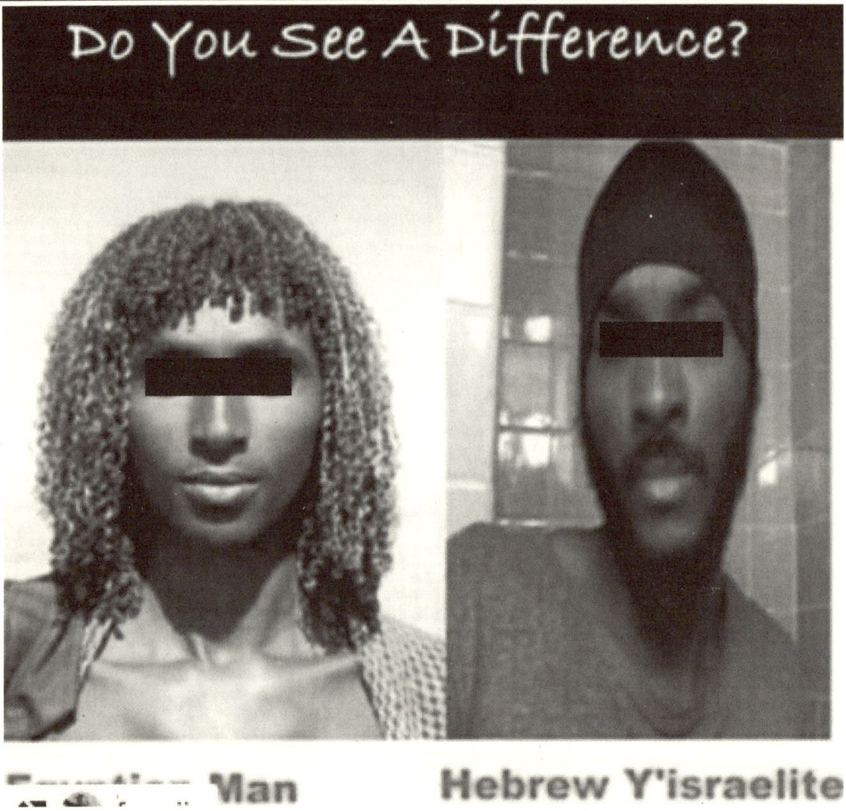

The above seeks to compare an African-American Hebrew Israelite cult member, whom, if a DNA test was conducted, would reveal that he has largely West African DNA with possibly some European and hence his browner complexion. Yet the false deductions made by the new-age Hebrew Israelite cults are that such a complexion denotes a link to either Eastern Africa or the Middle East?! This is nothing but the epitome of anti-black ignorance and colourist tomfoolery.

As for the ancient Egyptians, then some folios indicate how they deemed the races with whom they interacted, and some images distinguish the Nubian from the Asiatic and from the Egyptian. Although it is clear that the majority were of an African stock and not just the 25th Dynasty, as in the case of the earlier Pharaonic Dynasties, such as the First Dynasty of which the founding king was Narmer (Menes) and had clear African features. However, even some of the Kushite Pharaohs of the 25th Dynasty and their wives were depicted as reddish skinned within some of the hieroglyphics as in the case of Naparaye the daughter of Piye, she is buried at El-Kurru.

coupled with blatant distortion of facts. They therefore bring the most extreme example of tribal body modifications and decorations in order to show that they are not African, yet these same body modifications are also to be found in America! Furthermore, this would be like bringing the most extreme examples of Israelite practice as a proof that one is not a Hebrew Israelite. Indeed, it would be like putting together a placard depicting the advocacy of paedophilia, as preached by some Hebrew Israelites openly in New York, along with words saying "we are not Hebrew Israelites"! Or the examples of poor fathering and 'baby mothers' with numerous children abandoned by their Hebrew Israelites fathers without a father to cultivate them in the home and saying "we are not Hebrew Israelites". Yet we will suffice with refuting the credo of this cult.

6. Importantly, it is evident that the Hebrew Israelite cults have been deceptive in their presentation of Africa. Thus, we see that they totally forget to present on their propagation boards aspects of African civilisation, and particularly West African civilisation from which the black so-called Hebrew Israelites actually originate. They do not present the civilisation of ancient Ghana, ancient Mali and Songhay. They do not bring forth on their propagation boards the

---

However, Egypt's location would have meant that their ethnic make-up was quite diverse in any case and even among the black African ethnic group are a highly diverse phenotype in terms of facial features, skin tone and hair texture. The Masai Mara tribe look different from the Khoisan in Southern Africa and the Ashanti look different from the Igbo, etc.

Yet Egypt's location would have meant that as time even within antiquity, the gene pool of Egypt would have become increasingly varied and diversified. Evidence of this can be seen in the Fayyum Mummy Portraits which are from Fayyum in Egypt and date back to the 1st Century CE. Kemet Afrocentrics and Hebrew Israelites in their poor research will claim that the images of such people are of 'later Arabs', when the reality is that the images depict indigenous Egyptians from Fayyum from the 1st -3rd Centuries CE during the Imperial Roman Egyptian Era and not from after the 8th century CE and the Islamic Conquest. The people depicted resemble a North African ethnic stock and appearance and with some who possess more African features, and these are also plentiful within the Ptolemaic Era portraits which date from 305 BCE-30BCE. The Ptolemaic Kingdom was a Hellenistic Kingdom which was based in Egypt, the last Pharaoh of it being Cleopatra before the Roman Conquest of Egypt.

libraries of Timbuktu wherein African Muslims wrote on grammar, jurisprudence, creed, logic, science, geometry and mathematics. It is also possible that the reason they deny all of this is because it not only undermines their false claim that they "are not African" but it also demonstrates the civilisation of Islamic West Africa which the Hebrew Israelite cults want to hide and deny.

7. Moreover, when the Hebrew Israelite cults such as ISUPK bring forth these images of Animist and uncivilised tribes of Africa as a proof that they are not African yet at the same time the same tribal practices are found among the peoples whom the Hebrew Israelite cults try to curry favour with and claim are part of the "12 tribes of Israel". So for example, Hebrew Israelites claim that various South American peoples are also from "the tribes of Israel", such as the Native Americans for instance. Yet the Hebrew Israelites conveniently forget to mention their savage and barbaric cultural practices far from the teachings of the Prophets, such as scalping. These uncivilised cultural practices are also found with hunter gatherer tribes in the Brazilian Amazon for instance, such as the Piraha tribe, the Akuntsu tribe, the Yanomamo tribe, the Kayapo tribe, the Suya tribe etc. The beliefs of the Native Americans have been mentioned earlier.
8. Also, such extreme body decorations are found among the Apatani People of the Ziro Arunachal Valley in Pradesh in Northeast India (women from whom wear nose plugs, a practice which originated in order to keep away invading men from other tribes); teeth sharpening, as found among tribes in Bali and Vietnam; the kayan women of Northern Thailand who wear brass coils around their necks.
9. What also makes their assertions all the more odd is the fact that many of these above mentioned people hail from tribes which were not monotheistic whatsoever.

Four: Slavery of Israelites Confused With Trans-Atlantic Slavery

The Hebrew Israelite cults suggest that Africans captured Hebrew Israelites in West Africa and then sold them into slavery in the Americas. They argue that Deuteronomy 28:68 which talks about the descendants of Shem being taken by ships and sold into slavery is in fact intending the Trans-Atlantic Slave period. They not only to fail to bring a shred of historical evidence to support this contention, but they also perform a degree of biblical hermeneutical acrobatics in order to arrive at this supposition. The verse in Deuteronomy states:

> The Lord will send you back to Egypt in ships, by a route which I told you you shall never see again. There you shall be offered for sale to your enemies as male and female slaves, but none will buy you.
>
> [Deut. 28:68]

Moses according to the Bible said "the Lord will send you back to Egypt in ships" as the method in which the children of Israel left was via the miracle of the parting of the Red Sea (Exodus 14:21-22, 29), so the verse is not a prophecy rather a warning of punishment to Israel for disobedience.

Five: White People Are "Devil Edomites" Descended From Esau

The Hebrew Israelite Cults claim that white people and Ashkenazi Jews are "devil Edomites" that are descended from Esau. This is a merely another cult credo similar to the Nation of Islam belief that white people were grafted devil creatures created by a mad black scientist called Yakub. Such concepts are not the true religion of the Creator. According to the Bible, the Edomites were destroyed for their actions against Israel, not because they were white. Edom was located between modern Jordan and Israel, it was an ancient kingdom in Transjordan and its capital was Petra. 'Edom' means 'red' and is the son of Esau, the son of Issac, as per the Bible. After the Babylonian destruction of Jerusalem in 586 BCE, the Edomites were based in Judea, while in 163 BCE they were conquered by the Jewish Maccabees. They converted to Judaism and were based in Southern Judea and in the First Century CE they fought with the Jews against Rome and were vanquished, only a few of them escaped. As a result it is pseudo-history to say that white people came from them, as not only are the dates all messed up but it is more likely, as per the Bible, that Europeans are descendants of Japeth, also in the Bible in 1 Samuel an Edomite was hired by Saul, so how could they be "devil Edomites" and the like. So if Esau is from Shem, then Edomites are themselves Semites. This is merely black cult credo revamped in the garb of modern Hebrew Israelite cult language.

Hebrew Israelites claims that 'Edomites' were a group of white converts among the Khazars who eventually went on to father the Ashkenazi Jews. Blindly following the work of Koestler in *The Thirteenth Tribe*, and via the use of contorted historiography and ethnography, they assert that they are Edomites. There has also been some discussion about the Khazar Conversion to Judaism as some historians and geneticists hold that the Khazar Conversion theory has been somewhat overplayed. Nevertheless, that there was indeed a conversion of the Khazar Empire in the 8th century CE is not denied by historians. This was largely to enable them to better participate in the lucrative Silk Road trade between Germany and China which was controlled by Jewish traders. It was during this period that Yiddish developed as a language for trade. Shlomo Sand from Tel Aviv University states in his book *The Invention of the Jewish People:*

> From the sixth century on, Persian testimonies, followed by Muslim ones shed light on the early stages of the Khazar saga. They invaded the Sassanid kingdom and harassed its border inhabitants. They got as far as the area about Mosul in today's Iraq. In the early seventh century, during the reign of the Persian king Khosrau II, a marriage with the Khazar king's daughter sealed an alliance that enabled the Persians to build fortifications in the passes of the Caucasus Mountains.[674]

Sand also notes:

> The arrival of Jewish believers from Armenia, from today's Iraq, from Khorasan (which covered parts of modern-day Iran, Turkmenistan, Uzbekistan, Tajikistan, Afghanistan and Pakistan) and from Byzantium may well have triggered the conversion of that strange kingdom to Judaism. Proselytizing Jews were driven from the arena of rival monotheisms, Christianity or Islam, to the lands of paganism. As in other regions that witnesses mass Judaization, so in Khazaria, it began with immigrants who convinced the pagans that their faith was preferable. The great mass proselytizing campaign that began in the second century BCE, with the rise of the Hasmonean kingdom, reached its

674 Shlomo Sand, *The Invention of the Jewish People* (London and New York: Verso, 2010), p.214.

> climax in Khazaria in the eighth century CE.[675]

Sand therefore highlights:

> If in the nineteenth century scholars were doubtful about the conversion of the Khazar kingdom, today it is not in dispute. The spreading monotheism reached the Caucasus and the steppes of the Volga and the Don – today's southern Russia – and convinced rulers and tribal elites to believe in the many advantages of a single deity.[676]

Sand goes on to emphasise how the Khazar Empire wanted to remain independent from both the Abbasid Muslim Empire and the Orthodox Christian Byzantine Empire.

Eran Elhaik, an Israel-American geneticist and bioinformatician from the University of Sheffield, Department of Animal and Plant Sciences, has argued that according to his genetic analysis there is strong evidence for the Khazarian hypothesis accounting for the origin of European Jews. The Caucasus populations (i.e. Armenians, Georgians etc.) were very isolated and there is no historical evidence of any mass migration of Caucasus migration into East and Central Europe prior the fall of Khazaria and the Khazar conversion to Judaism.[677] In a 2016 study Wexler, Elhaik et al. argue that the first Ashkenazi populations to speak Yiddish came from areas near four villages in Eastern Turkey along the Silk Road whose names derived from "Ashkenaz" rather than from the Germanic lands. Elhaik and Wexler proposed that Iranians, Greeks, Turks and Slavs converted to Judaism in Turkey prior to migrating to Khazaria.[678] They propose the following:

---

675 Ibid.p.220

676 Ibid. p.221

677 Eran Elhaik, "The Missing Link of Jewish European Ancestry: Contrasting the Rhineland and the Khazarian Hypotheses." In *Genome Biology and Evolution*, Vol.5, issue 1, 1 January 2013, pp.61-74. See: https://academic.oup.com/gbe/article/5/1/61/728117 Accessed August 2018.

678 Eran Elhaik, Ranajit Das, Paul Wexler and Mehdi Pirooznia, "Localising Ashkenazic Jews to Primeval Villages in the Ancient Iranian Lands of Ashkenaz." In *Genome Biology and Evolution*, Vol.8, Issue 4, 1 April 2016, pp.1132-1149. See: https://academic.oup.com/gbe/article/8/4/1132/2574015 Accessed December 2018

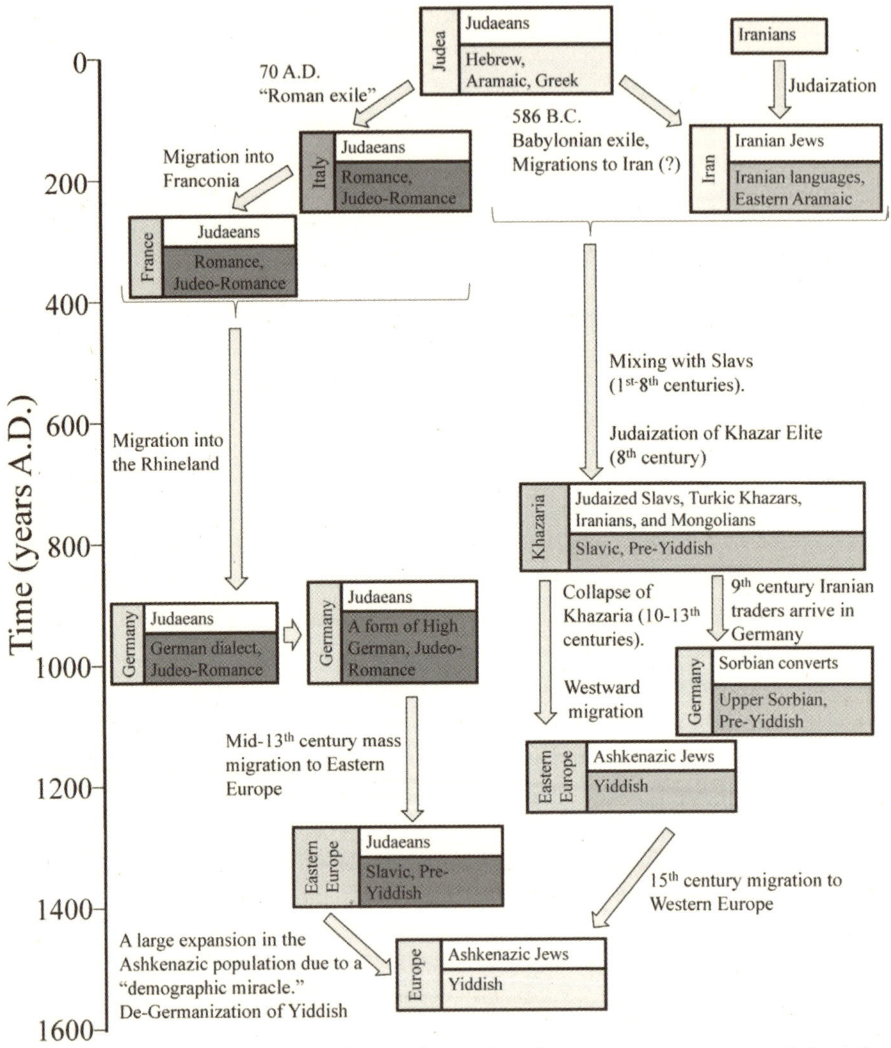

The above is an illustrated timeline for the events comprised by the Rhineland (blue arrows) and the Irano-Turko-Slavic (orange arrows) hypotheses. The stages of Yiddish evolution according to each hypothesis are shown through landmark events for which the identity of the proto-Ashkenazic Jewish populations and their spoken languages are noted per region. Dan Graur, Professor of molecular evolution at the University of Houston, and who was also Elhaik's doctoral supervisor, called Elhaik's conclusion that the Ashkenazi Jews originated in the Caucasus region and not the Middle East as "a very honest estimate".[679] While some have noted however that Armenians themselves already have Middle Eastern roots and hence their genetic similarity to Ashkenazi Jews in Elhaik's study.

Six: The Bible as Authoritative and the Hebrew Israelite Reliance on the King James Bible

The Hebrew Israelites rely much on the Bible, and not any Bible. For they have a fanatical and blind acceptance of the Kings James Bible, even claiming that King James was also a black man and a Hebrew Israelite?! First of all, from an Islamic perspective the Qur'ān mentions,

وَمَا لَهُم بِهِ مِنْ عِلْمٍ
إِن يَتَّبِعُونَ إِلَّا الظَّنَّ وَإِنَّ الظَّنَّ لَا يُغْنِي مِنَ الْحَقِّ شَيْئًا ۞ فَأَعْرِضْ
عَن مَّن تَوَلَّىٰ عَن ذِكْرِنَا وَلَمْ يُرِدْ إِلَّا الْحَيَاةَ الدُّنْيَا ۞

> And they have thereof no knowledge. They follow except assumption, and indeed, assumption avails not against truth at all. So turn away from whoever turns his back on Our message and desires not except the worldly life.
>
> [Al-Najm (53): 28-29]

فَوَيْلٌ لِّلَّذِينَ
يَكْتُبُونَ الْكِتَابَ بِأَيْدِيهِمْ ثُمَّ يَقُولُونَ هَٰذَا مِنْ عِندِ اللَّهِ لِيَشْتَرُوا بِهِ
ثَمَنًا قَلِيلًا فَوَيْلٌ لَّهُم مِّمَّا كَتَبَتْ أَيْدِيهِمْ وَوَيْلٌ لَّهُم مِّمَّا يَكْسِبُونَ ۞

> Woe (destruction) to those who write the "scripture" with their own hands, then say "This is from Allāh" in order to exchange it for a small price. Woe (destruction) to them for what their own hands have written and woe (destruction) to them for what they earn.

679 Rita Rubin, "'Jews a Race' Genetic Theory Comes Under Fierce Attack by DNA Expert." *The Forward*, 7th May 2013. See: https://forward.com/news/israel/175912/jews-a-race-genetic-theory-comes-under-fierce-atta/?p=all Accessed December 2018

[Al-Baqarah (2): 79]

Kenneth Cragg states about the New Testament:

> There is condensation and editing, there is choice production and witness. The Gospels have come through the mind of the church behind the authors. They represent experience and history.[680]

Von Tishendorf admitted that the New Testament had:

> …in many passages undergone such serious modification of meaning as to leave us in painful uncertainty as to what the Apostles had actually written.[681]

Dr Frederic Kenyon stated:

> Besides the larger discrepancies, such as these contradictions, there is scarcely a verse in which there is not some variation of phrase in some copies (of ancient manuscripts from which the Bible has been collected). No one can say that those additions or omissions or alterations are matters of mere indifference.[682]

Martin Kähler, a German theologian (1835-1912) stated in his 1892 book *Der Sogenannte historiche Jesus und der geschichtliche, biblische christus* [The So-Called Historical Jesus and the Historic, Biblical Christ]:

> We do not possess any sources for a 'life of Jesus' which a historian can accept as reliable and adequate. I repeat: we have no sources for a biography of Jesus of Nazareth which measure up to the standards of contemporary historical science.[683]

In 1957, the Jehovah's Witnesses published the headline "50,000 errors

---

680 Kenneth Cragg, *The Call of the Minaret* (London and New York: Oxford University Press, 1956), p.277

681 James Bentley, *Secrets of Mount Sinai: The Story of the World's Oldest Bible – Codex Sinaiticus* (Garden City, NY: Doubleday and Company, 1986), p.117

682 Frederic Kenyon, *Our Bible and the Ancient Manuscripts: Being a History of the Texts and its Translations* (London: Eyre and Spottiswoode, 1895) p.3.

683 Martin Kähler, *The So-Called Historical Jesus and the Historic, Biblical Christ* (Minneapolis: Augsburg Fortress Press, 1964, trans. C.E. Braaten), p.47. Relayed in Martin Kähler, "Against the Life-of-Jesus Movement" in James D.G. Dunn and Scot McKnight (eds.), *The Historical Jesus in Recent Research* (Winona Lake, Indiana: Eisenbrauns, 2005), p.69.

in the Bible" in their *Awake* magazine, writing: "There are probably 50,000 errors in the Bible, errors which have crept into the Bible text." Nevertheless, they go on to say: "as a whole the Bible is still accurate"!? In *The Story of the Manuscripts*, the Reverend George E. Mernil quotes Professor Arnold as stating: "There are not more than 1500 to 2000 places in which there is any uncertainty whatever as to the true text."[684] The *Five Gospels* written by the 'Jesus Seminar', a group of 74 renowned biblical scholars from biblical studies institutes and universities around the world,[685] was the result of six years of dedicated study. They state:

> In fact we do not have original copies of any of the gospels. We do not possess autographs of any of the books of the entire Bible. The oldest surviving copies of the gospels date from about 175 years after the death of Jesus, and no two copies are precisely alike. And handmade manuscripts have almost always been "corrected" here and there, often by more than one hand. Further, this gap of almost two centuries means that the original Greek (or Aramaic) text was copied more than once, by hand before reaching the stage in which it has come down to us.[686]

Peake's Commentary on the Bible notes:

> It is well known that the primitive Christian Gospel was initially transmitted by word of mouth and that this oral tradition resulted in variant reporting of word and deed. It is equally true that when the Christian record was committed to writing, it continued to be the subject of verbal variation, involuntary and intentional, at the hands of scribes and editors.[687]

Ehrman mentions:

> In any event, none of the original manuscripts of the books of the Bible now survive. What do survive are copies made over the

684 George Edmands Merrill, *The Story of the Manuscripts* (D. Lothrop, 1881), p.169

685 Robert W. Funk, Roy W. Hoover and the Jesus Seminar (trans. And eds.), *The Five Gospels: The Search for the Authentic Words of Jesus* (New York: Macmillan Publishing, 1993), pp.533-537

686 Ibid. p.6.

687 Arthur Samuel Peake, Matthew Black and Harold henry Rowley, *Peake's Commentary on the Bible* (London: Nelson and Sons, 1962), p.633

> course of centuries, or more accurately, copies of the copies of the copies, some 5,366 of them in the Greek language alone, that date from the second century down to the sixteenth. Strikingly, with the exception of the smallest fragments, no two of these copies are exact. No one knows how many different, or variant readings, occur among the surviving witnesses, but they must number in the hundreds of thousands.[688]

John Toland noted in his 1718 book *The Nazarenes*, a copy of which is in the British Library and which I accessed in 2005, observed:

> We know already to what degree, imposture and credulity went hand in hand in the primitive times of the Christian Church, the last being as ready to receive as the first was ready to forge books. This evil grew afterwards not only greater when the Monks were the sole transcribers and the sole keepers of all books good or bad, but in the process of time it became almost absolutely impossible to distinguish history from fable, or truth from error as to the beginning and original monuments of Christianity.[689]

Tishendorf uncovered over 14,800 corrections to just one ancient manuscript of the Bible, the *Codex Sinaiticus* – one of the two most ancient copies of the Bible available today, by nine or ten separate "correctors" which had been applied to this one manuscript over a period from 400 CE to circa 1200 CE.[690] In the preface of the *New Revised Standard Version of the Bible* we read:

> Yet the King James Version has serious defects. By the middle of the nineteenth century, the development of biblical studies and the discovery of many biblical manuscripts more ancient than those on which the King James Version was based, made it apparent that these defects were so many as to call for revision.[691]

---

688 Bart D. Ehrman, *The Orthodox Corruption of Scripture: The Effects of Early Christological Controversies on the Text of the New Testament* (Oxford and New York: Oxford University Press, 1996), p.27

689 John Toland, *The Nazarenes* (1718), p.73

690 Jack Finegan, *Light from the Ancient Past, vol.1: The Archaeological Background of the Hebrew-Christian Religion* (Princeton: Princeton University Press, 2015), p.345. Also see Bruce M. Metzger, *Manuscripts of the Greek Bible: An Introduction to Greek Palaeography* (Oxford: Oxford University Press, 1981), p.77

691 New Revised Standard Version of the Bible: Catholic Edition (Oxford and

The preface goes on to state:

> Occasionally it is evident that the text has suffered in the transmission and that none of the versions provides a satisfactory restoration. Here we can only follow the best judgement of competent scholars as to the most probable reconstruction of the original text.

Brueggemann states under 'History' in *Reverberations of Faith: A Theological Handbook of Old Testament Themes*:

> In fact, what happened is remote from us and to some great extent unrecoverable, because we lack access to what would count as verifiable data.

Then he states:

> In the last two generations however, new methodologies, perspectives, and ways of framing the question have resulted in a strong scholarly propensity to conclude that the biblical evidence itself is a poor and unreliable guide to what happened, because interpretive purposes and tendencies shape the biblical evidence and thus make it untrustworthy.[692]

This is the reality of the Kings James Version, and the Bible was illegal for the common people to read even by the 17th century. The scholar William Tyndale and his students were persecuted and branded as heretics by the church in the 16th century for merely translating the bible into the English language for the benefit of the masses who could not read Latin. Only qualified clergy could read it and up until this time the "layman" was outlawed from reading it. It took centuries before the Bible could be accessed by the lay people. Where does this fit in with the Hebrew Israelite cults? The vast majority of whom have difficulties in reading English, let alone Hebrew, which most of the cult followers are totally ignorant of comprehending. Tyndale is sometimes referred to as the "father of the English Bible".

He (i.e. Tyndale) was born in Gloucestershire and educated at Oxford where he gained a BA in 1512 and an MA in 1515, while at Cambridge

---

New York: Oxford University Press, 2000), p.xv.

692 Walter Brueggemann, *Reverberations of Faith: A Theological Handbook Old Testament Themes* (Louisville and London: Westminster John Knox, 2002), p.96.

he studied Greek. Tyndale's translation, which was completed while he was in exile in Germany, was the first published New Testament in the English language translated from Greek. Cuthbert Tunstall, Bishop of London at the time, bought copies of Tyndale's translation in huge numbers in order for them to be burnt in public. High Chancellor Sir Thomas More (considered a 'Saint' by the Catholic Church) published a dialogue in which he denounced Tyndale's translation as being "not worthy to be called 'Christ's Testament', but rather 'Tyndale's own testament' or the testament of his master – the Antichrist."[693] During his time in Antwerp, many attempts were made to lure him back to England. He was arrested by agents of Emperor Charles the 5th and taken to Vilvorde, six miles north of Brussels where he was imprisoned in a fortress on 21 May 1535. In August 1536 he was tried, found guilty of heresy, for having the nerve to translate the bible into English, and turned over to the secular power for execution. On 6th October 1536, William Tyndale was strangled and burned at the stake. John Wycliffe in the 14th century and his students, known as the Lollards, also suffered similar persecution for translating the Bible into English.

693 Frederick Fyvie Bruce, *History of the Bible in English* (Cambridge: The Lutterworth Press, 1961 First Print, 2002 Reprint), p.40; Watson E. Mills, Roger Aubrey Bullard and Edgar V. McKnight (eds.), *Mercer Dictionary of the Bible* (Macon, Georgia: Mercer University Press, 1990), p.249; John F.A. Sawyer (ed.), *The Blackwell Companion to the Bible and Culture* (Chichester, West Sussex: John Wiley and Sons, 2012), p.61.

Bibliography

Arabic Sources

Āl Salmān, Shaykh Abū 'Ubaydah Mashhūr Hasan (1426/2005). *Kutub Hadhara minha al-'Ulama*, vol.2, 3rd Edn. Riyadh, KSA: Dār us-Sumay'ī, Shaykh Bakr Abī Zayd, intro.

Al-Afrīqī, Muhammad al-Ameen bin Muhammad al-Mukhtār al-Jaknī ash-Shanqītī al-Mauritānī al-Mālikī (1417/1996). *Adwā' ul-Bayān fī Eedāh al-Qur'ān bi'l-Qur'ān,* vol.1. Beirut: Ihyā Turāth al-'Arabī, First Ed.

Bin Bāz, Shaykh 'Abdul'Azeez ibn 'Abdullāh, Eng. Trans. "Marriage, Casts and Compatibility". *Al-Istiqāmah* newsletter, no.7., Rabī' ul-Awwal 1418AH/ July 1997 CE). Online Version.

_______, *Naqd Qawmiyyatul-'Arabiyyah.* Cairo: Dār Imām Ahmad, 1425 AH/2004 CE.

_______, Eng. trans. "The Evils of Nationalism". *Al-Istiqāmah* Newsletter, no.2, Safar 1417 AH/July 1996 CE.

al-Maqdisī, al-Imām al-Faqeeh al-Muhaddith Abū 'Abdullāh Muhammad ibn Muflih (1419/1999). *al-Ādāb ash-Shar'iyyah wa'l-Minah al-Mar'iyyah, vol.3*. Beirut: Mu'assisat ur-Risālah, 3rd Edn., eds. Shu'ayb al-Arna'ūt and 'Umar al-Qayyām.

Ibn al-Jawzī, Abu'l-Faraj (1412/1993). *Tanwir al-Ghabash fi Fadl as-Sudan wa'l-Habash.* Sudan: Omdurman Islamic University Printing and Publishing House. Ed.Mohamed Barakat.

Ibn Fūdī, 'Uthmān (1978). *Bayān Wujūb ul-Hijrah 'ala'l-'Ibād.* Trans. & ed. F.H. al-Masri. Khartoum University Press and Oxford University Press.

_______________, *Islam Against Illusions.* Trans. & ed. Fazlur Rahman Siddiqi. (Kano: Department of Islamic Studies Bayero University (Quality Press), 1989.

Ibn Taymiyyah, Shaykh ul-Islām Ahmad bin 'AbdulHaleem bin 'AbdusSalām (1419/1999). *'Iqtidā' as-Sirāt ul-Mustaqeem li-Mukhālifa Ashāb al-Jaheem.* Riyadh: Dār Ishbilia. Ed. Dr Nāsir bin Abdil-Kareem al-'Aql.

___________, (1425/2004). *Majmū' al-Fatāwā,* vol.28. Madeenah al-Munawwarah, KSA: Majma' Malik Fahd. Eds. 'AbduRahmān bin Muhammad bin Qāsim and his son Muhammad.

al-Jāhiz (1981). "Fakhrus-Sudan 'Alā al-Baythān." In *The Islamic Quarterly,* Vol. 25, pp.3-26. Eng. Trans. T. Khalidi.

an-Nāsirī, Shaykh Abu'l-'Abbās Ahmad bin Khālid (1955). *Kitāb ul-Istiqsā' li-Akhbār Duwal al-Maghrib al-'Aqsa.* Ja'far and Muhammad an-Nāsirī (eds.), Vol.5. Dār ul-Baydā' [Casablanca]: Dār ul-Kitāb.

English Sources

Abbott, Elizabeth (2001). *A History of Celibacy.* James Clarke and Co.

Abd-Rahim, Muddathur (1969). *Imperialism and Nationalism in the Sudan: A Study of Constitutional and Political Development, 1899-1956.* Oxford: Clarendon Press.

Adams, Nehemiah (1847). *The Life of John Eliot: With an Account of the Early Missionary Efforts Among the Indians of New England.* Boston: Massachusetts Sabbath School Society.

Afigbo, A.E. (1980). "Prolegomena to the Study of the Culture History of the Igbo-Speaking Peoples of Nigeria" in B.K. Swartz and Raymond E. Dumett (eds.), *West African Culture Dynamics: Archaeological and Historical Perspectives.* The Hague and Paris: Mouton Publishers, pp.305-327.

Ahmed, Hassan Makki Mohamed (1989/1410). *Sudan: The Christian Design.* Leicester: The Islamic Foundation.

Ahmed, Maulana Saeed (2000). *Slavery in Islam.* Karachi: Darul-Ishāt, trans. Rafiq Abdur-Rehman.

Aidi, Hishām (Spring 2005), *Slavery, Genocide and the Politics of Outrage – Understanding the New Racial Olympics. Middle East Report.* Online.

al-'Awāyishāh, Husayn bin 'Awdah (Safar 1427/March 2006). *al-Fasl al-Mubeen fī Mas'ala wa Mufāraqat al-Mushrikeen*, trans. Aboo Maryam Ismaa'eel Alaracon, *A Conclusive Study on the Issue of Hijrah and Separating from the Polytheists.* New York: al-Ibaanah.

al-Bagdādī, Abd al-Rahmān (2001). *The Amusement of the Foreigner*, trans. Yacine Daddi Addoun and Renée Soulodre-La France. Toronto: Nigerian Hinterland Project, Toronto, Canada: York University. Accessed Online: www.yorku.ca/nhp/shadd/baghdadi.pdf

Aling, Charles (2005). "The Prelude to Amarna", in Glenn A. Carnagey Sr, Glenn Carnagey Jr and Keith N. Schoville (eds.), *Beyond the Jordan: Studies in Honor of W. Harold Mare.* Eugene, OR: Wipf and Stock Publishers.

Al-Shinnawy, Abdul Aziz (2002). *The Islamic Openings (al-Fatuhat al-Islamiyah)*, trans. Heba Samir Hendawi, revised by A.A. Mischler. Al-Mansura, Egypt: Umm al-Qura.

Asante, Molefi (1985). "Afrocentricity and Culture" in Asante and Kariamu Welsh Asante (eds.), *African Culture – The Rhythms of Unity.* Westport, CT: Africa World Press.

Austen, Ralph (1979). "The Trans-Saharan Slave Trade: A Tentative Census," in H.A. Gemery and J.S. Hogendorn (eds.), *The Uncommon Market: Essays in the Economic History of the Atlantic Slave Trade.* New York: Academic Press. pp.66-68.

Awad, Mohamed (1966). *Report on Slavery.* New York: UN.

Azami, Muhammad Mustafa (1992). *Studies in Early Hadith Literature.* Indianapolis: American Trust Publications, 3rd Edn..

Azumah, John Alembillah (2001). *The Legacy of Arab-Islam in Africa: A Quest for Inter-Religious Dialogue.* Oxford: One World.

Bairoch, Paul, *Economics and World History: Myths and World History.* Chicago: University of Chicago, 1993.

Baker, William W., *Theft of a Nation.* Las Vegas: Defenders Publications, 1982.

Barth, Heinrich (1965). *Travels and Discoveries in North and Central Africa ... in the years 1849-1855. London: Frank Cass.*

Batran, A.A. (1985). "The Ulamā of Fez, M. Ismail and the Issue of the Harātīn of Fas" in John Ralph Willis (ed.) *Slaves and Slavery in Muslim Africa*, vol.2. London: Frank Cass, pp.9-13.

Ben-Dor Benite, Zvi (2009). *The Ten Lost Tribes: A World History.* Oxford: Oxford University Press.

______________________ "Mormon Scripture and the Lost Tribes of Israel." *Bible Odyssey* website. Accessed 9th June 2017:

https://www.bibleodyssey.org/en/places/related-articles/mormon-scripture-and-the-lost-tribes-of-israel

Ben Jochannan, Yosef (1972). *Black man of the Nile and his Family.* Baltimore, MD: Black Classic Press.

Bentley, James (1986). *Secrets of Mount Sinai: The Story of the World's Oldest Bible, Codex Sinaiticus.* Garden City, NY: Doubleday and Company.

Beshir, Mohamed Omer, (1968) *The Southern Sudan: Background to Conflict.* London: C. Hurst & Co.

Bin Humaid, Saleh Abdullah (1415/1994). *A Refutation of Doubts About Current Issues.* Trans. Abdul Lateef S. Al-Khayat, Jeddah and Makkah: Al-Manara.

Bontemps, Arna and Conroy, Jack (1945). *They Seek a City.* New York: Doubleday.

Booth, Charlotte (2011). *The Myth of Ancient Egypt.* Stroud, Gloucestershire: Amberley Publishing.

Botticini, Maristella and Eckstein, Zvi (2012). *The Chosen Few.* Princeton University Press.

Brent Turner, Richard (1997). *Islam in the African American Experience.* Bloomington: Indiana University Press.

Brooks, Francis (1693; 2013). *Barbarian Cruelty.* London.

Bruder, Edith and Parfitt, Tudor (2012). *African Zion: Studies in Black Judaism.* Newcastle Upon Tyne: Cambridge Scholars Publishing.

Brueggemann, Walter (2002). *Reverberations of Faith: A Theological*

Handbook Old Testament Themes. Louisville and London: Westminster John Knox.

Carson, Clayborne (1991). *Malcolm X: The FBI File*. New York: Carroll and Graff.

Cheney, Victor T. (2006). *A Brief History of Castration*. Bloomington, Indiana: Author House, 2nd Edn.

Chireau, Yvonne (1999). "Black Culture and Black Zion: African American Religious Encounters with Judaism, 1790-1930, An Overview" in Yvonne Chireau and Nathaniel Deutsch (eds.), *Black Zion: African-American Religious Encounters with Judaism*. Oxford: Oxford University Press.

Clarence-Smith, William Gervase (2006). *Islam and the Abolition of Slavery*. London: Hurst and Co..

Clarke, John Henrik (1991). *Notes for an African World Revolution: Africans at the Crossroads*. Trenton, New Jersey: Africa World Press.

Clegg III, Claude Andrew (1997). *An Original Man: The Life and Times of Elijah Muhammad*. New York: St. Martin's Press.

Cogley, Richard W. (2009). *John Eliot's Mission to the Indians before King Philips War*. Cambridge, MT and London, England: Harvard University Press.

Cragg, Kenneth (1956). *The Call of the Minaret*. London and New York: Oxford University Press.

Curtin, Philip D. (ed.) (1967). *Africa Remembered: Narratives by West Africans from the Era of the Slave Trade*. Madison: University of Wisconsin Press.

ad-Damīrī, Abu'l-Bakr Muhammad Ibn Mūsā (1906-08). *ad-Damīrī's Hayat al-Hayawan – A Zoological Lexicon*. Trans. A.S.G. Jayakar of Bombay University. London: Luzac & Co., Bombay: Fort Printing Press, Volume 1: 1906; Volume 2: 1908.

Daniel, Norman (1997). *Islam and the West: The Making of an Image*. Oxford: One World.

Darnell, John Coleman and Manassa, Colleen (2007). *Tutankhamun's Armies: Battle and Conquest During Ancient Egypt's Late Eighteenth*

Century. Hoboken, New Jersey: John Wiley and Sons.

David, A. Rosalie (1993). "Akhenaten" in John R. Hinnells (ed.), *Who's Who of World Religions*. London and Basingstoke: The Macmillan Press, p.15.

Davidson, Basil (1993). *African Civilisation Revisited.* Trenton, New Jersey: African World Press.

____________, (1961; 1994) *Black Mother: The Years of the African Slave Trade.* Boston: Little, Brown & Co., 1961 and UK: James Currey Publications, 1994.

Davis, Robert C. (2004). *Christian Slaves, Muslim Masters: White Slavery in the Mediterranean, the Barbary Coast and Italy, 1500-1800.* Basingstoke and New York: Palgrave Macmillan.

ad-Dehlawee al-Madanee, Shaykh Ahmad ibn Muhammad (Ramadaan 1425/December 2005), *A History of the People of Hadeeth*, Shaikh 'Ali ibn Hasan ibn 'Ali ibn 'Abdul-Hameed (ed.), trans. Aboo 'Ubaidah 'Amr ibn Basheer. Birmingham: Salafi Publications.

Deogaonkar, S.G. and Deogaonkar, S.S (2002). *Native Americans and Native Indians.* New Delhi: Concept Publishing.

Diouf, Sylviane (1998). *Servants of Allah: African Muslims Enslaved in the Americas.* New York and London: New York University Press.

Diop, Cheikh Anta (1987). *Precolonial Black Africa.* Trans. Harold Salemson. New York: Lawrence Hill Books.

Doi, Abdur Rahman I. (1984). *Islam in Nigeria.* Zaria: Gaskiya Corporation Limited.

Dowling, Eva S. and Levi H. (1909). *The Aquarian Gospel of Jesus the Christ.* London: C.F. Cazenove and Los Angeles: Royal Publishing.

Drake, St. Clair and Clayton, Horace R. (1993). *Black Metropolis: A Study of Negro Life in a Northern City.* Chicago: University of Chicago Press.

Dubois, W.E.B. (1969). *The World and Africa.* New York: International Publishers Inc.

Dumeil, Lynn (1984). *Freemasonry and American Culture, 1880-1930.* Princeton, NJ: Princeton University Press.

Du Pasquier, Roger (1992). *Unveiling Islam.* Cambridge: Islamic texts Society, 1992.

Dupuis, Joseph (1824). *Journal of Residence in Ashantee.* London: Henry Colburn.

Edwards, Bryan (1794). *The History, Civil and Commercial, of the British Colonies in the West Indies,* 2 Vols. *2nd edn.* London: John Stockdale, Piccadilly, 1794.

Edwards, Paul (1789; 1969). *Equiano's Travels,* 1789; Reprint, London: Heinemann, 1969.

Ehle, John (1989). *Trail of Tears: The Rise and Fall of the Cherokee Nation.* New York, NY: Anchor Books.

Ehrman, Bart D. (1996). *The Orthodox Corruption of Scripture: The Effects of Early Christological Controversies on the Text of the New Testament.* Oxford and New York: Oxford University Press.

Elhaik, Eran (2013). "The Missing Link of Jewish European Ancestry: Contrasting the Rhineland and the Khazarian Hypotheses." In *Genome Biology and Evolution*, Vol.5, issue 1, 1 January 2013, pp.61-74. See: https://academic.oup.com/gbe/article/5/1/61/728117 Accessed August 2018.

Elhaik, Eran Das, Ranajit Wexler, Paul and Pirooznia, Mehdi (2016). "Localising Ashkenazic Jews to Primeval Villages in the Ancient Iranian Lands of Ashkenaz." In *Genome Biology and Evolution*, Vol.8, Issue 4, 1 April 2016, pp.1132-1149. See: https://academic.oup.com/gbe/article/8/4/1132/2574015 Accessed December 2018

El-Shahawy, Abeer and al-Misri, Mattah (2005). *The Egyptian Museum in Cairo A Walk through the Alleys of Ancient Egypt.* Cairo: American University in Cairo Press.

Essien-Udom, E.U. (1962). *Black Nationalism – A Search for an Identity in America.* University of Chicago Press.

Evanzz, Karl (1992). *The Judas Factor: The Plot to Kill Malcolm X.* New York: Thunder's Mouth Press.

___________,(1999). *The Messenger: The Rise and Fall of Elijah Muhammad.* New York: Pantheon Books.

Fauset, Arthur Huff (1944). *Black Gods of the Metropolis: Negro Religious Cults of the Urban North.* Philadelphia: University of Pennsylvania.

Favazza, Armando R. (1996). *Bodies Under Siege: Self-Mutilation and Body Modification in Culture and Psychiatry.* Baltimore and London: The John Hopkins University Press.

Fernheimer, Janice W. (2014). *Stepping into Zion: Hatzaad Harishon, Black Jews, and the Remaking of Jewish Identity.* Tuscaloosa: University of Alabama Press.

Finegan, Jack (2015). *Light from the Ancient Past, vol.1: The Archaeological Background of the Hebrew-Christian Religion.* Princeton: Princeton University Press.

Francis, Convers (1836). *Life of John Eliot, the Apostle to the Indians.* Boston: Hilliard Gray & Co and London: Richard James Kennett.

Funk, Robert W., Hoover, Roy W. and the Jesus Seminar (1993). *The Five Gospels: The Search for the Authentic Words of Jesus.* New York: Macmillan Publishing.

Gemery, H.A., and Hogendorn, J.S. (1979) (eds.). *The Uncommon Market: Essays in the Economic History of the Atlantic Slave Trade.* New York: Academic Press.

Gerber, Jane S. (2011). "Eldad Da-Dani" in Adele Berlin (ed.), *The Oxford Dictionary of the Jewish Religion.* Oxford: Oxford University Press.

Goldenberg, D. (2017). *Black and Slave: The Origins and History of the Curse of Ham.* Leck: Walter de Gruyter GmbH & Co KG.

Goldschmidt, Henry (2006). *Race and Religion Among the Chosen People of Crown Heights.* London and New Brunswick: Rutgers University Press.

Gomez, Michael A. (2005). *Black Crescent: The Experience and Legacy of African Muslims in the Americas.* New York: Cambridge University Press.

Gordon, Charles George (1885; 1961). *Khartoum Journal.* London: Kegan, Paul, Trench & Co., 1885 and Reprint, New York: Vanguard Press, 1961.

Greenberg, Gershon (1996). "American Indians, Lost Ten Tribes and Christian Eschatology" in Bryan F. LeBeau and Menahem Mor (eds.), *Religion in the Age of Exploration: The Case of Spain and New Spain.* Omaha, NB: Creighton University Press.

Guyatt, Nicholas (2007). *Providence and the Invention of the United States, 1607-1876.* Cambridge: Cambridge University Press.

Hallow, William H. (1993). "Babylon" in Bruce M. Metzger and Michael D. Coogan (eds.), *The Oxford Companion to the Bible.* Oxford: Oxford University Press.

Halkin, Hillel (2002). *Across the Sabbath River: In Search of a Lost Tribe of Israel.* Boston: Houghton Mifflin.

Harms, Robert (2013). "Introduction," in Robert Harms, Bernard K. Freamon and David W. Blight (eds.), *Indian Ocean Slavery in the Age of Abolition.* New Haven, London: Yale University Press.

Hathaway, Jane and Barbir, Karl (2014). *The Arab Lands Under Ottoman Rule: 1516-1800.* London and New York: Routledge.

Hathaway, Jane (1997). *The Politics of Households in Ottoman Egypt: The Rise of the Qazdaglis* (Cambridge and New York: Cambridge University Press.

Haley, Alex (1993). *The Autobiography of Malcolm X.* New York: Ballatine Books.

Henson, Maria Rosa (1999). *A Filipina's Story of Prostitution and Slavery under the Japanese Military.* Lanham: Rowan & Littlefield.

Higman, B.W. (1984). *Slave Populations of the British Caribbean, 1807-1834.* Baltimore, MD: John Hopkins University Press.

__________, (1976). *Slave Population and Economy in Jamaica, 1807-1834.* Cambridge, England: Cambridge University Press.

Hilliard, Constance (1997). *Islam Et Societies Au Sud du Sahara.* Paris: Fondation de la Maison des Sciences de l'-Homme, p.175.

Hiskett, Mervyn (1994). *The Sword of Truth: The Life and Times of the Shehu Usuman dan Fodio.* Evanston, Illinois: Northwestern University Press.

Hoffmeier, James Karl (2015). *Akhenaten and the Origins of Monotheism.*

Oxford and New York: Oxford University Press.

Howard, Keith (1996). *Korean Council for Women Drafted for Military Sexual Slavery by Japan: True Stories of the Korean Comfort Women.* London: Cassell Academic.

Huddleston, Lee Eldridge (1969). *Origin of the American Indians: European Concepts, 1492-1729.* Austin: University of Texas Press.

Ibn Kathīr (2000). *Tafsir (Abridged), Eng. Trans., Vol.4: Surat Al-A'raf to the end of Surah Yunus.* Riyadh, KSA: Darussalam Publishers and Distributers.

Ibn Majah (2007). *English Translation of Sunan Ibn Majah, vol.3.* Riyadh, KSA: Darussalam Publishers and Distributers.

Issac, Ephraim (1985). "Genesis, Judaism and the 'Sons of Ham'," in John Ralph Willis (ed.), *Slaves and Slavery in Muslim Africa, Vol.1: Islam and the Ideology of Enslavement.* London and New York: Frank Cass and Co. Ltd., pp.75-91.

Italian, Sidy 'Othman the (1994). *Ian Dallas: The Shaykh Who Has No Clothes: The True Realities of Shaykh 'Abdalqadir al-Murabit and the Murabitun World Movement.* Rome: n.p..

Jackson, Sherman (2005). *Islam and the Blackamerican: Looking Toward the Third Resurrection.* New York: Oxford University Press.

Jennings, Hargreave, and Redway, George (1884; 1982). *Phallicism: Celestial and Terrestrial, Heathen and Christian and its Connection with the Rosicrucians and Gnostics.* London: George Redway, 1884 and Reprint: Health Research, 1982.

Jestice, Phyllis G. (2004). *Holy People of the World: A Cross-Cultural Encyclopedia, Vol.1, Entries A-G.* Santa Barbara, California, Denver Colorado and Oxford, England: ABC-CLIO.

Johnson, Douglas H. (2004). *The Root Causes of Sudan's Civil Wars.* Indiana: Indiana University Press and Oxford: James Currey.

Kähler, Martin (1964). *The So-Called Historical Jesus and the Historic, Biblical Christ* (Minneapolis: Augsburg Fortress Press, trans. C.E. Braaten.

____________(2005) "Against the Life-of-Jesus Movement" in James

D.G. Dunn and Scot McKnight (eds.), *The Historical Jesus in Recent Research* (Winona Lake, Indiana: Eisenbrauns.

Karim, Benjamin (1992). *Remembering Malcolm.* New York: Carroll and Graf.

Karenga, Maulana (1989). "Black Religion." In Gayraud S. Wilmore (ed.), *African American Religious Studies: An Interdisciplinary Anthology.* Durham and London: Duke University Press.

Kati, Mahmood Kati ibn ul-Hajj al-Mutawakkil (1913; 1964). *Tarikh al-Fattāsh.* Paris: E. Leroux, 1913-14, Reprint Paris: Librairie d'Amérique et d'Orient Adrien-Maisonneuve, 1964. Trans. O Houdas and M. Delefosse.

Katz, Nathan (2000). *Who Are the Jews of India?* Berkeley and Los Angeles: University of California Press.

Kenyon, Frederic (1895). *Our Bible and the Ancient Manuscripts: Being a History of the Texts and its Translations.* London: Eyre and Spottiswoode.

al-Khajnadee, Muhammad Sultaan al-Ma'soomee (1414/1993). *Blind Following of Madhhabs,* Saleem al-Hilaalee (ed.), trans. Dawood Burbank. Birmingham: Al-Hidaayah.

Khani, Ahmad Mohammad (Muharram 1405/1985). *The Intellectual Origin of the Sokoto Jihad.* Ibadan, Nigeria: Iman Publications.

Kia, Mehrdad (2011). *Daily Life in the Ottoman Empire.* Santa Barbara, California and Oxford, England: ABC-CLIO.

Kramer, Samuel Noah (1986). *In the World of Sumer: An Autobiography.* Detroit: Wayne State University Press.

Kupperman, Karen Ordahl (1980). *Settling with the Indians: the Meeting of English and Indian Cultures in America, 1580-1640.* Totowa, NJ: Rowman and Littlefield.

Lafaye, Jacques (1987). *Quetzalcoati and Guadalupe: The Formation of Mexican National Consciousnes*s, *1531-1813.* Chicago and London: University of Chicago Press, trans. Benjamin Keen.

Landing, James E. (2002). *Black Judaism: Story of an American Movement.* Durham, NC: Carolina Academic Press.

Leeds, Josiah Woodward (1877). *A History of the United States of America:*

Including Some Important Facts Mostly Omitted in the Smaller Histories. Philadelphia: J.P. Lippincott & Co.

Le Roux, Magdel (2003). *The Lemba: A Lost Tribe of Israel in Southern Africa?* Unisa, South Africa: Unisa Press.

Lehman, H. Eugene (2011). *Lives of England's Reigning and Consort Queens.* Bloomington, IN: Authorhouse.

Leslau, Wolf (1951). *Falasha Anthology: The Black Jews of Ethiopia.* New Haven, Conn.: Yale University Press.

Levtzion, N., and Hopkins, J.F.P. (1981) (eds.). *Corpus of Early Arabic Sources for West African History.* Cambridge: Cambridge University Press.

Lovejoy, Paul (1983). *Transformations in Slavery: A History of Slavery in Africa.* Cambridge, England: Cambridge University Press.

al-Madkhalee, Shaykh Rabee ibn Haadee (1417/1997). *The Methodology of the Prophets in Calling to Allaah – That is the Way of Wisdom and Intelligence,* trans. Dawood Burbank. Birmingham: Al-Hidaayah Publishing.

Mamdani, Mahmood (2017). "Reading Ibn Khaldun in Kampala." *Journal of Historical Sociology*, 21 April 2017: https://onlinelibrary.wiley.com/doi/full/10.1111/johs.12148 Accessed 1 January 2019

McKenney, Tom C. (1994). *Please Tell Me... Questions People Ask about Freemasonry – and the Answers.* Lafayette, LA: Huntingdon House.

Madden, Richard Robert (1835). *A Twelve Months' Residence in the West Indies.* Philadelphia: Carey, Lea and Blanchard.

Malwal, Bona (1981). *People and Power in Sudan: The Struggle for National Stability.* London: Ithaca Press.

Marmon, Shaun E. (ed.) (1999). *Interdisciplinary Journal of Middle Eastern Studies: Slavery in the Islamic Middle-East, vol.7.* Princeton: Markus Wiener Publishers.

McLoughlin, William G. (2008). *The Cherokees and Christianity, 1794-1870: Essays on Acculturation and Cultural Persistence.* Athens and London: University of Georgia Press.

McMahon, Keith (2013). *Women Shall Not Rule: Imperial Wives and Concubines in China from Han to Liao* (Lanham, Maryland and Plymouth, UK: Rowman and Littlefield Publishers.

Merrill, George Edmands (1881). *The Story of the Manuscripts*. D. Lothrop.

Metzger, Bruce M. (1981). *Manuscripts of the Greek Bible: An Introduction to Greek Palaeography*. Oxford: Oxford University Press.

Mgbeafulu, Mathias Chinonyere (2003). *Migration and the Economy: Igbo Migrants and the Nigerian Economy 1900-1975*. Lincoln, NE and New York: iUniverse Inc.

Middleton, John (2005). *World Monarchies and Dynasties*. London and New York: Routledge.

Milton, Giles (2004). *White Gold: The Extraordinary Story of Thomas Pellow and Islam's One Million White Slaves*. London: Hodder and Stoughton Ltd, 2004 and Farrar, Straus and Giroux: 2nd edition, 2005.

Morrison, Uthman-Ibrahim (1997). *The Forbidden Dialogues: The Impact of Islam on the Future of the African Diaspora*. Norwich: Black Stone Press.

Muhammad, Elijah (1965). *Message to the Blackman in America*. Chicago: Elijah Muhammad.

Najovits, Simson (2004). *Egypt, Trunk of the Tree, A Modern Survey of an Ancient Land: Vol.II: The Consequences, How Egypt Became the Trunk of the Tree*. New York: Algora Publishing.

Onunwa, Udobata R. (2010). *A Handbook of African Religion and Culture*. Pittsburgh, Pennsylvania: Red Lead Press.

Owusu-Ansah, David (1991). *Islamic Talismanic Tradition in Nineteenth-Century Asante*. New York: Edwin Mellen Press.

Parfitt, Tudor and Egorova, Yulia (2006). *Genetics, Mass Media and Identity: A Case Study of the Genetic Research on the Lemba and the Bene Israel*. London: Routledge.

Peake, Arthur Samuel, Black, Matthew and Rowley, Harold Henry (1962). *Peake's Commentary on the Bible*. London: Nelson and Sons.

Philips, Abu Ameenah Bilal (1990). *The Ansar Cult in America*. Riyadh: Tawheed Publications.

Pinn, Anthony B., Finley Stephen C. et al. (2009). "Church of the Living God, Pillar of Truth for All Nations" in *African American Religious Cultures, Volume 1, A-R*. Oxford and Santa Barbara, California: ABC CLIO.

Popović, Alexandre (1999). *The Revolt of African Slaves in Iraq in the 3rd/9th Century*, trans. Léon King. Princeton: Markus Wiener Publishers.

Quinn A., Charlotte, and Quinn, Frederick (2003). *Pride, Faith and Fear: Islam in Sub-Saharan Africa*. Oxford: Oxford University Press.

Rashad, Adib (1995). *Islam, Black Nationalism and Slavery: A Detailed History*. Beltsville, MD: Wriers' Inc..

Reis, João José (1993). *Slave Rebellion in Brazil: The Muslim Uprising of 1835 in Bahia*, Trans. Arthur Brakel. Baltimore and London: Johns Hopkins University Press.

Roberts, Peter (2006). *HSC Ancient History*. Glebe, New South Wales: Pascal Press.

Robinson, David (2004). *Muslim Societies in African History: New Approaches to African History*. Cambridge: Cambridge University Press.

Rodney, Walter (1974). *How Europe Underdeveloped Africa*. Washington: Howard University Press.

Rodriguez, Junius P. (1997). *The Historical Encyclopedia of World Slavery, vol.1*. Santa Barbara, California and Oxford, England: ABC-CLIO.

Rogers, Joel Augustus (1967). *Sex and Race*. New York: Helga M. Rogers.

Ross, Jennifer C. and Steadman, Sharon R. (2017). *Ancient Complex Societies*. London: Routledge.

Rout Jr, Leslie B. (1976). *African Experience in Spanish America: 1502 to the Present Day*. Cambridge, England: Cambridge University Press.

Rubin, Rita (2013). "'Jews a Race' Genetic Theory Comes Under Fierce Attack by DNA Expert." *The Forward*, 7th May 2013. See: https://forward.com/news/israel/175912/jews-a-race-genetic-theory-comes-under-fierce-atta/?p=all Accessed December 2018.

Ruf, U.P. (1999). *Ending Slavery: Hierarchy, Dependency and Gender in*

Central Mauritania. New Brunswick, NJ: Transaction Publishers.

Sabry, Hussein Zulfakar (1982). *Sovereignty for Sudan*. London: Ithaca Press.

as-Saleh, Dr Saleh (ed.), *Dispraise of al-Hawā by Imām Ibnul Qayyim*. Jeddah: Dar Al-Khair Distributers, n.d.

Sand, Shlomo (2010). *The Invention of the Jewish People*. London and New York: Verso.

Sanderson, Lillian Passmore, and Sanderson, Neville (1981). *Education, Religion and Politics in Southern Sudan*. London: Ithaca Press and Khartoum University Press.

Sanneh, Lamin O. (1979). *The Jakhanke: The History of an Islamic Clerical People of the Senegambia*. London: International African Institute.

Santos, Marcel de Lima (2014). *The Ethnopoetcis of Shamanism*. New York, NY: Palgrave Macmillan.

Sassoon, John (1993). *From Sumer to Jerusalem: The Forbidden Hypothesis*. Oxford: Intellectual Books.

Schimmel, Annemarie (1992). *Islam: An Introduction*. Albany, New York: State University Press.

Segal, Ronald (2003). *Islam's Black Slaves: A History of Africa's other Black Diaspora*. London: Atlantic Books.

Shahak, Israel, *Jewish History, Jewish Religion: The Weight of Three Thousand Years*. London: Pluto Press, 1994.

Shatzmiller, Maya (1993). *Labour in the Medieval Islamic World*. Leiden: Brill.

Simpson, George Eaton (1978). *Black Religions in the New World*. New York: Columbia University Press.

Siuda, Tamara L. (2009). *The Ancient Egyptian Prayerbook*. New Lenox, IL: Stargazer Design.

Sookhdeo, Patrick, "The Blood of the Martyrs". *The Daily Telegraph*. Wednesday June 3rd 1998, p. 26.

Soyinka, Wole (1999). *The Burden of Memory, The Muse of Forgiveness*. New York: Oxford University Press.

Spencer, Patricia (2004). *The Egyptian Temple: A Lexicographical Study.* Abingdon, Oxon and New York, NY: Routledge.

Sulaiman, Ibraheem (1986). *A Revolution in History: The Jihad of Usman Dan Fodio.* London and New York: Mansell Publishing Limited.

At-Tabarī (1992), *The History of al-Tabari (ta'rik al-rusul wa'l-muluk), Volume XXXVI. The Revolt of the Zanj.* Albany: State University of New York Press. Trans. David Waines.

Tanaka, Yuki (2002). *Japan's Comfort Women: Sexual Slavery and Prostitution during World War II and the US Occupation.* London: Routledge.

Toland, John (1718). *The Nazarenes.*

Toledano, Ehud R. (1998). *Slavery and Abolition in the Ottoman Middle East.* Seattle and London: University of Washington Press.

_____________(1982). *The Ottoman Slave Trade and Its Suppression.* Princeton, New Jersey: Princeton University Press.

Toru, Miura & Philips, John Edward (2000). *Slave Elites in the Middle East and Africa: A Comparative Study.* London and New York: Kegan Paul International.

Tougher, Shaun (2009). *The Eunuch in Byzantine History and Society.* London and New York: Routledge.

Trimingham, J.S. (1983). *Islam in the Sudan.* London: Frank Cass.

Van Sertima, Ivan (ed.) (1992). *Golden Age of the Moor.* New Brunswick and London: Transaction Publishers.

Various Islamic Scholars, *Fatawa Islamiyah: Islamic Verdicts, Vol. 5.* Riyadh: Darussalam: 2002.

Varner, Gary A. (2007). *Mysteries of Native American Myth and Religion.* Raleigh, N.C.: Lulu Press.

Vikør, Kurt S. (1995). *Sufi and Scholar on the Desert Edge: Muhammad bin 'Ali al-Sanusi and his Brotherhood.* London: Hurst & Co.

Watkins-Owens, Irma (1996). *Blood Relations: Caribbean Immigrants and the Harlem Community, 1900-1930.* Bloomington: Indiana University Press.

Webster, J.B., and Boahen A.A., (1967). *The Revolutionary Years: West African States Since 1800.* London: Longman.

Wilks, Ivor (1967). "Abū Bakr al-Siddīq of Timbuktu" in Philip D. Curtin (ed.), *Africa Remembered: Narratives by West Africans from the Era of the Slave Trade.* Madison: University of Wisconsin Press.

Willis, John Ralph (ed.) (1985). *Slaves and Slavery in Muslim Africa*, vol.1. London: Frank Cass.

Winter, Michael (2003). *Egyptian Society Under Ottoman Rule, 1517-1798.* London and New York: Routledge.

Wolf, Lucien (2012). *Menasseh Ben Israel's Mission to Oliver Cromwell: Being a Reprint of the Pamphlets Published by Menasseh Ben Israel to Promote the Re-admission of the Jews to England, 1649-1656.* Cambridge: Cambridge University Press.

Yates, Donald (2014). *Old World Roots of the Cherokee: How DNA, Ancient Alphabets and Religion Explain the Origins of America's Largest Indian Nation.* Jefferson, North Carolina: McFarland & Co. Publishers.

Yoshimi, Yoshiaki (2000). *Comfort Women: Sexual Slavery in the Japanese Military during World War II*, Trans. S. O'Brien. NY: Columbia University Press.

Journals

Addoun, Yacine Daddi and Lovejoy, Paul (2007). "The Arabic Manuscript of Muhammad Kabā Saghanughu of Jamaica, c.1823". *SHADD: Studies in the History of the African Diaspora – Documents, 3*, pp. 10-11. Accessed Online 2011: http://yorku.ca/nhp/shadd/kaba/index.asp Also see Annie Paul and Kamau Brathwaite (eds.), *Caribbean Culture: Soundings on Kamau Brathwaite.* Kingston, Jamaica: University of the West Indies Press, 2007. 313-341.

Afroz, Sultana (2000). "The Jihad of 1831-1832: The Misunderstood Baptist Rebellion in Jamaica". *Journal of Muslim Minority Affairs* 21, pp.227-43.

Baepler, Paul (January 2004). "The Barbary Captivity Narrative in American Culture". *Early American Literature*, vol.39, no.2, p.217.

Barker, Hannah (2016). "Purchasing a Slave in Fourteenth Century

Cairo: Ibn al-Afkhānī's Book of Observation and Inspection in the Examination of Slaves." *Mamluk Studies Review 19*, pp.1-24.

Campbell, Carl (1975-76). "John Mohammad Bath and the Free Mandingoes in Trinidad: The Question of Their Repatriation of Africa, 1831-38". *Journal of African Studies,* no.2, pp.467-68.

De Wāl, Alex, "Sudan: Social Engineering, Slavery and War". *Covert Action Quarterly*. Spring 1997.

El-Cheikh, Nadia Maria (2005). "Servants at the Gate: Eunuchs at the Court of Al-Muqtadir." *Journal of Economic Social History of the Orient*, 48(2), p.1.

Al-Ghailani, Yusuf A (2015). "British Early Intervention in the Slave Trade, 1822-1873." *History Research*, Oct.-Dec., 2015, Vol. 5, No. 4, 225-238.

Hunwick, John (1999). "Islamic Law and Polemics over Race and Slavery in North Africa (16-19th Centuries)" in Shaun E. Marmon (ed.), *Interdisciplinary Journal of Middle Eastern Studies: Slavery in the Islamic Middle-East, vol.7*. Princeton: Markus Wiener Publishers, p.62.

Key, Andre (2014). "If Thou do not harken unto the Voice of the Lord thy God: A Critique of Theodicy in Black Judaism", *Black Theology*, vol.12, no.3, November 2014.

Macguire, Thomas E.R. (2000), "The Islamic Simulacrum in Henry Louis Gates Jr's 'Into Africa". *West Africa Review, no.1 (2),* January 2000.

Masonen, Pekka and Fisher, Humphrey J. (1996). *Not Quite Venus from the Waves: The Almoravid Conquest of Africa in the Modern Historiography of Western Africa*. University of Tampere. Online: http://www.uta.fi/~hipema/Venus.htm Originally published in the journal *History of Africa*, vol.23, 1996, pp.197-232

Nasseem, Zubairi B., and Marjan, Doka Wahib (June 1992). "The 'Nubians' of East Africa: A Discussion". *Journal of the Institute of Muslim Minority Affairs,* vol.13: 1.

Nicolini, Beatrice (1999). "Religion and Trade in the Indian Ocean: Zanzibar in the 1800s." *ISIM Newsletter* (Leiden), 1(3), p.28.

Reichmuth, Stefan (1999). "Murtada al-Zabidi (d. 1791) in Biographical and Autobiographical Accounts: Glimpses of Islamic Scholarship in the 18th Century CE". *Die Welt Des Islams: International Journal for the Study of Modern Islam*. Leiden, Boston and Koln: Brill, Vol. 39, No. 1, March 1999, p.70.

Ryle, John, *"Disaster in Darfur". The New York Review, vol. 51, no.13.* August 12 2004.

Shouk, Ahmed I., Hunwick, J.O. and O'Fahey, R.S., "A Sudanese Missionary to the United States: Sātti Majid, 'Shaykh ul-Islām in North America', and His Encounter with Noble Drew Ali, Prophet of the Moorish Science Temple Movement". *Sudanese Africa*, no.8 (1997), pp.137-91.

Shyllon, Folarin (1977). *Black People in Britain, 1555-1833*. London, New York and Ibadan: Oxford University Press, for the Institute of Race Relations.

Sikainga, Ahmad Alawad (1998). "Slavery and Muslim Jurisprudence in Morocco." *Slavery & Abolition: A Journal of Slave and Post-Slave Studies*, 19:2, 57-72.

Talhami, Ghada Hashem (1977). "The Zanj Rebellion Reconsidered." *The International Journal of African Historical Studies.*

Tinney, James (1973). "Black Jews: a House Divided" in *Christianity Today*, December 7th 1973.

Versteegh, Kees (2001). "Linguistic Contacts Between Arabic and Other Languages". *Arabica: Journal of Arabic and Islamic Studies, vol.4.* Leiden: Brill, Oct. 2001, p.494.

West, L.J., and Langone, M.D., "Cultism – A Conference for Scholars and Policy-Makers". *Cultic Studies Journal*, Vol.3, pp.117-134. Online Version.

Wolfson, Bernard J. (2000). "African American Jews: Dispelling Myths, Bridging the Divide" in Yvonne Patricia Chireau and Nathaniel Deutsh (eds.), *Black Zion: African American Religious Encounters with Judaism.* Oxford and New York: Oxford University Press.

Theses and Dissertations

Alawiye, Imran Hamza (August 1985). *Ibn al-Jawzi's Apologia on Behalf of the Black People & Their Status in Islam: A Critical Edition and*

Translation of Kitab Tanwir al-Ghabash fi Fadl as-Sudan wa'l-Habash. Ph. D Diss., School of Oriental and African Studies, University of London.

Boafo, Kwaku (2009). 'The Star in the Banner: Studies on North American Black-Jewish Communities.' *Ottowa Journal of Religion*, vol.1, p.140. Accessed 12 June 2017: https://ruor.uottawa.ca/bitstream/10393/26047/1/Boafo_Kwaku_2009.pdf

Bugaje, Usman Muhammad (March 1979). *The Contents, Methods and Impact of Shehu Usman Dan Fodio's Teachings, 1774-1804.* MA Dissertation, Institute of African and Asian Studies, University of Khartoum. Online Version.

Fernheimer, Janice Wendy *The Rhetoric of Black Jewish Identity Construction in America and Israel: 1964-1972* (Austin: University of Texas, May 2006, Phd Thesis), pp.39-40. Accessed 12 June 2017:

https://www.lib.utexas.edu/etd/d/2006/fernheimerd82976/fernheimerd82976.pdf

al-Hajj, M.A. (1973). *The Mahdist Tradition in Northern Nigeria.* Zaria, Nigeria: Ahmed Bello University. Unpublished PhD thesis.

Ingram, Paige Mandisa (2015). *Trials of Identity: Investigating al-Jahiz and the Zanj in Pro-Black Discourse.* Unpublished MA thesis. The University of Texas at Austin.

McLeod, Nicholas C. (2016). "Race, rebellion, and Arab Muslim slavery: the Zanj Rebellion in Iraq, 869 - 883 C.E." Electronic Theses and Dissertations. Paper 2381. https://doi.org/10.18297/etd/2381

Muhammad, Suad Mustafa (1981). *The Zanj Revolt (869-883) in the Abbasid Era.* Unpublished MA thesis. The University of Arizona. Accessed July 2018: https://repository.arizona.edu/bitstream/handle/10150/557872/AZU_TD_BOX170_E9791_1981_528.pdf?sequence=1

Audio Recordings

Adeeb, Dāwūd, "*The Love of this Life.*" Eid Khutbah.

Al-Halabī, Shaykh 'Ali ibn Hasan ibn 'AbdulHameed, Lectures on Īmān and Kufr. *Imām al-Albānī Centre for Islamic Research*, 'Ammān,

Jordan. March 2006 CE.

Al-Jāmī, Shaykh Muhammad Amān, *Rad 'alā't-Turābī.*

Al-'Uthaymeen, Shaykh Muhammad bin Sālih, *Sharh 'Iqtidā' as-Sirāt ul-Mustaqeem.* Istiqāmah Recordings: Riyadh and 'Unayzah, 1416 A.H, tape no. 13.

Newspaper Articles

Al-Dāwah Islamic Monthly Magazine (Riyadh), no.50, Shawwal 1426 AH/November 2005, p.29.

Associated Press, "Christian evangelist Franklin Graham blasts Islam, says will rebuild churches in Sudan". October 9 2006.

BBC Online News Edition, "EU 'to protect' sex slaves". Thursday 8 March 2001.

BBC Online News *Edition,* "Israel women trafficking soars". Thursday 24 March 2005.

BBC Online News Edition, "Italy's sexual slave trade". Wednesday 2 August 2000.

BBC World, "Sudan tribes agree ceasefire". *BBC Online Network.* Wednesday 10 March 1999.

Christian Science Monitor, "Slave 'Redemption' won't save Sudan". 26 May 1999.

Crawford, Sharon E., "Former Nuwaubian writes book, tells how York duped followers". *Macon Telegraph* (Georgia, USA). March 14 2005.

De Wāl, Alex, "Darfur's deep grievances defy all odds for an easy solution". *The Guardian* (UK). Sunday July 25 2004.

Elias, Richard, "Scotland's 6000 sex slaves". *The Daily Record* (of Scotland). 22 February 2006.

Graff, Peter, *Time Magazine.* November 3 1997, pp.50-51

Hecht, David, ""Slavery" African Style". BBC. February 14 1998.

Keily, Sam, "Sudanese Children Sold as Slaves". *The Times* (of London). 16th March 1996.

Lewis, Paul, "Nightmare world of suburban sex slaves". *The Guardian* (of

London). Monday May 8 2006.

Nelan, Bruce W., Dowell, William, Mutiso, Clive and Waller, Douglas. *Time Magazine.* July 27 1998, pp.24-28

The Independent on Sunday (London), "Scam in Sudan: An Elaborate Hoax Involving Fake African Slaves and Less-than Honest Interpreters is Duping Concerned Westerners". 24 February 2002.

The Irish Times, "The Great Slave Scam". 23 February 2002.

The Muslim News (London), "Christians have no right to dictate to Muslims." 28 August 1998, p.2.

______________________, *"Imam Warith in London".* May 28 1993.

The New York Times, "In Sudan – No Clear Difference Between Arab and African". 3 October 2004.

The Washington Post, "Ripping Off Slave 'Redeemers': Rebels Exploit Westerners Efforts to Buy Emancipation for Sudanese". 26 February 2002.

Wainwright, Martin, "Slavery returns to Britain on large scale, study says". *The Guardian* (of London), Monday February 26 2007.

Online Articles

Bostom, Andrew G. (2005). "Black Slaves, Arab Masters". *FrontPage Magazine.* April 18 2005. Online Version.

Green, 'AbdurRaheem (n.d.). "A Response to 'An African Asks Some Disturbing Questions of Islam'". Online.

Gutman, Matthew, "Pressured by US, Israel Battles a Burgeoning 'White Slave' Trade". *Forward* (New York), June 28 2002. Online.

Perry, Mark, *Perceptions of Race in the Arab World.* Online.

Progler, Yusuf (1999). *Islam and the Politics of Slavery in American Academia. Muslimedia,* June 1999. Online Version.

Trifkovic, Serge (2002). "Islam's Wretched Record in Slavery". *Frontpage Magazine,* 20 November 2002.

Reports

Human Rights Watch – Africa, *(1994) Civilian Destruction: Abuses By All Parties in the War in Southern Sudan.*

Sudan Foundation, *Allegations of Slavery and Slavery-Related Practices, Part 2; Open Letter to Caroline Baroness Cox.* Saturday 22nd March 1997.

Runnymeade Trust, *Islamophobia – Issues, Challenges and Action – A Report by the Commission on British Muslims and Islamophobia.* Stoke on Trent, UK and Sterling, USA: Trentham Books, 2004.

US State Department, *Country Reports on Human Rights Practices for 1990*, p. 387.

US State Department, *Country Reports on Human Rights Practices for 1991*, p. 391.

Verney, Peter, *"Slavery in Sudan". Sudan Update* and *Anti-Slavery International*, London, May 1997.

Conference Papers

Bernard K. Freamon, *Slavery and the Slave Trades in the Indian Ocean and Arab Worlds: Global Connections and Disconnections*, p.22, see:

https://glc.yale.edu/sites/default/files/files/indian-ocean/freamon.pdf Accessed March 2018.

From The Gilder Lehrman Center's 10th Annual International Fall Conference *Slavery* and the *Slave Trades* in the *Indian Ocean* and *Arab Worlds*: *Global Connections* and *Disconnections* November 7-8, 2008 Luce Hall Auditorium, Yale University, New Haven, Connecticut.

Documentaries

United Nations' Integrated Regional Information Unit (IRIN), *IRIN* interview with Dr Abu Doum. *Peace Under Fire – Sudan's Darfur Crisis.* Online documentary. April 8 2004.